DISCOVERY PROGRAMME REPORTS

DISCOVERY PROGRAMME REPORTS: 5

Royal Irish Academy/
Discovery Programme
Dublin 1999

THE DISCOVERY
PROGRAMME

AR THÓIR NA SEAN

First published in 1999 for the Discovery Programme
by the Royal Irish Academy,
19 Dawson Street, Dublin 2.
Copyright © Royal Irish Academy 1999.

All rights reserved. No part of this book may be
reprinted or reproduced or utilised in any electronic,
mechanical or other means, now known or hereafter
invented, including photocopying and recording, or
otherwise without either the prior written consent of
the publishers or a licence permitting restricted
copying in Ireland issued by the Irish Copyright
Licensing Agency Ltd, The Writers' Centre,
19 Parnell Square, Dublin 1.

ISBN 1 874045 69 0

British Library Cataloguing-in-Publication Data.
A catalogue record for this book is available from the
British Library.

Typeset in Ireland by Wordwell Ltd
Origination by Wordwell Ltd

Printed in Ireland by Colour Books

Cover: Aerial view of Dun Eochla, Inis Mór, Co. Galway (Claire Cotter).

CONTENTS

Preface		vii
Réamhrá		ix
Acknowledgements		xi
List of figures		xii
List of plates		xiv

1. AUTHORITY AND SUPREMACY IN TARA AND ITS HINTERLAND C. 950–1200 — Edel Bhreathnach — 1

2. LANDSCAPES OF MOVEMENT AND CONTROL: INTERPRETING PREHISTORIC HILLFORTS AND FORDING-PLACES ON THE RIVER SHANNON — Tom Condit and Aidan O'Sullivan — 25

3. WESTERN STONE FORTS PROJECT
Cahercommaun Fort, Co. Clare: a reassessment of its cultural context — Claire Cotter — 41

4. BALLYHOURA HILLS PROJECT
A survey of Carn Tigherna hillfort, Co. Cork (Barry Masterson) — Martin Doody — 97

5. KNOCKNALAPPA, CO. CLARE: A REAPPRAISAL — Eoin Grogan, Aidan O'Sullivan, Finola O'Carroll and Ines Hagen — 111

6. EXCAVATIONS AT MOOGHAUN SOUTH 1995
Interim report — Eoin Grogan — 125

7. ARCHAEOLOGICAL APPLICATIONS OF MODERN SURVEY TECHNIQUES — Barry Masterson — 131

PREFACE

The period covered by these reports was a time of considerable research activity for the Discovery Programme. Concentration was directed towards our four main projects: the Ballyhoura Hills Project, the North Munster Project, the Western Stone Forts Project and the Tara Project. Some of the papers published below deal directly with the results of excavations or with the reassessment of other excavations that are relevant to the investigations of the Discovery Programme. Wider issues, such as survey and the significance of fording-places, are also considered.

Martin Doody reviews recent work at Chancellorsland and on 'Chancellorsland-type' sites. He argues that, if enclosures of this type can be shown to date from the Bronze Age, this will greatly increase the visibility of settlement types of this period. He provides a note on the geophysical survey of a concentration of at least 22 ring-barrows near Elton, Co. Limerick, and also a note on the survey of three hillforts and their relationship to other monuments: Castle Gale, Co. Limerick, and Carn Tigherna and Caherdrinny, Co. Cork. He also contributes a note on the excavation of Chancellorsland Site A—a Bronze Age enclosure—and Chancellorsland Site C, indicating its use 'from the Middle Bronze Age, through the late Iron Age, Early Christian period and beyond'.

Barry Masterson's first article is a detailed survey of Carn Tigherna, Co. Cork, revealing previously unrecorded features, most notably the external outworks in the north-west quadrant. The survey revealed the complex nature of the defences, illustrating the potentially 'militaristic nature of the hillfort'.

Masterson's second article is concerned with the application to archaeology of modern survey techniques. He argues that archaeologists should have some understanding of the techniques involved in electronic surveying in view of the enormous potential of such techniques but also because of their cost. The stages involved in carrying out an electronic topographic survey are then outlined.

The article by Tom Condit and Aidan O'Sullivan draws attention to the importance of approaching the study of certain archaeological sites 'in terms of movement through the landscape' instead of the existing emphasis on 'static distributions of settlements and burials'. The article focuses on Killaloe on the River Shannon, where east–west and north–south routeways would have met. Archaeological evidence suggests that fording-places here were being used for thousands of years, from at least the late Neolithic period, when stone axes were deposited in their hundreds in the Shannon. By the Late Bronze Age the emphasis in artefact deposition had shifted from tools to weaponry, and routeways, to and from the river, were being 'controlled' by hillforts. In a sense, the river would have become a political feature, a boundary between territories. The article argues that we need to examine prehistoric fording-places in terms of their wider landscapes.

Eoin Grogan contributes an interim report on the excavations in 1995 of a number of areas at the Mooghaun hillfort. A second article by Dr Grogan and colleagues, Aidan O'Sullivan, Finola O'Carroll and Ines Hagen, consists of a re-examination of the results of the excavation in 1937 of a Late Bronze Age lakeshore platform at Knocknalappa, Co. Clare. The excavator, Dr Joseph Raftery, had concluded that the site was never occupied. However, as a result of the reappraisal of the evidence the authors put forward the view that there were two phases of activity at the site. The first phase dated from about 1600 BC. The second dated from the ninth century BC and showed definite evidence of domestic activity. The article concludes with a survey of eleven nearby (and probably related) sites, some of which were discovered during underwater surveying.

The major article by Claire Cotter, with contributions from Edel Bhreathnach, Raghnall Ó Floinn, Peter Woodman, Gabriel Cooney and Stephen Mandal, reassesses the dating evidence for the trivallate stone fort known as Cahercommaun,

Co. Clare. This important monument has been interpreted previously both as a prehistoric hillfort and as a cashel of the Early Christian period. The report of the excavation of the site in the 1930s has influenced the dating of stone forts since its publication. The article concludes that there were two principal stages of activity at the site, the first in the prehistoric (perhaps the early prehistoric) period and the second in the Early Christian period. Together with its various additional contributions, the article looks at the 'architectural, stratigraphic ... artefactual and ... literary/historical' evidence. The author also provides a broad reconstruction of the site's history during the Early Christian period.

Edel Bhreathnach's article based on the historical sources deals with the competition for supremacy over the region in which Tara is situated in the period between 950 and 1200. From the point of view of methodology she highlights the importance of pursuing a regional approach to the study of early historic Ireland as a means of 'building the database for the next survey on a national scale'. She emphasises the fact that beneath the apparent constant instability in the area was a local continuum, most vividly expressed through the persistence of the Déisi Breg, which lasted into the Anglo-Norman period. This stability must have existed to an even greater extent in other regions that were 'more remote or less open to outside influence'. She concludes her article with the observation that Dunshaughlin, which is normally thought of as a pre-Norman ecclesiastical site, may also have served as the 'caput' used by the Mac Gilla Sechnaill family and not simply as a church, as perceived from the surviving physical remains. Dr Bhreathnach suggests that a similar function could be argued for Duleek and Slane.

With this publication the Discovery Programme hopes to make available the results of its research activities and, in doing so, to contribute to wider archaeological and related studies.

George Eogan

George Eogan
Chairman

The Discovery Programme
Directorate
Professor George Eogan (Chairman)
Dr Terry Barry
Mr John Bradley
Professor Séamus Caulfield
Professor Gabriel Cooney
Ms Claire Foley
Mr Noel Lynch
Dr Billy O'Brien
Mr Paul Walsh

RÉAMHRÁ

Bhí cuid mhór taighde ar siúl faoin gClár Fionnachtana le linn na tréimhse a thagann i gceist sna tuairiscí seo. Díríodh aird ar cheithre phríomhthionscnamh dár gcuid: tionscnamh chnoic Bhaile Fheabhrach, tionscnamh Thuaisceart na Mumhan, tionscnamh Ráthanna Cloiche an Iarthair agus tionscnamh Theamhair. I gcuid de na páipéir atá foilsithe anseo thíos, pléitear go díreach le torthaí ar thochailtí nó le hathbhreithniú ar thochailtí eile a bhfuil baint acu leis na scrúduithe atá ar siúl ag an gClár Fionnachtana. Tugtar ceisteanna níos leithne i gcuntas chomh maith, mar shampla, suirbhé agus an tábhacht a bhaineann le hionaid thrasnaithe ar áth.

Breathnaíonn Martin Doody siar ar obair a rinneadh le gairid ag Oileán an tSeansailéara agus ar láithreacha den chineál céanna le hOileán an tSeansailéara. Áitíonn sé, más rud é gur féidir a léiriú gur ó dháta de chuid na Cré-Umhaoise bábhúin den chineál seo, gur fearr go mór a bheifear in ann cineálacha lonnaithe de chuid na tréimhse seo a fheiceáil. Tá nóta curtha ar fáil aige faoin suirbhé geoifisiciúil ar chomhchnuasach ina bhfuil ar a laghad dhá cheann is fiche de bharraí adhlactha fáinne gar d'Eiltiún, Co. Luimnigh, agus nóta freisin faoin suirbhé ar thrí ráth cnoic agus faoin mbaint atá acu le séadchomharthaí eile: An Chathair Gheal, Co. Luimnigh, agus Carn Tigherna agus Cathair Droinne, Co. Chorcaí. Tá nóta aige freisin faoin tochailt ar Láthair A in Oileán an tSeansailéara—bábhún de chuid na Cré-Umhaoise—agus Láthair C in Oileán an tSeansailéara ina léirítear an úsáid a baineadh aisti ó Lár na Cré-Umhaoise le linn dheireadh na hIarnaoise, ag tús Ré na Críostaíochta agus ina dhiaidh sin.

Is éard atá sa chéad alt ag Barry Masterson suirbhé mionchruinn ar Charn Tighearna, Co. Chorcaí, ina dtagann gnéithe chun solais a bhí gan chuntas roimhe seo, go háirithe na hoibrithe seachtracha sa cheathramhán thiar thuaidh. Léiríodh sa suirbhé a chasta is a bhí na cosaintí, agus feictear dá réir, dealramh an nádúir mhíleata ag an ráth cnoic.

Díríonn Masterson sa dara alt uaidh ar theicníochtaí nua-aimseartha na suirbhéireachta a chur ag obair sa tseandálaíocht. Áitíonn sé go mba cheart go mbeadh tuiscint éigin ag seandálaithe ar na teicníochtaí a bhaineann le suirbhéireacht leictreonach i ngeall ar an acmhainn iontach atá i dteicníochtaí den chineál seo agus chomh maith leis sin, i ngeall ar a gcostas. Leagtar amach ansin na céimeanna a thagann i gceist maidir le suirbhé leictreonach dinnseanchais a chur i gcrích.

Díríonn an t-alt ag Tom Condit agus Aidan O'Sullivan aird ar a thábhachtaí is atá sé dul i gceann staidéar a dhéanamh ar láithreacha áirithe seandálaíochta i dtéarmaí ghluaiseacht tríd an tírdhreach seachas an bhéim atá ann faoi láthair ar dháileadh statacha lonnaithe agus adhlacthaí. Breathnaítear go sainiúil san alt ar Chill Dalua agus ar Abhainn na Sionainne san áit a mbeadh na bealaí taistil soir siar agus thuaidh theas tagtha le chéile. Tá sé le tuiscint as fianaise na seandálaíochta go raibh ionaid thrasnaithe ar áth anseo in úsáid leis na mílte bliain, ar a laghad ó dheireadh na tréimhse Neoilití nuair a cuireadh tuanna cloiche ina gcéadta sa tSionainn. Faoi dheireadh na Cré-Umhaoise bhí an bhéim i ndeasca na ndéantán aistrithe ó uirlisí go hábhar airm, agus bhí bealaí taistil chuig agus ón abhainn 'á smachtú' ag ráthanna cnoic. Ar bhealach, bheadh an abhainn iompaithe ina gné pholaitiúil, ina teorainn idir chríocha. Áitítear san alt nach mór dúinn scrúdú a dhéanamh ar ionaid thrasnaithe ar áth de chuid na réamhstaire ag féachaint ar a dtírdhreach ina iomláine.

Tá tuairisc eatramhach ann ó Eoin Grogan ar na tochailtí in 1995 a rinneadh ar líon áirithe áiteanna ag ráth cnoic Mhúcháin. Is éard atá in alt eile ag an Dr Grogan agus a chomhleacaithe, Aidan O'Sullivan, Finola O'Carroll agus Ines Hagen, athscrúdú ar thorthaí na tochailte in 1937 a rinneadh ar ardán cois locha de chuid dheireadh na Cré-Umhaoise ag Cnoc na Leapa, Co. an Chláir. Bhí an tochaltóir, An Dr Joe Raftery, tagtha ar an tuairim nach raibh cónaí riamh sa láthair. Ach de thoradh ar athbhreithniú na fianaise cuireann na húdair an tuairim i láthair go raibh dhá chéim gníomhaíochta i gceist ag an láthair. Cuireadh dáta thart ar 1600 R.Ch. ar an gcéad chéim. Dáta de chuid an naoú céad R.Ch. a leagadh ar an dara céim anseo agus bhí fianaise dhearfa inti maidir le gníomhaíocht tí. I ndeireadh an ailt tá suirbhé ann ar aon láthair déag atá sa chóngar (agus ar dóigh go bhfuil ceangal eatarthu), a dtángthas ar chuid díobh le linn suirbhéireachta faoi uisce.

Sa phríomh-alt le Claire Cotter, ina bhfuil ábhar ó Edel Bhreathnach, Raghnall Ó Floinn, Peter Woodman, Gabriel Cooney agus Stephen Mandal, déantar athbhreithniú ar an bhfianaise maidir le dáta a leagan ar an ráth cloiche ina bhfuil trí bhalla fáil ar a dtugtar Cathair Comán, Co. an Chláir. Rinneadh léamh ar an séadchomhartha tábhachtach sin roimhe seo mar ráth cnoic réamhstaire agus mar chaiseal ó thus thréimhse na Críostaíochta. Ó foilsíodh í sna tríochaidí bhí tionchar ag an tuairisc faoin tochailt ar an láthair ar dhátú ráthanna cloiche. San alt, tagtar ar an tuairim go raibh dhá phríomhchéim gníomhaíochta ann ag an láthair; an chéad cheann sa tréimhse réamhstaire (b'fhéidir tús na réamhstaire) agus an dara ceann i dtréimhse thosaigh na Críostaíochta. In éineacht leis an ábhar breise éagsúil, breathnaítear san alt ar an bhfianaise ó thaobh ailtireachta, sraitheachais, déantán, agus na litríochta/staire de. Déanann an t-údar atógáil leathan freisin ar stair na láithreach le linn thréimhse thosaigh na Críostaíochta.

San alt ag Edel Bhreathnach, atá bunaithe ar na foinsí staire, dírítear aird ar an gcomórtas do cheannas ar an réigiún ina bhfuil Teamhair lonnaithe sa tréimhse idir 950 agus 1200. Maidir le modh oibre de, leagann sí béim ar a thábhachtaí is atá sé cur chuige réigiúnda a leanacht i gcúrsaí staidéir maidir le luathstair na hÉireann mar bhealach leis an mbunachar sonraí a chur le chéile don chéad suirbhé eile ar scála náisiúnta. Léiríonn sí go suntasach go raibh, taobh thiar den neamhsheasmhacht bhuan, de réir cosúlachta, a bhí sa cheantar, leanúnachas áitiúil a chuirtear in iúl go ríbhríomhar sa mhéid gur lean na Déisi Breg a mhair isteach sa tréimhse Angla-Normannach. Caithfidh go raibh an bhuanseasmhacht seo ann ar leibhéal níos mó fiú amháin, i réigiúin eile a bhí ní ba scoite amach nó nach raibh chomh mór sin faoi thionchar ón taobh amuigh. I ndeireadh an ailt deir sí maidir le Dún Seachlainn a meastar faoi de ghnáth gur láthair eaglasta réamh-Normannach atá ann, go dtiocfadh sé i gceist chomh maith mar an 'caput' a bhí in úsáid ag teaghlach Mhac Gilla Sechnaill agus nach mar eaglais amháin a úsáideadh é faoi mar atá le brath ó na hiarsmaí fisiciúla a tháinig slán. Tugann an Dr Bhreathnach le tuiscint go dtarlódh feidhm den chineál céanna ag Damhliag agus ag Baile Shláine.

Agus an foilseachán seo á chur ar fáil aige, tá súil ag an gClár Fionnachtana toradh ar an obair thaighde aige a sholáthar agus, dá réir, cur le léann seandálaíochta níos leithne agus le léann atá gaolmhar leis.

George Eogan
Cathaoirleach

ACKNOWLEDGEMENTS

The Discovery Programme is grateful to the Heritage Council, *Dúchas* and the Department of Arts, Heritage, Gaeltacht and the Islands for their continued support and assistance. The advice of many archaeologists and other specialists is also much appreciated. The cooperation of landowners is gratefully acknowledged too, and special thanks are due to Coilte Teoranta. The Western Stone Forts Project would like to thank all those who assisted with the project in 1995–6, and the Ballyhoura Hills Project continues to be indebted to a number of people in Emly, Co. Tipperary. Those who assisted the North Munster Project are also gratefully acknowledged.

LIST OF FIGURES

Authority and supremacy in Tara and its hinterland
1. Archaeological and natural features in the far and middle distance viewed from the Hill of Tara.
2. Sites and features in the hinterland of Tara mentioned in *Dindshenchas Érenn*.
3. The kingdom and petty kingdoms of Deiscert Breg: a hypothetical reconstruction.
4. Lands held by three intrusive families, Uí Murchada, Uí Ciarda and Uí Riacáin, within the barony of Skreen.
5. Sites mentioned in the annals from 950 to 1172.
6. Early Anglo-Norman settlements in Deiscert Breg.

Landscapes of movement and control
1. Distribution of prehistoric monuments and finds on the lower River Shannon.
2. Stone axes found during river-dredging operations at Killaloe.
3. Plan of Formoyle Beg hillfort, indicating earthen ramparts and location of adjacent archaeological sites.
4. Plan of Laghtea hillfort, indicating earthen rampart, contours and location of adjacent archaeological sites.
5. Map of the Killaloe area, indicating prehistoric monuments and general location of prehistoric finds.
6. Later prehistoric weaponry from the River Shannon at Killaloe.
7. Late Bronze Age sickle from the River Shannon at Killaloe.

Cahercommaun Fort, Co. Clare
1. Map showing location of Cahercommaun.
2. Map of settlement in the vicinity of Cahercommaun.
3. Plan of Caisleán Gearr, Co. Clare.
4. Westropp's plan and view of Cahercommaun.
5. Hill-shaded model of Cahercommaun.
6. Hencken's plan and sections of Cahercommaun, showing the areas excavated.
7. Hencken's post-excavation plan and sections of the inner enclosure.
8. The flint assemblage from Cahercommaun.
9. The stone axes from Cahercommaun.
10. Saddle querns from Cahercommaun.
11. Plan and section of souterrain B, showing the location of the human skull and findspot of the silver brooch.
12. Iron arrowhead, slotted and pointed object, and barrel padlock from Cahercommaun.
13. Zoomorphic penannular brooch fragment, head of enamelled brooch pin of copper alloy, and brooches and pins of iron and copper alloy.
14. Silver annular brooch: back and front.
15. Dynasties of Aran and north Clare *c.* AD 700.

The Ballyhoura Hills Project
1. Digital Terrain Model—Elton barrow cemetery.

A survey of Carn Tigherna hillfort, Co. Cork
1. Location map.
2. Outline plan with main features indicated.
3. Contour plan demonstrating height variations.
4. Hill-shaded plan highlighting structural features.
5. Profiles through the hill.
6. 3-D view of hill-shaded model from the south-east.
7. 3-D view of the north-west quadrant.
8. Profiles through outworks and north-west quadrant.

Knocknalappa, Co. Clare
1. Location map: the Mooghaun/Knocknalappa area of south-east Clare.
2. The Knocknalappa area around Rosroe and Fin Lough.
3. Plan of the Late Bronze Age platform at Knocknalappa.
4. Sections across Knocknalappa.
5. Sketch-plans of the 1937 excavations, redrawn from Dr Joseph Raftery's notebook.

6 Comparative profiles of Late Bronze Age necked jars from Knocknalappa, Mooghaun, Emain Macha and Ballinderry.

Excavations at Mooghaun South
1 Location of the excavations in 1995.
2 Excavations at Site C.
3 Site C: section through the middle rampart.

Archaeological applications of modern survey techniques
1 Digital linework plan of Dun Eochla, Inis Mór, Co. Galway.
2 Digital Terrain Model (DTM) and resulting contour plan and profiles of the complex earthen enclosure and mound at Rathanny, Co. Limerick.
3 DTM of a barrow cemetery at Elton, Co. Limerick.
4 DTM of a section of the foreshore at Carrigdirty Rock, Co. Limerick.
5 Hill-shaded model of Grianan Aileach, Co. Donegal.
6 Contour plan of an enclosure and barrow at Moanmore, Co. Tipperary.
7 Shaded relief map of the Chancellorsland complex, Co. Tipperary, with the magnetometry survey of site A superimposed over the model.
8 Perspective view of a shaded relief map of the Chancellorsland complex, Co. Tipperary, with the magnetometry survey of site A superimposed over the model.
9 A DTM of *fulachta fiadh* near Magh Adhair, Co. Clare, overlying a projected pre-monument ground surface.
10 Contour plan of the *fulachta fiadh* near Magh Adhair, Co. Clare.
11 DTM of a *fulacht fiadh* at Castlefergus, Co. Clare.
12 Contour plan of a *fulacht fiadh* at Ballyhickey, Co. Clare.

LIST OF PLATES

Landscapes of movement and control
1. Eel weirs at Killaloe, with rapids over the fording-points.
2. Dredging work in the 1880s at the Killaloe fords.
3. Aerial photograph of Formoyle hillfort.
4. Aerial photograph of Laghtea hillfort.
5. The ramparts of Laghtea hillfort.
6. Late Bronze Age bronze sword from Killaloe.

Cahercommaun Fort, Co. Clare
1. Aerial photograph of settlement in the vicinity of Cahercommaun.
2. Aerial photograph of Caisleán Gearr from south-west.
3. Niche III on the interior of the inner enclosing wall.
4. Vertical joint in the outer wall at Cahercommaun.
5. The upper and lower terrace and niches III and IV on the interior face of the inner wall at Cahercommaun.
6. The flint assemblage from Cahercommaun.
7. Saddle quern from Cahercommaun.
8. The inner enclosure after excavation, showing structures 4, 5, 6, 7, 8, 9, 10 and 11.
9. The skull buried in souterrain B.
10. Silver annular brooch.
11. Grave-slab, Teampall Bhreacáin.

The Ballyhoura Hills Project
1. Chancellorsland Site A—Structure 12 after excavation.
2. Chancellorsland Site C—Trench 1, Barrow 4 in background.

A survey of Carn Tigherna hillfort, Co. Cork
1. Aerial view of Carn Tigherna.
2. Look-out post built into the top of the cairn during World War II.
3. The dumped stone construction of the rampart as exposed on the south-west side of the hillfort.
4. Structural lines visible within the fabric of the dumped stone construction of the main rampart.
5. The entranceway through the main rampart viewed from the exterior, looking east.

Knocknalappa, Co. Clare
1. View of the site (centre) from north-east.

Excavations at Mooghaun South
1. Site C: the primary and secondary inner facings of the middle rampart from the north.
2. Site D: House 2 from the south.
3. Site I: Enclosure 4 from the south-west.

Archaeological applications of modern survey techniques
1. Surveying Carn Tigherna hillfort, Co. Cork, overlooking the Blackwater Valley with the Galtee Mountains in the distance.
2. Aerial view of Dun Eochla, Inis Mór, Co. Galway.
3. Total station equipped with a data-logger.

1. AUTHORITY AND SUPREMACY IN TARA AND ITS HINTERLAND C. 950–1200

Edel Bhreathnach

Introduction

The earliest historical sources available suggest that competition for supremacy over the region in which Tara is situated was intense and relentless.[1] This was a part of Ireland that was important owing to its economic richness, and also undoubtedly because of a lingering memory of some quasi-religious or sacral polity, which set it aside from the rest of the country.[2] The origin of and complex notions associated with certain place-names in the region—Banba, Brega, Cerna, Cera, Cerainn, Cermna and Cnogba, Loch Dá Gabor and Temair (to name but those commented upon to date)—appear to express topographically an ideology relating to kingship and sovereignty in which Tara played a pivotal role.[3] In common with, and even more acutely than, certain other economically and politically important regions in Ireland (for example, the plain of Kildare, the plains around Cashel and Crúachu, and the southern side of the Shannon Estuary), authority was reflected at two levels, the local and the intrusive. Layers of possession and dispossession can be detected in the sources. Around Tara, for example, population groups whose authority was at its height in the early historic (pre-AD 650), if not prehistoric, period survived as landed families into the pre-Norman period and later. The most prominent of these were the Déisi Breg, Cíannachta Breg, Gailenga and Luigne. Although they remained part of the polity of the region, their authority was gradually weakened, as they were replaced by the different branches of the Síl nÁedo Sláine. One branch of this confederation, Clann Chernaig Sotail, reputedly descended from Cernach Sotail, son of Diarmait mac Cerbaill (d. 664), was to play an important role in the political affairs of the region until the twelfth century.

The list of intruders who intervened is impressive. From the midlands came Clann Cholmáin (Uí Máelsechlainn), from the south the Éoganachta and later the Dál Cais (Uí Briain), from Leinster (from whom Brega may have been wrested in the early historic period) the Uí Dúnlainge and most especially the Uí Cheinnselaig, from the north the Ulaid (who held a position similar to the Laigin), the Airgialla and the northern Uí Néill dynasties, especially Cenél nEógain (Mac Lochlainn), from the midlands and the west in the later period Uí Briúin Bréifne (Uí Ruairc) and Uí Chonchobair, and also the Hiberno-Norse of Dublin. This region was therefore accustomed to intrusion and yet, despite this apparently unstable situation, a remarkable continuity can be detected in the exercise of local power. The family of Mac Gilla Sechnaill, for example, belonged to Clann Chernaig Sotail, who clung to their right to hold the kingship of Deiscert Breg (south Brega) down to the late twelfth century, despite frequent attempts by other dynasties to wrest it from them permanently.[4] Probably even more remarkable is the reappearance in the eleventh century of the Déisi Breg—those who had been removed from their position as kings of Lagore in the mid-eighth century[5]—in the guise of Gilla Fulartaig *rí na nDese Breg,* who was killed in 1034. The perpetrators of his death were the Uí Dúnchada and Uí Túathail of Leinster, who also killed Cathal mac Amalgaid, king of Uí Chellaig Chualann (south of Dublin), in the same incident.[6]

This study seeks to address the dynamics of how these different layers of authority and supremacy operated from the mid-tenth to the late twelfth century, and how the existing polity of the region contributed to the pattern of the Anglo-Norman intrusion in the late twelfth century.[7] In conjunction with the narrative and explanatory text, the study is accompanied by a series of maps which are based primarily on information provided in pre-Norman texts, namely *Dindshenchas Érenn,*[8] *Lebor na Cert,*[9] poems attributed to the poet Cináed úa hArtacáin (d. 975),[10] the eleventh- and twelfth-century memoranda preserved in the Book of Kells[11] and the annalistic record.[12] This information is supplemented by material extracted from later sources, the most important being *The song of Dermot and the earl,*[13] the Irish Pipe Roll of 14 John 1211–12,[14] the Chartularies of St Mary's Abbey, Dublin,[15] and of the monasteries of Llanthony Prima and Secunda,[16] documents relating to the de Lacy lordship of Meath[17] and other Anglo-Norman charter material,[18] and early Modern Irish poems.[19] The purpose of the maps is to illustrate the different types of sites which were perceived as important in the pre-Norman period and how this perception of the landscape continued or changed in the early Anglo-Norman phase. I have further tried to express through the medium of maps the diverse strands of authority in the pre-Norman era and to demonstrate how echoes of these strands are likely to have survived longer than hitherto acknowledged.

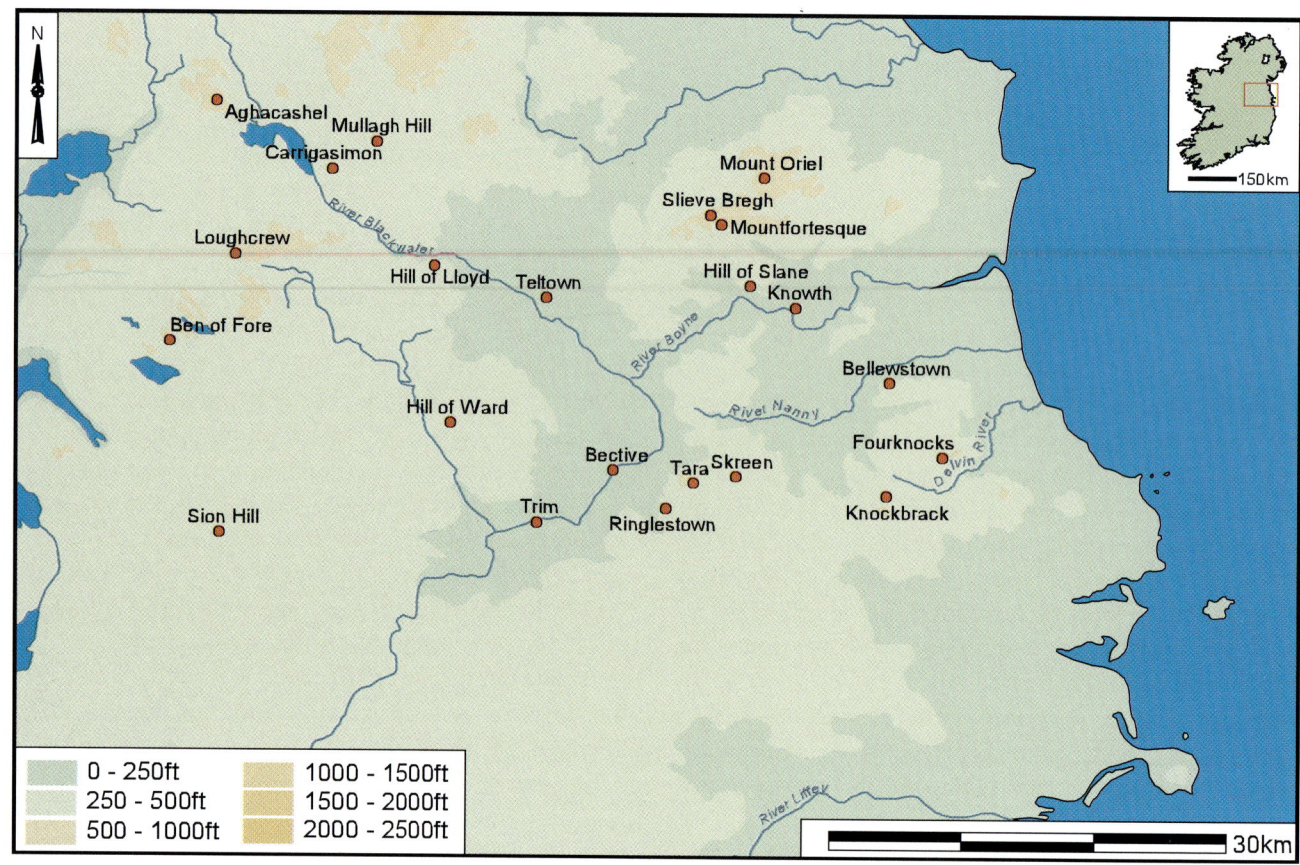

Fig. 1—Archaeological and natural features in the far and middle distance viewed from the Hill of Tara (after Fenwick).

Deiscert Breg (south Brega): geographical and political boundaries

Prehistoric monuments and natural features

There is a remarkable coincidence between the prominent features of this part of Ireland, as they are celebrated in the Middle Irish corpus of topographical texts collectively known as *Dindshenchas Érenn*, and those features (archaeological and natural) which can be seen from the Hill of Tara, both on the far horizon and in the middle distance[20] (Fig. 1). Even more remarkable is the overlap between prominent natural features and prehistoric archaeological monuments. These sites include Skreen (Achall), Fourknocks Hill, Knockbrack (near Naul, Co. Dublin: possibly Odba),[21] Uisnech, the Hill of Ward (Tlachtga), Loughcrew (Sliab na Callaige), the Hill of Lloyd (Mullach Aite), Slíab Breg, the Hill of Slane (Dumach Sláine) and the Boyne Valley passage tomb complex (Brug na Bóinde). Apart from Tara itself, *Dindshenchas Érenn*[22] praises the wonders and mythology of the following sites: Achall (Skreen), Tailtiu (Teltown), Cerna (possibly Carnes, barony of Upper Duleek, or Carn Hill, barony of Skreen), Mag mBreg (for definition see below), Tlachtga (the Hill of Ward), Tráig Tuirbe (Turvey), Inber n-Ailbine (estuary of the Delvin River), Ocha(n) (Faughan Hill), Ráith Ésa (unidentified), Bóand (River Boyne), Cnogba (Knowth), Odba (Navan or Mullahow, the latter being the most likely), Inber Cíchmaine (unidentified), Loch Dá Gabor (Lagore), Cléitech (?unidentified on the Boyne), Dún mac Nechtain Scéne (located at the confluence of the rivers Blackwater and Boyne, see existence of River Skane close to Tara), Bile Tortain (a sacred tree standing near Ardbraccan), Dubad (Dowth), Lind Féic (on the Boyne near Rosnaree), Druim Tairléime (on the Boyne near Rosnaree) and Duma Oena (unidentified) (Fig. 2). Both the view from Tara and the perception of the landscape of the region as portrayed in the *dindshenchas* texts are understandably influenced by dominant natural features, relatively low but visible hills which are often topped by monuments.[23] Deiscert Breg (south Brega) is an area bounded by the River Boyne to the north and west and the coast to the east, while the rivers Liffey and Rye afford a natural boundary to the south. This is an area which may be coterminous with Mag mBreg, 'the plain of Brega'.[24]

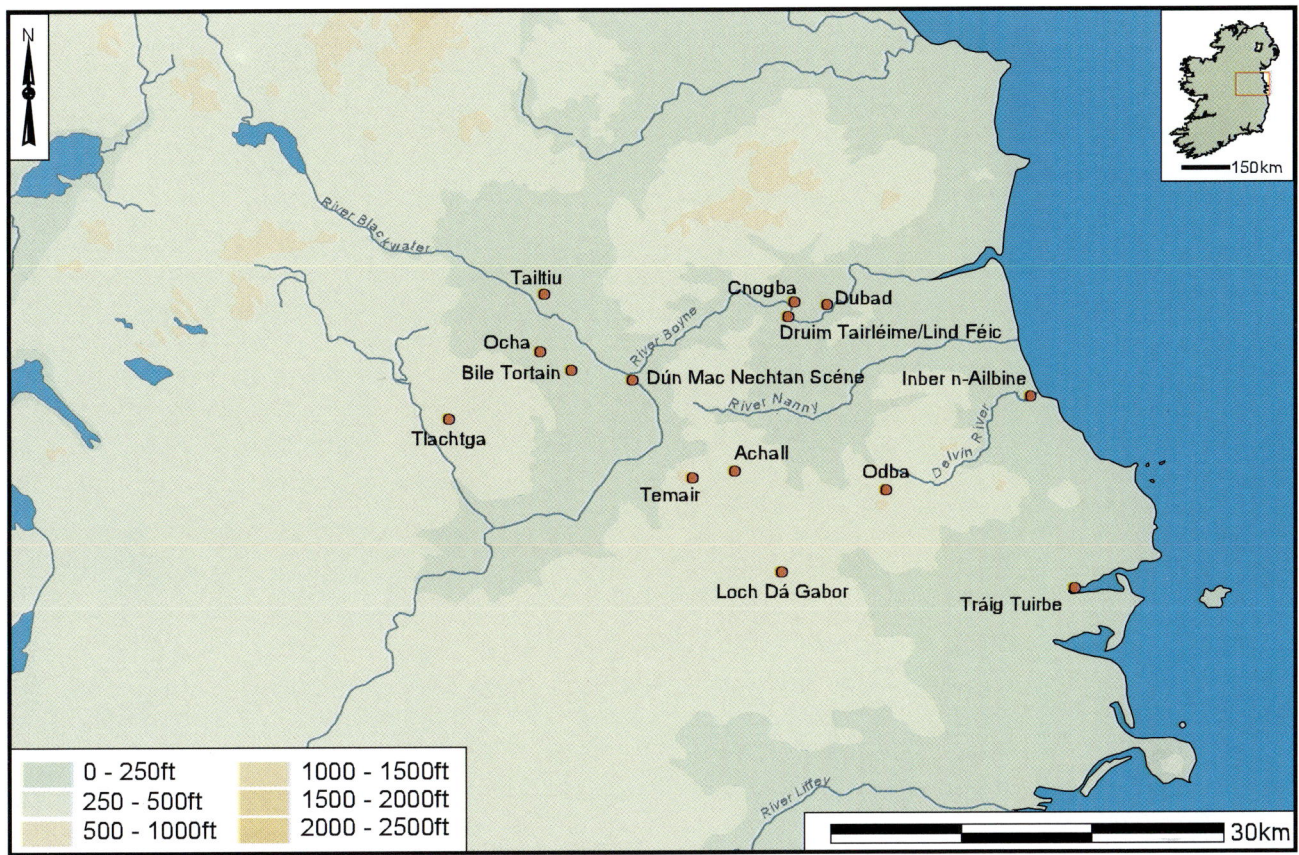

Fig. 2—Sites and features in the hinterland of Tara mentioned in Dindshenchas Érenn.

The kingdom and petty kingdoms of Deiscert Breg (Fig. 3)

During the period under consideration, there is compelling evidence to suggest that Deiscert Breg consisted of sub-kingdoms *approximately* coterminous with the baronies of Lower Deece and Ratoath (Clann Chernaig Sotail (Mac Gilla Sechnaill) and the earlier population group the Déisi Breg (Mac Gilla Fulartaig)), Balrothery East and West, Nethercross and Coolock (Saithne, Gailenga, Fine Gall), Upper and Lower Duleek (Uí Chellaig Breg) and Skreen (mensal lands of the kings of Tara and a variety of intruders). The region as a whole was recognised as a political entity, its kings being afforded the titles *rex* or *rí Locha Gabor* (see *AU* 785, 786, 805, 825, 836, 865, 868, 908, 960), *rex*, *rí* (in *AFM tighearna*) or *lethrí Deiscirt Breg* (see *AU* 751, 778, 797, 815, 826, 870, 1013, 1027, 1034, 1121, 1130, 1160, 1171) and *lethrí Breg* (*AU* 865). At times, as will be noted in the following narrative, some of these kings attained the more extensive title of *rí Breg*, which encompassed the wider territory of Deiscert Breg and of lands north of the Boyne stretching at least as far as Kells, if not further. The title of *rí Breg*, though probably of local importance, was not particularly significant beyond its own borders from the end of the tenth century, when Máel Sechnaill mac Domnaill (d. 1022) greatly lessened the independence of Brega and subsumed its power into the kingdom of Mide.[25] With regard to the use of the titles *rí* or *rex Locha Gabor* or *rí* or *rex Deiscirt Breg* in the early period, there is no clear pattern that would suggest that they are mutually exclusive or interchangeable. A considerable number of kings holding the title *rex Locha Gabor* were not succeeded by any descendant (Óengus mac Máele Dúin (d. 825); Coirpre mac Máele Dúin (d. 836); Tigernach mac Fócartae (d. 865 — he also held the title *lethrí Breg*); Diarmait mac Eterscéle (d. 868); Máel Ugrai (d. 908); Béollán mac Ciarmaicc (d. 969)), which arguably might imply that their rule was not sufficiently strong to merit the geographically more extensive title of *rí* or *rex Deiscirt Breg*.

(i) Clann Chernaig Sotail (Mac Gilla Sechnaill) and Déisi Breg (Mac Gilla Fulartaig)

The title *rex* or *rí Locha Gabor* became obsolete on the death of Béollán mac Ciarmaicc (d. 969). Price and Hencken, in their monumental report on the excavations at Lagore, took this to indicate, along

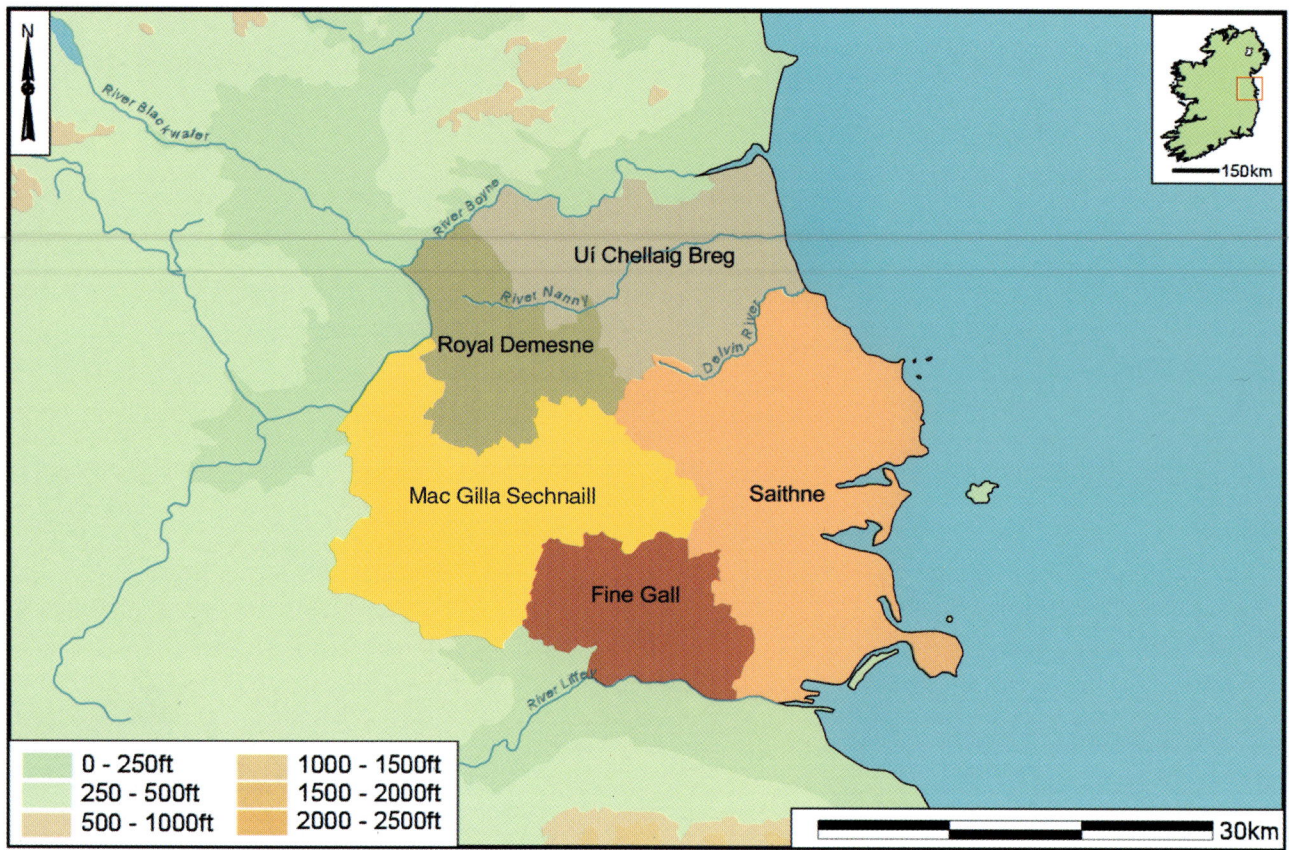

Fig. 3—The kingdom and petty kingdoms of Deiscert Breg: a hypothetical reconstruction.

with the destruction of Lagore by the Norse in 935,[26] that the site was abandoned in the late tenth century.[27] It is conceivable that Lagore was not subject to sudden abandonment but rather to a phased withdrawal or to increasing use of other important sites in the area, such as Dunshaughlin or Trevet. The peripatetic nature of Irish kingship should not be overlooked in the context of understanding the archaeology of Irish royal residences. Kings were constantly moving around, either feasting with their retinues in the houses of their most noble clients, going to assemblies or on military campaigns.[28] Béollán mac Ciarmaicc was not succeeded by his son. According to the Middle Irish list of the wives and mothers of Irish kings and their families, the *Banshenchas*, his daughter, Deichtire, was mother of Domnall mac Congalaig (d. 976), who belonged to the north Brega dynasty.[29] The descendants of his brother, Fogartach, who adopted the surname Mac Gilla Sechnaill (from Gilla Sechnaill mac Gilla Mochonna (d. 1034)), dominated the kingship of *Deiscirt Breg* from the eleventh century onwards. Mac Gilla Sechnaill[30] kings are accorded the title *rí* or *tighearna Deiscirt Breg* on six occasions during the period under consideration, in 1013, 1027, 1034, 1121, 1160 and 1171. They never succeeded in gaining recognition as kings of the whole of Brega or in obtaining the titles *rí Érenn*, *rígdamnae Temrach* or *rígdamnae Érenn*, which the north Brega dynasty attained under Congalach Cnogba (d. 956: *rí Érenn*), Muirchertach mac Congalaig (d. 964: *rígdamnae Temrach*), Domnall mac Congalaig (d. 976: *rí Breg*), and Donnchad úa Congalaig (d. 1017: *rígdamnae Érenn*).

Given the close connection between this family and Dunshaughlin, which can be seen not only by the adoption of the name Mac Gilla Sechnaill but also in that Donnchad mac Gilla Mochonna (d. 1027) was *comarba Sechnaill*,[31] it is highly likely that their primary residence was at Dunshaughlin. The poet Cináed úa hArtacáin (d. 975), who would appear to have belonged to Clann Chernaig Sotail himself,[32] portrayed the close association between this dynasty and Tara in the following geographical terms:[33]

Doluidh Diarmait leth re Gallaib a ndescert Breagh íarnata,
conid úaid síardes im Temraig Clann Chernaig meic Díarmad[a].

Diarmait went to south Brega facing towards
the Gaill [Norse of Dublin],
so that from him to the south-west around
Tara are (descended) the race of Cernach son
of Diarmait.

In his poem on the *dindshenchas* of Achall (Skreen), *Achall araicci Temair*, the same poet associated the Clann Chernaig Sotail with activities around Skreen:

gegnatar cúana cose
im tháebu úara Aichle.[34]

they have slain hosts till now round the cold flanks of Achall.

The continuing survival of a dynasty of the Déisi Breg, probably subject to Clann Chernaig Sotail and later Mac Gilla Sechnaill kings, is evident from the slaying of Gilla Fulartaig, *rí na nDése Breg*, in 1034. His son was slain with others in 1109 in a skirmish between Muirchertach Ua Máel Sechnaill (d. 1143) and Tigernán Ua Ruairc and Uí Briúin Bréifne.[35] His grandson (*mac mic Giollafhulartaigh*), who is described in the Annals of the Four Masters as *tigherna deiscirt Breagh*, was killed in another skirmish with Tigernán Ua Ruairc in 1130, in which also fell Diarmait Ua Máel Sechnaill, king of Tara, Amlaíb Ua Senáin, lord of the Gaileanga, and Óengus Ua Caindelbháin, lord of the kingdom of Láegaire. *Lebor na Cert*, as noted by Paul Walsh,[36] categorises both the Déisi Breg and their local lords Mac Gilla Sechnaill as Déisi: *Dligid rí Temrach na tuath ... caeca dam ón dáim Dési* 'The king of Tara of the tribes ... is entitled to fifty oxen from the people of the Déisi'[37] and *Dligid rí na nDési anocht fichi mart is fichi molt* 'The king of the Déisi tonight is entitled [from the king of Ireland] to twenty beeves and twenty wethers'.[38] The situation as portrayed in *Lebor na Cert* is also probably reflected in Hugh de Lacy's charter granting the barony of [Lower] Deece to Hugh de Hose or Hussy, 'all the land del Dies which Shaclin held'. Orpen rightly equates Shaclin with Gilla Sechnaill.[39] A grant by John de Hereford, which pre-dates his father Adam's death in 1216 since the latter witnesses the transaction along with Simon de Rochford, bishop of Clonard (d. 1224), confirms the possessions and ecclesiastical benefices to St Thomas's Abbey, Dublin:[40]

que sunt in mea parte terre de Desa, sicut ipsa dividitur inter dominum meum, Hugonem Heose, et me, et que ad meam spectant donationem

which are in my portion of Deece, as it is divided between me and my lord, Hugh Heose, and which belong to my donation [that is to the portion which I received].

A charter of Robert Poer of Dunshaughlin (variously recorded as *Dinelinsakelin* or *Dunelinsachlin*), which probably dates from *c.* 1188–91, mentions that the canons of St Thomas's Abbey, Dublin, had permitted his men the use of a roadway with their animals to the lake, *Lohgouer*, otherwise Lagore (*Ita tamen quod prior predictorum canonicorum concessit hominibus meis de Dunelinsachlin viam veniendi cum animalibus suis ad lacum qui dicitur Lohgouer*).[41] Apart from providing a twelfth-century reference to the landscape between Dunshaughlin and Lagore, and the reference to Lagore itself, the background to this charter offers more evidence as to the importance of Dunshaughlin, which seems to have been a *matrix ecclesia*, a church with dependent chapels. One such chapel, or *capella*, at Ratoath is mentioned in this specific charter. The ecclesiastical benefices of the fee of Dunshaughlin were granted by Hugh de Lacy to St Thomas's Abbey. On de Lacy's death in 1186, it is likely that Robert Poer was enfeoffed by John, lord of Ireland, who during this period attempted to retain the lordship of Mide in his own hands. The reoccurrence of references to Dunshaughlin in early Anglo-Norman sources associated with de Lacy suggest that it had been retained by Hugh de Lacy as his personal demesne, a fact which John wished to continue to his own good.[42]

(ii) Saithne (Uí Chathasaig)

As remarkable as the survival of the Déisi Breg to this period is the prominence of the Saithne and their kings, the Uí Chathasaigh. They belonged to the Dál Céin (Cíannachta, Gailenga, Luigne, Saithne), whose original old kingdom may have stretched from the Liffey to Druim Inasclainn (Dromiskin, Co. Louth). In the centuries under consideration in this paper, their lands were approximately coterminous with the baronies of East and West Balrothery.[43] Uí Chathasaig kings were sufficiently important in the eleventh and twelfth centuries to compete with the Uí Chellaig Breg for the kingship of Brega. The mid-eleventh-century Uí Chathasaig king, Gairbíth Ua Cathasaig, for example, was particularly active. He led the kingdom of Saithne and *fir Breg* to victory at Cassán Linne (Annagassan, Co. Louth) against Cenél nÉogain and the Airgialla in 1045.[44] He killed Flannacán Ua Cellaig, *rí Breg*, in 1062 and usurped the title himself. He is described in the same year in his obit as *rí Breg*.⁴⁵ The annals depict a sub-kingdom occupying a precarious position between competing spheres of influence—to the south the Norse of Dublin, whose lands of Fine Gall overlapped with those of the Uí Chathasaig,⁴⁶ to the north the lands of their rivals for the kingship of Brega, the Uí Chellaig Breg (see below), and to the west (the barony of Skreen) the demesne of the kings of Tara, the Uí Máel Sechnaill. Relations with the latter in the eleventh and twelfth centuries were difficult, which may in part have been caused by encroachments by the kingdom of Saithne on the land of the kings of Tara. In 1049, for example, Toirdelbach Ua Cathasaig, who was being kept as a hostage, was killed by Conchobar Ua Máel Sechnaill when a hosting of the Ulaid, Laigin and Norsemen invaded Mide.⁴⁷ Notably, according to *Lebor na Cert*, the king of Tara was entitled to far more from the Saithne than from the Déisi Breg:⁴⁸

> Cét sárbrat óna Saithnib,
> céd crána, is crod firthaicid
> 7 céd mart ar moigib
> is cét molt dia móroigid.

> A hundred fine cloaks from the Saithne, a hundred sows—prosperous stock—a hundred beeves on the plains and a hundred wethers for slaughter.

The king of Saithne was entitled to a horse, two score cows, a cauldron and a vat from the king of Ireland *uair ní lugu a ngoiri amach*, which the editor suggests might be translated 'for their closeness of kinship (*a ngoiri*) is no less'.⁴⁹ However, this aside could have an opposite meaning ('for their kinship is no less from outside [than others]'), which amounts to a twelfth-century comment on the prominence of the Saithne. Their king is listed in third position after *rí Mide* and *rí Breg* (a title to which, in any case, Uí Chathasaig kings frequently aspired in the eleventh and twelfth centuries) and ahead of the kings of the Déisi, Luigne and Gailenga.⁵⁰

Curiously, their precarious position as a type of buffer-kingdom may have contributed to their local importance, a phenomenon not unknown elsewhere, as witnessed by the role on a greater scale of Uí Cerbaill kings of Airgialla or Mac Gilla Pátraic kings of Osraige. In a possible reflection of the sub-kingdom of Saithne's buffer-type position continuing into the Anglo-Norman period, Giraldus Cambrensis mentions that one of the first actions undertaken by Philip de Worcester as justiciar in 1184 was 'to devote great care to restoring to the maintenance of the king's table the revenues of those lands which Hugh de Lacy had appropriated, comprising Ua Cathasaigh and a number of other territories' (*terras quas Hugo de Laci alienaverat, terram videlicet Ocadhesi et alias quam plures, ad regiam mensam cum omni sollicitudine revocavit*).⁵¹ This deed, which was an attempt by Henry II to curb Hugh de Lacy's activities, concerned the delimitation of the royal demesne of Dublin against the encroaching de Lacy lordship of Meath.

Some circumstantial evidence exists that the monastery of Lusk was subject to the competing interests of the Norse, the Uí Máel Sechnaill and the Saithne. In 1133, Conchobar Ua Máel Sechnaill, *rígdamna Temrach*, was killed by Donnchad mac Gillamocholmóc, *rígdamnae Laigen*. Donnchad was slain in revenge by the men of Meath, and Conchobar's brother, Domnall mac Murchada Uí Máel Sechnaill,⁵² plundered Fine Gall and east Leinster (*airther Laighean*). In the course of this campaign of revenge, Lusk, *co na teampal lán do dhaoinibh, 7 taiscceadhaibh* 'with its churches full of people and treasures',⁵³ was burnt. Domhnall mac Murchada Uí Máel Sechnaill died in 1137 at the hands of the people of east Meath (*airrther Midhi*) and the Saithne.⁵⁴ The intricacy of the relationship between Uí Chathasaigh and Uí Máel Sechnaill kings is best explained in the entry in the *Banshenchas*, which notes that *ingen hUi Chathasaig rig na Saidne* was the mother of Conchobar Daill Ua Máel Sechnaill, *comarba Finden* (abbot of Clonard, ? d. 1153).⁵⁵

A deed dated *c*. 1270 relating to the land in Kilreske (barony of Coolock) details land granted by Thomas son of John Leonis to John son of Rand:⁵⁶

> the land that was that of Macolursy [Mac Gilla Fulartaig] and McMony [Mac Maenaig], from the ditch of Hathchartalath to the bounds of Hachdundochely,⁵⁷ which Roger de Finglas held; and it goes from that ditch in the upper part of the great street that leads from Dublin to Grenoke⁵⁸ as far as the long ford of Donathor,⁵⁹ and from the land of Donathor to the fee of Kilsenethan,⁶⁰ namely the land William de Cadewelly held.

Archbishop Alen adds the following note on the estate of the tenement of Kilreske:⁶¹

> Before the conquest of Ireland Occadesi [Ó Cathasaig] was chief lord of the land aforesaid, and under that lord were freeholders, namely Mobolucy alias

Macullursy [Mac Gilla Fulartaig] and McMony [Mac Maenaig]; but after the last conquest there were four principal lords in succession, and five freeholders. The lords were Leonisius, his son John, and John's son Thomas, and the archbishop of Dublin ...

These texts hint at the location of the centre of the sub-kingdom of Saithne, an area in which lay no less than three possible high-status sites in the post-Norman period, Greenoge, Donaghmore and even Ratoath. I would contend that the reference to the land of Macolursy (*alias* Mobolucy and Macullursy) is none other than Mac Gilla Fulartaig of the Déisi Breg.

(iii) The intrusion of the north Brega dynasty (Uí Chellaig Breg)

The Uí Chathasaigh's main rivals for the title *rí Breg* in the eleventh and twelfth centuries were the Uí Chellaig Breg. They belonged to the north Brega dynasty of Síl nÁedo Sláine, who were descended from Congal son of Áed Sláine (d. 634). They were a collateral branch of the Uí Chongalaig, descendants of Congalach Cnogba (d. 956), and their main rivals in the early part of the period under consideration.[62] Flannacán Ua Cellaig, *rí Breg*, accompanied Sitric mac Amlaíb, *rí Gall*, on his pilgrimage to Rome in 1028. From Flannacán's time, members of this family are accorded the title *rí* or *tigerna Breg* in 1060–1, 1093, 1129, 1146, 1161, 1170 and 1295. The Uí Chellaig Breg had notable ecclesiastical connections insofar as the family of Conn na mbocht (d. 1059), a prominent ecclesiastical family in Clonmacnoise during the eleventh century, was somehow related to them. *AFM* s.a. 1056 includes a genealogy as part of its obit of Máelfindéin mac Cuind na mbocht, which concludes with the comment *do Uibh Ceallaigh Breagh*. Furthermore, *AFM* s.a. 1067 records the death of Célechair Mugdornach, bishop of Clonmacnoise, and unlike the other annals adds *Do Uibh Ceallaicch Breagh a chenél* 'his kin were of the Uí Chellaig Breg'. This apparent confusion between the Mugdornai (presumably the population group known as Mugdornai Breg, although it could refer to Mugdornai Maigen[63]) and the Uí Chellaig Breg, as pointed out by Ryan in his treatise on the monastery of Clonmacnoise,[64] raises the question of whether Célechair belonged by kin to the Mugdornai or to the Uí Chellaig Breg. He could have belonged to Mugdornai who were subsumed into Uí Chellaig Breg territory. Mugdornai Breg had interests in the church of Kilbrew (barony of Ratoath: its abbots on occasion were recorded as abbots of Slane[65]) and Domnach Mór Meic Laithbe (Donoghmore, barony of Slane).[66]

The significance of the link between these two population groups is that, if it can be construed from Célechair Mugdornach's obit that the Mugdornai were dominated by the Uí Chellaig Breg in the eleventh century, it provides a starting-point from which to delineate the lands of the Uí Chellaig Breg at the time. The annals, though not profuse in their evidence on the matter, refer to incidents involving Uí Chellaig Breg kings occurring at Duleek and Slane. According to the *Annals of the Four Masters*, Trénfher Ua Cellaig was killed in 1093 at Daimliac Chianáin by Ua Duibidir of Leinster.[67] The same fate befell Muirchertach Ua Cellaig and his wife Inderb, daughter of the Uí Chaindelbháin (king of Cenél Lóegaire), in Slane (*for lár Sláine*) in 1161 at the hands of Cathal Ua Ragallaig. Máel Sechnaill Ua Ruairc escaped from Cathal on that occasion.[68] The family interest in Duleek may be reflected through the endowment of the Augustinian priory of St Mary's, if Ware's comment concerning the foundation's origin is of any value: *Hoc cœnobium à Kellœo quodam diù ante Anglorum adventum in Hiberniam, fundatum fuisse*.[69] It has been suggested that the Kellœo (Uí Chellaig) referred to was the same Muirchertach who was killed in Slane in 1161.[70] Documents relating to the grange of Duleek belonging to Llanthony priory,[71] and specifically to land in the manor of Le Lowher (townland of Lougher on the Boyne), confirm the continuing interests of the Uí Chellaig in lands in this area. Reference is made in one of these, dated to 1287 and concerning an inquisition on land in Le Lowther, to the demesne of William Okelli (father and son) ... *et de dominico xxx acrarum cum pertinenciis ibidem quas Willelmus Okelly nuper tenuit* ...[72] 'and of the demesne of thirty acres with possessions which William Okelly held until now'. The detailed description of the manorial extent of the grange of Duleek dated to 1381 includes a section on the dwelling or manor (*mansio*) and land granted by William Okelli (Junior?) *natiuum et Hibernicum* to Llanthony priory:[73]

Ab antiquo ibidem fuit quedam mansio que modo est totaliter vasta et decasa et lx acre terre vnde per estimacionem sunt iij acre et dimidia prati, que quidem scitus mansionis et terre sunt infra manerium de Logher et pertinent et deuenerunt ad dictos religiosos per quemdam Willelmum Okelli natiuum et Hibernicum ...

From long ago until now there was a certain

dwelling which in manner (shape) is totally waste and decayed and sixty acres in land of which by estimation consist of three and a half acres and less of meadow-land. The site of this dwelling and land is within the manor of Logher and they belong and came into the possession of the said religious [Llanthony priors] through a certain William OKelli, native and Irish.

That the Llanthony priors did not gain possession of this land easily from William O Kelly is clear from a complaint made by him against the prior of St Michael's, Duleek, and brought before the justiciar at Drogheda in 1306.[74] The account of the conflict between William and the prior over the lands at Lougher, which is replete with claims and counter-claims of injuries inflicted on both parties, concludes with the legal question brought to the justiciar by William as to the rights of the priors of Llanthony to this land. He argued that 'the predecessors of the prior acquired their tenements of the Lougher after the statute of the king was enacted that lands should not come into mortmain' and that if the escheator of Ireland found that this was so, he should take the lands into the hands of the king.[75] This case may provide a rare instance of how an Irish family might have used the Anglo-Norman judicial system to resist the confiscation of their lands by the new intruders, in this case the Augustinian canons of Llanthony, who had been given their original grants of land at Colp near Drogheda and Duleek by Hugh de Lacy and his son Walter.[76]

If the lands of the Uí Chellaig Breg lay along the Boyne south of Slane, with its centre (*caput*) at Duleek, how far south did their lands extend? The competition between them and Uí Chathasaig kings for the title *rí Breg* suggests that their own lands could not have extended any further than the boundary between the baronies of Upper Duleek and Balrothery. The lands of the Déisi Breg and of Clann Chernaig Sotail (Mac Gilla Sechnaill) were on occasion subject to them, when they held the title *rí Breg*.

The demesne of Tara: Uí Máel Sechnaill and intruders

(i) Uí Máel Sechnaill

Paul Walsh defined Brega, in the sense of a minor kingdom, excluding subordinate territories, as 'in the heart of the present county of Meath, east and south of the River Boyne, where the barony of Skreen lies to-day'.[77] In this area lay Tara and Skreen; one site, though of immense traditional importance, was probably not inhabited, and the other was the site of a significant church from the tenth century onwards.[78] When Tara is referred to as a place rather than as a title of kingship or as a mythical location during this period, it is associated specifically with military campaigns. The battle of Tara was won in 980 by Máel Sechnaill Ua Domnaill over the Norse of Dublin and the Isles, and their allies, the Laigin, Gailenga, Fir Tulach and Mugdorna Maigen. Tara was not a coincidental choice of battleground. During the 970s the Norse of Dublin pursued an increasingly expansionist policy, effected primarily by their king Amlaíb Cúarán,[79] who was probably more powerful than any of the dynasts of Brega at the time. He defeated the king of Tara (of the northern Uí Néill), Domnall Ua Néill (d. 980), with the assistance of Domnall mac Congalaig Cnogba, *rí Breg* (d. 976), at the battle of Cell Móna, near Tara, in 970. The apparent attachment between Amlaíb and Skreen, as expressed in Cináed úa hArtacáin's poem on the *dindshenchas* of Achall (Skreen) and understood circumstantially from the annals, seems to confirm that his authority extended to this area (and probably beyond), the heart of Clann Cholmáin's symbolic kingship of Tara.[80] Once Máel Sechnaill mac Domnaill rid himself of the northern contender, Domnall Ua Néill, in 971[81] he turned his attention to the Norse of Dublin with a campaign which culminated in the battle of Tara. It is no coincidence that Brian Bóruma, with the Connachta, Osraige, Laigin and the Norse of Dublin, proceeded to Tara in 1000 in a show of force against Máel Sechnaill. He did not reach Tara because Máel Sechnaill overtook and slaughtered the Norse and Laigin, who were acting as an advance raiding party (*crech marcach* (*AU*), 'a raiding party of horsemen'). Máel Sechnaill and Clann Cholmáin's interests in Tara were not simply metaphorical or expressed in the title *rí Temrach*. Their military defence of this area implies that they regarded this territory (roughly coextensive with the barony of Skreen) as their estate land. The author of *Lebor na Cert* considers Temair and Mide as the same kingdom: *Ó ríg Themrach dano dá rígaib ⁊ do thuathaib na Midi* [82] 'now from the king of Tara to his kings and to the *túatha* of Mide'. It ends the section on the rights of the king of Tara thus: [83]

> Is ead sin dliges do chrua
> rí Midi cen mór-fordul;
> i Temraig buidi mar bís
> is ead sin uili a ardchís.

That is the amount of stock without error to which the king of Meath is entitled; in golden Tara where he dwells, that is the whole of his mighty rent.

In what seems to be a comment on Brian Bóruma's pretensions, one poem on the *dindshenchas* of Tara includes these verses as part of its final section:[84]

Ce beith ós Banbai braining
ríg amrai, ard a medair,
ni fuil rechtas ríg foraib
acht a ríg techtas Temair.

Maelsechlaind, géc co nglan-rath,
focheird síth ima sen-mag;
sech brón mbáis ós cach díniu,
robé i rígiu Temrach.

Though famous kings be over Banba of hosts, great their mirth, there is no royal authority over them, except for the king who possesses Tara. Máelsechnaill, branch of bright fortune, spreads peace over the old plain; free from the sadness of death beyond every generation, may he be in the kingship of Tara.

A poem lamenting the death of Máel Sechnaill in 1022, *A Midhe is maith da bamhair*,[85] expresses such sentiments as *Do dorchaidh gnúis mín Midhe, do bás rígh tigi Temra*[86] 'the fair face of Mide clouded over, the king of the house of Tara expired'. The theme of the Middle Irish text *Do Suidigiud Thellaich Themra*,[87] which may date from the eleventh century in its present form, tells of the dissatisfaction of the nobles of Ireland during the reign of Diarmait mac Cerbaill with the extent of the royal demesne of Tara. This royal demesne is described as *tellach Temra*, translated by the editor (with the context of the specific text in mind) as 'the manor of Tara',[88] although *tellach* mainly denotes 'a household, a hearth, entry (in the legal sense)'. A most apt depiction of the demesne of Tara in the same text is contained in the phrase *ba mór leo do thír aurland Temrach .i. maigen i mbátar secht radairc for cech leath*... 'they regarded as [too] great the land of the demesne of Tara, namely, where there were seven views on every side'.[89] Hogan, in his discussion of the land division known as *trícha cét*, noted the existence of *trícha cét Níalann*, which he identified as the mensal land of Cormac mac Airt, and though unable to ascertain its location he commented that 'the probability is that it was situated in and about Tara'.[90]

The titles *rí Temra(ch)* and *rígdamnae Temra(ch)* in the period under consideration were primarily confined to different branches of the Uí Máel Sechnaill.[91] The most notable exceptions to this rule were Donnchad Ua Congalaig (d. 991), Gallbrat Ua Cerbaill (d. 1058) and Congalach Ua Riacáin (d. 1059). Vestiges of the close association between the Uí Máel Sechnaill and Tara seem to survive in topographical evidence in the area. For example, Pope Celestine III confirmed the possessions of the convent of St Mary's at Clonard in a letter dated 26 February 1196 to the abbess, Agnes, possibly a niece or daughter of Murchad Ua Máel Sechnaill (d. 1153).[92] Included among the extensive list of churches and lands regarded as appurtenances of the nunnery in the papal letter were:[93]

> ... ecclesiam sante Marie de Scrin cum adiacenti campo Dumdonnuil cum pertinentiis suis, ecclesiam sancte Brigide de Odra cum ipsa villa et omnibus suis pertinentiis ...

> ... the church of St Mary's of Skreen with the adjacent field of Dumdonnuil [Dúin Domnaill] with its possessions, the church of St Brigit of Odder with its vill and all its possessions ...

The church of St Mary's lay south of Skreen, surrounded by, but not part of, the de Feipo lordship and the local parish structure.[94] While the name Dumdonnuil (presumably the genitive of *Dún Domnaill*) could have been an old name, it is also possible that it refers to Domnall Bregach, nephew of Murchad Ua Máel Sechnaill, who was recognised as king of east Mide until his death in Durrow in 1173 at the hands of his half-brother, Art. Domnall Bregach was somehow related to Agnes (probably a first cousin), abbess of St Mary's, Clonard, and was among the Irish kings who submitted to Henry II in 1171–2.[95] Dún Domnaill might be identified with a large (diam. 55m) raised circular enclosure with earthen bank and external fosse in Collierstown, the name of which originates from *Baile na Caillech*, alias Calliaghstown.[96]

(iii) Uí Murchada, Uí Ciarda and Uí Airt

In her study of Skreen and the early Normans, and specifically of the de Feipo family, Elizabeth Hickey drew particular attention to two parcels of land which are constantly mentioned in the de Feipo grants to St Mary's Abbey, Dublin.[97] These lands appear as the place-names *Balivmorkaid* (*Baliomorhechad*, *Balechuamorcaid*) and *Balivkerde* or *Hukerde*.[98] The land of *Balivmorkaid* was also known as *Rachgouney*.[99] Ó Conbhuí and Hickey demonstrated that these lands formed the greater part of the grange of Skreen owned by the monks of St Mary's Abbey.[100] Hickey noted that these lands were not part of the seigniory of Skreen and suggested that they might have been 'church or *termonn* lands'.[101] They may reflect a phenomenon which was prevalent in eleventh- and twelfth-century south Brega, that of outside intrusion in the guise of planted families. It is difficult to prove this conclusion decisively, and the nature of the documentary material necessitates that the following is based primarily on supposition. While the element Murchad in the place-name *Balivmorkaid* or *Baliomorhechad* might at first glance point in the direction of the descendants of Murchad Ua Máel Sechnaill, there is no indication that any branch of the Uí Máel Sechnaill adopted the surname Ua Murchada. The family name Uí Murchada in the genealogies is that of the Leinster kingdom of Uí Felmeda Thes, who are accorded the title *ríg húa Murchada* in the Book of Leinster.[102] Uí Felmeda Thes was situated in the barony of Ballaghkeen, Co. Wexford.[103] They took their name from Murchad mac Óengusa, an earlier king of Uí Felmeda Thes. A second branch of the family, also descended from this Murchad, are given the title *Húa Felmeda Thíri* in the Book of Lecan genealogies.[104] Another genealogy in the Book of Leinster notes that these were Uí Dublaich, kings of Fer Tulach (Fartullagh, Co. Westmeath),[105] which is confirmed in Seaán Mór Ó Dubagáin's topographical poem, *Triallom timcheall na Fódla*.[106]

If the suggestion that the Uí Murchada family of *Balivmorkaid* or *Baliomorhechad* originated in south Leinster is plausible, a possible explanation for this—and for the siting of another branch of the same family in the midlands —lies in the intervention of Diarmait mac Murchada, king of Leinster (d. 1171), in this region. When Toirdelbach Ua Conchobair, king of Connacht and claimant to the high-kingship of Ireland, divided the kingdom of Mide in 1144, Diarmait was apportioned the eastern half of the kingdom and Tigernán Ua Ruairc was given the western half.[107] Domnall Bregach Ua Máel Sechnaill, styled king of east Mide, submitted to Diarmait mac Murchada in 1170, and possibly to Henry II in 1171–2. Diarmait may have felt that it was in his gift to grant parcels of the mensal lands of the kings of Tara to his own subordinates in Leinster, a position in which the Uí Murchada of Uí Felmeda Thes found themselves, given the geographic location of their kingdom in Leinster. Two of Diarmait mac Murchada's charters allude to the connection between him and the Uí Murchada. Gilla Pátraic Ua Murchada witnessed Diarmait's charter in favour of Ferns,[108] while the same Gilla Pátraic Ua Murchada and his brother, Domnall Rúad,[109] witnessed a grant of lands in the territory of the Benntraige in favour of the Cistercian abbey of Killenny, Co. Kilkenny, also made by Diarmait mac Murchada.[110] Notably, Diarmait mac Murchada probably had a local ally in south Brega insofar as Donnchad Ua Cellaig Breg seems to have been fostered in Uí Chennselaig, if his name, *Donnchadh Ceinnsealach Ua Cealaigh*, as recorded in *AFM* s.a. 1169, is to be thus understood.

The second place-name associated with the grange belonging to St Mary's Abbey, variously referred to as *Balivkerde* or *Hukerde*, provides additional, if equally tentative, evidence to support the supposition that these place-names reflect the interventionist policy of Diarmait mac Murchada or other kings. Hickey suggested an interpretation of *Balivkerde* as 'the farmstead of the O'Murphys', presumably *Baile uí Murchada*.[111] While this interpretation is persuasive, the alternative form of the parcel of land in question, *Hukerde*, implies another interpretation. It may be that the surname involved is not *Ua Murchada* but *Ua Ciarda*. This name was that of the family who held the sub-kingdom of Cairbre, who were transplanted from the kingdom of Mide or Tethba and planted in the barony of Carbury in north-west Kildare, possibly under the patronage of Diarmait mac Murchada, in the mid-twelfth century.[112] The Uí Ciarda suffered singularly at the hands of Tigernán úa Ruairc, king of Bréifne (d. 1172), who killed their king Domnall in 1138, probably caused their annexation to Leinster in 1158 and attacked their kingdom in 1162 in revenge for their killing of his son that same year.[113] They also participated in internal feuds between rival Uí Máel Sechnaill claimants to the kingship of Mide in the mid-twelfth century. When Gilla Got Ua Ciarda was slain in Clonard by Donnchad Ua Máel Sechnaill in 1155, the latter was deposed as king of Mide and replaced by his brother, Diarmait mac Domnaill. Within three years, however, in 1158, the Uí Ciarda turned on Diarmait and supported Donnchad. Diarmait, with the assistance of Tigernán Ua Ruairc, defeated them at the battle of Áth Maigne and expelled Donnchad and the Uí Ciarda of the kingdom of Cairpre Gabra to Leinster. The close relationship between them and Uí Máel Sechnaill kings may be reflected in the entry in the *Banshenchas* which notes that Domnall Bregach Ua Máel

Sechnaill's mother was Ailbe, daughter of Uí Chiarmaic *do Chairpri o Ciarrda*.[114] Máel Ruanaid Ua Ciarda, *ríg Cairpre* (?1155–74), witnessed the memorandum of 1161 in the Book of Kells concerning the protection of the church at Ardbraccan.[115]

The influence of Diarmait mac Murchada's arch-rival, Tigernán Ua Ruairc, in the region is also worth noting. He granted lands to St Mary's Abbey, Navan, and may have founded an Arrouaisian house there, as shown by the confirmation of 1189 of these lands by John de Courcy:[116]

> hac presenti carta mei confirmasse deo & eccesie sancte Marie de Novan & canonicis regularibus ... omnes terras quas tenuerunt de donaciona hibernicorum ante adventum anglicorum in hibernia ... et totam terram quam O Roirke eis dedit ...

> by this my present charter confirmed to God and to the church of St Mary of Navan and the canons regular ... all the lands which they held by gift of the Irish before the coming of the English into Ireland ... and all the land which O'Rourke gave them [details specific lands].

Among the lords of Tara mentioned by Ó Dubhagán in his topographical poems is Ó hAirt, a family which, like Ua Ruairc, originated in Tethbae.[117] Orpen suggested that the lands referred to in the *Song of Dermot and the earl* as *la terre de Rathenuarthi*, which was granted to Adam Dullard, could be interpreted as 'Raithin O'hArtaigh, the little rath of OhAirt, *anglice* O'Hart'.[118]

(iii) Uí Duind and Uí Riacáin

Earlier intrusions by dynasties from outside Brega and even Mide also left their imprint on the toponymy of Tara's hinterland. During the period 1023–59 the title *rí Breg* was claimed on a number of occasions by the Uí Riacáin and Uí Duind, who may have belonged to the Uí Failge or Uí Chellaig Cualann of Leinster or were possibly of Dál Cais origin in Munster.[119] In 1023 Donnchad (Dúnchad) úa Duind, *rí Breg*, was seized by the Norse *ina n-airiucht fein* 'in their own assembly' (*AU*) in violation of the protection of the *coarb* of Colum Cille.[120] Donnchad was killed in 1027 following a series of related incidents, which finally led to his death. the *Annals of the Four Masters* provides the most extensive account of these events (which accords well with descriptions in the other annals):

> Scrín Cholaim Chille do orgain do Raen [úa Máelsechnaill], ⁊ boraimhe mór do breith esde. Scrín Mocholmócc do arccain lá hAmhlaoibh ⁊ la Dunchadh tighearna Breagh. Slóicceadh lá Sitriocc, mac Amhlaoibh ⁊ lá Dunchadh, tighearna Breagh i Midhe co Léicc mBladhma co comharnacthar friú fir Midhe im Roen Ua Maoileachlainn. Fearthar cath eatorra. Maidheadh for Gallaibh, ⁊ for fhiora Breagh. Cuirthear a nár im Dhúnchadh, mac Duinn, tighearna Breagh, agus im Ghiollaausaille mac Giollacaoimhghin, tighearna Ua mBriúin Chualann. Soiter for Roen doridhisi ⁊ maideadh fair, ⁊ marbhthar Roen, tighearna Midhe co sochaidhibh oile.

> Scrín Cholaim Chille [Skreen, Co. Meath] was plundered by Raen[121] and a large booty was taken from it. Scrín Mocholmóc [Staholmog, barony of Lower Slane[122]] was plundered by Amlaoibh and by Dunchad lord of Breg. A hosting by Sitriocc mac Amhlaoibh [king of Dublin] and by Dunchad, lord of Breg, into Mide as far as Léicc Bladma [Lickbla, barony of Fore[123]] and they encountered the men of Mide including Roen Ua Maoileachlainn. A battle was fought between them. The Norse and the men of Breg were defeated. They were slaughtered including Dúnchad mac Duinn lord and Giolla Ausaille, lord of Uí Briúin Cualann. They set upon Roen again and defeated him and slew Roen, lord of Mide with many others.

This series of events demonstrates the layers of intrusion in the region and the various and often shifting alliances of the period, evidenced by the alliance between Ua Duind and his erstwhile enemies, the Norse of Dublin (see 1023), and also Ua Duind and elements of the Laigin. Notably, in the following year (1028) Sitric, king of Dublin, went to Rome accompanied by Flannacán Ua Cellaig (of Uí Chellaig Breg), *rí Breg*.[124]

During the same period, another apparent intruder, Mathgamain Ua Riacáin, competed for the title *rí Breg*. His interest in the region is first recorded in 1025, when Gerr Gaela, *rí Breg*, was killed by him and by the people of Deiscert Breg.[125] He seized Amlaím, *rí Gall*—son of the king of Dublin, Sitric, who went to Rome—in 1029 and extracted a large payment from him as a pledge for keeping the peace.

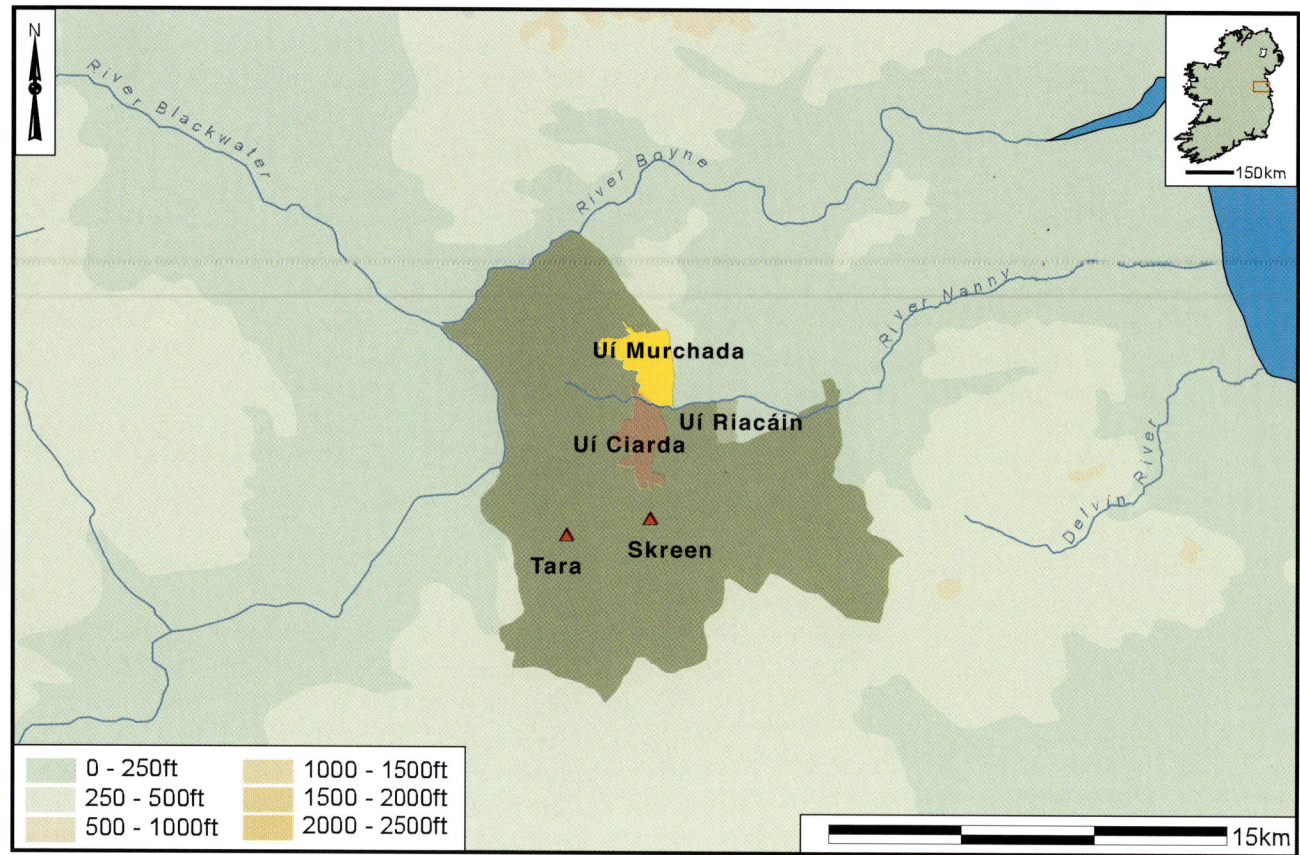

Fig. 4—Lands held by three intrusive families, Uí Murchada, Uí Ciarda and Uí Riacáin, within the barony of Skreen.

The pledge included 1200 cows, 120 Welsh (*bretnach*) horses, 60 ounces of gold and the sword of Carlus, an accumulation which, despite possible annalistic exaggeration, is a statement of the wealth of the Norse of Dublin.[126] Mathgamain Ua Riacáin was killed by Domnall Ua Cellaig, Flannacán's son, in 1032.[127] Uí Riacáin interests resurfaced in 1053, when they killed Máelcrón mac Cathail, styled as *rí Breg* by *AU* and *AFM* and as *rí deiscirt Breg* by *ATig*, and then proceeded to attack the Norse.[128] The last notice of Uí Riacáin activity is found in 1059, when Congalach Ua Riacáin, *rídomna Temrach*, was killed by Murchad, son of Diarmait mac Máel na mBó (d. 1070). It would seem, however, from evidence other than the annals that the Uí Riacáin may have maintained a presence in the region. Ó Dubhagáin includes the family among the nobility of Tara,[129] as well as including the Uí Duinn as an afterthought, *Tógbham tuilleadh ar Teamhraigh … Ó Duinn ar thíribh Teamhrach*.[130] Two post-Norman charters preserve the name Uí Riacáin in lands in the barony of Skreen. Robert de Aveni endowed the Hospital of St John the Baptist in Dublin (*c.* 1190) with two pieces of land, part of which was in his tenement of *Criuirigan*, namely the territory of the Uí Riacáin.[131] A certain Ranulph granted 'all that land which is called *Tworubragan*' to St Mary's Abbey, Dublin.[132] Hickey interpreted this place-name as *Tír uí Riagáin*,[133] although it might equally represent *túath uí(b) Riacáin*. More significantly, Hickey located *Crích Uí Riacáin* as 'an open field near Danestown' in the barony of Skreen (Fig. 4).[134] Uí Riacáin settlements in the region probably also account for a place-name such as Rathregan, in the barony of Ratoath, in the vicinity of which there exists a ringfort, a church and the site of a deserted settlement.[135]

The Norse of Dublin and the kingdom and petty kingdoms of Deiscert Breg

A further element of intrusion in Deiscert Breg from the ninth century onwards was that of the Norse, and especially the Norse of Dublin. The relationship between the Norse of Dublin and the various petty kingdoms alluded to in this paper merits a separate study, but some initial observations may be made.[136] In their analysis of the economic needs and resources of Dublin during this period, Bradley and Wallace have tackled the dynamics relating to the supply of food and other raw materials to the town.[137] It is argued that Dublin was dependent on the surrounding hinterland for up to 90 per cent of its meat diet, for raw materials such as mineral ores, fruit and nuts, timber (both for building and firewood), and other building materials (wattles, straw, stone, brushwood, fern, moss). Bradley maintains that, since the hinterland supplied the town with its everyday needs,[138] 'it is difficult to envisage that it was farmed by the native Irish, who could cut off supplies to the town, if the occasion arose. Rather it would have been essential for the continued existence of the town that this area should be farmed by Scandinavians, or at least by Hiberno-Scandinavians who were part and parcel of the Dublin polity.'

This hinterland around Dublin, Bradley contends, is best expressed by the term *Dyflinskiri*, a phrase which appears in twelfth- and thirteenth-century Icelandic sagas. The northern part of Dyflinskiri was Fine Gall, an area which extended from the Liffey to the north of Skerries.[139] In his discussion, Bradley comments that a distinction needs to be made between control and colonisation, and that there were areas in Dyflinskiri which were 'occupied by Irish tribes, over whom the Scandinavians exerted control'.[140] However, the situation is likely to have been far more complex than hitherto portrayed. If Dublin depended on its hinterland for such a large and constant supply of food and raw materials, was it feasible to rely solely on estates in Dyflinskiri? Much of Dyflinskiri was subject from time to time to control by Irish kings, whether local or provincial, and the situation changed constantly.

The battle of Tara in 980 can be seen as a landmark in the polity of this region, and particularly in the relationship between the Norse of Dublin and the kings of Brega and Mide. There is ample evidence to suggest that prior to that date the Norse of Dublin, especially in the guise of their king Amlaím Cuarán (d. 980), exercised considerable control over this area and possibly much further north.[141] The *Banshenchas*, for example, notes that Ragnailt, daughter of Amlaím [Cuarán], was the mother of Muirchertach Ua Congalaig (d. 995). Muirchertach belonged to the north Brega dynasty of Knowth. Dúnlaith, daughter of Muirchertach mac Néill Glúndub (d. 943), was the mother of both Máel Sechnaill mac Domnaill (d. 1022) and of Glúniarn, son of Amlaím Cuarán (d. 988).[142] That such blood relationships meant some form of alliance is evident from events recorded in the annals. Muirchertach Ua Congalaig raided Domnach Pátraic (Donaghpatrick, barony of Upper Kells, near Tailtiu) with the Norse of Dublin in 995, *sed Deus uindicauit in morte ipsius in fine eiusdem mensis* 'but God avenged it by the latter's death at the end of the same month'.[143]

A combination of defeat at the battle of Tara, the death of Amlaím Cuarán and the increasing interest of Irish kings in Dublin in the eleventh century must have affected the ability of the Norse of Dublin to control independent estates within Dyflinskiri, and even in Fine Gall. For example, Murchad, son of Diarmait mac Máel na mBó, was made king of Dublin in 1052 when his father expelled Echmarcach mac Ragnaill, king of the Norse of Dublin.[144] As king of Dublin and joint ruler of Leinster with his father, Murchad presumably could have guaranteed supplies to the town without depending solely on estates in Dyflinskiri, which had contracted since the reign of Amlaím Cuarán. Perhaps this increasing dominance of Dublin by Irish kings in the eleventh and twelfth centuries can explain to a degree relations between the kingdoms of Deiscert Breg and the Norse of Dublin at the time. Dublin was attacked *hi taidhe* 'in stealth' by the people of Deiscert Breg in 1004.[145] The Norse killed Ainbíth Ua Cathasaig, king of Saithne, in 1023 and Cúgaileng mac Gilla Sechnaill, *rí Breg*, in 1121. Glúniarn, son of Sitric (1031), Raghnall mac Torcaill (1146) and Brodar mac Torcaill (1160) were all killed by the people of Deiscert Breg. It seems likely, on the basis of the entries relating to the deaths of Cúgaileng mac Gilla Sechnaill and of Brodar mac Torcaill, slain by Máelcrón mac Gilla Sechnaill in 1160, that there was particular enmity between the Norse and the Mac Gilla Sechnaill kings of Deiscert Breg.[146] This enmity would appear to have had a long history, if there is any truth in the annalist's comment on the death of Gilla Mo-Chonna mac Fogartaig, *rí deiscirt Breg* and forebear of the Mac Gilla Sechnaill, in 1013: *Leis do-rata na Gaill fon arathar ⁊ da Ghall ic foirsed asa tiaghaibh 'na ndiaigh* 'By him the foreigners were yoked to the plough, and two of them made to harrow after them [and sow seed] from their satchels'.[147]

Relations with the kings of Saithne were more ambiguous. The lands of the Uí Chathasaig were within Fine Gall and, as mentioned above, they probably acted as a buffer between the Norse and the other kingdoms of the region. The kings of Saithne may have held an economically important position insofar as they may have had the power of facilitating or cutting off any supplies coming from Irish kingdoms to Dublin. In 1023, when the Norse plundered Deiscert Breg and raided Duleek, they killed Ainbíth Ua Cathasaig, king of Saithne.[148] When Máel Sechnaill mac Conchobair, king of Tara, was defeated by the Leinstermen and the Norse in 1086 at the battle of Crincha (on the northern bank of the Liffey), Máelciarán Ua Cathasaig fell in the battle.¹⁴⁹ Alliances were ever-changing and by 1146 the Norse were acting in consort with Flaithbertach Ua Cathasaig and killing Cellach Ua Cellaig, king of Brega.¹⁵⁰ Places singled out for attack included Domnach Pátraic (995: with Muirchertach Ua Congalaig), Termonn Feichín (1014: with the Leinstermen), Duleek (1023), Scrín Mocholmóc (1027: with Donnchad Ua Duind in revenge for an attack on Scrín Choluim Cille), Duleek and Scrín Choluim Cille (1039), and possibly, though unlikely, Scrín Choluim Cille (1127). Lusk, which is identified with the Norse and within Fine Gall, was plundered by the Uí Máel Sechnaill in revenge for the death of Conchobar mac Murchada Uí Máel Sechnaill in 1133.¹⁵¹

The conduct of the Norse when acting in consort with or as part of an intrusive campaign in this region is also worth noting. While the evidence is meagre, two patterns seem to emerge. The Norse of Dublin were often allied to the Laigin when they attacked Brega (1005, 1014, 1049, 1086), and when Brega was attacked from outside it was often as part of a campaign against Fine Gall or north Leinster, although, as with so many patterns of this period, this could vary, depending on shifting alliances and motives for the attack. In 1090, for example, Muirchertach Ua Briain with the Munstermen and the Norse of Dublin plundered a district of Leinster and Brega as far as Áth Buide (Athboy) (*co ro indairset cendtar Laigen ⁊ Fir[u] Bregh co Ath mbuidhi*).¹⁵² In 1100 Domnall Ua Lochlainn came south and plundered Brega and Fine Gall.¹⁵³ In a manner similar to their relations with the Mac Gilla Sechnaill, there is some evidence of a particular enmity between the Norse and the Uí Máel Sechnaill. This enmity may have stemmed from Máel Sechnaill mac Domnaill's rout of them at the battle of Tara in 980. As noted previously, the Norse acted in alliance with Donnchad Ua Duind and with Gilla Ausaille mac Gilla Caemgin, king of Uí Briúin Chualann, in 1027 against Roen Ua Máel Sechnaill. In 1133, when Murchada Ua Máel Sechnaill avenged the death of his son Conchobar, who was killed by Donnchad mac Gilla Mocholmóc, *rígdamnae Laigen,* and by the Norse, the Uí Máel Sechnaill burnt Lusk and then proceeded to plunder Fine Gall and east Leinster.¹⁵⁴

There is an occasional glimpse of the military role played by the Norse, most notably in their seafaring capacity, as witnessed in 1005 by their progress by sea to their stronghold, presumably Dublin, as part of Brian Bórama's host returning from Armagh, while the Laigin travelled overland across Brega: *Lothar imorro Laighin dar Breagha fodheas dia ttír, ⁊ Gaill for muir timcheall tair dia ndún* 'Then the Laigin went over Brega southwards to their land, and the Gaill overseas around to the east to their fort'.¹⁵⁵ They seized Donnchad Ua Duinn, king of Brega, in 1023 and took him overseas (*a bhreith dar muir*) despite the protection of the *coarb* of Colum Cille (abbot of Kells).¹⁵⁶

From the kingdom of Deiscert Breg to the de Lacy lordship of Meath: elements of continuity

The question arises as to the extent to which subsequent patterns of land division, settlement and defence were predetermined by the landscape itself and by existing patterns. This is of particular relevance with regard to the degree of continuity or change manifest in the twelfth century—from the immediately pre-Norman settlement and territorial divisions to the patterns which emerge with the intrusion of the first wave of Anglo-Norman settlers. One conclusion which is evident from this study is that the polity of south Brega operated at different levels: the local dynasties, who were relatively constant, as evident from the continuing presence of families such as Mac Gilla Fulartaig, Mac Gilla Sechnaill and the Uí Chathasaig; neighbouring but extremely influential dynasties, especially the Uí Máel Sechnaill and the Norse of Dublin; and the intrusions by kings of other provinces. An idea of these different layers, what Máire Herbert in her discussion of the Kells charter material aptly describes as 'a window on to a microcosm of Irish society on the eve of the Norman conquest',¹⁵⁷ may be gained from the memorandum in the Book of Kells concerning the church of Ardbraccan, dating from 1161. The guarantors to the agreement are listed as follows in the text: Gilla mac Liac, *comarba Pátraic*; Muirchertach mac Lochlainn, *ríg Érend*; Diarmait mac Domnaill meic Murchada, *ríg Mide*; Étrú Úa Miadachán, *epscop Mide*; Congalach mac Shenán, *ríg Galeng*; Ímar Úa Cathasaig, *ríg Saithne*; Domnall Úa Brain, *ríg Luigne*; Máelruanaid Úa Ciarda, *ríg Cairpre*; Móelcrón mac Gilli Shechlaind, *ríg Deiscirt Breg*; Murchad Úa Findulláin, *ríg Delbna;* and mac Rónán, *ríg Cairpre Gabra*.¹⁵⁸ If a region was subject to so many layers of control and intrusion in the eleventh and twelfth centuries, the initial reaction of the local dynasties to the coming of the Anglo-Normans may not have been so great. Despite the obvious cultural difference, the intrusion might have been seen as a continuation of an already regular occurrence. This view would have been strengthened by the alliance between the

Anglo-Normans and Diarmait mac Murchada, whose influence in the region was not insignificant.

Contending with the Anglo-Normans may not have been an immediate priority for the local dynasties either. Mac Murchada went to Mide in 1170 and burnt Kells, Dulane and Slane. Domnall Bregach Ua Máel Sechnaill, king of Brega (possibly in name only), submitted to Mac Murchada in the same year,[159] and probably to Henry II, along with Ua Cathasaig, king of Saithne, in 1171–2. Of greater concern to the local polity may have been the raids by Tigernán Ua Ruairc, king of Bréifne, on the kingdom of Saithne and Deiscert Breg in 1171. Mac Gilla Sechnaill, likely to be Máelcrón *rí deisceirt Bregh* who witnessed the memorandum of 1161 in the Book of Kells, was killed during this campaign.

To what extent were Anglo-Norman land grants and settlement or defensive sites predetermined by existing territorial divisions, high-status and strategic sites of pre-Norman kings and by the landscape itself? Evidence suggests that the pre-Norman kingdoms of south Brega consisted primarily of the lands of Mac Gilla Sechnaill (incorporating the lands of Mac Gilla Fulartaig), Uí Chellaig Breg, Uí Chathasaig, mensal lands of the kings of Tara (and intruders), with Fine Gall (Norse of Dublin) to the south and probably overlapping with parts of Mac Gilla Sechnaill and Uí Chathasaig lands. In his consideration of the de Lacy lordship of Meath, Robert Bartlett suggested that it is best regarded as quite a new political identity, in that its boundaries were created by the exercise of military power and did not exactly mirror those of any single earlier political unit.[160] It could be argued, however, that the new political identity was shaped by the region's dominant geographical features—as might be expected—and by existing territorial units. The primary influence of the first wave of Anglo-Norman settlers was in the administrative, cultural and military spheres. What changed in this region were not the boundaries but those who controlled the different territorial divisions. Those whose status was most affected by the new administration were the local dynasties, who either submitted to the latest intrusion (as the king of Saithne did) or who baulked at it for some time, which might explain the late resistance of a member of the Uí Chellaig Breg to the impositions of the prior of Llanthony at Duleek. If we take the pre-Norman lands as proposed above and explore what became of them in the hands of the de Lacys, there is a remarkable continuity between the two phases. Hugh de Lacy granted Hugh Hose or Hussey 'all the land of Deece which Shachlin (Mac Gilla Sechnaill) held',[161] thus clearly replacing one local king with an intrusive knight in a pre-existing territory. As noted earlier, the comment made by Giraldus Cambrensis concerning the lands of Ocadhesi (Uí Chathasaig), in which he stated that Philip of Worcester restored its revenue, which Hugh de Lacy had appropriated, to the royal demesne,[162] is probably partially explained with reference to the pre-Norman status of the kingdom of Saithne, that of a minor buffer between Dublin, Fine Gall and the rest of Brega. Henry II was curbing Hugh de Lacy's activities, and in this instance using a pre-existing territorial division to delimit the extent of his royal demesne of Dublin against de Lacy's lordship of Meath.[163] With regard to the lands around Tara and Skreen, this is the land which was granted by Hugh de Lacy to Adam de Feipo, according to *The song of Dermot and the earl* : '*E scrin ad pus en chartre, Adam de feipo lad pus done*' 'And Skreen he then gave by charter, To Adam de Phepoe he gave it'.[164] That Tara was part of the original grant can be inferred from the dispute which arose between Richard de Feipo and Randulph de Repentiny concerning Tara. The Pipe Roll of 14 John 1211–12 records that de Feipo rendered a fine to the king for bringing a writ of *praecipe* for one knight's fee with appurtenances at Ataneracht (*leg.* Taueracht), which he claimed against de Repentiny.[165] The de Repentiny family held on to their lands at Tara, as witnessed by late twelfth- or early thirteenth-century charters made in favour of St Mary's Abbey, Dublin, by Ralph de Repentiny and by his son Peter of *marcam unam mei redditus in villa de Tauerach annuatim percipiendam*[166] 'one mark of my income in the vill of Tara, payable annually'.

What of settlement and defence? Comments made in a recent paper by Marie Therese Flanagan are particularly relevant to this discussion and need to be reiterated:[167]

> Discussion of the siting of mottes was for too long focused on neutral geographical and strategic features as the most significant determinant in their choice of location and pattern of distribution, without sufficient attention being paid to pre-Norman settlement and political organisation. In recent years there has been a recognition that Anglo-Norman mottes frequently occur in close proximity to pre-Norman ecclesiastical sites. The royal residences or status sites of pre-Norman kings also have to be taken into consideration (bearing in mind that these too might be located near ecclesiastical sites).

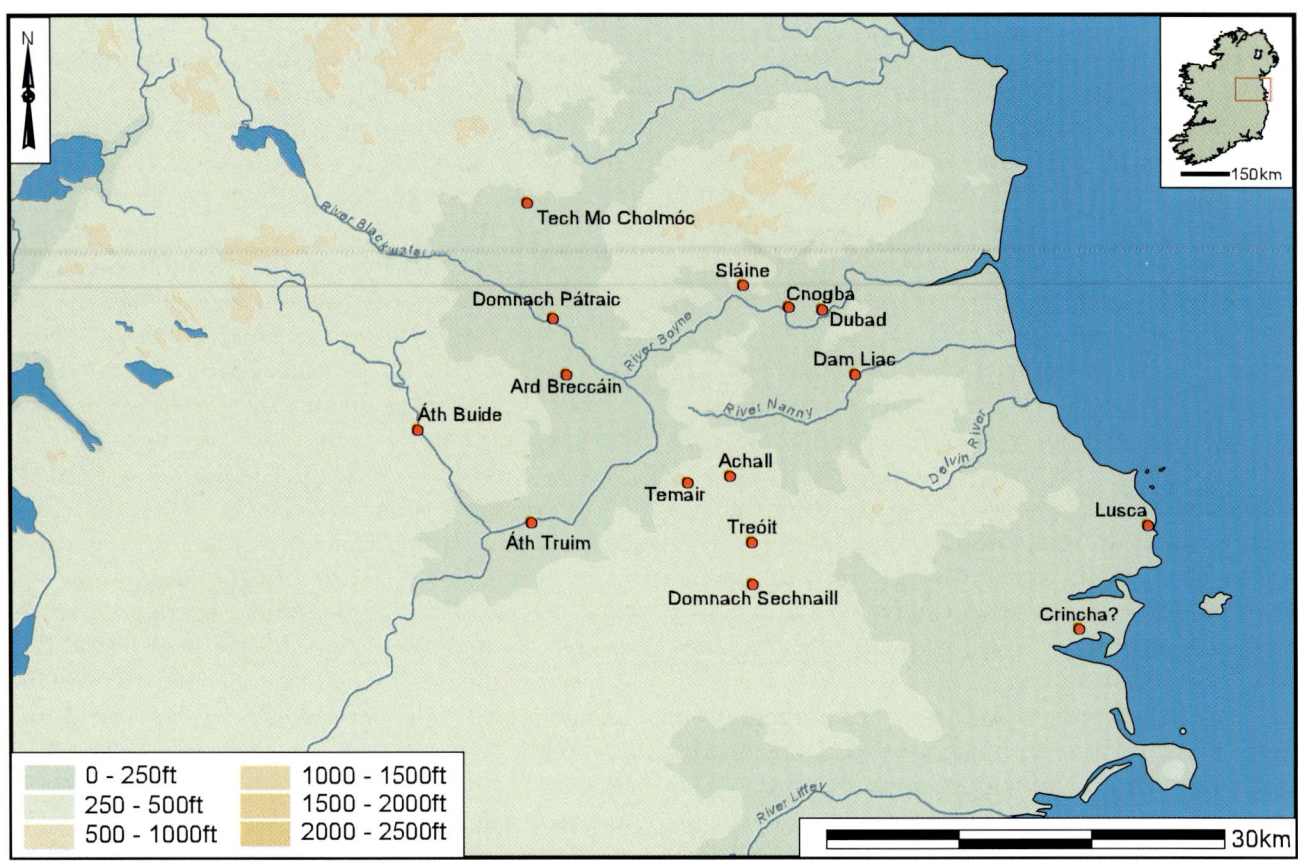

Fig. 5—Sites mentioned in the annals from 950 to 1172.

An indication of the most important sites in the pre-Norman period can be deduced from places mentioned in the annals, which tend to concentrate on the locations of battles or raids, often strategic locations or sites of significant population and power. The places in this region which are referred to in the annals during the period 950–1172 are listed below, along with the date and event involved (Fig. 5).

Tara	980: battle
	1000: hosting towards
	1104: hosting to
	1169: hosting to
Donaghpatrick	995: raid
Duleek	1023: raid
	1039: plundered
	1093: killing of *rí Breg*
	1123: House of Murchad úa Máelsechnaill, *rí Temrach,* and 80 other houses burned
Dunshaughlin	1026: raid
	1152: plundered
Skreen	1027: plundered
	1039: plundered
	1058: plundered
	?1127: raid
	1152: plundered
Staholmog	1027: plundered
Knowth	1039: burned
Drochet Átha[168]	1039: burned
	1136: battle
	1157: consecration of monastery
Lusk	1053: captives taken
	1133: burned
Dowth	1059: burned and plundered
Crincha	1086: battle
Athboy	1090: hosting to
Ardbraccan	1109: burned and captives taken
	1115: burned
Trim	1128: burned
Trevet	1152: plundered
Slane	1161: Máelsechnaill úa Ruairc's house seized and Muirchertach úa Cellaig, *rí Breg,* killed there

When this list is compared with the spread of Anglo-Norman settlements in this region, there is a marked similarity between them (Fig. 6). *The song of Dermot and the earl* refers to Ardbraccan, Skreen and Trim,[169] while Giraldus Cambrensis in *Expugnatio Hibernica* mentions Trim, Duleek and Skreen.[170] The *Miscellaneous Irish Annals* for the year 1176 notes that the Anglo-Norman castles built in this period were at Dunshaughlin, Trim, Skreen, Navan and Knowth.[171] It adds that in the same year Richard Fleming built a castle at Dumach Sláine,[172] which may be identified with the Hill of Slane.[173] The Irish Pipe Roll of 14 John 1211–12 is more detailed in its inclusion of Anglo-Norman settlements since it lists many judicial and economic transactions in Meath, but for the purposes of this paper references to the following sites may be noted: Drogheda, Kilsallaghan, Coolock, Duleek, Galtim, Athboy, Clonee, Trim, Donaghmore, Trevet, Tara, Slane and Rathfeigh. It is reasonable to conclude that Dunshaughlin, Skreen, Duleek, Lusk, Knowth, Drogheda (albeit not exactly where the Anglo-Norman town flourished), Dowth, Trim and Slane were important in the pre-Norman period and that these were recognised as such by the new settlers.

This conclusion is borne out to some extent by the annals (with due recognition for the possibility of exaggeration). In 1123, for example, the Gailenga burned Murchad Ua Máel Sechnaill's house in Duleek and, according to *AU*, 7 *ochtmogha taighi ime* 'and eighty houses around it'. Trim was burned in 1128 *cona thempluibh* 'with its churches'. Other sites of a lesser importance might have included Ratoath, Greenoge and Rathregan. Far from entering virgin territory and creating a new landscape,[174] the Anglo-Normans found in south Brega an established pattern of territorial division and of settlement, an established structure of authority, no doubt with a concomitant system of economic distribution and collection of tribute or taxes, and an evolving, parallel ecclesiastical framework. Rather than ignore this existing polity, they proceeded to mould it according to their own administrative, economic and military structures.

Deiscert Breg: the archaeology of stability and intrusion

In archaeological terms, the evidence for these patterns of continuity and of change needs to be addressed in any discussion of settlement models for the period. Initial examination of the monuments recorded at sites of pre-Norman and Anglo-Norman importance in this region point towards two types of complex.[175] The first is the more advanced site, in which all or many of the following elements are found: tumuli, souterrain(s), field-system(s), ringfort(s), large enclosure(s) and other earthworks,

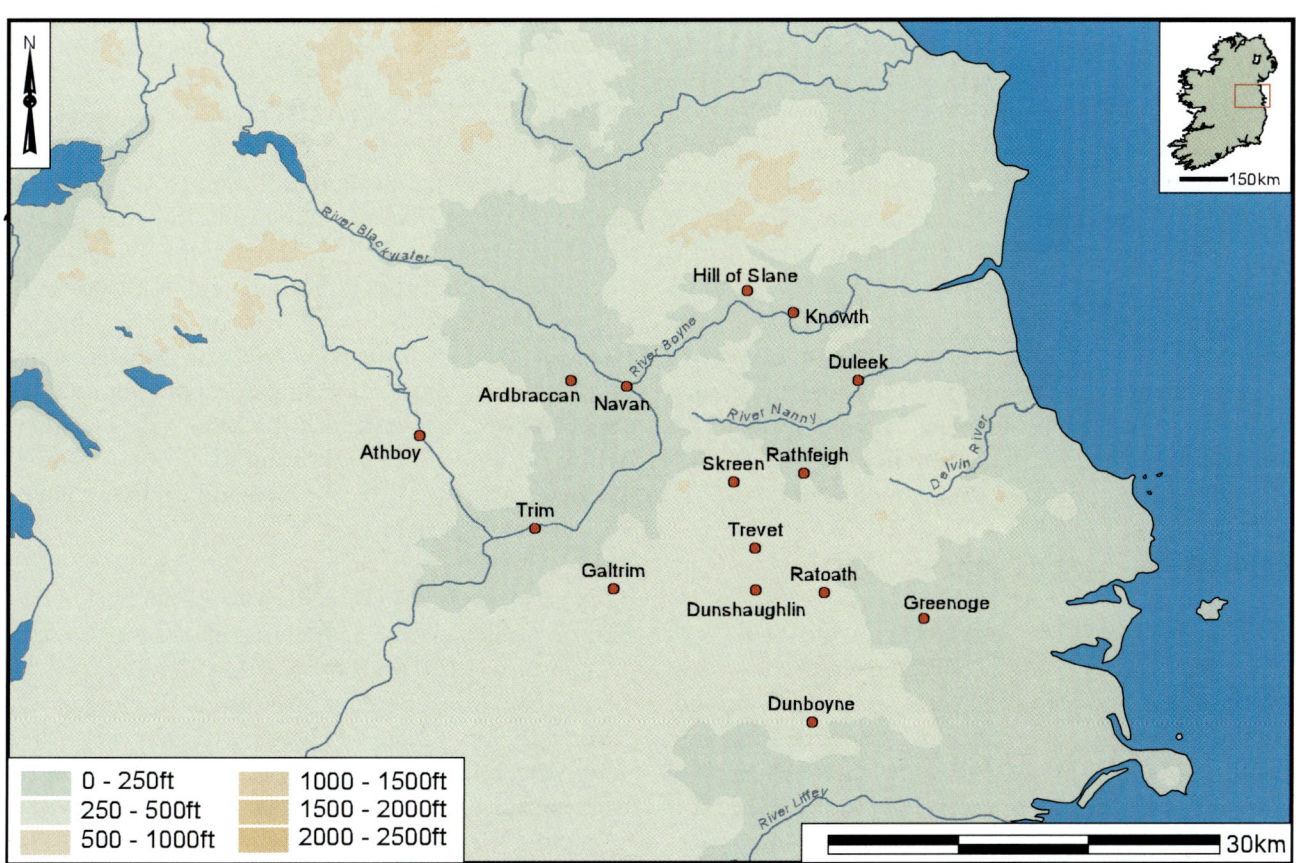

Fig. 6—Early Anglo-Norman settlements in Deiscert Breg.

church(es), cross(es), motte site, tower-house(s), gatehouse(s) and bridge(s). Duleek, Skreen, Knowth, Dowth, Athboy, Trim, Trevet, Ratoath and Slane belong to this category. The second type is a less complex site, with perhaps no more than two of the elements listed above. Sites of this category include Dunshaughlin (church and motte), Staholmog (ringfort and church), Ardbraccan (tumulus, souterrain, church), Greenoge (tumulus and church), Rathregan (tumulus, ringfort, church, deserted settlement), Rathfeigh (church and motte) and Galtrim (church site and motte). Some of these elements are clearly pre-Norman, and even prehistoric, while others have always been regarded as Anglo-Norman. The remains at Staholmog, for example, point in the direction of a pre-Norman settlement. But what of a site such as Trevet, important both in pre-Norman and Anglo-Norman sources? Trevet is recorded as incorporating a tumulus, a rectilinear enclosure, a field-system, a church, a ringfort, a bivallate ringfort and an earthwork.[176] Since it is known from the sources that Trevet (*Treóit*) was significant to Síl nÁedo Sláine from the early medieval period (and to their descendants in the area, Clann Chernaig Sotail and Mac Gilla Sechnaill) and to the Anglo-Norman family de Essocot, how do these various cultural associations manifest themselves in the archaeological evidence? Perhaps it may not be necessary always to seek a different type of monument to equate with a change in dynasty or even an intrusion. Existing buildings could be reused, depending on the function required of them by the newcomers and on the pace of the adoption of new practices. The main lesson of this study for the interpretation of a particular landscape is that neither the historical nor the archaeological record can be explained by neat one-dimensional models. If the documentary sources portray such complex relationships between different layers of authority in a region, the archaeological record must also reflect these intricacies in some manner.

Conclusion

The material brought together in this paper will hopefully stimulate further insights into the actual exercise of authority in early medieval Ireland. Methodologically, two conclusions emerge. It would seem that before any further wide-ranging survey of early medieval Ireland is undertaken in the future it is worth pursuing a regional approach, whereby a greater understanding may be gained from detailed regional and chronological studies. This type of work could be regarded as building the database for the next survey on a national scale. Such a study also illustrates how much information can be gathered from material which is disparate in style, in cultural background and in original purpose. One can only conclude that Brega, and in this specific case south Brega (*Deiscert Breg*), attracted incomers in every age. Beneath apparent constant instability was a local continuum, most vividly expressed through the persistence of the Déisi Breg. If such a continuum existed in this region, which succumbed so often to intrusion, it is likely that local stability' must have existed to an even greater extent in other regions which were more remote or less open to outside influence. While the nature of source material causes historians to continue to work mainly on either side of a pre- and post-Norman dividing line, greater attention to the local detail of specific bodies of material is likely to show that the earlier period spills into the later to a larger degree than hitherto acknowledged.

It is useful to speculate as to what significance this study might have for considerations regarding settlement and archaeological monuments. Identification of pre-Norman high-status sites and the link between them and existing monuments, which in many instances seem superficially to be Anglo-Norman, requires some reassessment of the division between the two. Dunshaughlin emerges from this study as a case most worthy of examination. While normally regarded as a pre-Norman ecclesiastical site, it is as likely to have been the *caput* used by the Mac Gilla Sechnaill family and not simply a church, as perceived from the surviving physical remains. A similar function could be argued for Duleek and Slane. How patterns of continuity and of intrusion, be it Irish or Anglo-Norman, left an imprint on the landscape and in source material is a subject which offers much to practitioners of many disciplines. This paper has sought to advance the topic a little further.

Acknowledgements

This paper is dedicated to the late Elizabeth Hickey, Skryne Castle, whose pioneering work on the local area inspired this study. I wish to thank Dr Terry Barry, Mr John Bradley, Mr Brian Lacey and in particular Dr Marie Therese Flanagan for their comments on an earlier draft on this paper. The maps were produced by Mr Barry Masterson and Mr Paul Synnott, Discovery Programme. I wish to thank Mr Joseph Fenwick for allowing me to reproduce the panoramic view of Tara as a map.

Notes

1 F.J. Byrne, *Irish kings and high-kings* (London, 1973), 87–105; E. Bhreathnach, 'Temoria: caput Scotorum?', *Ériu* **47** (1996), 67–88.

2 Byrne, *Irish kings*, 48–69; C. Swift, 'Pagan monuments and Christian legal centres in early Meath', *Ríocht na Midhe* **9**, no. 2 (1996), 1–26: 2–3; R. Ó Floinn, 'Artefacts in context: personal ornament in early medieval Ireland' (forthcoming).

3 W.A. Borgeaud, 'Hibernica: Echu-Echoch, Echoid-Echdach, Temair', *Beiträge zur Namenforschung* **6** (1971), 40–4; M.A. O'Brien, 'Varia IV: 12. *Banba*', *Ériu* **11** (1932), 167–8; T. Ó Concheanainn, 'Topographical notes — I. Cermna in Meath', *Ériu* **22** (1971), 87–96; T. Ó Cathasaigh, 'The semantics of *síd*', *Éigse* **17** (1977–9), 137–55; Ó Cathasaigh, 'The eponym of Cnogba', *Éigse* **23** (1989), 27–38; P. Ní Chatháin, 'Traces of the cult of the horse in early Irish sources', *Journal of Indo-European Studies* **19** (1991), 123–31.

4 For discussion of the segments of the Síl nÁedo Sláine in south Brega see P. Walsh, 'Ancient Meath according to The Book of Rights', *Leaves of history*, Series 1 (Drogheda, 1930), 3–51: 7–13; P. Walsh, 'Meath in the Book of Rights', in J. Ryan (ed.), *Féilsgríbhinn Eoin mhic Néill* (Dublin, 1940), 508–21: 516–17; L. Price, 'The history of Lagore, from the annals and other sources', in H. Hencken, 'Lagore Crannog: an Irish royal residence of the 7th to 10th centuries A.D.', *Proceedings of the Royal Irish Academy* **53C** (1950), 18–34; F. J. Byrne, 'Historical note on Cnogba (Knowth)', appendix to G. Eogan, 'Excavations at Knowth, Co. Meath, 1962–1965', *Proceedings of the Royal Irish Academy* **66C** (1967–8), 383–400: 390–400 and tables 1 and 2. The genealogies of Clann Chernaig meic Diarmada or Clann Chernaig Sotail, extending to the eleventh and twelfth centuries, are preserved in the Book of Ballymote (80d38).

5 *AU* 758, *Niallghus m. Boith rex na nDeisse mBregh [mortuus est]*.

6 *AU* 1034 records the slaying of Gilla Sechnaill mac Gilla Mochonna (Clann Chernaig Sotail king of south Brega) and of Gilla Fulartaig, king of Déisi Breg, without noting the perpetrators. *AFM* 1034 adds that Gilla Sechnaill mac Gilla Mochonna was killed by Fir Ruis, that Muirchertach Ua Ceallaigh slew Gilla Colaim Ua Riacáin, and then follows with the more expansive notice of Gilla Fulartaig's death.

7 Among the works which this study merely supplements are Walsh, 'Meath in the Book of Rights', Price, 'Lagore', Byrne, 'Cnogba (Knowth)', and M.T. Flanagan, *Irish society, Anglo-Norman settlers, Angevin kingship. Interactions in Ireland in the late twelfth century* (Oxford, 1989).

8 E. Gwynn, *The Metrical Dindshenchas* (5 vols) (Dublin, 1903–35) (Todd Lecture Series; reprinted in 1991 by the Dublin Institute for Advanced Studies).

9 M. Dillon, *Lebor na Cert. The Book of Rights* (Dublin, 1962) (Irish Texts Society 46).

10 K. Meyer, 'Mitteilungen aus irischen Handschriften: Cináed úa hArtacáin .cc.', *Zeitschrift für celtische Philologie* **12** (1918), 358–9.

11 G. Mac Niocaill, *Notitiæ as Leabhar Cheanannais 1033–1161* (Dublin, 1961); G. Mac Niocaill, 'The Irish "charters"', in P. Fox (ed.), *The Book of Kells, MS 58, Trinity College Library Dublin: commentary* (Luzern, 1990), 153–65.

12 Primarily the *Annals of Ulster* (*AU*), *Annals of Tigernach* (*ATig*), *Annals of Clonmacnoise* (*AClon*) and *Annals of the Four Masters* (*AFM*).

13 G.H. Orpen (ed.), *The song of Dermot and the earl* (London, 1892).

14 O. Davies and D.B. Quinn, 'The Irish Pipe Roll of 14 John, 1211–1212', *Ulster Journal of Archaeology* **4** (supplement) (1941), 1–76.

15 J.T. Gilbert (ed.), *Chartularies of St Mary's Abbey, Dublin* (2 vols) (London, 1884–6) (Rolls series).

16 E. St John Brooks, *The Irish cartularies of Llanthony Prima & Secunda* (Dublin, 1953) (Irish Manuscripts Commission).

17 See primarily Gilbert, *Chartularies of St Mary's Abbey*; J.T. Gilbert, *Register of the abbey of St Thomas the Martyr, Dublin* (London, 1889) (Rolls series); E. Curtis, *Calendar of Ormond deeds 1172–1350 A.D.* (Dublin, 1932) (Irish Manuscripts Commission); St John Brooks, *Llanthony cartularies*.

18 For example, E. St John Brooks, 'A charter of John de Courcy to the abbey of Navan', *Journal of the Royal Society of Antiquaries of Ireland* **63** (1933), 38–45.

19 Most notably the section in the poem *Triallom timcheall na Fódla* composed by Seaán Mór Ó Dubhagáin and edited in J. Carney, *Topographical poems by Seaán Mór Ó Dubhagáin and Giolla-na-Naomh Ó Hidhrín* (Dublin, 1943), 1–6.

20 J. Fenwick, 'A panoramic view from the Hill of Tara, Co. Meath', *Ríocht na Midhe* **9,** no. 3 (1997), 1–11.

21 D. Keeling, 'A group of tumuli and a hill-fort near Naul, County Dublin', *Journal of the Royal Society of Antiquaries of Ireland* **113** (1983), 67–74. This

22 Gwynn, *Metrical Dindshenchas*, vol. 5 (index).

23 *Ibid.*, vol. 1, 38.10, *Mag mBreg co n-ilar drummann* (Mag Breg with numerous hills).

24 The question as to whether Brega and Mag mBreg covered the same territory requires further detailed consideration (for a basic, if not always completely accurate, survey see E. Hogan, *Onomasticon Goedelicum locorum et tribum Hiberniae et Scotiae. An index, with identifications, to the Gaelic names of places and tribes* (Dublin and London, 1910; reprinted Dublin, 1993), 123–4, 514).

25 See comments in F.J. Byrne, 'The trembling sod: Ireland in 1169', in A. Cosgrove (ed.), *A new history of Ireland. Vol. II. Medieval Ireland, 1169–1534* (2nd edn, Oxford, 1993), 1–42: 19.

26 *AU* 935, *Inis Locha Gabhar do thogail la hAmhlaibh h. hImair. Huam Cnoghbhai do thogail dó isint sechtmain cetnai.* For comments on the context of these raids see B. Jaski, 'The Vikings and the kingship of Tara', *Peritia* **9** (1995), 310–53: 330.

27 Hencken and Price, 'Lagore', 7, 24.

28 For the most recent comments on this matter see R. Warner, 'On crannogs and kings (Part 1)', *Ulster Journal of Archaeology* **57** (1994), 61–9.

29 M.C. Dobbs, 'The Ban-Shenchus', *Revue celtique* **47** (1930), 312; **48** (1931), 188, 226.

30 Walsh (*op. cit.*, 517) quotes Fr Woulfe as suggesting that the derivatives of the surname Mac Gilla Sechnaill were M'Kintaghlin, Mac-A'Taghlin and MacTaghlin. It is interesting to note that in the Elizabethan fiants (*The Irish fiants of the Tudor sovereigns during the reigns of Henry VIII, Edward VI, Philip & Mary, and Elizabeth*, vol. 2 (*The Irish fiants of Queen Elizabeth 1, 1558–1586*) (Dublin, 1994: reprinted by Éamonn de Búrca), 241, no. 1799) one Hugh M'Kintaghlin, horseman, was pardoned with William Flemyng fitz Patrick of Perston (Piercetown, south of Dunshaughlin) in 1570–1.

31 *AU* 1027, *Donnchad m. Gilla Mo-Conna, comarba Sechnaill, sapientisimus Scotorum, in Colonia quieuit.* Donnchad was Gilla Sechnaill's brother.

32 *AU* 975, *Cinaed H. Artugan* (marginal gloss in TCD MS H.1.8: *.i. do sil Cernaigh Sotail*) *primecess Erenn, quieuit.*

33 Meyer, 'Mitteilungen', 359.

34 Gwynn, *Metrical Dindshenchas*, vol. 1, 46–53: 50, lines 79–80.

35 *ATig* 1109, *Sluagad la Muirchertach Húa mBriuin co feraib Muman ⁊ Midhe a Condachtaib a n-Uib Briuin Brefne, co tuc bu ⁊ brait moir, ⁊ co ndechatar for indsib Locha hUachtair, co tucsad bruid estib. Tanic iarsin Húa Ruairc ⁊ Húa Briuin, cor'cuirsed Húa MaelSechlainn asa longport ⁊ tucsat ár fer Midi im mac Gilla [F]ulartaigh et alios cum eo.*

36 Walsh, 'Meath in the Book of Rights', 516–17.

37 Dillon, *Lebor na Cert*, 1481–4.

38 *Ibid.*, 2182–3.

39 G.H. Orpen, *Ireland under the Normans, 1169–1216*, vol. 2 (Oxford, 1911), 85, note 5.

40 J.T. Gilbert, *Register of the Abbey of St Thomas the Martyr, Dublin* (London, 1889) (Rolls series), 123–4 (CXLIII).

41 *Ibid.*, 26.

42 I am indebted to Dr Marie Therese Flanagan for unravelling the complexities of this charter and other related material in the context of the present paper. Dr Flanagan points further to the granting of Ratoath (a dependent chapel of Dunshaughlin, also mentioned in the charter of Robert Poer as granted to St Thomas's Abbey) by Walter de Lacy to his brother Hugh de Lacy II, and to the possibility that John's grant to Robert Poer was overturned by Walter de Lacy when he gained seisin of Mide with the help of Richard I in 1194. It is recorded that Robert Poer was temporarily deprived of lands in England for siding with John, during the latter's rebellion against Richard I.

43 Walsh, 'Meath in the Book of Rights', 519; Brooks, *Irish cartularies of Llanthony*, xiv–xvii; M. T. Flanagan, '*Historia Gruffudd vab Kenan* and the origins of Balrothery, Co. Dublin', *Cambrian Medieval Celtic Studies* **28** (Winter 1994), 71–94: 71–6.

44 *AU*, *ATig*.

45 *ATig*.

46 Note the wording of the charter of John, son of Henry II, dated about 1189–90, confirming to Archbishop Cumin the possessions of the see of Dublin, including *medietatem decimarum terre Okadesi de Finegall* ('half of the tithes of the land of Okadesi of Finegall'): G. Mac Niocaill, 'Charters of John, lord of Ireland, to the see of Dublin', *Reportorium Novum* **3**, no. 2 (1964), 282–306: 294, line 19; Flanagan, '*Historia Gruffudd vab Kenan*', 75–6.

47 *AFM*, *ATig*.

48 Dillon, *Lebor na Cert*, 1501–4.

49 *Ibid.*, 2178–81. With regard to the translation of the last line see Dillon 103, footnote 2.

50 *Ibid.*, 2169–89.

51 A.B. Scott and F.X. Martin (eds), *Expugnatio Hibernica. The Conquest of Ireland by Giraldus Cambrensis* (Dublin, 1978), 198–9; Flanagan,

'Historia Gruffydd vab Kenan', 74–5, 82–3.

[52] *AFM* 1133 claims that his death was avenged by his father Murchad, while *ATig* s.a. 1133 (ed. W. Stokes, *Revue celtique* **18** (1897), 59) states that another brother, Donnchad, plundered Lusk. The *AClon* s.a. 1135 (edited by D. Murphy, *The annals of Clonmacnoise being annals of Ireland from the earliest period to A.D. 1408 translated into English A.D. 1627 by Conell Mageoghagan* (Dublin, 1896; reprinted Llanerch Publishers 1993), attributes the burning of Lusk to Domnall mac Murchada.

[53] *AFM* 1133.

[54] *ATig* 1137 (Stokes, *Revue celtique* **18** (1897), 155). *AClon* 1137 (p. 196) adds that Domnall was killed by the east of Meath (*sic*) 'for being in rebellion against his father and Meath men'.

[55] Dobbs, 'The Ban-Shenchus', *Revue celtique* **48** (1931), 192; see also P. Byrne, 'The community of Clonard, sixth to twelfth centuries', *Peritia* **4** (1985), 157–73: 163.48.

[56] C. McNeill, *Calendar of Archbishop Alen's register c. 1172–1534 (being an extra volume of the Royal Society of Antiquaries of Ireland for 1949)* (Dublin, 1950), 134.

[57] Possibly Athdunsochely. See Dunsoghly, Co. Dublin.

[58] Greenoge, barony of Ratoath, Co. Meath.

[59] Donaghmore, barony of Ratoath, Co. Meath.

[60] Kilsallaghan, barony of Nethercross, Co. Dublin.

[61] McNeill, *Archbishop Alen's register*, 134–5.

[62] Congalach Cnogba's father, Máelmithig mac Flannacáin (d. 919), was the brother of Cellach (d. 895) from whom Uí Chellaig Breg descended. Note the relationships as expressed in a Middle Irish poem (Book of Ballymote, 81a) quoted in Walsh, 'Book of Rights', 509: *Do luid Congal a cnoc Temra/ co Temraig naird nodradaigh/ conadh o Chongal ro clannaidh/ clann Ceallaig clann Congalaigh* ('Congal went to Temair's hill,/ to Temair, high and much disputed;/ from Congal have descended Clann Chellaig and Clann Chongalaig'). This is the same poem ascribed to Cináed úa hArtacáin which is edited by Kuno Meyer in *Zeitschrift für celtische Philologie* **12**, 358–9.

[63] Byrne, 'Cnogba (Knowth)', 390, 394.

[64] J. Ryan, *Clonmacnois. A historical summary* (Dublin, 1973), 37–8; A. Kehnel, *Clonmacnoise—the church and lands of St Ciarán. Change and continuity in an Irish monastic foundation (6th to 16th century)* (Münster, 1997), 271 (B20). Dr Kehnel suggests that Célechair was most likely another son of Conn na mBocht.

[65] M.A. O'Brien, *Corpus genealogiarum Hiberniae*, i (Dublin, 1962; reprinted 1976), 152: 142b39–40: *Sord a quo Sordraigi la Cremthaine de quibus epscop Ibair for Fobrech*.

[66] *Ibid.*, 152: 142b43–4: *Mes-snuibi a quo Snobraigi la hUltu Mugdorn de quibus epscop Eithern mac Laithbe i nDomnuch Mór Meic Laithbe*.

[67] For references to Ua Duibidir genealogies see S. Pender, 'A guide to Irish genealogical collections', *Analecta Hibernica* **7** (1935), 143.

[68] *AU, AFM*.

[69] J. Ware, *De Hibernia et antiquitatibus ejus* (London, 1654), 166.

[70] N. Hadcock, 'The origin of the Augustinian order in Meath', *Ríocht na Midhe* **3**, no. 2 (1964), 124–31: 128.

[71] For an extensive discussion of the layout of the manor of Duleek see A. Simms (with an appendix by J. Bradley), 'The geography of Irish manors: the example of the Llanthony cells of Duleek and Colp in County Meath', in J. Bradley (ed.), *Settlement and society in medieval Ireland. Studies presented to F.X. Martin, o.s.a.* (Kilkenny, 1988), 291–326.

[72] Brooks, *Llanthony cartularies*, 230, no. 34.

[73] *Ibid.*, 301, no. 98.

[74] *Calendar of Justiciary Rolls 1305–07*, 173–4.

[75] *Ibid.*

[76] For example see Brooks, *Irish cartularies of Llanthony*, 220–1.

[77] Walsh, 'Book of Rights', 509.

[78] On pre-Norman Skreen see E. Bhreathnach, 'The documentary evidence for pre-Norman Skreen, County Meath', *Ríocht na Midhe* **9**, no. 2 (1996), 37–45; C. Doherty, 'The Vikings in Ireland: a review', in H.B. Clarke, M. Ní Mhaonaigh and R. Ó Floinn (eds), *Ireland and Scandinavia in the early Viking Age* (Dublin, 1998), 288–330: 301–5.

[79] Jaski, 'Vikings and Tara', 343–8.

[80] Bhreathnach, 'Pre-Norman Skreen', 41–3.

[81] *AU: Domnall H. Neill, ri Temhrach, do innarbu a Midhe do Claind Colmain*.

[82] Dillon, *Lebor na Cert*, 1399–1400.

[83] *Ibid.*, 1524–7.

[84] Gwynn, *Metrical Dindshenchas*, vol. 1, 44, lines 69–76.

[85] *Book of Uí Maine,* 155Ra23.

[86] *Ibid.,* 155Rb35–6.

[87] R.I. Best, 'The settling of the manor of Tara', *Ériu* **4** (1910), 121–72.

[88] See Best's note on this translation, 164.

[89] *Ibid.*, 124.

[90] J. Hogan, 'The tricha cét and related land measures', *Proceedings of the Royal Irish Academy* **38C** (1928–9), 148–235: 212.

[91] P. Walsh, 'The Ua Maelechlainn kings of Meath',

Irish Ecclesiastical Record **57** (1941), 165–83.

[92] For accounts of this foundation see J. Brady, 'The nunnery of Clonard', *Ríocht na Midhe* **2** (1960), 4–7; N. Hadcock, 'The origin of the Augustinian order in Meath', *Ríocht na Midhe* **3** (1964), 124–31: 125–6.

[93] M.P. Sheehy, *Pontificia Hibernica. Medieval papal chancery documents concerning Ireland 640–1261*, i (Dublin, 1962), 84 (no. 29). For the complex relationship of this family see M. T. Flanagan, 'Mac Dalbaig, a Leinster chieftain', *Journal of the Royal Society of Antiquaries of Ireland* **111** (1981), 5–13: 9.

[94] E. Hickey, *Skryne and the early Normans* (Meath Archaeological and Historical Society, 1994), 76–7. Hickey notes that the modern townland Collierstown derives its name from Calliaghtowne (*Callaghton* in the Civil Survey) and further from *Baile na gCailleach*.

[95] Flanagan, *Irish society*, 311.

[96] M.J. Moore, *Archaeological Inventory of County Meath* (Dublin, 1987), 65 (no. 581).

[97] Hickey, *Skryne and the early Normans*, 83–90; see also Fr C. Ó Conbhuí, 'The lands of St Mary's Abbey, Dublin', *Proceedings of the Royal Irish Academy* **62C** (1961–3), 21–84: 75–8.

[98] Gilbert, *Chartularies of St Mary's Abbey*, i, 86, 88, 91, 196.

[99] *Ibid.*, i, 196, no. 164 (charter of confirmation of Simon de Feipo of churches and benefices to St Mary's Abbey: *et totam terram de Rachgouney, que alio nomine vocatur Baliumorkayd, in qua grangia eorum est sita, cum suis pertinenciis, que terra est dos predicte ecclesie et liberum sanctuarium*).

[100] Ó Conbhuí, 'The lands of St Mary's Abbey', 77–8; Hickey, *Skryne and the early Normans*, 83–90.

[101] Hickey, *Skryne and the early Normans*, 86.

[102] O'Brien, *Corpus genealogiarum Hiberniae*, 430: 337b1.

[103] Hogan, *Onomasticon*, 670.

[104] Lec. 93Va 32; see O'Brien, *Corpus genealogiarum Hiberniae*, 354: 317cb21.

[105] *Book of Leinster* (facsimile), 391b. Note also the death in 1127 (*AFM*) of Domhnall Dall Ua Murchada, *airdéaccnaid Laighean*.

[106] Carney, *Topographical poems*, 3: 57–8 (*Ó Dubhlaoich fa díoghainn rath, rí Fear ttriathuasal tTulach*).

[107] Flanagan, *Irish society*, 224–5.

[108] W. Dugdale, *Monasticon Anglicanum* (reprint, London, 1846), vi, II, 1141.

[109] They were the sons of Donnchad Ua Murchad and they terminate the genealogies of the Uí Murchada as preserved in the Book of Leinster (O'Brien, *Corpus genealogiarum Hiberniae*, 430).

[110] C.M. Butler and J.H. Bernard, 'The charters of the Cistercian abbey of Duiske in the County of Kilkenny', *Proceedings of the Royal Irish Academy* **35C** (1918–20), 1–188: 7–8.

[111] Hickey, *Skryne and the early Normans*, 86, 203 (footnote 7).

[112] Byrne, *New history of Ireland*, vol. II, 20; Flanagan, *Irish society and Anglo-Norman settlers*, 225 (footnote 166).

[113] *AFM*.

[114] Dobbs, 'The Ban-shenchus', *Revue celtique* **48**, 192.

[115] Mac Niocaill, *Notitiæ as Leabhar Cheanannais 1033–1161*, 36: 14–15.

[116] St John Brooks, 'A charter of John de Courcy', 38–45: 39–40; Sheehy, *Pontifica Hibernica*, ii, 23 §186.

[117] Carney, *Topographical poems*, 2: 26.

[118] Orpen, *Song of Dermot*, 3164–5; 315n.

[119] O'Brien, *Corpus genealogiarum Hiberniae*, 433: 337f1; 237: 152b31–2 (Muintir Donn-chuan); 238: 152b50.

[120] *AU, AFM*. *ATig* records that he was *Dondchad Hua Duinn chuan rí Breagh*.

[121] For comments on references to Roen's career see S. Duffy, 'Ostmen, Irish and Welsh in the eleventh century', *Peritia* **9** (1995), 378–96: 382–3.

[122] Hogan, *Onomasticon*, 593. See alternative names *Tech Mocholmóc* and *Dísert Mocholmóc*.

[123] Walsh, 'Ua Maelechlainn kings of Meath', 168.

[124] *AU, ATig, AFM* 1028.

[125] *AU, ATig, AFM* 1025.

[126] *AU, ATig, AFM*.

[127] *AU* 1032; *AFM* 1032 and 1039.

[128] *AU, AFM, ATig*. *ATig* reads *Mael-cron mac Cathail, rí desceirt Bregh, do marbadh do Uib [MS sic] Riacan aidhchi luan chasc, ₇ crecha lais for Gallaib*.

[129] Carney, *Topographical poems*, 2: 25–6: *Ríogha na Teamhrach i ttám, Ó hAirt ríoghdha is Ó Riagán*.

[130] *Ibid.*, 5: 121–4.

[131] E. St John Brooks, *Register of the hospital of S. John the Baptist without New Gate, Dublin* (Dublin, 1936), 172, no. 250.

[132] Gilbert, *Chartularies of St Mary's Abbey*, i, 228.

[133] Hickey, *Skryne and the early Normans*, 128. A further possibility is that *Tworubragan* might be a version of *Tír Uí Brecáin*.

[134] *Ibid.*, 107. Danestown incorporates the surname de Aveni, as proven by earlier versions Daneneystown or Danystown.

[135] Moore, *Archaeological Inventory of County Meath*, nos 857, 1487, 1691.

[136] On this matter see J. Bradley, 'The interpretation of Scandinavian settlement in Ireland', in J.

137 Bradley (ed.), *Settlement and society in medieval Ireland. Studies presented to F.X. Martin o.s.a.* (Kilkenny, 1988), 49–78: 56–62.
137 Bradley, 'Scandinavian settlement', 52–3; P. F. Wallace, 'The economy and commerce of Viking Age Dublin', in K. Düwel, H. Jankhun, H. Siems and D. Timpe (eds), *Untersuchungen zu Handel und Verkehr der vor- und frühgeschichtlichten Zeit in Mittel- und Nordeuropa iv: der Handel der Karolinger- und Wikingerzeit* (Gottingen, 1987), 200–45.
138 Bradley, 'Scandinavian settlement', 53.
139 Ibid., 57–8.
140 Ibid., 58.
141 Bhreathnach, 'Pre-Norman Skreen', 40–1.
142 Dobbs, 'The Ban-shenchus', 188, 227.
143 *AU*.
144 For comments on Murchad's role in defending the northern frontier of Leinster and control of Dublin see D. Ó Corráin, 'The career of Diarmait mac Máel na mBó, king of Leinster', *Journal of the Old Wexford Society* 3 (1970–1), 27–35: 31; Flanagan, *Irish society*, 88.
145 *AFM*.
146 The year 1160 provides an accurate reflection of the local enmities. Brodar mac Torcaill was slain by Máelcrón mac Gilla Sechnaill, Diarmait Ua Cathasaig was slain by Muirchertach Ua Cellaig (Breg) and Domnall mac Gilla Sechnaill was killed by Murchad mac Domnall Uí Máel Sechnaill.
147 *AU, AFM*.
148 *AU, AFM*.
149 *ATig*.
150 *AFM*.
151 *AFM*: *Lusca co na teampal lán do dhaoinibh, 7 taiscceadhaibh do losccadh for Fine nGall don lucht chédna a ndíoghail meic Murchadha .i. Chonchobhair. Móirchreach lá Murchadh Ua Maoileachlaind a ndíoghail a mhic, co ro airce Fine Ghall, 7 airther Laighean.*
152 *AFM, ATig*.
153 *AFM, AU*.
154 *AFM, ATig*.
155 *AFM*.
156 *AU, AFM*.
157 M. Herbert, 'Charter material from Kells', in F. O'Mahony (ed.), *The Book of Kells. Proceedings of a conference at Trinity College Dublin, 6–9 September 1992* (Aldershot, 1994), 60–77: 77.
158 Mac Niocaill, *Notitiæ*, 36.
159 *ATig*.
160 R. Bartlett, 'Colonial aristocracies of the High Middle Ages', in R. Bartlett and A. MacKay (eds), *Medieval frontier societies* (Oxford, 1989), 23–47: 31.
161 Orpen, *Ireland under the Normans*, vol. 2, 85, note 5.
162 Scott and Martin, *Expugnatio Hibernica*, 198–9.
163 For comments on this event and on Hugh de Lacy's custodianship of Dublin see Flanagan, *Irish society*, 264, 286–8.
164 Orpen, *Song of Dermot*, 230: 3156–7.
165 Davies and Quinn, *The Irish Pipe Roll*, 30–1. The text also mentions another case taken by Richard de Feipo against Walter de Essocot for one knight's fee with appurtenances in Trevet.
166 Gilbert, *Chartularies of St Mary's Abbey, Dublin*, 37–8, no. 12; 43–4, no. 19.
167 M. T. Flanagan, 'Anglo-Norman change and continuity: the castle of Telach Cail in Delbna', *Irish Historical Studies* **28**, no. 112 (1993), 385–9: 389.
168 On the location of pre-Norman Droichet Átha and the development of the Anglo-Norman settlement at Drogheda see J. Bradley, 'The topography and layout of medieval Drogheda', *Journal of the County Louth Archaeological and Historical Society* **19**, no. 2 (1978), 98–127: 103–6.
169 Orpen, *Song of Dermot*, 3145, 3156, 3223, 3262.
170 Scott and Martin, *Expugnatio*, 140–1, 195 (*castellum Ade de Futepoi*).
171 S. Ó hInnse, *Miscellaneous Irish Annals (A.D. 1114–1437)* (Dublin, 1947), 60–1.
172 Ibid., 62–3.
173 The *dindshenchas* (Gwynn, *Metrical Dindshenchas*, vol. iv, 270–1) tells how Sláine, king of the Fir Bolg, was buried at Duma Sláine, alias Druim Fuar, and refers to his grave as 'the mighty mound' (*in duma dímór*) and continues: *conidh Sláine is ainm don chnuc* 'and that Sláine is the name of the hill'.
174 B.J. Graham, 'Anglo-Norman settlement in County Meath', *Proceedings of the Royal Irish Academy* **75C** (1975), 223–48. For more recent comments on the concept of continuity during this period see B. J. Graham and L. J. Proudfoot, *An historical geography of Ireland* (London, 1993), 66–70.
175 This superficial examination is based primarily on the monuments recorded in Moore, *Archaeological Inventory of County Meath*, and adheres to the terminology used in the inventory.
176 Ibid., nos 222, 896–7, 1294, 1521.

2. LANDSCAPES OF MOVEMENT AND CONTROL: INTERPRETING PREHISTORIC HILLFORTS AND FORDING-PLACES ON THE RIVER SHANNON

Tom Condit and Aidan O'Sullivan

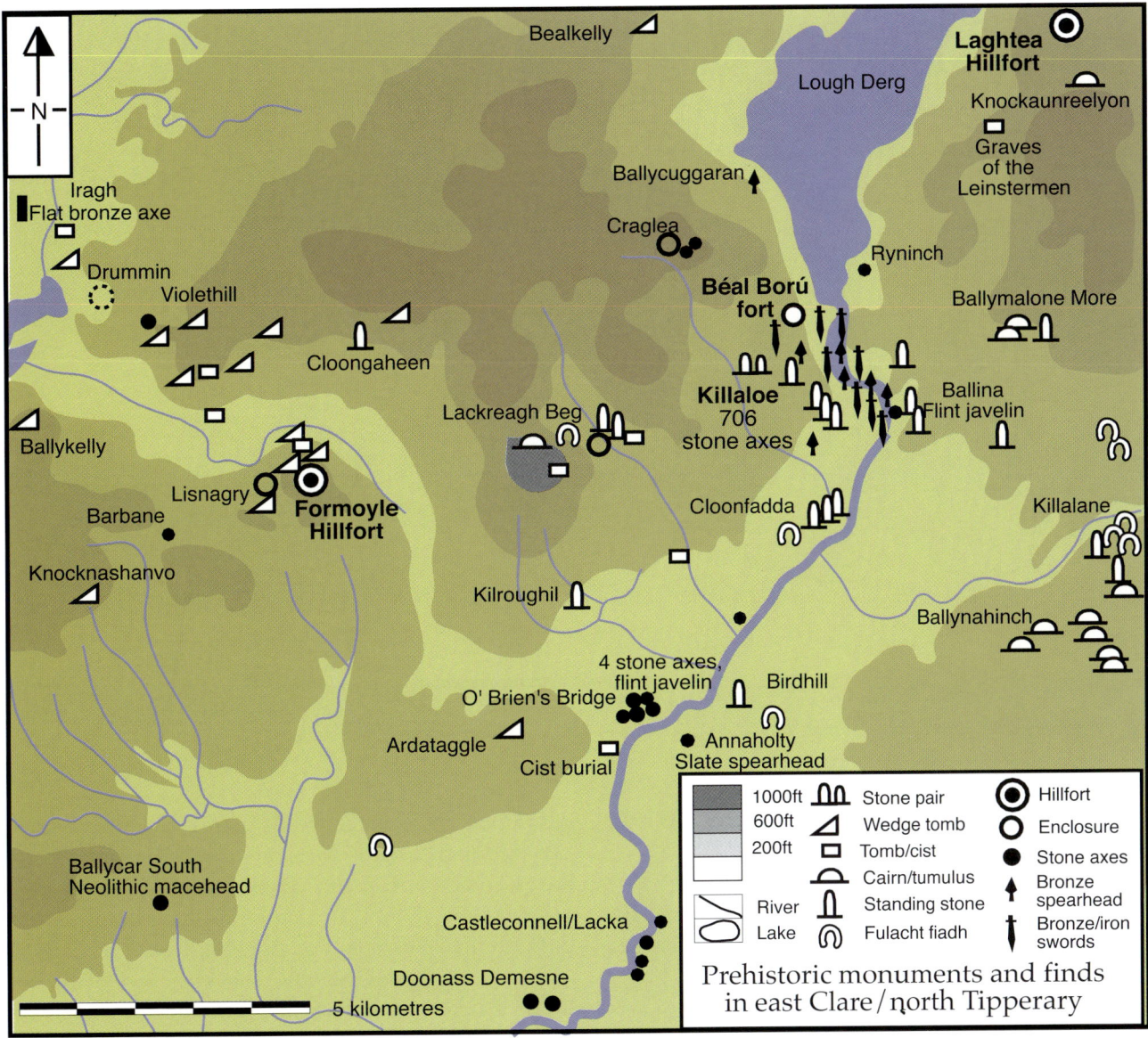

Fig. 1—Distribution of prehistoric monuments and finds on the lower River Shannon.

Introduction

In later prehistory, it is notable that some of the larger and more unusual archaeological monuments, such as hillforts, occur at strategic locations in the landscape—on hilltops, cliffs, ridges and other eminent positions. There are a number of reasons why such topographical features were chosen: high visibility, defensibility, extensive views, proximity to early prehistoric monuments. However, it may also be the case that hillforts were placed to control routeways and communications. In this paper it is argued that we need to approach the archaeological record in terms of movement through the landscape rather than to emphasise static distributions of settlements and burials, as routeways were an important means of defining territories and views across landscapes were used to locate places of importance.

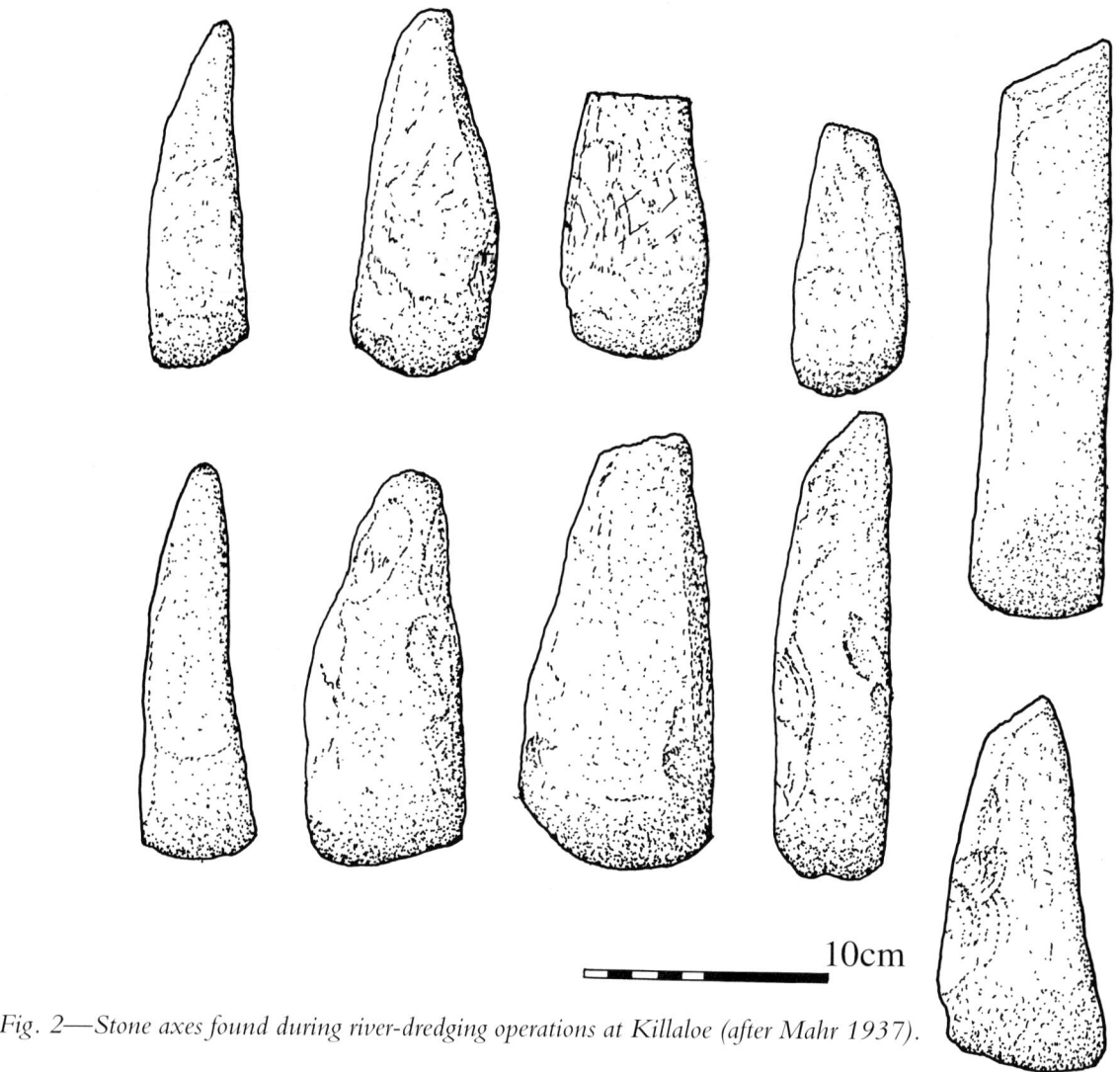

Fig. 2—Stone axes found during river-dredging operations at Killaloe (after Mahr 1937).

The physical landscapes of the River Shannon at Killaloe

It has been suggested that in pre-glacial times the lower Shannon would originally have flowed westwards along the Scarriff Gap between the Slieve Aughty Mountains and the combined Slieve Bearnagh/Arra mountain ranges before eventually cutting a route through the present Slieve Bearnagh Mountains on the west and the Arra Mountains on the east to form the Killaloe Gorge (Whittow 1974, 188–91; Davies and Stephens 1978, 113–14). The interpretation of the former course of the River Shannon is of course hypothetical, and the behaviour of the Shannon at Killaloe is one of Ireland's greatest geological puzzles. But whatever the origins of the River Shannon valley, the result is that it follows a peculiar topography with a number of east–west river valleys being dissected by the Shannon as it flows north–south towards Limerick.

In essence, then, the landscape to be discussed here is dominated by a large river flowing out from a large lake, through a narrow gorge and out again into a broad river flood-plain. Thus geology, topography and drainage govern the natural routeways and access through the landscape. Lough Derg, one of the largest lakes on the River Shannon, lies to the north, its shores flanked by hills to the east and mountains to the west. Although obviously navigable by boat, the lake would have been a major obstacle to travel. The River Shannon, as it flows southwards, passes through a narrow gorge and is overlooked by high mountains to either side. To the south the river flows through poorly drained, marshy gley soils and bogs, which in prehistory would have been a difficult landscape to traverse. However, prior to modern drainage there were a number of shoals and shallow fording-places in the Killaloe area which would have been an obvious attraction to travellers moving east and west. The effect of this physical landscape on prehistoric settlement meant that travel and communications became focused on one place where east–west and

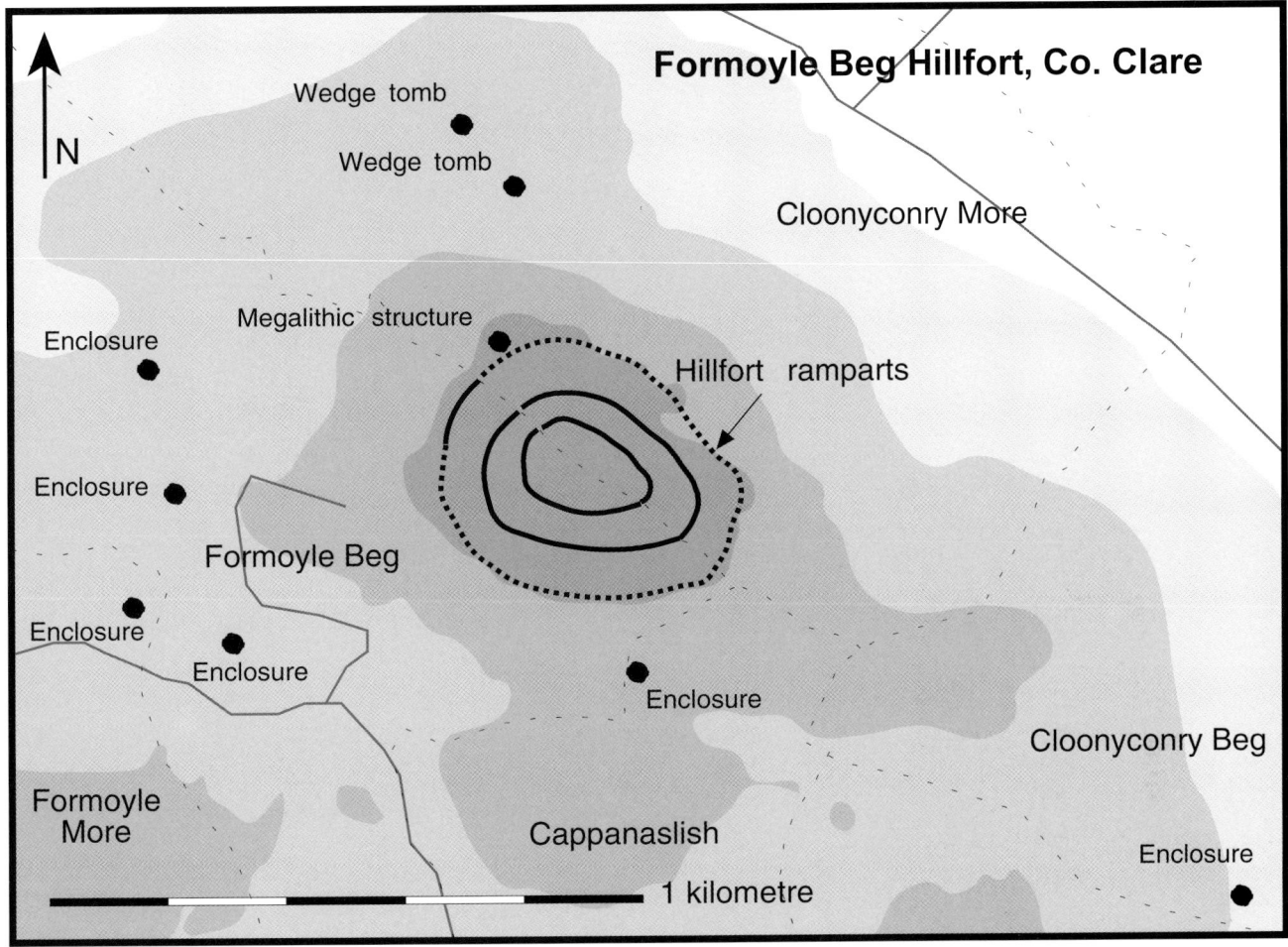

Fig. 3—Plan of Formoyle Beg hillfort, indicating earthen ramparts and location of adjacent archaeological sites.

north–south routeways would have met. This place was Killaloe.

The present town of Killaloe, with its fords and weirs, commands this important intersection. In terms of dryland transport and communication between the east and west, the principal focus is on the Broadford Gap on the west side of the river and on a number of key fording-points at Killaloe, O'Briensbridge and Castleconnell. There are other geological and mineral forces at play in this routeway landscape. For example, the Broadford Gap and Killaloe fords would have been the most direct route between the prehistoric landscapes of south-east Clare and the extensive copper deposits of the Silvermines on the Tipperary side of the Shannon (Jackson 1979).

Previous archaeological research

The importance throughout prehistory of the mountain passes and the fording-points over the River Shannon is also reflected in the history of archaeological research in the region. Most of it has been focused on megalithic tombs and prehistoric finds from the river fords. T.J. Westropp, W.C. Borlase and M. Timoney have all published descriptions of sites in east Clare (e.g. Westropp 1916; 1912; Timoney 1971). More recently, the Megalithic Survey of Ireland has published descriptive catalogues and plans of prehistoric tombs in the east Clare and north Tipperary region (de Valera and Ó Nualláin 1961; 1982; Ó Nualláin 1989). The River Shannon at Killaloe has also been subject to a long history of industrial dredging, particularly in the 1840s, in 1911 and between 1929 and 1942. These engineering works produced thousands of archaeological finds, particularly stone axes, leading Adolf Mahr to propose the existence of a 'Riverford culture' in prehistoric Ireland (Mahr 1937, 297–300; Grogan 1989; Byrnes 1995). The North Munster Project has also been studying later prehistoric settlement in the region (Grogan and Condit 1994a; Grogan *et al.*1995). Finola O'Carroll's forthcoming catalogue of prehistoric finds from north Munster will enable more detailed analyses of this artefactual record. Other important

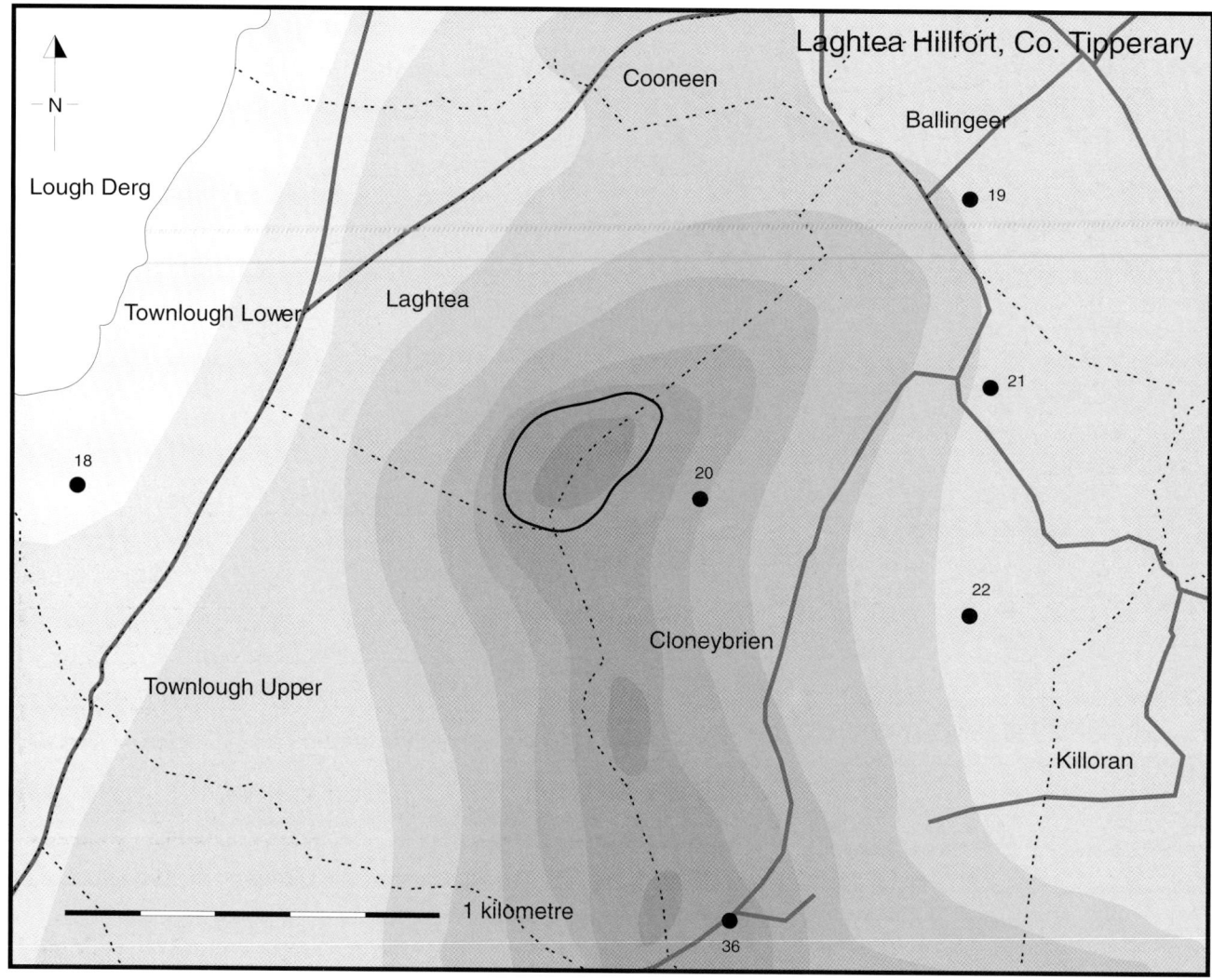

Fig. 4—Plan of Laghtea hillfort, indicating earthen rampart, contours and location of adjacent archaeological sites.

research includes the recent discovery of Bronze Age hillforts at Formoyle, Co. Clare, and at Laghtea, Co. Tipperary, an important contribution to both local and regional prehistoric studies (Condit 1995).

Early prehistoric landscapes

Neolithic/Early Bronze Age

There is, as yet, no evidence for Mesolithic hunter-gatherer activities on the lower River Shannon. It is presumably possible that the stone axes found at Killaloe and the slate spearhead from Annaholty, Co. Tipperary, are Mesolithic in date. Stone axes of shale and mudstone, similar to those recovered from the fords, and slate spearheads have been found on several Irish Late Mesolithic occupation sites (e.g. O'Sullivan 1998, 45–59). In any case, the distribution of wedge tombs, stone axes and flint and slate javelinheads indicates that the Broadford Gap and the River Shannon fords were established as locations on prehistoric routeways by at least the Late Neolithic (c. 3000–2500 BC). The wedge tombs represent the south-eastern fringe of the denser concentration found in the southern Burren area of north Clare. In east Clare, they are typically found on upland slopes with extensive views over mountain ranges and rivers. Particular clusters occur around Violethill at the mouth of the Broadford Gap, and further eastwards, deeper into the middle of the valley, there is a cluster of wedge tombs and megalithic structures around Formoyle Beg. There are also single isolated wedge tombs in uplands at Ballykelly, Ardataggle, Bealkelly, Knockshanvo and Killokennedy (de Valera and Ó Nualláin 1961; 1982; Ó Nualláin 1989).

The distribution of Neolithic stray finds complements this pattern of preference for mountain valleys and fording-places. Three stone axes are known from 'near Broadford' and stone axes are also known from the wedge tomb concentration in the

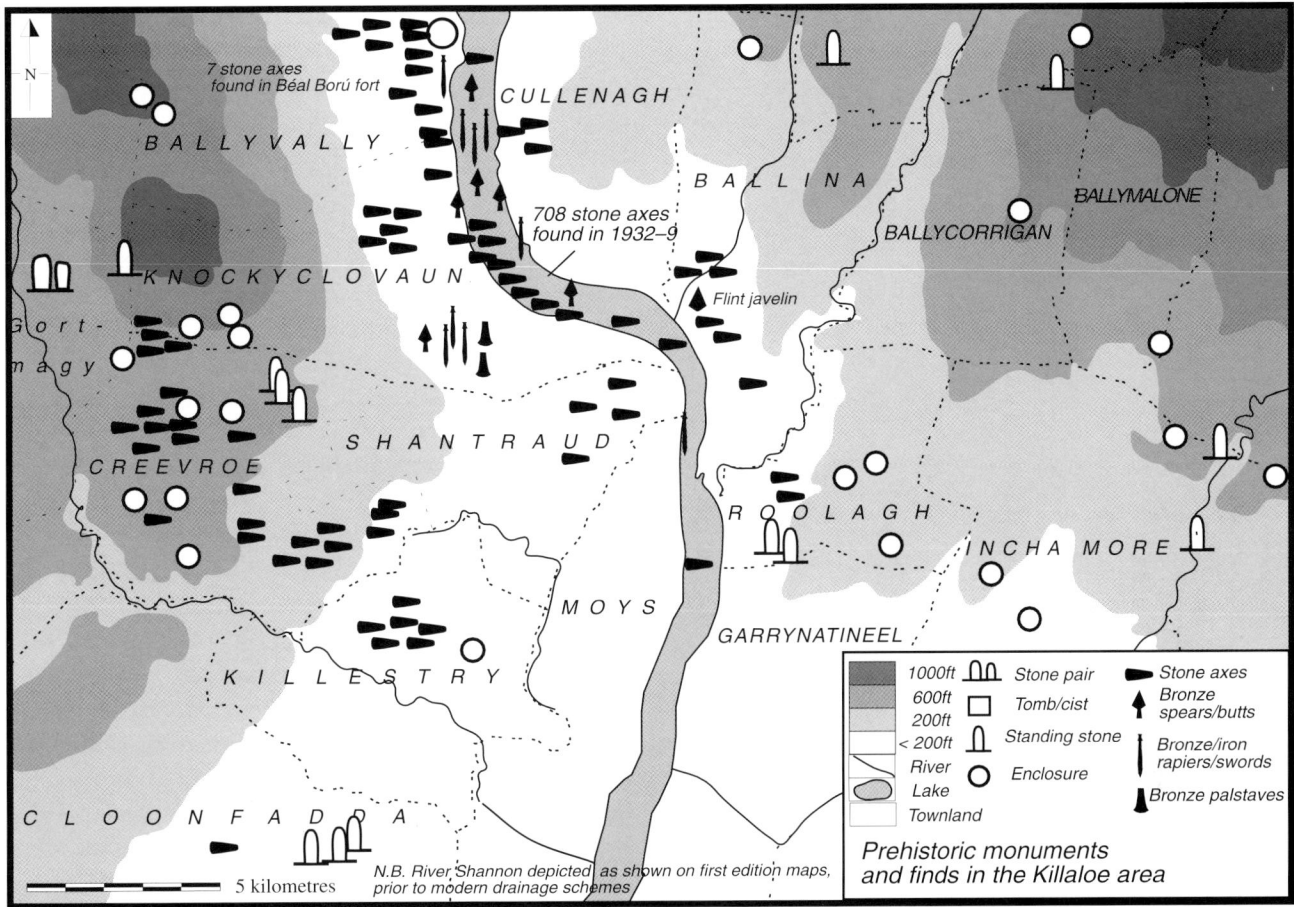

Fig. 5—Map of the Killaloe area, indicating prehistoric monuments and general location of prehistoric finds.

Broadford Gap between Violethill and Barbane. Stone axes have been found along the lower River Shannon, indicating that fording-places were in use there in the Neolithic. These include four stone axes from O'Briensbridge, two from a depth of 3.65m in Red Bog, and a stone axe and two stone adzes/chisels from Doonass Demesne. Stone axes are also known from across the River Shannon at Castleconnell and Lacka (in World's End Bog), Co. Limerick, probably indicating the use of the natural fording-point across the river above the waterfalls. Neolithic flint javelinheads have been found at Ballina and O'Briensbridge, a slate spearhead was recovered from a bog at Annaholty, Co. Tipperary, and a single Late Neolithic stone macehead was found at Ballycar South (F. O'Carroll, pers. comm.).

Stone axes also provide a clue to the dating of earthen monuments in the region. Six stone axes and seven fragments of stone axes were found at the ringfort of Béal Ború (Gleeson 1938; Grogan 1989). This site is located on a small but distinct promontory which overlooks the fording-points across the River Shannon. Béal Ború fort is generally dated to the late eleventh century AD, being associated with the medieval Ua Briain dynasty. Archaeological excavations at the site revealed a shallow, round-bottomed ditch which pre-dated the ringfort habitation (O'Kelly 1962). Neolithic finds included a chert end-scraper and a sherd of coarse pottery decorated with bird bone or stick impressions, possibly representing Ballyalton/Carrowkeel pottery (Grogan 1989). At least twelve stone axes have been found in the neighbouring townland of Ballyvally. Although the nature of the Neolithic occupation phase at Béal Ború is as yet unclear, the pottery and scraper certainly seem to indicate some domestic Neolithic occupation adjacent to the fords.

Stone axes at Killaloe

It is at Killaloe itself that we find the largest concentration of stone axes ever found in Ireland. At least 768 have been recorded from either the riverbed, the riverbank or the townlands in the vicinity (Grogan 1989; Byrnes 1995). Most were apparently dredged from the middle of the riverbed, particularly between Killaloe and Béal Ború fort on the Clare side. This dredged material was spread over the banks and many finds must have been taken from the spoil

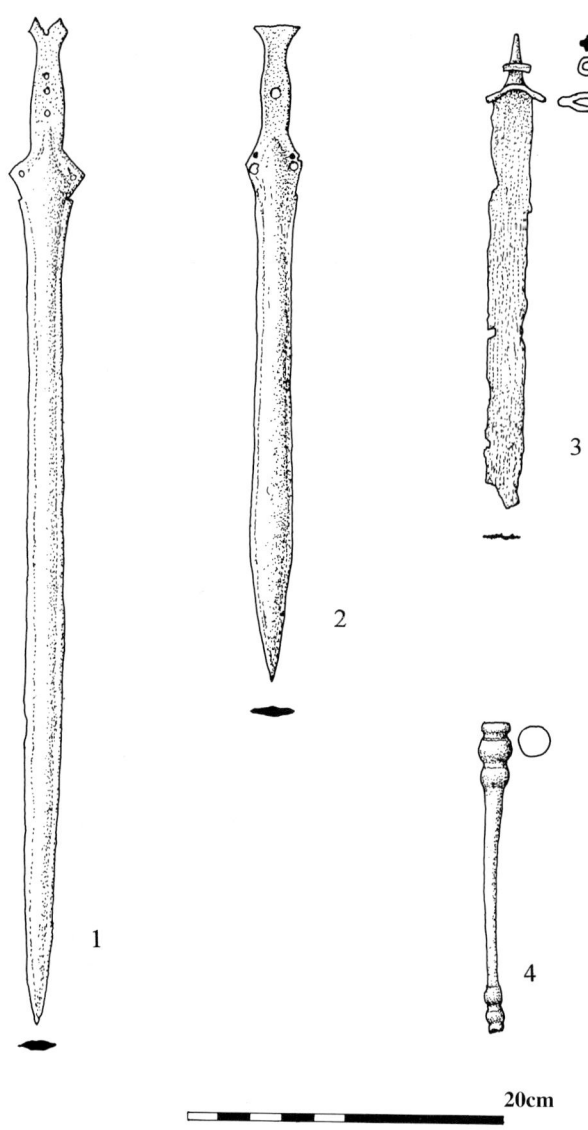

Fig. 6—Later prehistoric weaponry from the River Shannon at Killaloe: 1, 2, Late Bronze Age swords (after Eogan 1965); 3, Iron Age sword (after Raftery 1983); 4, Iron Age bronze spearbutt (after Raftery 1983).

Knockyclovaun may indicate settlements in these areas.

The stone axes from the riverbed could be interpreted in a number of ways. Firstly, they could simply be the result of accidental loss during the construction of wooden fishtraps in the river. However, this seems a somewhat unlikely argument in the face of the very large numbers of axes recovered. Secondly, it is also possible that some axes came to lie on the riverbed as a result of deposition through the riverine erosion of settlement deposits on the adjacent bank. But this would assume the existence of fairly extensive settlement, for which there is little other evidence, and in any case stone axes are not a particularly common find from settlement sites. In conclusion, it seems most likely that the stone axes from Killaloe are evidence of Mesolithic or Neolithic ritual activities at the fording-places, the deliberate deposition of artefacts at a sanctified location in the landscape.

An interesting feature of some of the dryland stone axe finds at Killaloe is the occurrence of collections of both whole and fragmentary stone axes. Six stone axes were found in Creevroe while a drain was being dug through a marshy field, and a further five axes were found in topsoil in the same townland. Several stone axes were found as fragments. It is important to point out that these axes may have been deposited on the drylands in recent times, as the gravels and silts from Killaloe are historically known to have been used for fertilising farmland. However, if they are in their original locations, then it is possible we are looking at evidence for the storage or production of stone axes in the vicinity of the fords. Most of the Killaloe stone axes are made of natural water-rolled pebbles and working is confined to the ground edges, apart from some faceting along the sides (E. Byrnes, pers. comm.). Stone axes can be ground out of shale in under 30 minutes. There may have been a tradition of grinding axes from local stone, solely for use as symbolic or ritual objects for deposition at the fording-places. It is also possible that hoards of axes were carried by travellers to Killaloe at particular times of the year for deliberate deposition at the fording-place. The use of broken axes in such rituals might imply that a symbolic axe would be sufficient, rather than an actual functional tool. In any case, the importance of Killaloe as a place on a routeway seems to have been established at an early time.

Early/Middle Bronze Age landscapes

A single Early Bronze Age burial is known in east Clare, and finds from the period (c. 2500–1500 BC)

in subsequent years. However, there are also a number of stone axes which may have been found on the adjacent drylands rather than in the river, particularly in the townlands of Creevroe, Knockyclovaun, Ballyvally and Killestry. Indeed, finds from the hills north of Killaloe include two axes from Craglea, a stone axe from Feenlea and a stone axe from a bog in Ballycuggaran. Stone axes are also known from along the eastern banks of the river, at Cullenagh, Ballina, Roolagh and Ryninch in County Tipperary. Grogan (1989) has suggested that the concentrations of finds in Creevroe, Ballyvally and

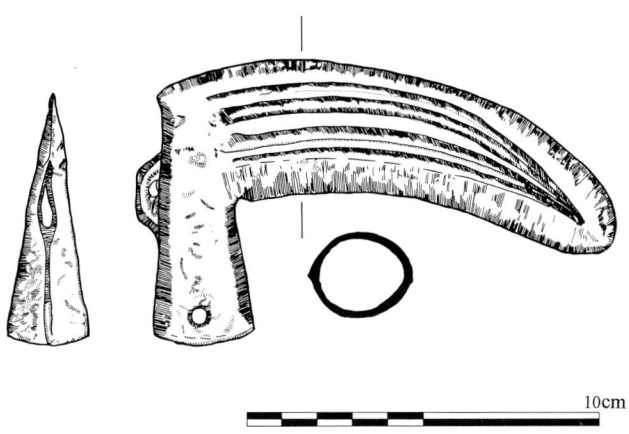

Fig. 7—Late Bronze Age sickle from the River Shannon at Killaloe (after Mahr 1937).

are relatively sparse in the region. The burial was a cist containing pottery, bone and ashes, found at O'Briensbridge in 1941 (Waddell 1990, 56). A single flat bronze axe with decoration is known from Iragh, on Lough Reavagh at the mouth of the Broadford Gap. In contrast, by the Middle Bronze Age (*c.* 1500–1200 BC) there seems to be some increase in activity. The evidence indicates strong elements of continuity with the Neolithic, the Broadford Gap continuing as an access routeway through the east Clare mountains and the Killaloe fording-places remaining important on those routeways.

Bronze Age *fulachta fiadh* are known from Lackreagh Beg, Cloonfadda and Coolderry. In 1996, a *fulacht fiadh* was located and excavated at Knockyclovaun, just to the north of Killaloe. The site was located on the riverbank and test excavations revealed the characteristic burnt mound and charcoal-flecked soil (Gowen 1997). These burnt mounds, which typically date from the Middle to Later Bronze Age (*c.* 1600–1000 BC), are now, of course, ubiquitous archaeological monuments in Ireland, although debate has generally been focused on their chronology and perceived function as cooking-places or saunas (Brindley *et al.* 1989–90; Buckley 1990; Barfield and Hodder 1987). However, it is being increasingly recognised that *fulachta fiadh* are not isolated monuments, but can often be linked to nearby Bronze Age domestic settlements and ritual sites. Indeed, they also seem to be located on lakeshores and in river valleys that are between, rather than adjacent to, Bronze Age settlement sites. This might imply that they served as meeting places amongst contemporary farming communities. In addition, there are some sites in south-east Clare which may only have been accessible during the summer and autumn months owing to seasonal flooding, and hence it is possible to suggest a seasonal element to their use, perhaps even around the time of the autumn harvest. In any case, it could be argued that *fulachta fiadh* can also be seen in terms of their role in the landscape of movement and mobility (O'Sullivan and Condit 1995; O'Sullivan 1998).

Standing stones, as single monuments and in groups, are known from Cloonagaheen, Kilroughil, Lackreagh Beg, Cloonfadda and Creevroe. Some form extended stone alignments, with two at Lackreagh Beg and three each at Creevroe and Cloonfadda. There is a single, as yet unconfirmed, report of a stone circle at Drummin (Timoney 1971). An archaeological site described by the Megalithic Survey at Gortmagy seems to be a stone pair. It apparently consists of two stones, set 60cm apart and standing 1m and 1.5m in height (de Valera and Ó Nualláin 1961). The strong association between cairns, standing stones, *fulachta fiadh* and an enclosure at Lackreagh Beg and between three standing stones and a *fulacht fiadh* at Cloonfadda suggests particular concentrations of Middle Bronze Age settlement. These may be the territorial centres of families or an extended kin-group. Similar clusters of standing stones, *fulachta fiadh* and possible earthen barrows can also be seen in the adjacent areas of north Tipperary, particularly at Ballymalone More, Killalane and Ballynahinch.

There are a range of Middle Bronze Age finds from the region. The blade-tip of a Middle Bronze Age dagger or rapier was found in a field on the bank of the river at Ballyvally, north of Béal Ború fort. There are also two bronze daggers and three further rapiers from the bed of the River Shannon at Killaloe, for which no more precise provenance has been retained. This group of rapiers includes a single example each of the Group II, III and IV types (Burgess and Gerloff 1981). Irish Middle Bronze Age rapiers show a number of interesting features. Many of the unprovenanced examples have a heavy patination, suggesting that they too were deposited in watery contexts, and the slightness of the blades suggests that they could hardly have functioned as efficient weapons. It has been suggested that rapiers were intended only for ostentation and display, much like the ceremonial swords used on parade grounds today (Ramsey 1995). Other Middle Bronze Age weaponry includes a base-looped bronze spearhead found during dredging at Killaloe, and a socket-looped spearhead with a kite-shaped blade from a bog in Ballycuggaran. There are also a number of Middle Bronze Age woodworking tools, including two unlooped palstaves found near Killaloe.

Pl. 1—Eel weirs at Killaloe, with rapids over the fording-points (Kierse 1995).

Later prehistoric landscapes

Introduction

By the Late Bronze Age and Iron Age in Ireland, the archaeological evidence suggests the emergence of an increasingly warlike, hierarchical society active in the consolidation of regional and local territories. Society seems to have been structured around the power of 'tribal' groups or perhaps individual families, who derived status and influence from the control of economic and industrial resources. It is also likely that the more intensive forms of agriculture, increasing population and an unstable climate made the control of land a matter of the highest importance. Indeed, the analysis of such evidence as later prehistoric hillfort distributions, barrow cemetery clustering and metalwork hoard deposition patterns indicates an increasingly forceful identification with both wider territories and specific natural places of high status. There is a range of evidence for Late Bronze Age and Iron Age activity in the River Shannon valley. Interestingly, two large hillforts—a trivallate example and a large univallate example—have been identified in the wider Killaloe region, at Formoyle near the town of Broadford and at Laghtea on the Tipperary side of the Shannon.

Formoyle hillfort

The hillfort was discovered through analysis of vertical aerial photographs of the east Clare mountains and confirmed through subsequent fieldwork (Condit 1995). The site is located in the middle of the Broadford Gap, on the south side, with extensive views across the valley floor to the mountains beyond. Its ramparts encircle the level summit of the hill, which reaches a height of 795ft OD. The slope of the hill is relatively gentle on all sides except on the north-east, where it falls steeply to the valley bottom. The hillfort lies within the modern townlands of Cloonyconry More on the north and Formoyle Beg on the south. The ramparts are clearly traceable in the townland of Formoyle Beg, where most of the remains are covered with peat 20–30cm deep. On the northern side of the townland boundary in Cloonyconry More, where the hilltop has been reclaimed for pasture, the remains are presently indistinct.

The hillfort has three concentric ramparts,

Pl. 2—Dredging work in the 1880s at the Killaloe fords (Kierse 1995).

enclosing a subcircular area. Two of the ramparts survive intact, and there are substantial remains of a third on the western slope. The inner enclosure has a maximum dimension of *c.* 210m, while the middle enclosure is *c.* 350m, maintaining a distance of 50–80m from the inner enclosure. The remains of the third enclosure, traceable in the north-western quadrant of the site, can be clearly distinguished for a length of *c.* 120m at a distance of *c.* 100m from the middle enclosure. A small cairn is located north-west of the summit of the hill.

All three ramparts appear to be of uniform construction. The overall width of the bank and external ditch is 6–7m; the ditch has an average width of 2.5m, while the bank, which stands up to 1.5m above the ditch, is 4–5m wide. At some points along the bottom of the innermost rampart on the interior there are traces of a small ditch, *c.* 30cm wide, defined again by the presence of grass and the absence of peat. It is difficult to determine the exact material which makes up the bank, but it is most likely the stone and earth which lie immediately under the peat and are exposed in small areas where peat-cutting has taken place. No obvious gaps or entrance features can be detected in any of the ramparts.

Laghtea hillfort, Co. Tipperary

Laghtea hillfort is situated on the opposite side of the River Shannon, *c.* 10km north-east of Ballina in the northern foothills of the Arra Mountains. The hillfort encloses the summit of Laghtea Hill, about 1.6km north of Tountinna, which is the highest peak in the range. Laghtea Hill itself rises to a height of 1088ft, from where there are extensive views over Lough Derg to the north and west and over the valley of the Nenagh River to the north-east. The ridge of the hill runs in a line roughly north–south, with smooth but steep slopes on the west, north and south. The eastern side of the hill is defined by steep cliffs and crags. To the south, a col which dips down to 800ft links Laghtea Hill with the rest of the Arra range. Forestry plantations currently cover much of the western slopes of the hill, reaching the 800ft contour. Dense furze with an average height of 70cm covers most of the rest of the hill.

The hillfort, located in the townlands of Laghtea, Cloneybrien and Townlough Upper, consists of a single enclosing element which is clearly traceable on the north, west and south, running along the contour of the hill at about 900ft. The rampart could not be identified on the eastern side of the hill where the

Pl. 3—Aerial photograph of Formoyle hillfort (NMP).

hillslope consists of a series of bluffs and crags. There is no evidence to suggest that this side of the hill was ever enclosed. The rampart, consisting of a double bank with an intervening ditch, is 7–8m wide. The ditch, *c.* 2.5m wide at the bottom, is grass-covered. The outer bank stands *c.* 0.5m high from the bottom of the ditch and is *c.* 2m wide at the base. The inner bank, on average *c.* 2.5m wide, stands up to *c.* 2.5m high from the bottom of the ditch and *c.* 0.7m above the inside. For the most part the entire rampart is covered by peat and furze, while the ditch, which was dry at the time of inspection, was visible as a grassy track running through the furze. The course of the rampart can be traced around most of the summit of the hill, except where it is interrupted by small cliffs and crags on the south-west.

Where the rampart returns eastwards at the north end of the hillfort the possible remains of a circular platform (*c.* 20m in diameter) can be traced. The presence of this enclosure is detectable under more verdant furze growth. Within this there is evidence for the existence of a stone-edged well. It is difficult to establish the exact relationship of this circular platform with the hillfort enclosure, but it would appear to be at least contiguous with the hillfort rampart.

Discussion

In recent years it has become clear that hillforts in Ireland have their origins in the Late Bronze Age, as indicated by excavations at Mooghaun, Co. Clare (Grogan and Condit 1994b), Haughey's Fort, Co. Armagh (Mallory 1991; 1995; Mallory and Warner 1988), Rathgall, Co. Wicklow (Raftery 1994), and Dun Aonghusa (Cotter 1996), which were all constructed at the beginning of the Late Bronze Age. Of particular interest to the Formoyle and Laghtea hillforts are the recent results of excavations at Mooghaun hillfort in south-east Clare, where the stone ramparts appear to have been built and renewed over several phases in the Late Bronze Age. Large, defended entrances controlled access into the hillfort. The later phases of construction led to the incorporation into the ramparts of large amounts of discarded domestic food debris (cattle and pig bone), a saddle quern, coarseware pottery and small bronze artefacts and waste. Mooghaun hillfort is also situated in a region with extensive evidence for Middle and

Pl. 4—Aerial photograph of Laghtea hillfort (NMP).

Late Bronze Age settlement and sacred landscapes (Grogan and Condit 1994a; Grogan *et al.* 1995).

Bronze Age hillforts appear not to have been fortified settlement sites in the normal sense, apparently being empty not long after the final phases of their construction. If anything, it is the Bronze Age lakeshore settlements and unenclosed settlements that were the focus for both high-status and ordinary domestic activities. It may be that the hillforts were intended to be used as places of storage or as refuges at times of particular danger. It is also probable that some measure of community status was involved in their construction: they may, in other words, have been used for display, being primarily meant to be seen from a distance by the local community and also by travellers passing by. In this way, hillforts on the skyline would have reminded people that they were within the boundaries of specific political territories. Strategically placed hillforts could have dominated routeways through mountain valleys.

Formoyle Beg is a classic type of Irish trivallate hillfort and is situated in an area of uplands which contains several early prehistoric wedge tombs, megalithic structures and enclosures. Indeed, the siting of the hillfort itself was clearly influenced by the presence of the earlier wedge tombs, as a small cairn is situated off the summit of the hill. This is unsurprising as the reuse of wedge tombs is well known in Middle and Late Bronze Age Ireland: weapons, ornaments and industrial debris of the period were often placed in the chambers and cairns of these monuments (O'Brien 1993). The location of the hillfort at Formoyle may also be related to other symbolic or mythological associations which added force to the hillfort's control of the landscape. The trivallation at Fermoyle is likely to be a feature which confirms the site as being Late Bronze Age in date. The univallate Laghtea hillfort is also likely to date from the same period on the basis of its large scale. Although the two hillforts are some distance apart, they effectively form a pair situated to either side of the fords at Killaloe. If they are contemporary, and that is by no means proven, then they could be interpreted as two rival centres of regional or local political territories. This could also be the reason why they both appear to control access, through a mountain valley and along the lakeshore, on a routeway towards Killaloe. Indeed, as will be shown below, there are also elements of aggressive activity and community investment at the Killaloe fords, where there is little other evidence for monumental construction.

Pl. 5—The ramparts of Laghtea hillfort (NMP).

Later Bronze Age/Iron Age finds at Killaloe

Although the actual number of Late Bronze Age and Iron Age artefacts does not match the number of early prehistoric stone axes recovered from the River Shannon at Killaloe, it is clear nonetheless that significant numbers of bronzes were cast into the river during the Late Bronze Age (c. 1000–500 BC) and into the Iron Age (500 BC–AD 500). As discussed above, in the early prehistoric period it seems likely that it was stone axes that were most commonly placed in the river. These could have been used as tools, weapons or symbols of status. In later prehistory there appears to be a definite and unambiguous emphasis on the deposition of weaponry rather than tools, with spearheads and swords the typical finds. At least five bronze spearheads have come from the River Shannon at Killaloe, including a Late Bronze Age socketed, leaf-shaped spearhead, a looped spearhead and a bronze spearhead with lunate openings. A bronze socketed spearhead with lunate openings is also known from Cullenagh on the Tipperary side of the river. At least five bronze swords (a single example of Eogan's Class IV and two Class V types) were recovered by dredging from Killaloe, one of them from 'near the sluice-gate' near the town (Eogan 1965). One bronze sword may have been found as a fragment. There are some Late Bronze Age artefacts which might be agricultural or woodworking tools. Two sickles were found in the riverbed in about 1936; one was a socketed and looped bronze sickle with curved blade (Mahr 1937), and a second bronze sickle is also known (Byrnes 1995). A bronze chisel was also found in 1881 on the riverbed at Killaloe (Byrnes 1995).

The tradition of placing weaponry into the river at Killaloe seems to have continued into the Iron Age. Finds from the period include an early (La Tène Type I) iron sword and a bronze spearbutt, which were recovered through dredging at Killaloe in the early 1930s (Raftery 1983), and another, more recently discovered La Tène sword from the river between Ballyvally and Cullenagh (F. O'Carroll, pers. comm.). A possible Early Christian iron sword is also known from the river (Byrnes 1995). Mahr (1937, 300) suggested that most of the later prehistoric material came from the riverbed further north of Killaloe, particularly along the stretch opposite Béal Ború. This would confirm that this locality continued in importance through the later prehistoric period.

Conclusion

For the early prehistoric period, the distribution of stone axes, wedge tombs and megalithic structures indicates a widely dispersed settlement pattern along the Broadford Gap. Moreover, there seem to have been several important fords in early prehistory across the River Shannon, mainly at Killaloe, O'Briensbridge, Castleconnell and Doonass

Pl. 6—Late Bronze Age bronze sword from Killaloe (NMP).

Demesne. By the later prehistoric period there is an increased emphasis on one fording-place only, that at Killaloe. There may also have been a local shift in emphasis in later prehistory, northwards and slightly upstream from Killaloe itself, towards the fording-places at Kincora and Béal Ború. By this period we can also see an increased emphasis on the control of long-established routeways through the region. The placing of a hillfort in the Broadford Gap at Formoyle Beg and on the summit of Laghtea Hill indicates a concern with controlling movement towards and away from the fords. In particular, the increased emphasis on weaponry suggests that these fords were more and more important in political and territorial terms.

The evidence both of the Formoyle and Laghtea hillforts and of the Killaloe weaponry deposits argues that warfare and political conflict were central to the emerging regional identities of Late Bronze Age and Iron Age communities on the lower River Shannon. This is unsurprising, as it has been pointed out that for later prehistoric communities the 'triad of politics, warfare and religion' were amongst the most important forces which motivated social groups. Periodic raiding, ritual combat, warrior élites, complex and constantly varying tribal alliances and shifting enmities must also have been significant elements in Late Bronze Age social organisation (Randsborg 1995; Dark 1995). It is clear that society attached great importance both to symbols of warfare and to boundaries, whether physical, political or supernatural. In archaeological interpretation, the deposition of weaponry in wet places has usually been examined to understand the *reasons for deposition* (i.e. ritual action, temporary concealment, conspicuous consumption of economic surplus, etc.) rather than the *place of deposition*. It may be time to start enquiring why particular lakes, fords or bogs were chosen. The evidence from the River Shannon suggests that Killaloe, already redolent of myth and supernatural associations from early prehistory, was being tied into local regional territories and recreated as a place of political significance.

The hillforts and fording-places also indicate the importance of controlling routeways through the landscape. In prehistoric Ireland, rivers were an obvious means of defining a territorial boundary, as they naturally restricted travel across the landscape and focused routeways on particular nodes at fords and shallows. The community controlling access across such a ford could have derived power from their strategic location, as well as economic benefits. Indeed, it is also possible that routeways themselves were an important means of defining territories and ownership of a landscape. At a local and sub-regional scale, the construction of wooden trackways across wetlands is most common in the Middle and Late Bronze Age (Raftery 1996). This may well be due to a wetter and colder climate leading to more waterlogged bogs, but the frequency and continuity of these reconstructions signal a determination amongst local communities to keep routeways open and to maintain access to farmland and outside contacts. Similarly, in the Iron Age one of the largest monuments in Ireland was the massive oak-plank trackway, Corlea 1, which appears to have been an oversized routeway constructed to enhance the prestige of local communities (Raftery 1996). The importance of rivers and fording-places in defining

Iron Age territories can also be seen at the Doon of Drumsna, Co. Roscommon, where a massive earthen rampart was constructed, not to enclose a promontory but to control access to the shallows and fords in the River Shannon (Condit and Buckley 1989). Several other rivers have also produced large amounts of later prehistoric metalwork, namely the River Erne, the River Bann and the River Barrow. In conclusion, it is clear that prehistoric fording-places in Ireland need to be investigated in terms of their wider landscapes.

Acknowledgements

The authors would like to thank Finola O'Carroll and Eoin Grogan for their advice and information on finds in the region, and Emmett Byrnes for allowing us to read his report on the Killaloe finds. We thank Aoife Daly for her help with illustrations, and Sarah Cross, Eamonn O'Donoghue and Leo Keohane for their great assistance in aerial photography. Plates 1 and 2 are reproduced from *Portraits of Killaloe* by Sean Kierse (Boru Books, 1995).

References

Barfield, L. and Hodder, M. 1987 Burnt mounds as saunas and the prehistory of bathing. *Antiquity* **61**, 370–9.

Brindley, A.L., Lanting, J.N. and Mook, W.G. 1989–90 Radiocarbon dates from Irish fulachta fiadha and other burnt mounds. *Journal of Irish Archaeology* **5**, 25–33.

Buckley, V.M. (ed.) 1990 *Burnt offerings: International contributions to burnt mound archaeology*. Dublin.

Burgess, C. and Gerloff, S. 1981 *The dirks and rapiers of Great Britain and Ireland*. Praehistorische Bronzfunde, Abteilung IV, Band 7. Munich.

Byrnes, E. 1995 Preliminary catalogue of the finds from Killaloe Town and the neighbouring townlands in Counties Clare and Tipperary. Unpublished report, Irish Stone Axe Project, Dublin.

Condit, T. 1995 Hillfort discoveries near Killaloe, Co. Clare. *Archaeology Ireland* **31**, 34–7.

Condit, T. and Buckley, V. 1989 The Doon of Drumsna, the gateways to Connacht. *Emania* **6**, 12–14.

Cotter, C. 1996 Western Stone Fort Project. Interim report. *Discovery Programme Reports* **4**, 1–14.

Dark, K. R. 1995 *Theoretical archaeology*. London.

Davies, G.L.H. and Stephens, N. 1978 *Ireland. The geomorphology of the British Isles*. London.

De Valera, R. and Ó Nualláin, S. 1961 *Survey of the megalithic tombs of Ireland, Vol. I. Co. Clare*. Dublin.

De Valera, R. and Ó Nualláin, S. 1982 *Survey of the megalithic tombs of Ireland, Vol. IV. Cos Cork and Tipperary*. Dublin.

Eogan, G. 1965 *Catalogue of Irish bronze swords*. Dublin.

Gleeson, D.F. 1938 Find of stone axes at Kincora fort, Co. Clare. *Journal of the Royal Society of Antiquaries of Ireland* **68**, 148–9.

Gowen, M. 1997 Knockyclovaun: fulacht fiadh. In I. Bennett (ed.), *Excavations 1996*, 9. Bray.

Grogan, E. 1989 The early prehistory of the Lough Gur region; Neolithic and Early Bronze Age settlement patterns in north Munster south of the River Shannon. Unpublished Ph.D. thesis, National University of Ireland.

Grogan, E. and Condit, T. 1994a The later prehistoric landscape of south-east Clare. *The Other Clare* **18**, 8–12.

Grogan, E. and Condit, T. 1994b New hillfort date gives clue to Late Bronze Age. *Archaeology Ireland* **28**, 16–20.

Grogan, E., Condit, T., O'Carroll, F. and O'Sullivan, A. 1995 A preliminary assessment of the prehistoric landscape of the Mooghaun study area. *Discovery Programme Reports* **2**, 47–56.

Jackson, J. 1979 Metallic ores in Irish prehistory: copper and tin. In M. Ryan (ed.), *The origins of metallurgy in Atlantic Europe*, 107–25. Dublin.

Kierse, S. 1995 *Portraits of Killaloe*. Killaloe.

Mahr, A. 1937 New aspects and problems in Irish prehistory. *Proceedings of the Prehistoric Society* **3**, 262–436.

Mallory, J. 1991 Excavations at Haughey's Fort 1989–90. *Emania* **8**, 10–26.

Mallory, J. 1995 Haughey's Fort—Macha's other twin. *Archaeology Ireland* **31**, 28–30.

Mallory, J. and Warner, R.B. 1988 The date of Haughey's Fort. *Emania* **4**, 5–20.

O'Brien, W.F. 1993 Aspects of wedge tomb chronology. In E. Shee-Twohig and M. Ronayne (eds), *Past perceptions; the prehistoric archaeology of south-west Ireland*, 63–74. Cork.

O'Kelly, M.J. 1962 Béal Ború, Co. Clare. *Journal of the Cork Historical and Archaeological Society* **67**, 1–27.

Ó Nualláin, S. 1989 *Survey of the megalithic tombs of Ireland, Vol. V. Co. Sligo*. Dublin.

O'Sullivan, A. 1998 *The archaeology of lake settlement in Ireland*. Discovery Programme Monographs 4. Dublin.

O'Sullivan, A. and Condit, T. 1995 Late Bronze Age settlement and economy by the marshlands of the upper Fergus estuary. *The Other Clare* **19**, 5–9.

Raftery, B. 1983 *A catalogue of Irish Iron Age antiquities*. Veroffentlichung des vorgeschichtlichen seminars. Marburg.

Raftery, B. 1994 *Pagan Celtic Ireland*. London.

Raftery, B. 1996 *Trackway excavations in the Mount Dillon Bogs, Co. Longford 1985–1991*. Irish Archaeological Wetland Unit Transactions 3. Dublin.

Ramsey, G. 1995 Guaranteed Irish. *Archaeology Ireland* **31**, 14–17.

Randsborg, K. 1995 *Hjortspring: warfare and sacrifice in early Europe*. Aarhus.

Timoney, M.A. 1971 Ancient monuments in the neighbourhood of Broadford, Co. Clare, compiled by Lieutenant-Colonel William Audrey Bentley. *North Munster Antiquarian Journal* **14**, 3–16.

Waddell, J. 1990 *The Bronze Age burials of Ireland*. Galway.

Westropp, T.J. 1912 Types of the ring-forts remaining in eastern Clare (Killaloe, its royal forts and their history). *Proceedings of the Royal Irish Academy* **29**, 186–212.

Westropp, T.J. 1916 Types of the ring-forts remaining in eastern Co. Clare (Clonlara, Broadford, Cullaun and Clooney). *Proceedings of the Royal Irish Academy* **32**, 58–77.

Whittow, J.B. 1974 *Geology and scenery in Ireland*. Bungay.

3. CAHERCOMMAUN FORT, CO. CLARE: A REASSESSMENT OF ITS CULTURAL CONTEXT

Claire Cotter

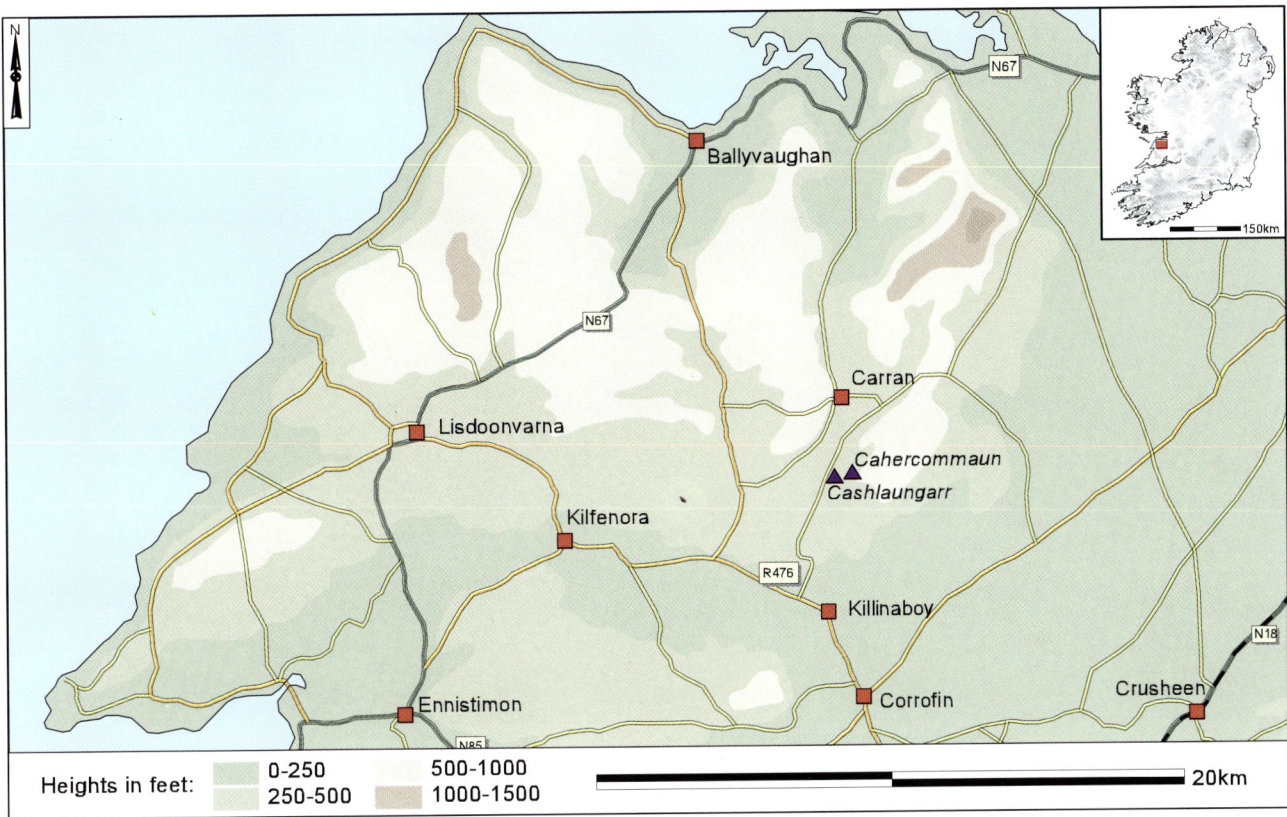

Fig. 1—Location of Cahercommaun.

Introduction

The trivallate stone fort of Cahercommaun (Cathair Chomáin; Tullycommon Td; NGR R12819, 19649; SMR CL010:064/03) is located in the south-eastern part of the Burren, Co. Clare, 5km north of Killinaboy and 2.5km south of the village of Carran (Fig. 1). It is dramatically sited at the north-western edge of the extensive limestone plateau of Tullycommon/Glasgeivnagh Hill, an area regarded locally as providing the best winter grazing for cattle in the whole of the Burren. Along the south, this plateau overlooks the catchment area of the River Fergus—a low-lying, lake-filled zone which forms a natural boundary between the Burren and the lowlands of south Clare.

In the immediate vicinity of the fort, the northern side of the plateau drops vertically to a narrow gorge about 30m below (Pl. 1; Fig. 2). The spectacularly sited stone fort of Caisleán Gearr (CL010:057) (Fig. 3; Pl. 2) stands at the entrance to this gorge, 0.6km west of Cahercommaun. This substantial fort occupies the entire summit of a high rock pinnacle; its highly defensive character and its strategic location beside a natural routeway suggest that it was built to control access into the area. Over twenty cashels or enclosures have been recorded on the plateau itself (County Clare Sites and Monuments Record), the most substantial being Moheracarton (CL010:064/35), 2km east-north-east of Cahercommaun. Four wedge tombs, a cist grave and a number of prominently sited groups of cairns attest to prehistoric activity in the immediate area (Fig. 2).

Cahercommaun fort was marked but not named on the first edition (1842) of the OS 6-inch map, though the OS Letters, Name-books and Memoranda do not include any reference to it. The earliest published account of the site was by Dunraven, who considered it 'a great discovery' (1875, 18). Westropp visited the site in 1896 and published a plan (Fig. 4), view and description (1896–7, 154–7). The fort was excavated over a six-week period in 1934 by the Third Harvard Archaeological Expedition to Ireland, led by Hugh O'Neill Hencken. Thirty-seven workmen and six archaeological assistants were associated with the project; the entire inner enclosure was excavated, in addition to eight areas in the outer enclosure and six in the middle enclosure. The results

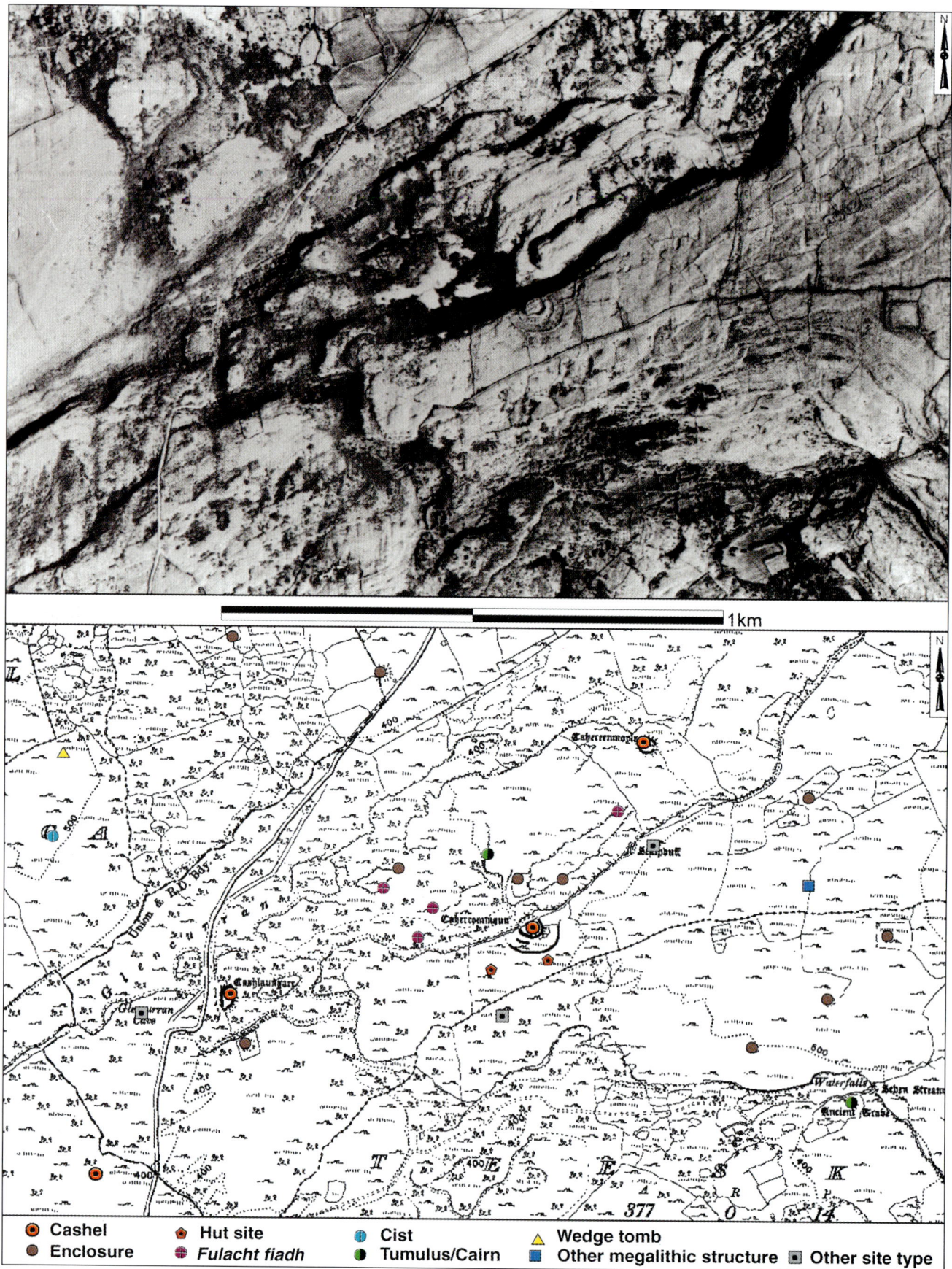

Pl. 1 and Fig. 2—Aerial photograph and map of settlement in the vicinity of Cahercommaun (map based on SMR for County Clare).

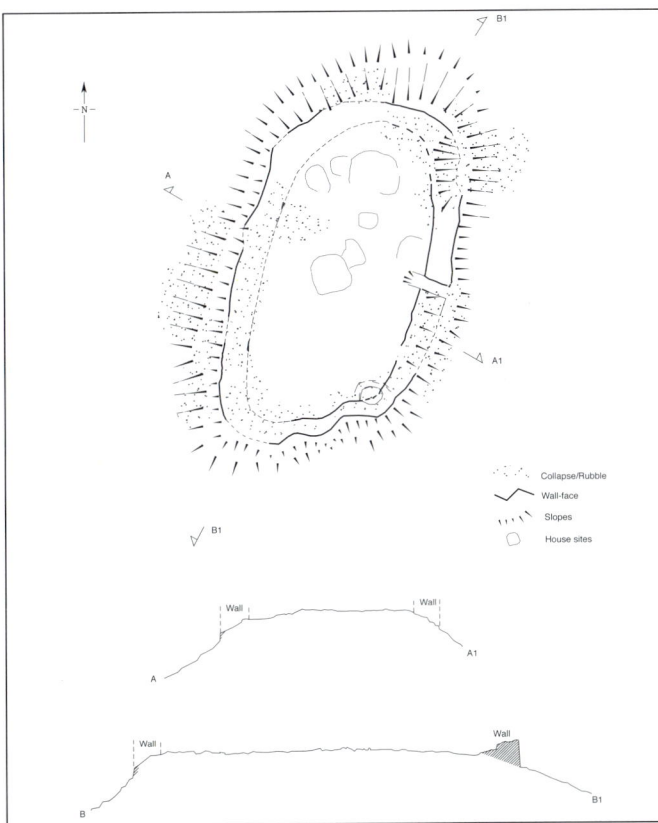

Fig. 3—Plan of Caisleán Gearr, Co. Clare (with additions; based on survey by Martin FitzPatrick and Kieran Goucher, reproduced courtesy of Dúchas).

were published as an extra volume of the *Journal of the Royal Society of Antiquaries of Ireland* in 1938.

In the opening pages of the report Hencken briefly summarised the results of the excavation and suggested that the fort had been built in the early part of the ninth century AD by a chief of north Clare. The dating framework for the site rested mainly on three objects (a silver annular brooch, the enamelled head of a brooch-pin and a fragment of a bronze zoomorphic penannular brooch), all of which Hencken considered to date from the period around AD 800. The general similarity of the objects from Cahercommaun to those from another site excavated by the Harvard expedition—the crannog of Lagore in County Meath—also appeared at the time to support a ninth-century date (Hencken 1938, 3). On the basis of a mid-seventh-century historical reference, Hencken, in a subsequent publication, revised his dating framework for Lagore and also suggested revised chronologies for the founding of Cahercommaun and of Ballinderry II, Co. Offaly (1950, 17–18). The revised chronology for Cahercommaun rested solely on the presence at the site of the zoomorphic penannular brooch (E4:358; Fig. 13.1; Hencken 1938, 33–4). Only one miniature example of this type of brooch had been found at Lagore, and Hencken concluded that the type had

Pl. 2—Aerial photograph of Caisleán Gearr from south-west (Claire Cotter).

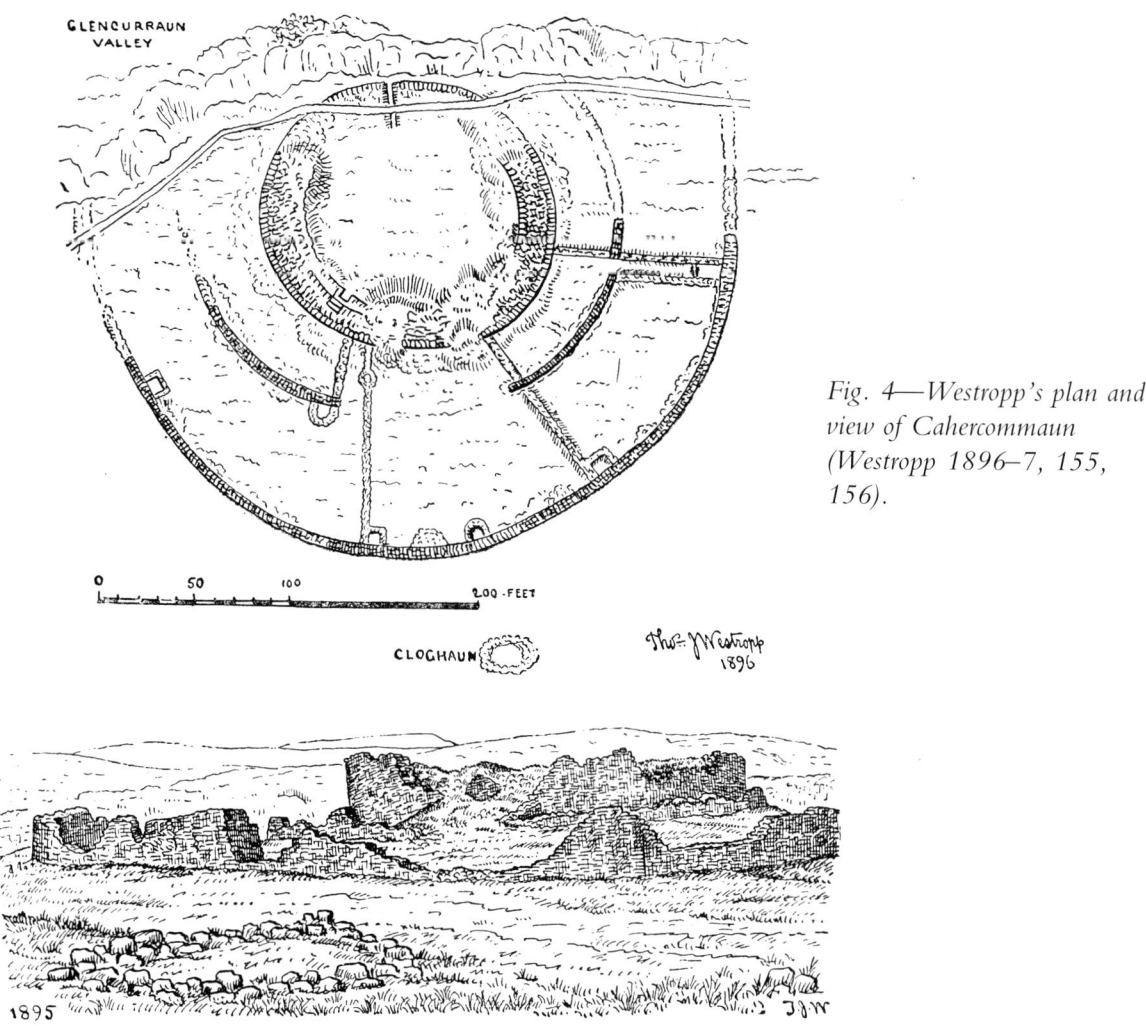

Fig. 4—Westropp's plan and view of Cahercommaun (Westropp 1896–7, 155, 156).

'gone out of fashion' by the mid-seventh century (1950, 17). The presence of a zoomorphic penannular brooch at Cahercommaun therefore 'presumably put the date of its founding back at least to the first half of the seventh century', although some time-lag for the spread of ideas might be expected (*ibid.*). The silver brooch was still considered reliable evidence, however, that Cahercommaun had continued to be occupied in the ninth century.

Hencken's dating of Cahercommaun has long been a matter of controversy in Irish archaeology. Twenty-five years ago Barry Raftery examined the dating framework for the site and concluded that the ninth-century AD date assigned to the fort by Hencken was tenuous in the extreme, and that 'Cahercommaun and a number of Irish sites, hitherto dated to the second half of the first millennium AD, may well have to be back-dated by at least half a millennium' (1972, 53). Almost ten years later Caulfield suggested that Cahercommaun may have been built before the introduction of the rotary quern and thus its construction and initial occupation 'could potentially have a BC rather than AD date' (1981, 210). However, both Laing (1975, 147–9) and Lynn (1983, 49–50) argued that the evidence of the artefacts indicated a date in the Christian period for the main occupation of the fort and, according to Lynn, 'it would seem reasonable to assume that the construction of the fort took place immediately before the chief period of occupation'. In summary, whilst most commentators (including Barry Raftery, pers. comm.) support a date in the second half of the first millennium AD for the *main* occupation of the fort, the date of its construction and the possibility of an earlier horizon of activity at the site remain a matter of debate. This difference of opinion is reflected in the two classifications of the site which have appeared in the literature during the last 25 years or so, i.e. hillfort and cashel.

As Cahercommaun is included in that group of stone forts being studied by the Western Stone Forts Project, its cultural context is of particular interest. It is often compared to Dún Aonghasa on the Aran Islands, the most striking similarity between the two being their cliff-edge location. In addition, both forts are multivallate and have a number of similar architectural features, notably the strong inner citadels and terraced enclosing walls. The presence of a *chevaux de frise* at Dún Aonghasa and the finding of a bronze fibula at the site in the last century have in the past provided the only clues to its construction date, and an Iron Age date has frequently been suggested. The presence of saddle querns at Cahercommaun also raised the possibility of a late prehistoric date for its construction, and there appeared to be a case, therefore, for arguing that both sites might fill the long gap between the demise of the Late Bronze Age hillfort and the emergence of the Early Medieval ringfort.

The recent excavations at Dún Aonghasa have pushed the initial construction date of the monument back into the Late Bronze Age but have not satisfactorily resolved the question of Iron Age activity at the site. In that light, therefore, the dating of Cahercommaun is of particular interest. In addition, despite the lapse of over half a century, Cahercommaun remains the most extensively excavated Early Medieval settlement in the west of Ireland. As such, it provides the best comparable data for many of the stone forts being studied by the project—Dún Aonghasa and Dún Eoghanachta on Inis Mór, Aran Islands, for example, have both produced Early Medieval cultural assemblages.

The main aim of this paper is to reassess a number of aspects of Hencken's excavations at Cahercommaun with a view to integrating this information into the overall project at a later stage. The architecture of the fort is examined in Part 1. Part 2 reassesses the evidence for prehistoric activity at Cahercommaun and includes a reassessment of the flint assemblage from Hencken's excavations by Peter Woodman (University College Cork); Gabriel Cooney and Steve Mandal (Stone Axe Project) have re-examined the stone axe assemblage; analysis of the saddle querns is based on an MA thesis (1993) by Anne Connolly (Archaeological Services Unit Ltd, Oranmore, Co. Galway). The ringfort phase of occupation is reviewed in Part 3 and includes a reassessment of the dating of the metal ornaments from the site by Raghnall Ó Floinn (National Museum of Ireland). The contemporary political and social conditions which might have prompted the construction of such a prestigious fort as Cahercommaun are examined by Dr Edel Bhreathnach (Discovery Programme) in Part 4. In addition to providing an opportunity to look at the broader historical context of the site, it is hoped that this study will ultimately shed some light on the possible political and economic affiliations between the mainland and the Aran Islands in the Early Medieval period. From the work of the project over the last number of years there is some evidence to suggest that the period of contemporaneity of all seven stone forts on the Aran Islands may have been during the later part of the first millennium AD. The presence of seven large forts on a relatively small land mass at this time requires some explanation and the fluctuating political fortunes of its nearest neighbours in north Clare may be particularly relevant in this regard.

Unfortunately, it did not prove possible to trace any archival material relating to Hencken's excavations at Cahercommaun and Parts 2 and 3 are therefore based solely on the published report. Some of the original photographs in that report (taken by T.H. Mason) are reproduced here. During excavation some (or possibly all) finds were numbered in a field catalogue (Hencken 1938, 27), and the objects illustrated in the published excavation report were referred to by these numbers. Subsequently the finds were deposited in the National Museum of Ireland, where all were renumbered and given the excavation prefix E4. For ease of reference both sets of numbers are included here.

Acknowledgements

I am grateful to my colleague Edel Bhreathnach for her contribution to this paper and for lengthy discussions on the subject of stone forts in general; to Peter Woodman for his analysis of the flint assemblage; to Gabriel Cooney and Steve Mandal for reassessing the stone axes; to Anne Connolly for permission to include extracts from her unpublished MA thesis and for reading a draft of the section on saddle querns; to Raghnall Ó Floinn for his re-evaluation of the dating of the metal ornaments from the site, for his helpful comments on the artefacts in general and for reading a draft of this paper; to Finola O'Carroll for information on prehistoric artefacts from the Burren and for kindly allowing this to be published in advance of her own work; to Mary Cahill (National Museum of Ireland) for her assistance with the artefact assemblage and in attempting to trace archival material from Hencken's excavations; to Andy Halpin for permission to publish his comments on the iron arrowhead; to Caroline Donaghy for permission to refer to her unpublished MA thesis (1991); to Conor Newman for his comments on the metalwork in general; and to Gina Johnson

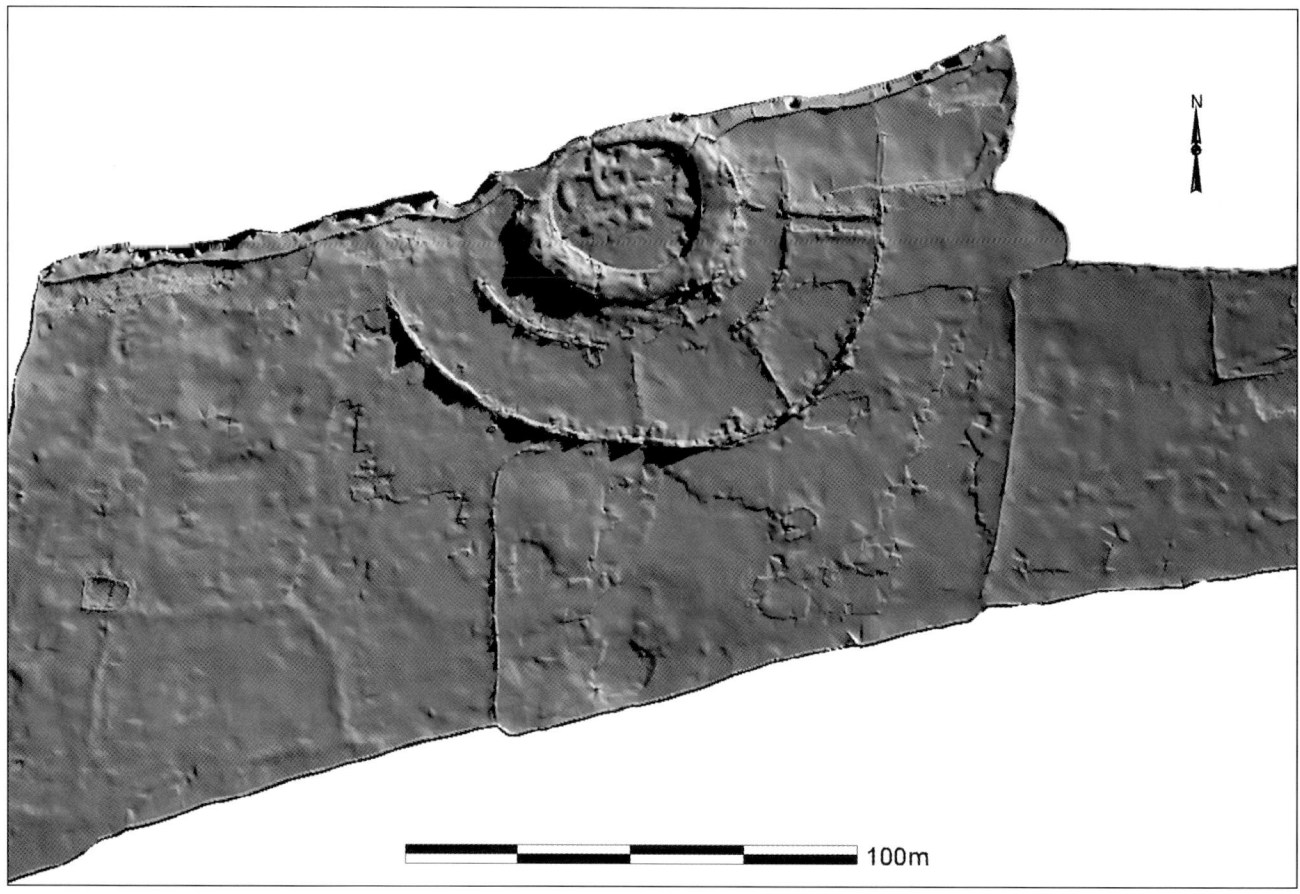

Fig. 5—Hill-shaded model of Cahercommaun (based on survey by Martin FitzPatrick and Kieran Goucher, reproduced courtesy of Dúchas).

(University College Cork) for initially examining the flint assemblage. I would also like to thank Eamon Cody (Ordnance Survey of Ireland) for his help with the OS archives, and Anne Lynch (*Dúchas*) for permission to publish the topographic surveys (Figs 3 and 5) carried out on behalf of *Dúchas* by Martin FitzPatrick (Archaeological Consultancy, Athenry) and Kieran Goucher (Margaret Gowen & Co.). I am also grateful to the Royal Society of Antiquaries of Ireland for permission to reproduce the illustrations from Hencken's original report and those from Westropp's account of Cahercommaun, and to the National Museum of Ireland for Plates 3 and 8. Figure 8 was drawn by Ursula Mattenberger and Figs 1, 2, 3 and 5 have been prepared by Barry Masterson (Discovery Programme).

Finally I would like to thank Sharon Weadick and Maria FitzGerald (Western Stone Forts Project) for their assistance in writing this paper, and Paul Walsh (Ordnance Survey of Ireland) for his critical comments.

PART 1. The architecture of the fort

A recent topographic survey of Cahercommaun carried out on behalf of *Dúchas* (Fig. 5) has highlighted the accuracy of Hencken's pre-excavation plan (Fig. 6). After excavations were completed at the site, the terraces and niches visible on the internal face of the inner wall were blocked up (or partly blocked up) in the interests of conservation (Hencken 1938, 14), and the entrance also appears to have been deliberately blocked. Hencken took great care to record the extent of the rebuilding, marking the original level of the terraces with V-shaped notches which are still visible at the site today (Pl. 3).

Earliest accounts

The earliest comprehensive account of the site (Westropp 1896–7, 154–7) does not differ substantially from Hencken's description of the fort prior to excavation. Westropp recorded the majority of the herdsmen's huts noted by Hencken in the middle and outer enclosures (Fig. 6). Both Dunraven (1875, 18) and Westropp recorded the entrance

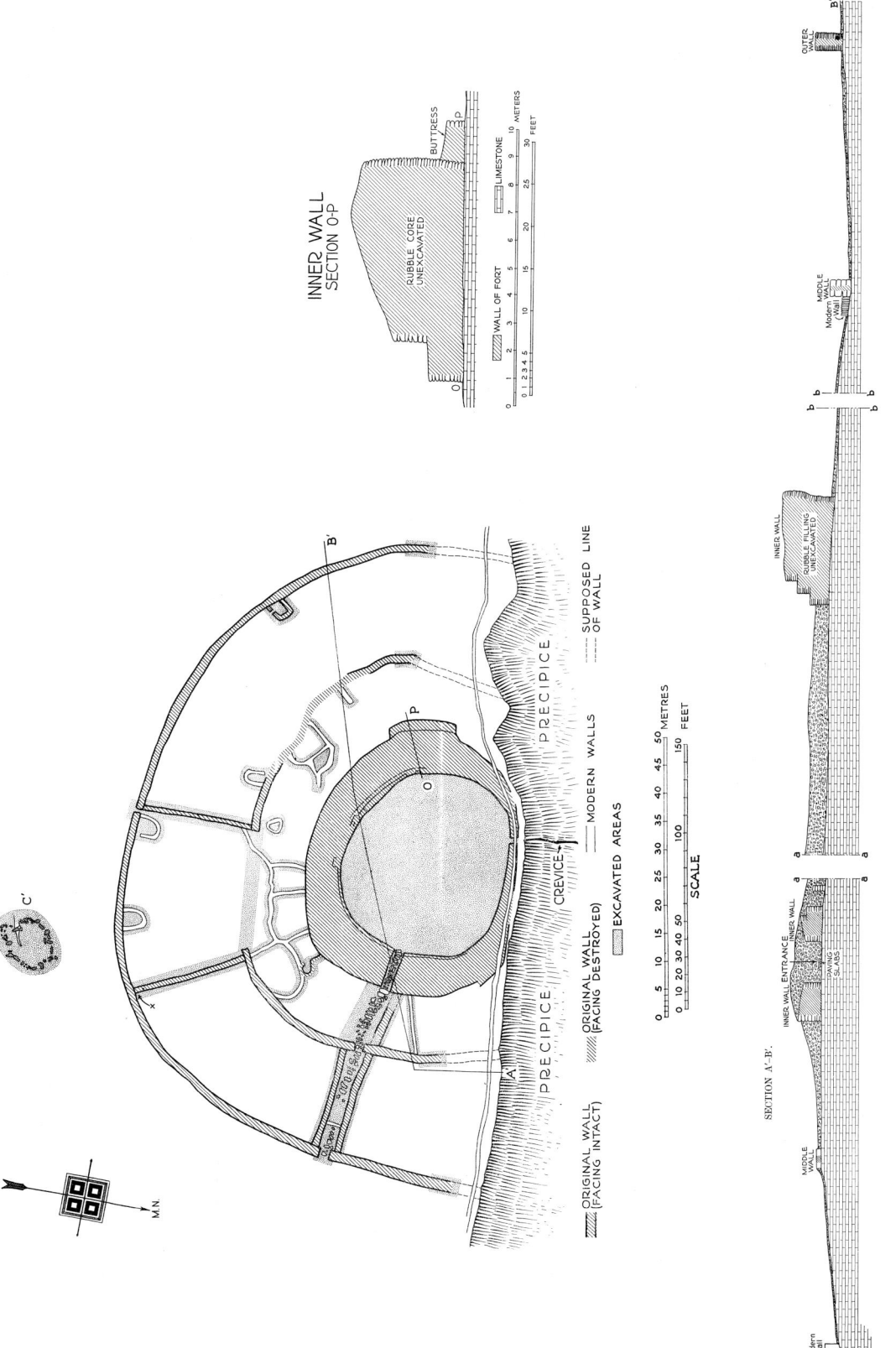

Fig. 6—Hencken's plan and sections of Cahercommaun, showing the areas excavated (Hencken 1938, pl. II, figs 2 and 6).

Pl. 3—Niche III on the interior of the inner enclosing wall. One of the V-shaped notches made by Hencken can be seen on the wall to the left. These marked the surviving upper surfaces of the terraces prior to conservation work on the site (Claire Cotter).

passage in the south-east sector, but described the inner and outer walls as unbreached at each end of the passage—the entrances may have been blocked up or concealed by collapse at the time of their visits. Apart from souterrain A, described 'as a rock-cut passage probably forming the only gate to the caher', Westropp did not record any structures in the interior of the inner enclosure. He noted a recess on the internal face of the inner wall in the south-west sector from which 'shallow steps built of flags led to a second platform or to the summit' (1896–7, 157). Dunraven also noted the presence of steps 'about 3 feet wide' leading up to the terrace (1875, 18). These were not recorded by Hencken and may have collapsed in the interim. Westropp also carried out some exploratory digging in what he described as 'a rock-cut drain' (this may have been souterrain B) and found bones of 'oxen, deer and swine', as well as 'shapeless iron implements greatly decayed' (1913, 254).

Site description

The fort was defended by three concentric stone walls and enclosed a total area of 0.81ha (1.96 acres). The less substantial outer and middle walls terminated at the cliff along the north, but the massive inner wall continued as a slighter wall along the cliff edge and enclosed a roughly oval area measuring 32.5m east–west by 28.6m north–south. The interval between the outer and middle walls ranged from 18m to 21m, and that between the middle and inner walls averaged 10m.

The outer wall enclosed a maximum area of 116m east–west by 69m north–south; at the time of excavation it varied in thickness from 1.25m to 2m and survived to a maximum height of 2.5m. It had been repaired or rebuilt in a number of places, and Hencken considered that this secondary work was of comparatively recent date (1938, 7). The middle wall survived to a maximum height of 1.7m and was up to 1.5m thick. It had been extensively robbed out along the south and west, so much so that Westropp suggested that it had been partly demolished when the outer wall was built (1896–7, 156). However, Hencken's suggestion that the robbing out of the wall took place at a later period, when the small enclosures and huts were built in the middle enclosure, seems more likely (1938, 7). Two radial walls and four hut sites were visible in the outer enclosure, and a series of low walls and associated huts or shelters occupied the central area of the middle enclosure. The inner wall was by far the most massive; it had a maximum basal width of 8.5m and was terraced on the interior. The external face survived to a maximum height of 4.3m along the south-west sector but was badly ruined on the south side; a low buttress of unknown date extended for a distance of 11m along the external wall face at the west. The wall along the cliff edge was much slighter, and at the time of excavation it measured 1.17m in maximum thickness and averaged 0.5m in height externally.

The walls are of drystone construction made up of a rubble core which is faced internally and externally with coursed limestone flags—the flaggy nature of the local limestone makes the overall finish somewhat rough. Based on an average external height of 4.5m and width of 7m along the terraced west, east and south façades, and a height of 2m and width of 1.5m along the cliff-edge section (and allowing a 20% reduction for voids), an estimated 16,500m^3 of stone were needed to build the inner wall alone. The extensive quarrying necessary to provide this volume of stone has undoubtedly altered the topography in and around the fort. For example, if the quarrying were confined to the immediate vicinity, then an area twice that of the fort itself would have had to be stripped of 1m of rock.

Hencken identified nine vertical joints in the masonry of the outer wall; matching sets of joints were visible on both inner and outer faces, but they did not appear to continue down to foundation level (Pl. 4). This is a feature of a number of other forts in County Clare and suggests that the foundations were laid out first as a single unit. The middle wall was too ruinous to preserve any traces of jointing, but no clearly marked vertical joints were evident in the well-preserved sections of the inner wall. A joggled joint was visible on the external face of the inner wall at the north-east and appeared to Hencken 'as though two parties of builders had failed to make their work join' (1938, 13). This feature is not visible today—the external wall face is low along the north-east sector and is partly concealed by collapse. According to Hencken, the wall beyond this joint to the north appeared to be largely rebuilt. Vertical joints are visible at a number of other stone forts in the Burren, and Westropp suggested that these may have resulted from the walls being built in sections, possibly by more than one party of builders (1902, 647). Vertical joints are not a marked characteristic of the stone forts on the Aran Islands. There are no very definite examples evident at Dún Aonghasa, for example, though meandering joints are common, particularly in the middle wall. These are most likely unintentional and may in some cases be exaggerated by subsequent settling of the stonework. A number of vertical joints are evident on the external face of the inner wall at Dún Chonchúir, Inis Meáin (particularly along the north-western sector), and an irregular joggled joint occurs along the north-eastern sector at

Pl. 4—Vertical joint in the outer wall at Cahercommaun (Hencken 1938, pl. 1, fig. 2).

Pl. 5—The upper and lower terrace and niches III and IV on the interior face of the inner wall at Cahercommaun (Hencken 1938, pl. V, fig. 2).

a point 32m north of the entrance. Here it may also be the result of an irregular junction between original and secondary walling.

At Cahercommaun, only the inner wall preserved evidence for terracing. The middle wall did not survive to a sufficient height to determine whether it was terraced or not, but no terracing was evident on the well-preserved sections of the outer wall. The remains of an upper and lower terrace were visible along the south-western sector of the inner wall. The terraces ranged from 0.4m to 1m in width and stood 1.5m and 2.5m above bedrock respectively. The combined width of the surviving terracing was therefore confined to the inner 1.8m of the wall thickness. As the enclosing wall averaged between 7m and 8.5m wide this arrangement allowed only very restricted outward visibility. The evidence from well-preserved stone forts (e.g. Staigue, Co. Kerry) and an examination of restored examples such as Cahergel, Co. Kerry, and Dún Chonchúir, Aran Islands, suggest that a width of *c.* 1m was optimum for the upper parapet. It seems likely, therefore, that there were originally additional terraces at Cahercommaun.

According to Hencken (1938, 13), each of the surviving terraces at Cahercommaun appeared to begin at the level where the one below left off. A collapsed section of the lower terrace presently allows a keyhole view of the construction technique and appears to confirm Hencken's opinion that the inner wall was built as a single unit and stepped back on the interior to form the terraces. As far as can be established, therefore, this inner enclosing wall does not appear to have been built in vertical sections, as was the case, for example, at Dún Aonghasa (Cotter 1993, 8–9).

Westropp also recorded that the enclosing walls at the stone forts of Feenagh (SMR CL002:033/04), Ballyalaban (SMR CL005:094), Caherbullog (SMR CL005:002) and probably Ballykinvarga (SMR CL009:059/12) were formed of 'a series of thinner layers, one behind the other, and each complete in itself' (1902, 648–9). At Dún Aonghasa this *murus duplex* type of construction allowed an earlier, slighter wall to be incorporated into the more massive later defences. The main reason for adopting this technique, however, was probably an engineering one, as vertical sections of walling gave greater stability on uneven ground. In the Burren, in particular, this building technique allowed the fort-builders to take maximum advantage of small, elevated rock plateaux.

Prior to the excavations at Cahercommaun, five rectangular niches were visible on the interior face of the inner wall along the south-west sector (Fig. 7; Pl.

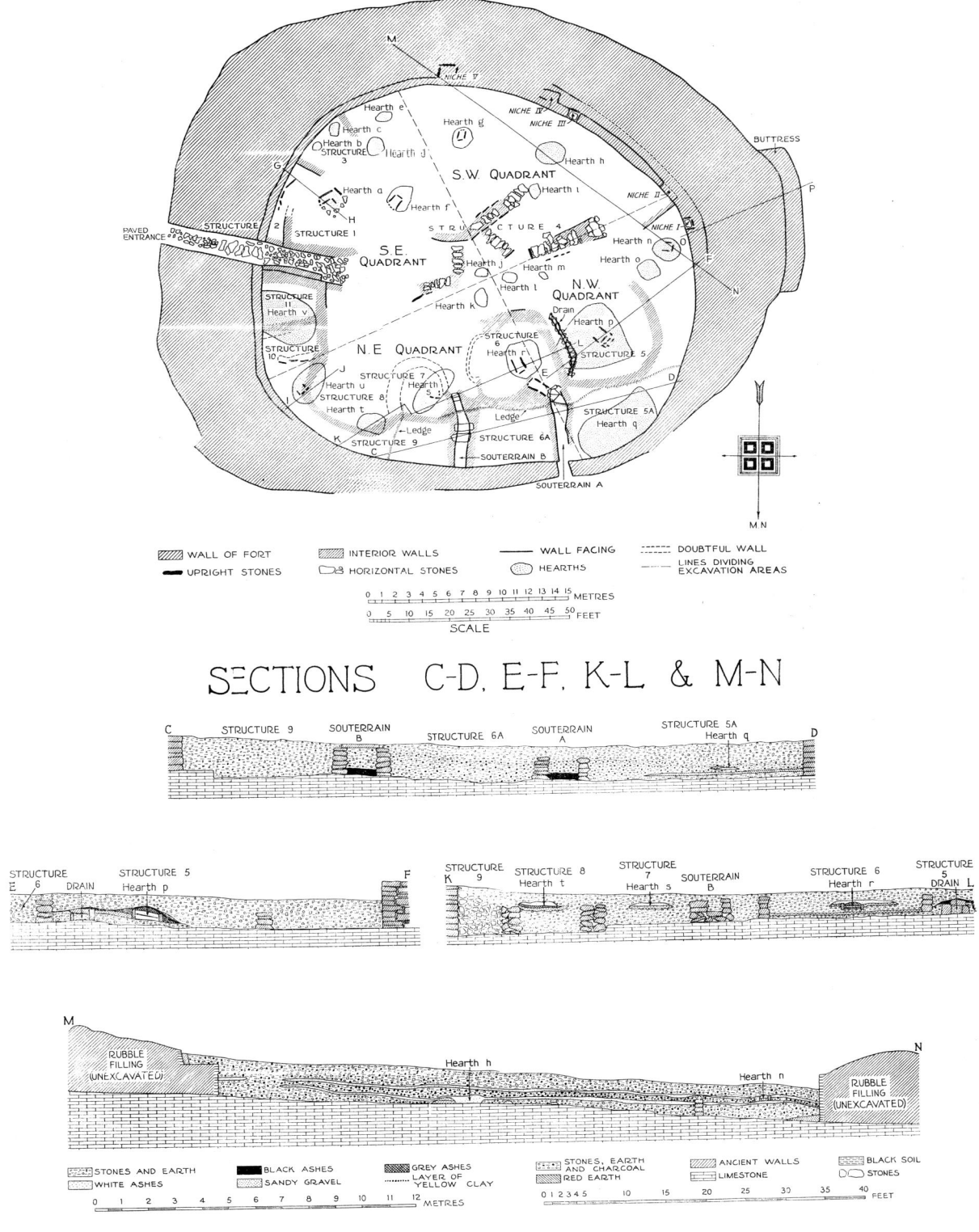

Fig. 7—Hencken's post-excavation plan and sections of the inner enclosure (Hencken 1938, pls VI and VII).

5). These ran back into the thickness of the wall, three being located on the lower terrace and two on the upper. The sides and back of some of the niches were lined with uprights and a number were floored with flat slabs. During excavation a thin layer of 'yellowish material' was found on the base of two of the lowermost examples; subsequent analysis revealed that this deposit was composed of 'fine yellow clay and lime with traces of vegetable humus and wood charcoal dust with a few grains of sand'. In one of the niches this material was sealed by a layer of ashes and charcoal, leading Hencken to suggest that they may have functioned as hearths (1938, 14).

Only two of the niches identified by Hencken in the lower terrace (niches I and III) and the remains of another on the upper terrace (niche V) are visible at the site today. They average 0.85m in width by 0.85m deep and vary from 0.5m to 1m in height. Westropp recorded one of the niches in the lower platform (probably Hencken's niche III) and a flight of shallow steps built of flags on the terrace above it (1896–7, 157). He suggested that the niche may have been a recess for a ladder, and altogether a stairwell of some form seems a more likely functional explanation. Surviving examples of steps at a number of other stone forts in the Burren indicate that inset vertical flights were the most common local form.

The main entrance at Cahercommaun lay in the east sector and consisted of a paved pathway, flanked by sidewalls, with unelaborated faced gaps forming gateways through the defences. The flanking walls had been almost wholly rebuilt prior to excavation, but the original foundations remained along most of their length (Hencken 1938, 10). On analogy with a number of other stone forts (e.g. Dunbeg and Leacanabuaile, Co. Kerry) it seems likely that the upper terraces on the inner wall continued over a lintelled door passage. At some stage during the occupation of the fort, refurbishment of the buildings which stood immediately inside the entrance to the inner enclosure gave the overall effect of extending the entrance passage for some distance into the interior. No evidence as to how the entrance was defended was found during the excavations.

The architectural features at Cahercommaun belong to a repertoire restricted to a select group of impressive stone forts. In terms of morphology, the majority of these forts appear to belong to the cashel class (i.e. they are defended settlements dating from the Early Medieval period), with a small proportion belonging to the promontory fort class. Excavations at the coastal promontory fort of Dunbeg, Co. Kerry, produced no definite dating evidence for the substantial terraced stone rampart (Barry 1981, 308). The presence of a souterrain and a radiocarbon date of 1150 ± 75 BP (680–1020 cal. AD; UB-2215) from wood charcoal at the base of the inner fosse (*ibid.*, 306) suggest that the final remodelling of the rampart took place in the Early Medieval period. This raises the possibility that other promontory forts with atypically massive stone defences (e.g. the coastal promontory forts of Dúchathair, Aran Islands, and Doonamo, Co. Mayo, and the inland promontory fort of Caherconree, Co. Kerry) may also have been remodelled sometime during the second half of the first millennium AD. A small number of these impressive stone forts are not readily classifiable as cashels (e.g. Ballykinvarga, Co. Clare, and Dún Chonchúir, Aran Islands) either (in the case of the former) because of the presence of a *chevaux de frise* or (in the case of the latter) because of its unusually large size. The architecture of both of these sites, however, also strongly suggests that the final phase of building took place during the Early Medieval period.

In terms of distribution, the only notable concentrations of these distinctive forts occur in the Burren, Co. Clare, south Clare, the Aran Islands, Co. Galway, and to a lesser extent the Dingle and Iveragh peninsulas in County Kerry; occasional isolated examples occur in other western counties. Within this group Cahercommaun is distinguished by two features—the strength of its inner enclosing wall (equalled only at Dún Chonchúir) and its trivallate defences. Trivallate forts with closely spaced defences like Cahercommaun are generally seen as part of the ringfort tradition. Initial studies on a countywide basis indicate that (with the notable exception of County Meath) the proportion of ringforts with more than two enclosing banks or walls rarely exceeds more than 1% of the total. Multivallate raths are far more common than multivallate cashels. Indeed, the total number of trivallate cashels in the country is probably less than half a dozen, and only one other example (Cahercalla, SMR CL034:150) has been recorded in County Clare. In the case of raths the number of enclosing banks is often viewed as an expression of status, and Warner has suggested that multivallation may be one of the distinguishing features of a royal site (1988, 67). In the case of stone ringforts the massiveness of a single enclosing wall may have been the characteristic used to symbolise the power, wealth or status of the owners. Within the cashel class Cahercommaun is unusual in that it combines both elements, i.e. multivallation and a strong inner citadel.

Despite Westropp's suggestion that the middle wall at Cahercommaun may have been demolished when the outer wall was built, the question of multiphase construction was not considered by Hencken, nor has it been raised by subsequent commentators. The concentric layout of the fort certainly suggests that the defences were designed and built as a single entity. No evidence for any major secondary modifications was recorded during the excavation, but whether or not this can be accepted as conclusive proof that there were none is debatable. Excavations at the raths of Lisleagh I and II, Co. Cork (Monk 1995, 105–15), indicated that both the form of the enclosing elements and the size of the settlements there changed considerably over a period of some 200–300 years. At Lisleagh I the original bank was slighted and replaced when the fort was enlarged, and at Lisleagh II the primary bank and ditch were replaced by a short-lived ditch and timber palisade (*ibid.*, 113). The absence of any ground-cutting features (e.g. ditches or palisade slots) at cashels means that it is extremely difficult to identify similar developments. In addition, the nature of most drystone walls is such that secondary refurbishments very often mask or even obliterate earlier work. For example, at Dún Aonghasa, Aran Islands, the fact that an earlier slighter wall had been incorporated into the present massive inner enclosing wall might have gone undetected were it not for the fortuitous photograph taken by Dunraven (Cotter 1993, pl. 3) prior to the nineteenth-century restoration work at the site.

PART 2. The evidence for prehistoric activity at Cahercommaun

The evidence for prehistoric activity at Cahercommaun rests on an assemblage of prehistoric artefacts. The currently recognisable prehistoric artefacts are four stone axes, three or more saddle querns, three or possibly four flint end-scrapers and a blade-like flake of chert. Some of the other stone objects recovered at the site—e.g. six keeled rubbing stones (Hencken 1938, fig. 34, 486) and a granite ball (*ibid.*, fig. 37, 90)— could also be of prehistoric date, but as none of these are chronologically diagnostic, this remains a matter of opinion and they are not discussed here.

The context of the prehistoric artefacts

In the course of the excavations the entire internal façade of the inner enclosing wall was exposed down to foundation level. It is not clear to what extent the external foundations of the wall were exposed, but Hencken's site plan (Fig. 6) shows the excavated cuttings abutting the external wall face at six separate points. A substantial part of the middle wall appears to have been excavated, including a 20m-long stretch where the wall had been largely robbed out. Seven cuttings abutted the inner face of the outer wall and two of these extended across the robbed-out foundations of the northern and southern terminals of the wall. No evidence for any activity pre-dating the walls was uncovered and, according to Hencken, the foundations of all the walls rested on bedrock (Hencken 1938, 15; Figs 6 and 7). The absence of any archaeological deposits pre-dating the middle and outer walls is not surprising, however, as there was no evidence for any domestic activity in the outer and middle enclosures.

Stratigraphically the earliest occupation deposit identifiable in the inner enclosure was the layer of black earth mixed with stones and charcoal which Hencken interpreted as flooring. In section M–N (Fig. 7) this layer underlies Hencken's primary habitation level (represented by the lower layer of ashes) and in places is up to 0.5m in depth. In the south-western quadrant the layer was stratified over thin patches of original humus but elsewhere it lay directly on the bedrock. The nine phase 1 hearths identified by Hencken (Fig. 7) were on a similar level to this 'flooring material'. They were set on the bedrock or into a layer of sand or gravel and were mainly concentrated in the southern half of the fort where the 'flooring material' was deepest. It would appear, therefore, that both the hearths and the 'flooring material' belonged to the same occupation horizon and represented the earliest *in situ* habitation surface in the southern half of the site. Similar flooring material was evident in the northern part of the fort underlying the hearths or occupation deposits in structures 5, 5a and 6. As none of the structures appear to have been paved, and only structure 5 was provided with a drain, the flooring deposit would have been essential for drainage purposes. The main question is whether this flooring deposit represented the (possibly disturbed) remains of an earlier occupation horizon or whether the material had been deliberately laid in conjunction with the construction of the ringfort-phase buildings.

The spatial distribution of the artefacts gave no indication that there was any *stratified* prehistoric material pre-dating the hearths at the site. Hencken lists twelve finds from over the bedrock and under the area of ashes in the north-west, south-west and south-east quadrants, though none appear to have been sealed (1938, 72, footnote, but see also p. 46). The range of finds included a number of iron objects and a fragment of a bone comb, as well as part of a saddle quern and a flint scraper. Part of a rotary quern lay on the bedrock in the north-eastern quadrant and, according to Hencken, was so large that it appeared 'unlikely that it had sunk through the fill' (1938, 60). A barrel padlock (Fig. 12) was found on the bedrock in structure 5a stratified below a stone axe. None of the prehistoric artefacts were associated with any of Hencken's phase 1 hearths, nor do they appear to have been concentrated in any particular zone in the interior. The north-eastern and south-eastern quadrants each yielded two saddle querns and two stone axes; a flint scraper, a scraper or waisted blade of flint and a blade-like flake of chert were also found in the south-eastern quadrant. A saddle quern and a fragment of another were recovered from the south-western quadrant, and finally two flint scrapers and a saddle quern came from the north-western quadrant. Contextual information was recorded for only six of these objects; the upper and lower ash layers produced two axes and a saddle quern, an axe was recovered from the occupation level in structure 5a, and two of the flint scrapers were found on the bedrock in the north-west and south-east quadrants.

Thus, while the presence of these artefacts points to some prehistoric activity on the site, there is no *stratigraphic* evidence to link this activity with the enclosing walls of the fort or with any of the features uncovered during the excavations. The prehistoric assemblage was dispersed throughout the interior, and three of the six contexted prehistoric artefacts were recovered from later occupation layers. On the other hand, the artefacts recovered from the earliest stratified features at the site (the phase 1 hearths) indicated that the latter belonged to the ringfort phase (Hencken 1938, 70–1). In addition, the foundations of the inner enclosing wall, and of the ringfort-phase buildings which abutted it (structures 1, 2, 3, 10 and 11), all rested directly on the same bedrock plane. This suggests that any levelling off or quarrying of the bedrock was carried out during the construction of the fort and not after it was built. Thus a dispersed residual artefact assemblage seems more likely to belong to a phase pre-dating the extant monument. On present evidence, therefore, the arguments for an earlier cultural horizon on the site rest solely on a residual assemblage of prehistoric artefacts which has no demonstrable relationship to the extant monument. The only clue as to the possible extent of any settlement pre-dating the fort is the fact that the prehistoric assemblage was confined to the area of the inner enclosure. As the site is located on a plateau it seems unlikely that erosion alone could account for the lack of any occupation evidence in the outer part of the fort. It is possible that the extensive quarrying carried out to provide the building stone for the fort resulted in the removal of any earlier habitation layers. The relatively level surface of the bedrock shown in sections A–B (Fig. 6) and M–N (Fig. 7) certainly suggests that some quarrying was carried out within the fort. On analogy with similar ground conditions at Dún Aonghasa, however, it could reasonably be expected that, had there been any prolonged occupation in the area between the inner and outer walls, some residue of domestic rubbish would have survived within the bedrock grykes.

THE LITHIC ASSEMBLAGE FROM CAHERCOMMAUN
P.C. WOODMAN

The lithic assemblage from Cahercommaun consists of five struck artefacts, of which four are of flint and one of chert.

E4:590 (Fig. 8; Pl. 6): max. length 30mm+. This is a small chert blade-like flake whose extreme distal end has been broken off. Its large, comparatively smooth striking platform suggests that it has been struck with a hard hammer percussion technique. The left edge and distal end are both slightly serrated, probably through use.

E4:418 (Fig. 8; Pl. 6; Hencken 1938, fig. 37, 78): max. length 26mm. This is a small convex end-scraper made on a thin flake, covered with a white patina. It has been made with steep peripheral retouch which extends in part down both lateral edges. This scraper lacks the invasive retouch of small scrapers which are often thought to be characteristic of Bronze Age assemblages.

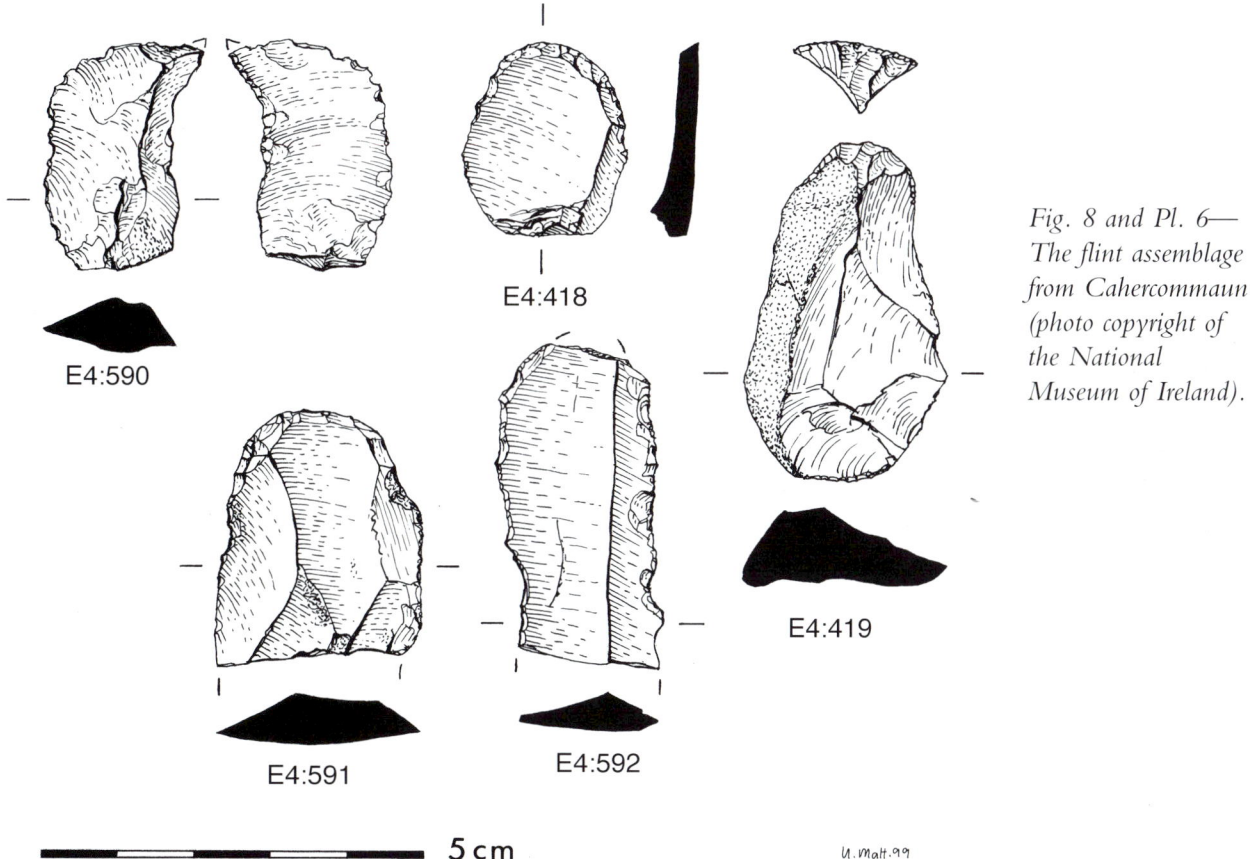

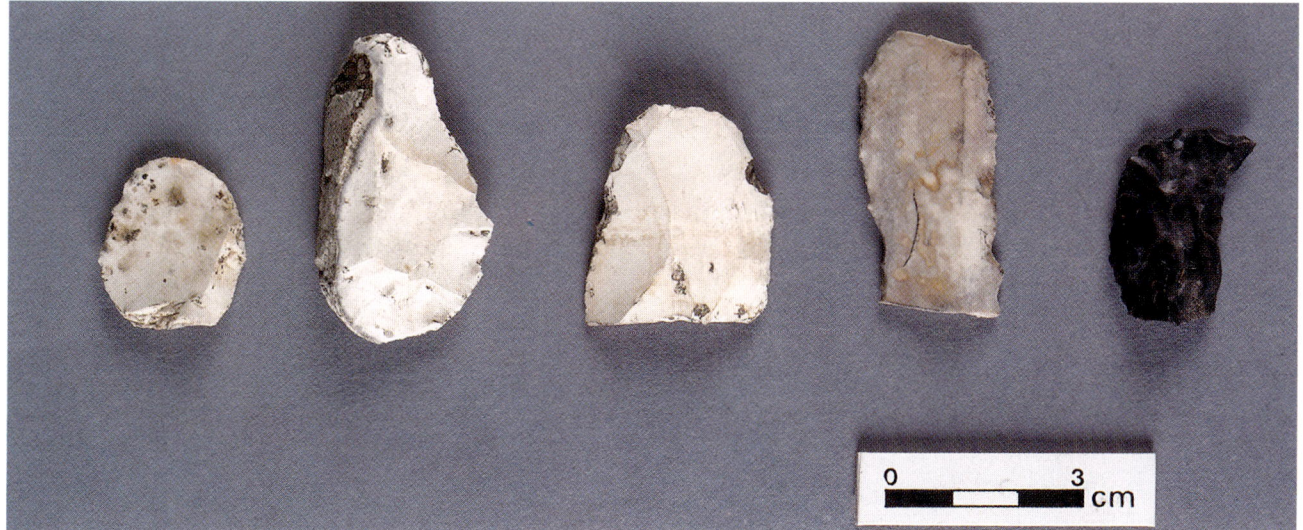

Fig. 8 and Pl. 6—The flint assemblage from Cahercommaun (photo copyright of the National Museum of Ireland).

E4:419 (Fig. 8; Pl. 6; Hencken 1938, fig. 37, 580): max. length 45mm. This is a convex end-scraper made on a large flake which still retains a significant area of cortex. The cortex is more weathered than water-rolled. The flint itself is exceptionally heavily patinated—a deep white in colour—with some of the lateral edges rounded off. The flake, although narrow, does not run at right angles to the striking platform, which is large and smooth. The functional edge is formed by steep semi-invasive retouch to create a narrow functional edge.

E4:591 (Fig. 8; Pl. 6; Hencken 1938, fig. 37, 767): max. length 31mm+. Convex end-scraper. This is a fragment of a large end of blade (?) scraper which may originally have been more than 50mm in length. The piece has lost its proximal end as a result of recent fracture, perhaps as a result of damage during excavation. This fractured surface shows that only a tiny sliver of flint retains its original dark grey colour and that the white patina is not superficial and virtually the whole body of the artefact has undergone a change. As in the case of E4:419, weathering has caused a rounding of the edges of the scraper. The original retouch was steep and peripheral and is confined to the distal end and the immediate lateral edges. Traces of edge damage also occur on the two lateral edges.

E4:592 (Fig. 8; Pl. 6; Hencken 1938, fig. 37, 236): max. length 40mm+. End-scraper/waisted blade (?). This is the medial portion of a particularly fine blade which has a more mottled white patina than the other flint artefacts. It is possible that there may have been a scraping edge at the distal end as one small area of fine abrupt retouch still exists at the left distal end. The right lateral edge retains an extensive run of invasive flake scars on both faces. While two of the flake scars retain differential patina it is probable that most were created at the initial period of use. The left lateral edge retains areas of abrupt peripheral retouch though these usually exist as short irregular runs.

Summary

These artefacts represent the residue(s) of one or more episodes of prehistoric activity, with some of the pieces being created by extremely competent flint-knappers who produced blades from a comparatively good source of flint not usually seen on the beaches on the west coast of Ireland. Some of the pieces are so weathered and patinated (in fact by Irish standards they are weathered to an exceptional degree for specimens not found adjacent to a beach) that it is likely that they lay exposed on an open surface for a very significant length of time.

Scrapers are not usually diagnostic, and while these objects may belong to several episodes of occupation it is probable that blade no. 592 is of Neolithic date; the scrapers are very unlikely to post-date the Neolithic period, and given their very weathered condition it is possible that they are earlier.

THE STONE AXES FROM CAHERCOMMAUN

Gabriel Cooney and Stephen Mandal

The four stone axes from Cahercommaun (Fig. 9) are all made from shale, a widely available local stone in this area. This is consistent with the pattern of shale being the dominant source material for axe production in County Clare (Cooney and Mandal 1995, 976; 1998, 108). The fact that the faces of two of the axes (E4:99; E4:351) are formed from bedding planes might suggest that the primary method of manufacture was to cleave thin slabs out of shale bedrock. On the other hand, the most common evidence of primary manufacture on the axes is for flaking, and it seems probable that at least one of the axes (E4:145) was manufactured from a beach or river cobble (see discussion in Cooney and Mandal 1995). This use of secondary sources of shale would appear to have been very common. The widespread occurrence of shale outcrop and secondary sources in the form of cobbles, combined with the facility with which axes can be made from shale, would have made it a very important, but also low-quality, local source material.

None of the axes are complete; all show signs of use, and their state is consistent with a domestic function. On the other hand, it seems clear that the upper portion of the axe represented by E4:162, which is almost 10cm in length, comes from an object that was probably at least twice as long (over 20cm) when complete. It is also the most carefully made of the four. Its large size and the effort expended on its production suggest that it may have been seen as more than just a functional object.

In terms of date, shale axes have been found on sites of widely varying age. They occur on Mesolithic (e.g. Newferry, Co. Antrim; Woodman 1977), Neolithic (e.g. Lough Gur, Co. Limerick; Ó Ríordáin 1954; Grogan and Eogan 1987) and Bronze Age sites (e.g. Clonfinlough, Co. Offaly; Moloney et al. 1993). They also occur on sites of later date, where they are interpreted as evidence either for earlier activity on the site or for continued use of stone axes as a basic functional artefact or as talismanic objects.

In the case of the axes from Cahercommaun, given the occurrence of other prehistoric activity on the site, the axes are perhaps best interpreted as fitting in with this phase. Given the very wide date range of shale axes, in the absence of other prehistoric activity it would be very difficult to tie them in with a particular phase of activity on the site.

Catalogue of Cahercommaun stone axes

A standard format has been devised by the Irish Stone Axe Project for cataloguing stone axes. It has been abbreviated for this report and a sequence is used which is broadly similar to that in other Project reports (e.g. Cooney and Mandal 1998; Mandal and Cooney 1996). Locational and contextual details are followed by the petrographical identifications based on macroscopic analysis. This is followed by details of the method of manufacture. Details based on specific descriptive categories for all features are then given. The drawn face is referred to as face 1, the obverse as face 2. The cutting edge is called 'the edge' and the part of each face above the edge is referred to as 'the blade'. The opposite end is 'the butt'. The lateral junctions between the two faces are called 'the sides' and the side view is referred to as 'the profile'.

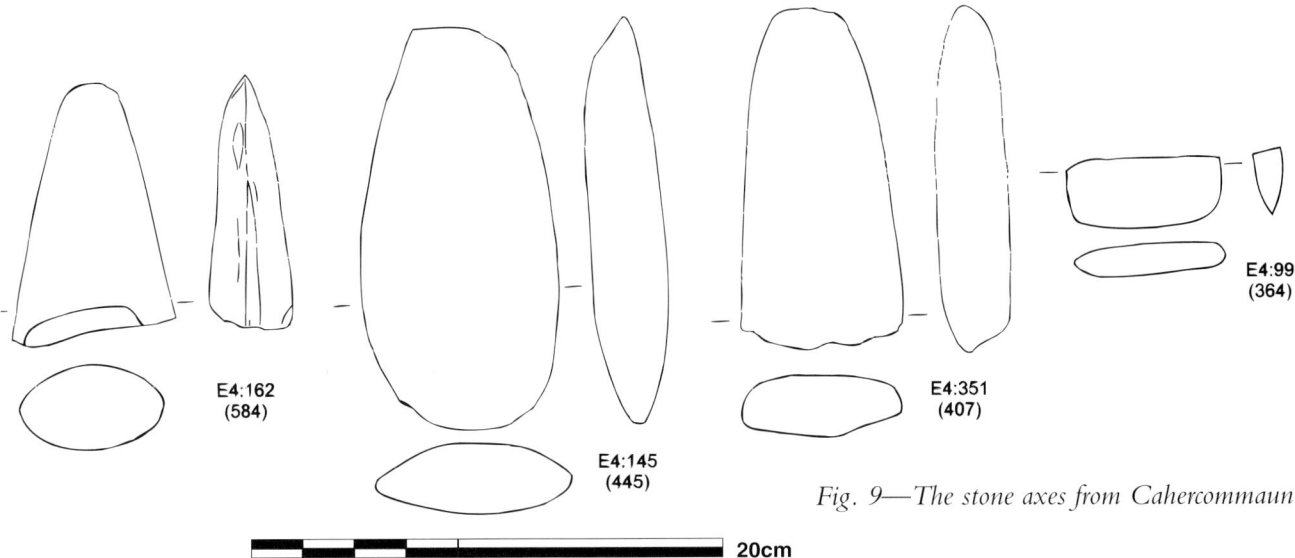

Fig. 9—The stone axes from Cahercommaun

Dimensions: maximum length, width and thickness measurements in centimetres are followed by weight in grammes and are abbreviated as follows; length = L., width = W., thickness = T. and weight = Wt. The present collection is then given, with museum or other registration numbers where applicable. The Irish Stone Axe Project number is also appended. Any previous publications are listed.

TULLYCOMMON, CO. CLARE
OS 6-inch sheet 10
Circumstance of discovery: Archaeological excavation (Cahercommaun). *Context:* Found in the north-east quadrant of the excavation (Hencken 1938, 55).
Petrography: Shale.
Axe, upper portion: Partially ground and polished. Right side straight, rounded, well polished, smooth. Left side more convex, with a lot of flake damage, face 2. Face 1 ground bedding plane, face 2 has large relatively recent flake damage on right side. Butt rounded pointed, with some damage. Present lower end of the axe defined by clean break perpendicular to length. Profile is unknown, cross-section is narrow oval.
L. 13.2cm, W. 6.3cm, T. 2.6cm, Wt. 335g.
National Museum of Ireland (NMI E4:351)
ISAP: 1322
Hencken 1938, 55, fig. 34, 407.

TULLYCOMMON, CO. CLARE
OS 6-inch sheet 10
Circumstance of discovery: Archaeological excavation (Cahercommaun). *Context:* From the upper layer of white ashes in the south-west quadrant (Hencken 1938, 55).
Petrography: Shale.
Axe: Ground and partially polished. Right side convex, deliberately faceted (fine facets). Left side more convex, naturally flattened upper portion, flaked lower portion. No junctions with edge. Edge badly damaged, numerous flakes. Face 1 convex, face 2 slightly flatter, grinding marks remain on upper portion. Butt oblique, damaged. Profile is asymmetrical: thin; cross-section is narrow oval.
L. 15.5cm, W. 7.4cm, T. 2.7cm, Wt. 480g.
National Museum of Ireland (NMI E4:145)
ISAP: 1324
Hencken 1938, 55, fig. 34, 445.

TULLYCOMMON, CO. CLARE
OS 6-inch sheet 10
Circumstance of discovery: Archaeological excavation (Cahercommaun). *Context:* From the layer of black ashy fill in the lower part of structure 5A (Hencken 1938, 55).
Petrography: Shale.
Axe, blade only: Ground and partially polished. Remaining portion of sides: right side rounded, left side with subtle facets. No junctions with edges, though sharp curve. Edge sharp, straight, virtually undamaged. Remaining portion of faces ground bedding planes, unpolished. Present upper end of axe defined by clean break perpendicular to length. Profile is unknown; cross-section is narrow oval.
L. 2.8cm, W. 5.9cm, T. 1.2cm, Wt. 32g.
National Museum of Ireland (NMI E4:99)
ISAP: 5352
Hencken 1938, fig. 34, 364.

TULLYCOMMON, CO. CLARE
OS 6-inch sheet 10
Circumstance of discovery: Archaeological excavation (Cahercommaun). *Context:* Found in the lower layer of white ashes in the south-west quadrant (Hencken 1938, 55).
Petrography: Shale.
Axe, upper portion: Ground and polished. Sides straight, splayed from butt, both have several ground facets. Face 1 rounded, ground; face 2 flatter, ground. Butt has fine damage chips. Very well-finished axe. Present lower end of the axe defined by clean break oblique to length. Profile is unknown; cross-section is oval.
L. 9.8cm, W. 6cm, T. 3.3cm, Wt. 211g.
National Museum of Ireland (NMI E4:162)
ISAP: 8648
Hencken 1938, fig. 34, 564.

THE SADDLE QUERNS
CLAIRE COTTER

Hencken recorded a total of eight seemingly complete quernstones and 34 quern fragments from the site; all were made from sandstone (1938, 58). They consisted of two upper rotary quernstones and 33 rotary quern fragments, and six saddle querns and a fragment of another (*ibid.*, 60). None of the saddle querns were associated with any of the structures at the site, but one complete example (no. 433, not illustrated) came from the upper layer of white ashes and, according to Hencken, belonged 'at least to the later period of occupation' (*ibid.*). Two of the saddle querns were illustrated in the excavation report. No. 410 (Fig. 10; Pl. 7), described as the largest example recovered, was 620mm long, 310mm wide and 90mm thick and had a concave grinding surface. It came from the area of ashes in the north-west quadrant. No. 286 (Fig. 10) was the smallest example recovered and came from the south-east quadrant. It measured 280mm long, 130mm wide and 63mm

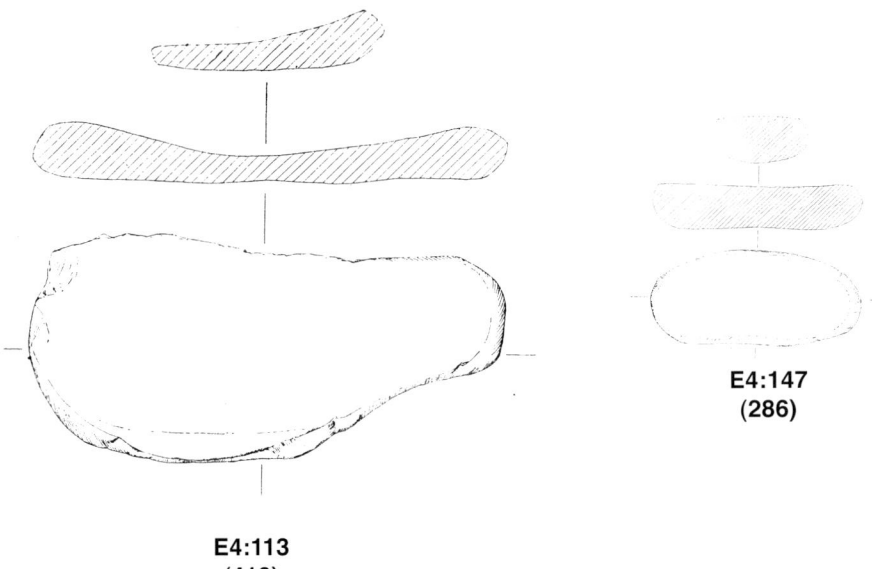

Fig. 10 and Pl. 7—Saddle querns from Cahercommaun: scale 1/10 (Hencken 1938, fig. 36; photo courtesy of the National Museum of Ireland).

thick and was concave along its long axis but slightly convex along its shorter axis. None of the other saddle querns were described in the report and only three examples appear to be housed in the National Museum of Ireland. These include the two querns described above (no. 410, renumbered E4:113, and no. 286, renumbered E4:147). The third example (reclassified as a whetstone during the subsequent cataloguing of the finds and numbered E4:168) is of similar form to no. 286 but slightly smaller in size; both were manufactured from split boulders or cobbles, have flat upper surfaces and measure less than 300mm in length.

The morphology and distribution of Irish saddle querns has recently been studied by Anne Connolly (1993; 1994), and I am grateful to her for permission to publish the following information. At the time of her study some 228 saddle querns had been recorded in Ireland; this number has now increased to 250 (Connolly 1994, 35). Approximately 151 examples could be provenanced, and their geographical distribution showed a marked concentration in the east of the country. The querns varied in length from 0.26m to 0.67m, and Connolly noted a wide diversity in the shape both of the stones themselves and of the grinding surfaces. Though none of the three saddle querns which survive from Cahercommaun could be described as classic prehistoric saddle querns, the typological characteristics of the two smaller examples do nonetheless conform to the broader classification of 'grinding stone'. Similar ground stones have been found in a definite Late Bronze Age context at Clonfinlough, Co. Offaly (Moloney 1993, figs 109, 110 and 113). It seems very unlikely, however, that either of the two smaller examples from Cahercommaun was ever used for grinding grain.

Of the 150 or so querns which could be provenanced by Connolly, approximately 117 were found on or near archaeological monuments, 26 were recovered during agricultural work, three were surface finds, five were recovered from bogs and four were found in sandhills or on the seashore. Ten of the saddle querns recovered from archaeological sites came from Ballygalley Head, Co. Antrim, and at least three of these came from definite Neolithic contexts. One of four saddle querns found during excavations at the multiperiod enclosure at Raffin Fort, Co. Meath, came from a Neolithic context, and a surface find of a saddle quern from Feltrim Hill, Co. Dublin, may also be of Neolithic date. A saddle quern found at the passage tomb on Baltinglass Hill, Co. Wicklow, may belong to a Neolithic phase of activity on the hilltop or alternatively it may be related to the later hillfort. A number of saddle querns from Whitepark Bay, Co. Down, were considered by Knowles to be of Neolithic date, but a question mark now lies over this dating (Connolly 1994, 31). A single example found adjacent to the main mound at Knowth, Co. Meath, came from an unstratified context. Six saddle querns were recovered during excavations from, or in the immediate vicinity of, Bronze Age cists. Nineteen examples were found at hillforts (Rathgall, Co. Wicklow, and Haughey's Fort, Co. Armagh); recent excavations at the hillforts of Mooghaun, Co. Clare (Eoin Grogan, pers. comm.), and by the writer at Dún Aonghasa on the Aran Islands have also yielded a number of saddle querns. Sixty-five other saddle querns came from excavated contexts of known or likely Late Bronze Age date (Aughinish, Co. Limerick; Belderg, Co. Mayo; Ballinderry II, Co. Offaly; Carrigillihy, Co. Limerick; Clonfinlough, Co. Offaly; Dalkey Island, Co. Dublin; Knocknalappa, Co. Clare; Killymoon, Co. Tyrone; Lough Eskragh, Co. Tyrone; Lough Gara, Co. Sligo; Moynagh Lough, Co. Meath). Eight saddle querns recovered from either crannogs, mounds of stone or areas of black soil might also be included in this category. A pair of saddle querns were found at an oval stone enclosure (20.5m by 13.5m) of unknown date at Sheeauns, Connemara, Co. Galway. Two saddle querns were recovered from a ploughed field beside Rathcrandhun ringfort in Mullamast, Co. Kildare, an area of known later prehistoric activity (all information from Connolly 1993 and catalogue in Connolly 1994, 33–5).

Excluding the examples from Cahercommaun, only two excavated ringforts have produced saddle querns—a saddle quern and a trough quern were recovered during excavations at a small univallate cashel in Rinnaraw Townland, Co. Donegal (Fanning 1987; 1998; 1990), and rescue excavations at a large D-shaped cashel in Carn Townland, Co. Fermanagh (Brannon 1981–2), also produced a single saddle quern. The site at Rinnaraw consisted of a small rock-platform some 25m in diameter with slight remains of an enclosing wall—the enclosure was designated as a cashel on the later editions of the Ordnance Survey maps. Excavations indicated that the site had been occupied in the Early Medieval period; a large house in the interior probably belonged to the final phase of occupation during the first quarter of the second millennium AD (Fanning 1987; 1988; 1990). The saddle quern was found below the sod layer outside the house and had been partly reworked and used in conjunction with metalworking (Connolly 1993, 158).

The univallate cashel in Carn Townland, Co.

Fermanagh, was located on the edge of a steep escarpment at a height of 500ft OD. A local tradition of a cairn in the immediate vicinity attested to possible prehistoric activity in the area (Brannon 1981–2, 60). The fort had an internal diameter of *c*. 73.2m by 44.6m—an extremely large size for a cashel—and the poorly preserved enclosing wall may have been *c*. 6–8m thick originally. Surface stripping in advance of quarrying meant that little archaeological evidence was preserved in the interior. A small quantity of iron slag, animal bone and five unstratified artefacts were recovered in the course of the excavation. These consisted of the saddle quern, two hammerstones, a stone disc described as a palette, and a bone spindle-whorl with dot-in-circle decoration (*ibid*., fig. 2). The fort has now been completely removed. Its large size and substantial rampart are atypical features of the cashel class generally, but the (undated) large stone enclosures which Lacy has identified in County Donegal (Lacy *et al*. 1983, 116) may be a possible parallel.

Two other saddle querns have been recorded as casual finds at ringforts—one from the trivallate fort of Gearta Mor at Carrowmore, Co. Mayo (MA049:139), and the second from near the entrance to a souterrain at a cashel in Deer Park, Co. Sligo (Connolly 1993, 182). Westropp (1901, 273–92; 1902, 635) also refers to primitive corn-crushers described as 'long hollowed stones' found at or near stone forts in the townlands of Ballycahill (Caherahooan, CL005:054), Moheramoylan and Ballyganner in the Burren, Co. Clare, but there appears to be no further record of these objects.

Based on a study of the provenanced examples, Connolly concluded that, in Ireland, the saddle quern is rare on Neolithic sites. It has (to date) appeared mainly in a funerary context in the Middle Bronze Age, and there is substantial evidence to support the argument that it is mainly a Late Bronze Age artefact (1993, 80–2). The scarcity of securely dated Iron Age settlement sites in Ireland does not permit any general statements to be made about the role of the saddle quern during this period but Connolly suggests that Caulfield's quern replacement theory is not upheld in England, where there is evidence for a 'definite though declining use of the saddle quern throughout the Iron Age' (*ibid*., 82).

It is also evident from Connolly's study that the occurrence of saddle querns at ringforts is extremely uncommon. Despite the large number of ringforts which have been excavated in the country, only three appear to have produced saddle querns. There are a number of interesting conclusions to be drawn from this, but in the context of this article Connolly's study shows overwhelmingly that, despite being highly visible and portable objects, saddle querns were rarely transported onto Early Medieval settlement sites. There is a strong case to be made, therefore, for concluding that the presence of the saddle querns at Cahercommaun is a reliable indicator of prehistoric activity at the site. Statistically, Connolly's study indicates that this earlier activity is more likely to be Late Bronze Age in date but, given the lack of datable Iron Age settlements, a later prehistoric date cannot be ruled out. The weight of evidence also indicates that the saddle quern was primarily a domestic artefact. In this respect the absence of pottery at Cahercommaun may be significant—all five Late Bronze Age hillforts excavated to date have produced coarse cooking pottery, and other domestic settlements of similar date, e.g. Aughinish, Co. Limerick (Kelly 1974, 21), Clonfinlough, Co. Offaly (Moloney *et al*. 1993, 129–31), and Knocknalappa, Co. Clare (J. Raftery 1942, 53–72), have also produced similar pottery. Hencken was already familiar with Irish prehistoric pottery from his excavations at Poulawack (1935, 210) and remarked on its absence at Cahercommaun (1938, 2).

SUMMARY AND DISCUSSION
CLAIRE COTTER

Whilst the presence of the stone axes, saddle querns and flint/chert artefacts at Cahercommaun testifies to prehistoric activity on the site, it is less certain that the assemblage can be considered a discrete one. The flint assemblage is unlikely to post-date the Neolithic, the stone axes are chronologically undiagnostic and, whilst the saddle querns are more likely to be of late prehistoric date, they could conceivably date from any period from the Neolithic to the Iron Age. All the objects appear to be consistent with activity of a domestic nature, though this too is uncertain, as all three classes of artefact have also been recorded in ritual or funerary contexts. The weathered appearance of the flint scrapers testifies to exposure over a long period, possibly indicating that there was no substantial buildup of any associated occupation layers. The absence of coarse cooking ware also raises doubts as to whether there was any intensive or extensive Late Bronze Age occupation at the site—it seems highly unlikely, for example, that there was ever a hillfort at this location during this period, but the overall evidence is too meagre to draw any further conclusions.

There is no stratigraphical evidence to link any of

these objects to the fort itself and, in terms of context, the only common factor appears to be that all were recovered from within the inner enclosure. The prehistoric activity on the site may therefore have focused on the area close to the cliff edge. No traces of any features pre-dating the construction of the fort were uncovered during Hencken's excavations. It is possible that the extensive quarrying associated with its construction resulted in the removal of any earlier structures or (if the site was enclosed at this time) that a relatively insubstantial enclosing wall was later enveloped by the vast bulk of the present inner enclosing wall. Over 2500 undated 'enclosures' have been recorded by the SMR in County Clare. At present it is not possible to date these on morphological grounds—in the Burren the morphological distinction between cashels, 'enclosures' and even fields becomes blurred at a certain point. A large number of the recorded enclosures are likely to have been associated with animal husbandry (i.e. fields, pens, booleying complexes, fenced-off natural hazards, etc.) but it seems probable that some proportion represent the remains of past human settlement. Excavations at a small enclosure (one-eighth of an acre in extent) within an extensive field-system in Parknabinnia Townland (4km south-east of Cahercommaun) indicated that the site was first occupied in the Final Neolithic/Early Bronze Age period, with a secondary phase of settlement taking place in the Early Medieval period (Jones 1995; Jones and Walsh 1996). Recent fieldwork by Christine Grant (1995) in Fannygalvin Townland (3km west-north-west of Cahercommaun) has also highlighted possible chronological and spatial associations between a number of enclosures and a complex of prehistoric funerary/ceremonial monuments.

A number of stone enclosures are visible today on the plateau at Tullycommon (e.g. CL010:064/17); these range from *c.* 10m to 20m in internal diameter and are generally defined by low collapsed walls, often less than 1.5m in width. The relatively insubstantial nature of the enclosing element suggests that, if such an enclosure formerly existed at Cahercommaun, its removal would leave little or no trace.

In summary, therefore, whilst the prehistoric artefacts from Cahercommaun may be seen as the residue(s) of one or more episodes of prehistoric activity on the hilltop, the nature or extent of such activity can only be guessed at now. There is ample evidence for a dynamic Neolithic and Bronze Age presence in the Burren. To date, the majority of the excavated evidence relates to burial monuments, with sites such as the portal tomb at Poulnabrone (Lynch 1988; Lynch and Ó Donnabháin 1994) and the cairn at Poulawack (Hencken 1935; Ryan 1981; Brindley and Lanting 1991–2) both producing Neolithic dates. Four wedge tombs lie within a 1.5km radius of Cahercommaun, and a dense concentration of at least fourteen others (the Roughan–Leana group; Jones and Walsh 1996, 98) has been recorded in the Parknabinnia area, which lies 4km to the south-south-west. None of these tombs have been excavated, but radiocarbon dates from a number of excavated wedge tombs in the south-west of the country indicate a Final Neolithic/Early Bronze Age context for the earliest use of these monuments, with ritual use of the tombs extending into later prehistoric times (O'Brien 1993, 73).

A number of stone cairns on the Tullycommon and Parknabinnia plateaux could also be of early prehistoric date. Four of these prominently sited groups of cairns occur in close proximity to wedge tombs; a fifth group on Glasgeivnagh Hill at the south-eastern edge of the plateau (1.6km south-south-east of Cahercommaun) commands a spectacular long-range view, with the Atlantic Ocean visible on the skyline to the south-west.

Evidence for activity in the Burren during the second millennium BC is also provided by a number of stray finds, e.g. a bronze dagger from Gortaclare (midway between Carron and Turlough Hill), a bronze razor found at Gragans West, near the top of Corkscrew Hill (Cotter 1989), a trunnion chisel from Blakesmountain (at the western side of Slieve Elva), and bronze rapiers found at Ballykeel (north of Kilfenora) and Ballyconnoe South, east of Lisdoonvarna (O'Carroll, forthcoming). Many of these objects were found during peat-cutting in the areas where the acid shales intersect with the limestone, the rate of recovery in the exclusively pastoral landscape of the limestone plateaux being not surprisingly low. A stone mould for a flanged axe and razor/knife found by the landowner at an Early Medieval settlement in Gragans West Td (Cotter 1989) provides the only evidence to date for the manufacture of bronze implements in the area.

The majority of the *fulachta fiadh* recorded by the SMR in the Burren may also date from the second millennium BC. Over 30 *fulachta fiadh* have been recorded on the lower-lying limestone terraces below Tullycommon/Glasgeivnagh; at least seven others have been identified in the townlands of Fahee North and Fahee South, which lie towards the eastern end of the Carron depression. Excavations at a *fulacht fiadh* in Fahee South (CL010:024), 2.5km north-north-east of

Cahercommaun, indicated usage in the period 1431–1134 cal. BC (3050 ± 35 BP; GrN-11437; O'Drisceoil 1988).

The Gleninsheen/Poulgorm area, located *c.* 7km north-west of Cahercommaun, is one of a number of other upland plateaux in the Burren which preserve evidence for intensive activity over a long period. The Late Bronze Age gold collar found in a rock crevice in Gleninsheen Townland (Gleeson 1934) suggests that these areas of upland pasture remained central to the economic wealth of the inhabitants throughout the later prehistoric period. Secondary burials of Bronze Age date were inserted into the burial monuments at Poulawack (Ryan 1981; Brindley and Lanting 1991–2) and Poulnabrone (Lynch 1988), and coarseware pottery recovered during recent excavations by James Eogan at a burial cairn (CL006:044) in Coolnatullagh Townland (*c.* 3.5km north-east of Fahee South) may also be linked to Bronze Age activity at this site (Eogan 1998, 5–6).

Only a small number of definitively dated Iron Age objects are known from the north Clare area (Waddell 1991, 70). The majority of these are items of horse trappings found near Lough Inchiquin, along the south-eastern edge of the Burren, but a beehive quern found at Cohy, north of Kilfenora (Caulfield 1977, fig. 21, C), and a possible horse pendant from the Fanore area (information from Finola O'Carroll) provide some tangible evidence for an Iron Age presence in the Burren itself.

There is thus abundant evidence for activity in the general Cahercommaun area at various stages throughout the prehistoric period. Whilst the large number of wedge tombs in the immediate vicinity of Cahercommaun might seem to support a Late Neolithic dating for the known prehistoric assemblage from Hencken's excavations, the emergence of the wedge tombs may itself represent an intensification of earlier activity in the area (Cooney and Grogan 1994, 93). It seems clear, however, that by the end of the Neolithic period upland plateaux like Tullycommon had become the focus of fairly intensive human activity. Indications are that this trend continued into the later prehistoric period, and the distribution of Early Medieval cashels in the Burren also reflects a similar pastoral focus, with the greatest concentrations of these forts occurring in sheltered locations either up on the plateaux or on the terraces along their margins. The construction of the stone fort at Cahercommaun is also best seen as but one phase in a much longer history of human activity on the surrounding plateau.

PART 3. The cultural context and date of the main occupation

Summary of Hencken's excavation

Apart from two small hut sites and a few scraps of animal bone, no trace of any occupation activity was evident in the middle and outer enclosures. The subdivision of these enclosures by radial walls suggested to the excavator that this part of the fort had probably been used mainly for housing livestock (Hencken 1938, 10). In the course of his excavation of the inner area Hencken identified eleven drystone structures, numbered 1–11, and two annexes, 5a and 6a (Fig. 7; Pl. 8). Of these he considered that only seven (1, 2, 3, 4, 5, 5a and 6) had been regularly occupied, and that the six remaining structures (6a, 7, 8, 9, 10 and 11) had been filled up with loose stones from the time the fort was built—the fill of loose stones functioning either as a support for the inner face of the wall or as a raised living surface. Structures 6 and 7 were each associated with a souterrain (B and A respectively). The most westerly of these (souterrain A) led through an opening in the wall of the fort to a vertical crevice in the cliff face. At the southern end of souterrain B, a human skull 'surrounded by flat stones carefully laid' (*ibid.*, 23) was interpreted by Hencken as a foundation deposit.

In the southern half of the interior two phases of occupation were identified (*ibid.*, 2). The two-phase division was based on two extensive layers of ashes separated by a layer of loose stones and earth, which occurred near structure 4. According to Hencken, numerous detached hearths in the vicinity fell into two corresponding stratigraphic groups separated by the same reflooring layer of stones and earth. The two-phase division was not evident in the northern half of the site and Hencken considered that the reflooring of the southern half of the interior had taken place after the structures in the northern half had been constructed. With the exception of one detached wall in the west sector, all the structural walls sat directly on bedrock. Hencken concluded, therefore, that the same structures had remained in use during both phases of occupation. Finally, charcoal contained in the upper fill of the interior led him to suggest that, at some date after the abandonment of the fort, it was temporarily reoccupied, but 'not for a sufficiently long period to leave any distinct traces' (*ibid.*, 15).

Based on the distribution and status of individual artefacts, Hencken proposed a hierarchical spatial organisation within the fort, with structure 6 being

Pl. 8—The inner enclosure after excavation, showing structures 4, 5, 6, 7, 8, 9, 10 and 11 (Hencken 1938, pl. VIII, fig. 2).

the principal dwelling occupied by the owners of the fort, followed by structures 5 and 5a, whose occupants were only of 'slightly less importance' (*ibid.*, 19). The extensive layers of ashes and the relative frequency of querns in the vicinity of structure 4 indicated that this was 'the kitchen quarters' (*ibid.*, 68), and the lack of luxury items in the southern quadrants of the fort led Hencken to conclude that these were 'poor areas', occupied by people of lesser status such as the iron-smelters and serving people (*ibid.*, 68–9). He estimated that the maximum number of occupants at the fort at any given time was 40–50 people.

It is not possible, based on the published evidence at any rate, to reassess the excavations at Cahercommaun in close stratigraphical detail. Unlike Ballinderry and Lagore, where some well-defined occupation levels were identified and illustrated on plans, sections etc., very little stratigraphy appears to have been recorded at Cahercommaun. For much of the interior the only recorded archaeological horizon consisted of a 'brown or black layer of loose earth and stones containing charcoal, animal bones and artefacts'. In fairness to Hencken, however, it must be said that the excavations were conducted according to the best standards of the day. Undoubtedly over much of the site it was extremely difficult to distinguish chronologically different episodes of activity. The dry,

loose nature of the deposits, the absence of any negative features and the constant reworking of occupation soils are factors which sound all too familiar from similar site conditions encountered by the writer during excavations at Dún Aonghasa. The following aspects of the published report, however, place limitations on the extent to which the results of the excavation can be interrogated.

The distinction between occupation layers, abandonment levels and post-occupation collapse of the buildings was not made in the report and most of the deposits excavated were described as 'earth and stone fill' or 'the main fill layer'. The amount of post-abandonment disturbance at the site was also unstated. Though the animal pens and 'herdsmen's huts' were confined to the outer part of the fort, most of the buildings in the interior (particularly the structure 4 complex) appear to have been partly robbed out. The only living surfaces identified at all levels were hearths and associated ash spreads, and the absence of any sections across the full width of the interior means that it is difficult now to correlate the occupation sequences in each of the four quadrants. The division of the site into two phases based on 'the two layers of ashes separated by a layer of fill' (Hencken 1938, 2) does not appear to have been relevant to most of the interior. Apart from section M–N (Fig. 7), this horizontal division is not indicated elsewhere, and in the list of the distribution of animal bones at the site (*ibid.*, 74) those 'from the level of ashes' were recorded for the south-western and north-western quadrants only. In a footnote to the same list Hencken also stated that 'the two layers of ashes were not clearly divided in most places and thus the animal bones from both were kept together'. In the northern half of the site, Hencken's belief that souterrain B with its 'foundation burial' had to be a primary feature heavily influenced his interpretation of the occupation sequence in this area. As a result, any activity pre-dating or post-dating either the souterrains or the structures associated with them was considered to have been only of a temporary nature.

In the following reappraisal the site is examined firstly from the perspective of the surviving buildings and secondly from the perspective of the artefacts with the overall aim of establishing some chronological framework for the date and duration of the settlement. Hencken's two-phase division is re-assessed and an alternative three-phase sequence is suggested. The construction date of the fort itself is discussed in the final summary.

The structural sequence

Apart from buildings which appear to have gone out of use (structures 1, 10 and 11) and the rebuilding of the walls flanking the entrance passage (i.e. the northern and southern walls of structures 1 and 11 respectively), there is no recorded building sequence in the published report. There are a number of reasons for suggesting, however, that the same buildings did not remain in use throughout the entire occupation of the fort. The reflooring of the southern area significantly raised the floor level within the structures there—the phase 2 floor level in structure 1 lay *c*. 0.5m above that of phase 1, whilst the phase 2 hearths in structure 3 sat on 0.5m of 'earthy fill mixed with animal bones' (1938, 17). Structure 1 also appears to have been enlarged during phase 2—the occupation floor during this later phase extended over a raft of rubble (either collapse or deliberate fill within structure 2) and abutted the enclosing wall (*ibid.*, fig. 7). By the time the fort was abandoned, the occupation level in this part of the fort had risen to the level of the lower terrace.

At the centre of the site Hencken identified five primary hearths (h, i, j, k and l) which he considered to be contemporary with his structure 4. However, as these hearths were located either outside or along the wall line of that complex of buildings (Fig. 7) this seems unlikely. In discussing the two extensive layers of ashes near the structure 4 complex, Hencken considered the possibility that there had been 'two successive wooden structures which had burned down' but concluded that this was not the case as 'the postholes of the second should have been detectable in the ashes of the first' (1938, 2). However, the apparent absence of any structures in much of the south-western quadrant (where the two extensive layers of ashes were most evident) could best be explained by successive phases of thatched timber buildings which had burnt down. Given the site conditions, the absence of recognisable post-holes is not surprising. In addition, sizeable timber posts appear to have been rarely used on dryland sites in the Early Medieval period, and smaller stakes appear to have been the norm. The stratigraphy associated with the structure 4 complex itself is unclear and there are no sections of this area. However, as the paving associated with the refurbishment of the entrance passage led directly to this group of buildings, it seems more likely that they belong to the later phase of occupation at the site.

In the northern half of the fort, the backfilling of structures 10 and 11 (Hencken 1938, 26) and the existence of a number of hearths and occupation spreads overlying this fill indicate a sequence of occupation in this area also. A large hearth post-dated the abandonment of structure 7 (Fig. 7, section K–L; *ibid.*, 24). A portion of a rotary quern was incorporated into the wall of structure 6 (*ibid.*, 60), indicating that this building was either secondary or had been refurbished at some stage. Both souterrains were essentially overground features masked by stone and earth fill and by the rubble platform which extended from the entrance to the fort on the east as far as structure 5a on the west. The construction of this platform post-dated the abandonment of structures 10 and 11; the party wall between 5 and 6 was described by Hencken as being of the same type as that revetting the platform (1938, 19), and on plan appears to be a continuation of it. The fill which buttressed the souterrains (Hencken's structure 6a) and the rubble making up the platform both incorporated habitation material and a number of finds (*ibid.*, 24–6 and 73).

There is thus some evidence to suggest that the souterrains were secondary features, and it is possible that the conjoined houses 5 and 6 were also constructed at this later stage. No occupation surfaces were recorded within structures 7 and 8; both are conjoined and on plan at least appear contemporary. As souterrain B was accessed from structure 7, there is a strong likelihood that structures 7 and 8 were contemporary with the 5/6 complex of buildings.

There is insufficient evidence now to suggest any layout of this area in a possible pre-souterrain phase. The sticky reddish-brown clay deposit at the southern end of souterrain B (Fig. 11) may indicate that the lower ledge of rock in this area of the fort was levelled off immediately prior to the construction of the souterrains—similar sterile clay deposits were occasionally associated with quarrying at Dún Aonghasa. If this was the case, any earlier occupation layers in this area are likely to have been removed or reworked at this time. Thus any residue of a pre-souterrain horizon may be represented only by occupation material incorporated in the fill which buttressed both souterrains. The occupation layers within 10/11 and 5a may also belong to a pre-souterrain phase—that within 5a does not appear to have any direct relationship with the rather vague structure defined by Hencken (Fig. 7), whilst the activity within 10/11 was sealed by the rubble platform which also concealed the souterrains.

In the southern area, whilst a number of different stratigraphical horizons were recorded, these are not always unequivocally related to the structures identified by Hencken. Indeed, the majority of Hencken's phase 1 hearths appear to be unrelated to any of the surviving buildings. However, there is no evidence now to link these with a pre-souterrain phase at the site. In the case of structure 4, for example, even if this complex of buildings post-dates Hencken's phase 1 hearths, it is unclear whether it belongs to the period when the 5/6/7/8 complex was in use or whether it was built after this complex had either been downgraded or had gone out of use.

The structures

Four of the five buildings located along the internal face of the enclosing wall appear to have been rectangular in plan (structures 2, 3, 10 and 11) and some may have been of lean-to type. The fifth structure (no. 5a) had very little definition. It may have formed part of the conjoined series of circular or curvilinear houses in the northern part of the fort. It is equally possible, however, that in its final form structure 5a was simply a passageway which gave access to souterrain A. At Dúcathair a similar passage runs behind a group of houses to an intramural chamber. Structures 5 and 6 were conjoined circular houses and formed part of a cellular complex, which also included the less well-defined circular or curvilinear buildings nos 7 and 8. This complex of buildings lay in the northern sector of the site, where the enclosing wall ran along the cliff edge. From the point of view of attack, this was the safest part of the fort, thus possibly explaining why the principal dwellings (i.e. those with souterrains) were located here. Of the remaining structures identified by Hencken, no. 2, which was located directly inside the entrance to the fort, was described as a passageway which gave access to the guard chamber (i.e. structure 1). Hencken's structure 4 appears to have been a complex of rectangular buildings which occupied the central area of the fort. The more robust construction and central location of this complex also distinguished it from the remaining structures at the site.

Apart from the walls themselves, there were few surviving architectural details at any of the structures. The ope for the doorway survived only in structure 4, but its wide splay and its location at the angle of the building raise doubts as to its being an original feature. Formal hearths were evident only in structures 1, 5 and 6. No evidence for the method of roofing was apparent in any of the structures; the ash layers in the southern part of the fort suggest that the buildings there were timber-roofed and thatched. It is possible that the cellular buildings at the northern end had corbelled stone roofs, but the thinness of the individual walls would seem to preclude this. In addition, field observation suggests that stone clocháns may not have been part of the architectural repertoire in the Burren (or in County Clare generally).

It is also possible that there were a number of timber buildings within the fort. The majority of the phase 1 hearths in the southern area could have been associated with a phase of timber buildings. Some of the phase 2 hearths were also unassociated with any of the stone buildings and there may have been a sequence of timber buildings (possibly worksheds) in the southern half of the fort. Excavations at the cashel of Loher, Co. Kerry, produced possible evidence for timber houses pre-dating the stone examples (O'Flaherty 1985, 27), but a transition from timber to stone as a building material is best evidenced at ecclesiastical sites such as Church Island (O'Kelly 1958) and Reask (Fanning 1981) in County Kerry.

The surviving stone buildings at Cahercommaun therefore included both rectangular and circular or curvilinear types. Lynn (1978; 1994) has argued that there was a transition from circular to square or rectangular houses within ringforts during the later part of the first millennium AD. The limited information available from excavated cashels supports this chronological sequence, though at some sites (e.g. Cahergal, Co. Kerry (O'Sullivan and Sheehan 1996, 187), and Ballynavenoooragh, Co. Kerry (Cuppage *et*

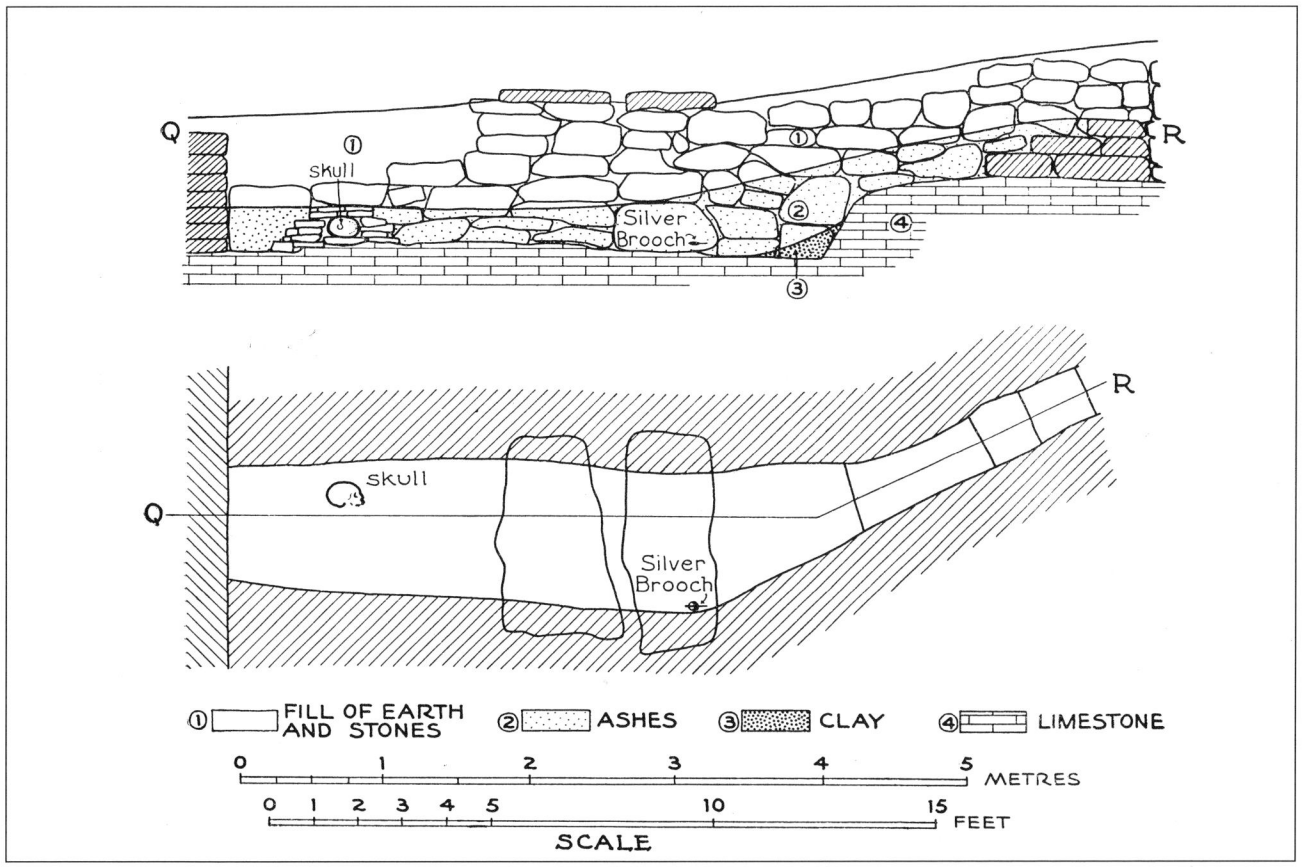

Fig. 11—Plan and section of souterrain B, showing the location of the human skull and findspot of the silver brooch (Hencken 1938, fig. 9).

al. 1986, 192)) the principal buildings remained circular throughout. At the stone forts of Loher (O'Flaherty 1985, 27) and Leacanabuaile (Ó Ríordáin and Foy 1941) in County Kerry the principal buildings were 'upgraded' from circular to rectangular structures, and it is possible that the same sequence occurred at Cahercommaun. At Ballynavenooragh, Loher and Leacanabuaile the principal houses were all either directly associated with souterrains or had annexes with souterrains. Hencken's structure 4 complex could therefore belong to a late (post-souterrain?) phase in the development of the settlement. The complex occupied a central position in the interior and was described as being far better built than any of the other structures. It seems very unlikely, therefore, that this group of buildings had a subsidiary function within the settlement, and there is no evidence at all to support Hencken's theory that structure 4 was the kitchen quarters. This interpretation was based on the presence of the two ash layers and the fact that 'more querns were found there than elsewhere' (1938, 2). However, although one complete upper stone and 21 fragments of rotary quern were recovered from the south-western quadrant (*ibid*., 60), only two fragments of rotary quern are listed as being associated with structure 4. Both were derived from fill which could not definitely be attributed to any particular phase of activity (*ibid*., 70). It seems somewhat more likely that the structure 4 complex ultimately became the principal dwelling (or group of dwellings) within the fort. This development may have taken place at a late stage in the occupation sequence. The fact that relatively fewer artefacts were associated with structure 4 (*ibid*., 70) may reflect the declining economic status of the occupants at this time rather than any functional layout within the fort.

The guard cell and souterrains

Hencken's interpretation of structure 1 as a guard cell accessed by a passage (structure 2) opening off the entrance seems a reasonable one. Structure 2 at any rate would have had the appearance of an intramural passage located immediately inside the door to the fort. Intramural guard chambers occur at the stone forts of Knockdrum, Co. Cork (Power *et al*. 1992, 224), and Dunbeg, Co. Kerry (Barry 1981, 307); there may also have been an example at Doonamo, Co. Mayo (Westropp 1912, 203). At O'Boyle's Fort, Co. Donegal, two intramural passages which opened

Pl. 9—*The skull buried in souterrain B (Hencken 1938, pl. X, fig. 2).*

off opposite sides of the main entrance allowed the occupants to gain direct access to the interior or to the wall top. Two intramural passages at Grianán Aileach, Co. Donegal, may also have communicated directly with the main entrance passage at one time.

Although there is as yet no absolute dating available, current evidence suggests that intramural chambers and passages are relatively late features at Irish cashels and represent a development of the stone-built souterrain. Until relatively recently there was very little independent dating evidence for Irish souterrains. At ringforts where both E-ware and souterrains occurred, the latter were generally found to be secondary features post-dating the E-ware horizon. The introduction of the souterrain in a domestic context therefore seemed unlikely to have taken place prior to the eighth century AD. Present indications are that it was not widely adopted until much later. A timber souterrain excavated at Coolcran ringfort, Co. Fermanagh, produced a dendrochronological date of 822 ± 9 (Williams 1985, 75). The main period of souterrain-building at Knowth, Co. Meath, appears to have been in the ninth/tenth century (George Eogan, pers. comm.), and a tenth-century date is also suggested for the construction of the souterrains at Deer Park Farms, Co. Antrim (Chris Lynn, pers. comm.).

In his re-evaluation of the metalwork from Cahercommaun, Ó Floinn (see below) suggests that the deposition of the silver brooch found in souterrain B is likely to have taken place in the ninth century. The brooch was found in the roofed southern end of the souterrain passage. It was stratified over an ash layer 50mm in depth and was sealed by another ashy layer (up to 400mm deep at this point) which Hencken considered had in part drifted down from the entrance (1938, 23). The brooch therefore provides a broad *terminus ante quem* for the construction of the souterrain. It might equally provide a *terminus post quem* for its abandonment, as there is no way of knowing now when the layers of ashes accumulated on the floor of the passage. The survival of the roof lintels in that part of the passage where the brooch was found suggests, however, that the souterrain was still in use when the brooch was deposited. At any rate, it was certainly in existence during the later ninth century, and (on analogy with the above-mentioned ringforts) a construction date sometime during the ninth century could be argued for in this case.

The human skull (complete except for the lower jaw), which Hencken considered to be a foundation deposit, lay 2.5m further north along the same souterrain passage (Fig. 11; Pl. 9). Unlike the brooch, the skull and its stone surround 'were embedded in but not covered by the deposit of ashes on the floor of the passage' (Hencken 1938, 23). This northern section of the passage was also unroofed, and a number of other (seemingly unrelated) human bone fragments were found in the immediate vicinity. The weight of evidence suggests, therefore, that the burial (or possibly burials) post-dated the abandonment of the souterrain. There are no known parallels for Hencken's 'foundation burial' theory, and on the few occasions when human remains are found in souterrains interment likewise appears to have taken place after the souterrains had gone out of use (Mark Clinton, pers. comm.).

In summary, therefore, the sequence of occupation at Cahercommaun appears to have been somewhat more complex than that outlined by Hencken. Though there is no definite instance of any building being replaced, some (structure 2, and possibly the structure 4 complex) were repaired or remodelled and others (structures 1, 10/11 and possibly 5a) were certainly abandoned during the occupation of the fort. The cellular complex (5/6/7/8) also appears to have fallen into disuse prior to the abandonment of the fort.

The fact that the foundations of all the extant stone buildings apparently rested on bedrock may be significant. If these buildings were secondary, then either there was little or no buildup of earlier habitation material inside the fort or their wall foundations were laid in trenches. The latter seems very unlikely. For example, when the opposing walls of structures 1 and 11 were refurbished, the additional thickness of wall was laid directly on the contemporary ground surface, and this seems to have been the usual practice in Early Medieval Ireland. On the other hand, if the stone buildings were primary features it seems unlikely that (even if refurbished from time to time) they could have remained in use for more than a few generations at most. Lynn has estimated that the wooden houses at Deerpark Farms were replaced every 30 years. Though stone houses may have been more durable, the likelihood is that they too were replaced or rebuilt at intervals— particularly if (as seems to have been the case at Cahercommaun) they had timber roofs. The surviving house walls at Cahercommaun were relatively well preserved (some stood to a height of 1m or more), and on balance it seems likely that the majority were in use during the later stages of the occupation.

A reinterpretation of the structural sequence

Based on the structural evidence and the limited stratigraphical evidence from the site, a possible reinterpretation of the occupation history can be attempted.

Phase A (pre-souterrain occupation): None of the extant structures can definitely be associated with this phase. The buildup of the 'flooring material' and some of Hencken's phase 1 hearths in the southern area may date from this period, but this is uncertain. In the northern half, the ashy occupation layer in 5a, the occupation layers within structures 10 and 11, and the artefacts and domestic debris in the material buttressing the souterrains may represent the remains of this early horizon.

Phase B (main occupation): This comprised the 5/6/7/8 cellular complex of stone buildings and both souterrains. The location of this cellular complex in that sector of the interior which was furthest from attack, the relatively large number of artefacts seemingly associated with these buildings (Hencken 1938, 72–3) and the construction of the souterrains during this phase suggest that this was the floruit of the fort. Timber buildings, possibly worksheds, may have occupied much of the southern half of the fort. It is unclear what the form or function of any buildings at the centre of the site may have been in this period. During this phase the upper and lower terraces of the enclosing wall were relatively unimpeded and functioned as wall-walks. The construction of the low platform against the interior of the north wall strengthened the weaker defences in the northern area, masked the souterrains and provided support for the roofs of the conjoined complex. An additional defensive feature was the passage which gave access to the guard chamber immediately inside the entrance.

Phase C: During this phase the southern area was refloored and the rectangular complex (structure 4) may have been constructed at the centre of the site. The door passage was repaved and the flanking walls rebuilt so that the entrance now led directly to structure 4. Access to the guard chamber was blocked off and, if the structure 4 complex was now the principal dwelling within the fort, it was located in a far more vulnerable part of the site than any of the earlier dwellings. The higher occupation level in the southern half meant that the lower terrace ceased to function as a wall-walk. Habitation material accumulated on the surface of the lower terrace in the south-east sector and on the stone platform along the interior of the enclosing wall in the north sector; the ladder recesses or steps in the south-western sector were reused as hearths. By this time, therefore, defence may no longer have been a primary consideration. In the northern half of the site structures 5 and 6 may have continued to be occupied for a time, but the remainder of this complex possibly fell into disrepair and was replaced by dwellings associated with hearths s, t and u.

The dating of these phases is examined in the final summary.

The date and duration of the occupation: the evidence of the artefacts

The majority of the objects recovered at Cahercommaun belong to the group usually assigned to the Early Medieval period. Over 1000 objects were found, ranking Cahercommaun with sites like Lagore and Ballinderry in terms of the number of artefacts recovered. In terms of comparative wealth, however, the occupants of Cahercommaun appear to have possessed fewer objects made of precious materials such as silver or bronze. The assemblage included 524 whetstones, 36 pounding or rubbing stones, 63 iron knives, 52 fragments of lignite rings or bracelets, eighteen beads made from blue glass, stone or bone, 107 pins or pin fragments (82 bone, nineteen iron and six bronze), 55 spindle-whorls, fourteen bone points, and a small number of bone awls, needles and 'spears'. There was no evidence for the production of high-status goods at the site and there was little that could be considered exotic among the artefact assemblage itself. The sheer number of artefacts and the presence of objects such as a barrel padlock, a silver brooch and an enamelled pinhead nonetheless distinguish Cahercommaun from the majority of other excavated ringforts.

Analysis of the distribution and associations of the artefacts recovered is limited by the information available. Hencken lists twenty artefacts which can be attributed to his earlier phase of the occupation and c. 28 which can be attributed to his later phase (1938, 70–4). None of the other artefacts could be assigned to any definite phase and most were recovered from 'the fill' within the structures or from 'fill'

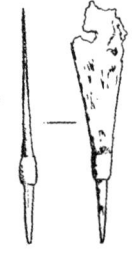

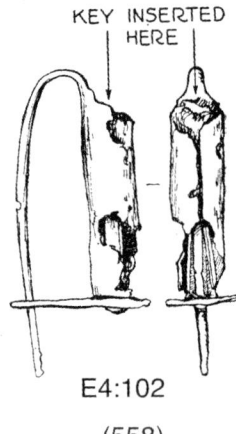

Fig. 12—Iron arrow-head, slotted and pointed object, and barrel padlock from Cahercommaun: scale 1/2 (Hencken 1938, fig. 32, 728 and 657; fig. 29, 558).

unassociated with any particular structure. From the little evidence available, there is no discernible difference in the range or type of artefacts from the earlier and later phases of the occupation. Whether this can be taken to indicate that there was no significant time-lapse between Hencken's earlier and later phases of occupation is a matter of debate.

Currently the majority of the artefacts cannot be closely dated within the period, and in a number of instances it is only by association that an Early Medieval (rather than a pre-Christian) date is assigned to many of the objects. Over half of the artefacts recovered consisted of whetstones or scored sharpening stones, probably indicating intensive smithing activity on the site. Iron was smelted (Hencken 1938, 54) and a wide range of domestic and agricultural iron implements were found. The number of whetstones, however, appears excessive in terms of solely servicing the needs of the occupants, who may have been engaged in the production of iron goods. The assemblage gave no clue as to what these goods might have been. Apart from a sword tip and an arrowhead no weapons were recovered, and the number of iron knives, nails etc. appears to be fairly typical for this type of site. A study of the scored sharpening stones might provide some clue as to what was being produced.

The bone artefacts

No typologies exist at present for most types of simple bone pins, and the range of bone pin types found at Cahercommaun can be paralleled either singly or as a group with pins from other Irish ringforts and crannogs, urban Hiberno-Norse sites and—further afield—Pictish and Norse habitation sites in Scotland. As an assemblage, their large size and finely polished finish would place them firmly in the last quarter of the first millennium AD.

Hodkinson has remarked on the exceptionally large number of spindle-whorls recovered at Cahercommaun, and has also suggested that the bone 'spears' from the site may have been pin beaters (1987, 49). No typology exists for spindle-whorls at present, and the ox femora type in particular appears to have had a long history (see Ó Floinn, below). Many of the Cahercommaun spindle-whorls appear to be lathe-turned, but as the date when the lathe became widely used in Ireland is unknown this sheds no light on their period of use. The presence of only a single pair of shears at the site (as opposed to seven pairs at Garryduff ringfort; O'Kelly 1963, 44) may mean that the occupants were not themselves directly involved in producing fleeces but rather that the raw wool was collected and brought to the site to be processed. The stage to which this processing was carried out is unknown, but it is not beyond the bounds of possibility that woven garments were produced on site. The fact that the majority of the Cahercommaun spindle-whorls were still intact when discarded may mean that these objects were considered to be relatively disposable—thus the loss of 55 spindle-whorls over an unspecified length of time may have no particular significance. Alternatively, such a large concentration may indicate that there was one or more intensive periods of wool-processing at the site. A large number of spindle-whorls were also recovered at the royal site of Knowth, Co. Meath, in ninth/tenth-century contexts (George Eogan, pers. comm.). According to Kelly (1998, 448–9), the division of the assets of a marriage as outlined in *Cáin Lánamna* suggests that women were responsible for the combing, spinning and weaving of wool. It is possible, therefore, that at both of these high-ranking settlements we are seeing some tangible evidence for a strong female presence (free or unfree).

Three double-sided bone combs were illustrated by Hencken (1938, fig. 26, 10, 87 and 717), and a few other tooth-plate fragments were also recovered. None are closely datable and Dunlevy assigns them to her class D1, which dates broadly from the period between the fifth and the tenth centuries AD (1988, 359). Number 10 (Hencken 1938, 42, fig. 26) can be paralleled by a comb recovered from a late ninth/tenth-century context at High Street in Dublin (Dunlevy 1988). Hencken mentions that the corresponding one-sided type was also present (1938, 42), but none of the surviving combs from the site appear to belong to this class.

The metal artefacts

The iron shears, knives, socketed and pronged tool, awls and rings recovered at Cahercommaun can be closely paralleled at sites such as Garryduff (O'Kelly 1963, fig. 5, 478 and 376), Lagore (Hencken 1950) and Garranes (Ó Ríordáin 1942). The object described by Hencken as an iron tool with small tang (1938, fig. 32, 728), recovered from the north-east quadrant, has been identified by Andy Halpin (pers. comm.) as a tanged leaf-shaped arrowhead of Scandinavian origin which, in an Irish context, cannot be dated to earlier than the ninth century AD. Similar arrowheads are known from urban contexts, from Lagore and the Dunbell raths; this type of arrowhead disappeared with the coming of the Normans in the twelfth century.

Seven slotted and pointed iron objects were recovered by Hencken (1938, 53) (Fig. 12). One of these came from structure 6, but all are described as unstratified. These complex objects (variously interpreted as tools for weaving organic material, augurs or fire steels) can be paralleled at Irish sites such as the ninth-century Viking cemetery at Islandbridge in Dublin (Edwards 1990, fig. 91) and Lagore crannog, Co. Meath (Hencken 1950, fig. 51, 154 and A); a recent example recovered by the writer at the stone fort of Dún Eoghanachta on the Aran Islands also came from a likely ninth-century context.

An iron barrel padlock from Cahercommaun (Fig. 12, E4:102; Hencken 1938, 46) has been classified by

Donaghy (1991) in her Type 1b. The only other complete examples of this type from Ireland are an antiquarian find from Dromcliffe, Co. Sligo, and a padlock from the upper habitation levels at Garryduff, Co. Cork (*ibid.*, 15–17). Donaghy's Type 1b differs only in slight detail from her Type 1c; an old find from Lagore and a padlock from Moylarg crannog, Co. Antrim, are the only recorded Type 1c examples. Though all of the above examples were recovered from Early Medieval or likely Early Medieval contexts, none have been closely dated.

In conclusion, only a very small number of the items discussed above are chronologically diagnostic at present. Those that can be more closely dated (i.e. the decorated bone comb, the slotted and pointed tools and the iron arrowhead) appear to fit comfortably into the ninth/tenth centuries. To a large extent, this dating relies on closely dated parallels from Viking or Hiberno-Norse sites, and it could be argued that the poorer chronologies currently available for seventh/eighth-century settlements unduly influence the overall picture. The dynamism evident in some aspects of the material culture of Early Medieval Ireland is also rarely apparent in the ordinary functional objects which make up the bulk of the assemblage at Cahercommaun. In this respect the date range of the more luxury items may be of greater significance in determining the time-span of the occupation.

The following is a reassessment by Raghnall Ó Floinn of the more prestigious metal ornaments from the site. Of the fifteen objects discussed, eleven are contexted only to quadrant (seven from the north-east quadrant, three from the south-east quadrant and one from the south-west quadrant). The contexts of the remaining four objects were as follows: the silver brooch was found in souterrain B; the iron pin (no. 76) came from the fill of structure 5a; the iron ringed pin (no. 497) was found in the fill of structure 4; and the copper-alloy pin (no. 190) was found in the entrance passage between structures 1 and 2. Ó Floinn also suggests that the material culture of Early Medieval Ireland (spanning the period from the fifth to the early tenth century) can be broadly divided into four phases (EM1–4) and examines the occupation history of Cahercommaun from this perspective.

THE DATE OF SOME METALWORK FROM CAHERCOMMAUN REASSESSED

RAGHNALL Ó FLOINN

Introduction

Since its appearance 60 years ago the Cahercommaun excavation report has assumed an important place in consideration of the date of stone forts, ringforts and cashels (for a summary see Laing 1975, 147–9, and Lynn 1983, 49–50). Although the excavator does make occasional references to stratified features and artefacts associated with them (Hencken 1938, 2, 69–73), the excavated deposits may be regarded to all intents and purposes as unstratified. The dates ascribed to the metalwork have therefore been central to the arguments put forward in the original excavation report (and by subsequent commentators) in dating the occupation of the site.

This paper re-examines some of the metalwork from Cahercommaun, taking into account in particular more recent evidence from excavated contexts which enables a closer dating of some of the artefact types. The objects will first be discussed by type in chronological order. The subsequent discussion will suggest a relative chronology of first-millennium AD artefact types based on evidence from recently excavated sites with stratified deposits and will attempt to indicate where Cahercommaun fits into this sequence.

Penannular brooch of iron (E4:403)

The damaged hoop of an iron brooch with a single surviving simple scrolled-out terminal and part of its accompanying pin were discovered in the north-east quadrant (Fig. 13, 1; Hencken 1938, 37 and fig. 22, 73). Although the original length of the pin cannot be determined, it would appear to have been greater than the diameter of the hoop. The size of the hoop indicates that the object functioned as a brooch rather than a pin with a decorative head. In his report, Hencken merely recorded its presence on the site without any discussion of parallels.

The brooch may now be identified as a penannular brooch of Elizabeth Fowler's Class B, defined as having 'terminals either coiled or simply bent outwards from the ring and always in the same plane as the ring. The pin is slightly arched' (Fowler 1960, 152). Fowler noted that the type was not very prolific 'and the few dated examples are either first century B.C. or A.D.', but conceded that the single Irish example known to her, from Cahercommaun, appeared to be post-Roman in date (ibid., 157). She drew attention to the existence of almost identical brooches from Iberia, illustrating one from Castro de Sabroso (ibid., 158 and fig. 5). The British distribution of Type B penannulars is very localised, centred on Wiltshire (ibid., fig. 8). Unlike most other penannular brooch forms, which are of copper alloy, those of Fowler's Class B are almost exclusively of iron.

It is now recognised that many of Fowler's

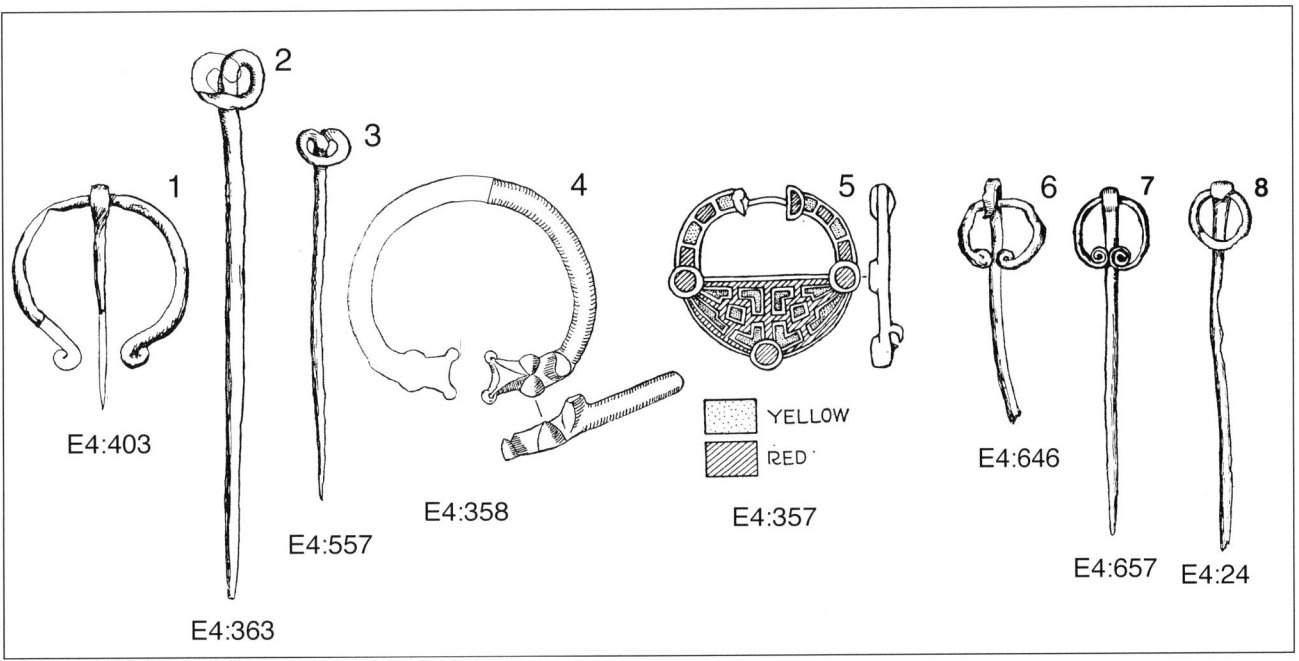

Fig. 13—1–3. Brooches and pins of iron and copper alloy (scale 1/2); 4. zoomorphic penannular brooch fragment; 5. head of enamelled brooch-pin of copper alloy (scale 1/1); 6–8. brooches and pins of iron and copper alloy (scale 1/2) (Hencken 1938, figs 18, 19 and 22).

penannular brooch groups, which are based principally on the form of the terminal, contain distinct subgroups separated widely in time and space. Thus, for example, reassessments by James Graham-Campbell and Tanya Dickinson of her Type G have shown that it contains at least four distinct groups ranging in date from the fourth to the ninth centuries, and that the Type G brooches from Ireland and Scotland belong to the latter end of this range (summarised in Dickinson 1982, 42–3). This appears to be the case also with her Type B brooches, in that *some* of the British brooches from apparently Iron Age contexts may form a discrete chronological and chorological series. It should be noted that Fowler lists a number of British and Continental Type B brooches which were recovered from Saxon and Migration Period contexts as late as the fourth and fifth centuries (Fowler 1960, 172–4).

The Irish Type B series, like the British, is primarily of iron—only two Irish copper-alloy brooches of the type are known, and both are unlocalised (for an illustration of one see Coffey 1909, fig. 19). As brooches of iron are less likely to be picked up as stray finds, this would account for the scarcity of known examples, the majority of which have been discovered through excavation. Since Fowler's publications, excavations have increased substantially the number of Irish brooches of Type B, and all are of iron.

Several examples identical to that from Cahercommaun are known from the excavations at Dooey, Co. Donegal (Ó Ríordáin and Rynne 1961, 62). The excavators identified four phases of occupation at this site: the first three were interpreted as habitation and the site was used as a cemetery in its final phase. The stratified Class B brooches appear to have come from Phases I and II. Phase III contained an extensive area of habitation and metalworking which was dated to the eighth or ninth century, on the basis of some decorated moulds (O'Meadhra 1987, 36–7), offering a *terminus ante quem* for the earlier phases. More recently, Catryn Power has obtained three radiocarbon dates for the Phase IV cemetery (UB-3652, 1428 ± 41; UB-3653, 1331 ± 34; UB-3654, 1359 ± 43) with a calibrated range at the two-sigma level of AD 552–773 which give a *terminus ante quem* for Phase III of the eighth century (at the latest), which is somewhat earlier than the art-historical and typological date range suggested above. (I am grateful to Catryn Power for permission to quote these dates, and she would like to acknowledge the Heritage Council, which provided the funding for the dates.)

Phase I at Dooey contained the well-known motif-piece of antler dated, by reference to its ornament, to the fifth or sixth century (Ó Floinn in Youngs 1989, no. 152). The same level produced a nail-cleaners and finger-ring, both of late Roman type (E. Rynne, pers. comm.; for a decorated Irish ring of the same form as that from Dooey see Ó Floinn in Youngs 1989, no. 29, where it is dated to the fifth/sixth century), which would support a date in the fifth or sixth century for Phase I and therefore for the Type B penannulars. Further support for such an early date comes from the discovery of two brooches of this type on the shoulders of an unburnt crouched burial of a female in excavations by Eamonn Kelly of a cemetery at Betaghstown, Co. Meath, which has produced a radiocarbon date (OxA-2652, 1565 ± 60: Kelly 1987–8; E. O'Brien 1993, 96–7 and fig. 3, a, b) giving a calibrated range at the two-sigma level of AD 344–638. The Betaghstown burial also provides us with evidence that these brooches were worn in pairs, on the shoulders, and that they were items of female dress.

As discussed above, Fowler thought that Class B penannular brooches in Britain were Iron Age or Roman but left over the possibility that they lasted until the end of the Roman period (Fowler 1963, 147, 149). A date more in keeping with the Dooey and Betaghstown excavation evidence for at least some of the British series is suggested by the occurrence of three examples in Anglo-Saxon graves, two of which are dated to the sixth century (White 1988, 9). A date for the Cahercommaun brooch sometime in the fifth or sixth century therefore seems likely.

Iron pins with looped wire heads (E4:363 and 557)

Two iron pins with heads formed by bending the broader end of the head into a loop may be of the same date as the iron penannular brooch (Fig. 13, 2 and 3; Hencken 1938, 38 and fig. 22, 146, 826). Pins of this type were absent from Dooey, which produced a range of iron brooch and pin types. A similar iron pin was discovered in excavations at a crannog in Lough Faughan, Co. Down (Collins 1955, fig. 9, 37), but its stratigraphic position was not noted. The site produced evidence of occupation, dated by the excavator to between the seventh and tenth centuries on the basis of the range of finds, which were comparable to those from Lagore (*ibid.*, 71). A single copper-alloy pin with looped wire head from an unknown context at Drumbo, Co. Monaghan, is known (Raftery 1984, fig. 87, 4). Iron pins with looped or coiled wire heads may somehow be related to the wire projecting ring-headed pins of the Scottish later Iron Age with suggested contexts of between the second and fourth centuries AD (Stevenson 1955, 288 and fig. B, 2). Most recently Foster (1990, 153) has noted that 'Plain wire projecting ring-heads are probably the most chronologically insensitive of all IA [Iron Age] metal pins, and an extremely wide date range is suspected'. The Scottish evidence, however, suggests that these pins are pre-seventh-century, and a similar *terminus ante quem* may be proposed for the Cahercommaun pins.

Copper-alloy zoomorphic penannular brooch (E4:358)

This fragmentary copper-alloy object, consisting of approximately half the hoop of a zoomorphic penannular brooch, was found in fill in the north-east quadrant (Fig. 13, 4; Hencken 1938, 33 and fig. 18, 372). Hencken concluded that brooches of this type 'would seem ... to have been disappearing by about 800'. He cited as evidence in support of this the absence of similar brooches at Lagore, which at the time of writing was dated by him to the late eighth to tenth century, and their presence at Ballinderry 2, which he dated 'slightly earlier' (*ibid.*, 34). Elizabeth Fowler, in an appendix to her discussion of Celtic metalwork of the fifth and sixth centuries, classified the Cahercommaun brooch fragment as belonging to her Type E1 but did not discuss it in the text (Fowler 1963, 137 and fig. 2, 10). Laing (1993, 12) has recently argued that 'her [Fowler's] E1 category consists of an assortment of very different brooches that need not be in any way related to the E group at all', and suggests that the Cahercommaun brooch 'appears to be a descendant of some Irish F brooches' (*ibid.*). There are, in fact, no direct parallels for the Cahercommaun brooch among the Irish zoomorphic penannular brooches. Its small size sets it apart from the main series and is reminiscent of Kilbride-Jones's 'small' or pseudo-zoomorphic penannular brooches (Kilbride-Jones 1980, fig. 52), regarded by him as being early in the series, yet the terminal has more in common with more developed (and later) brooches. The Cahercommaun brooch appears to have been unknown to Kilbride-Jones and was therefore not discussed by him. It would seem superficially to be a variant of his Group D, one of the characteristics of which is a pronounced spur where the snout joins the hoop. It also shares with Group D brooches the pronounced projecting 'ears', but differs from the latter in having 'eyes' otherwise absent in brooches of the type. Group D brooches, and a related series of pins, can be placed in the late fifth–seventh centuries by the association of a terminal waster with imported B-wares at Clogher (Warner in Youngs 1989, no. 193) and with E-ware from Phase I at Gransha, Co. Down (Lynn 1985, 84 and fig. 3). Given its unique form, all one can suggest is that the Cahercommaun brooch belongs closer to the end than to the beginning of the zoomorphic penannular series, and is therefore datable perhaps to the sixth or seventh century.

Given that there is no evidence for metalworking from the site, the fragmentary copper-alloy zoomorphic penannular brooch cannot be interpreted as a piece of scrap metal introduced to the site and it may therefore be regarded as being an accidental loss. It is also perhaps worth noting that the Cahercommaun example lies well outside the main distribution of zoomorphic penannular brooches (Kilbride-Jones 1980, fig. 19), there being only one other brooch of this type from County Clare, that from Toomullin townland (*ibid.*, no. 31). If the Cahercommaun zoomorphic penannular is to be associated with brooches and pins of Group D, then it is even more of an outlier as the latter are confined to the north of Ireland, with provenanced examples from Tyrone, Down and Armagh and with evidence for the manufacture of Group D brooches at Clogher, Co. Tyrone (Kilbride-Jones 1980, 65–9).

Head of an enamelled copper-alloy brooch-pin (E4:357)

This object was found in the north-east quadrant (Fig. 13, 5; Hencken 1938, 34, 36 and fig. 19, 575). It was described in the original report as a 'ring-headed pin' (*ibid.*, 36), and the terms 'pseudo-penannular ring-brooch' (Fanning 1994, 5 and 2), 'hinged pin' (Stevenson 1987, 92) and 'ring brooch' (Laing 1975, 316–18), among others, have been applied to dress-fasteners of this type. Despite these differences in terminology, all are agreed that these functioned as pins rather than brooches, given that their shanks are much longer in proportion to their heads than true brooches and that the type is derived from more elaborate annular brooches such as the Tara or Hunterston brooches. It is proposed to use the term 'brooch-pin' here, in conformity with the terminology used in the '*Work of Angels*' catalogue (Ó Floinn 1989, 90). Two types of brooch-pin are known—those with pins which move freely on the ring and those with fixed pins. The Cahercommaun brooch-pin belongs to the latter category. The distinguishing feature of this type of ring-headed dress-fastener is that the movement of the pin was restricted and was designed to swivel on a hinge or bar confined between buffers.

The majority of the heads of brooch-pins with

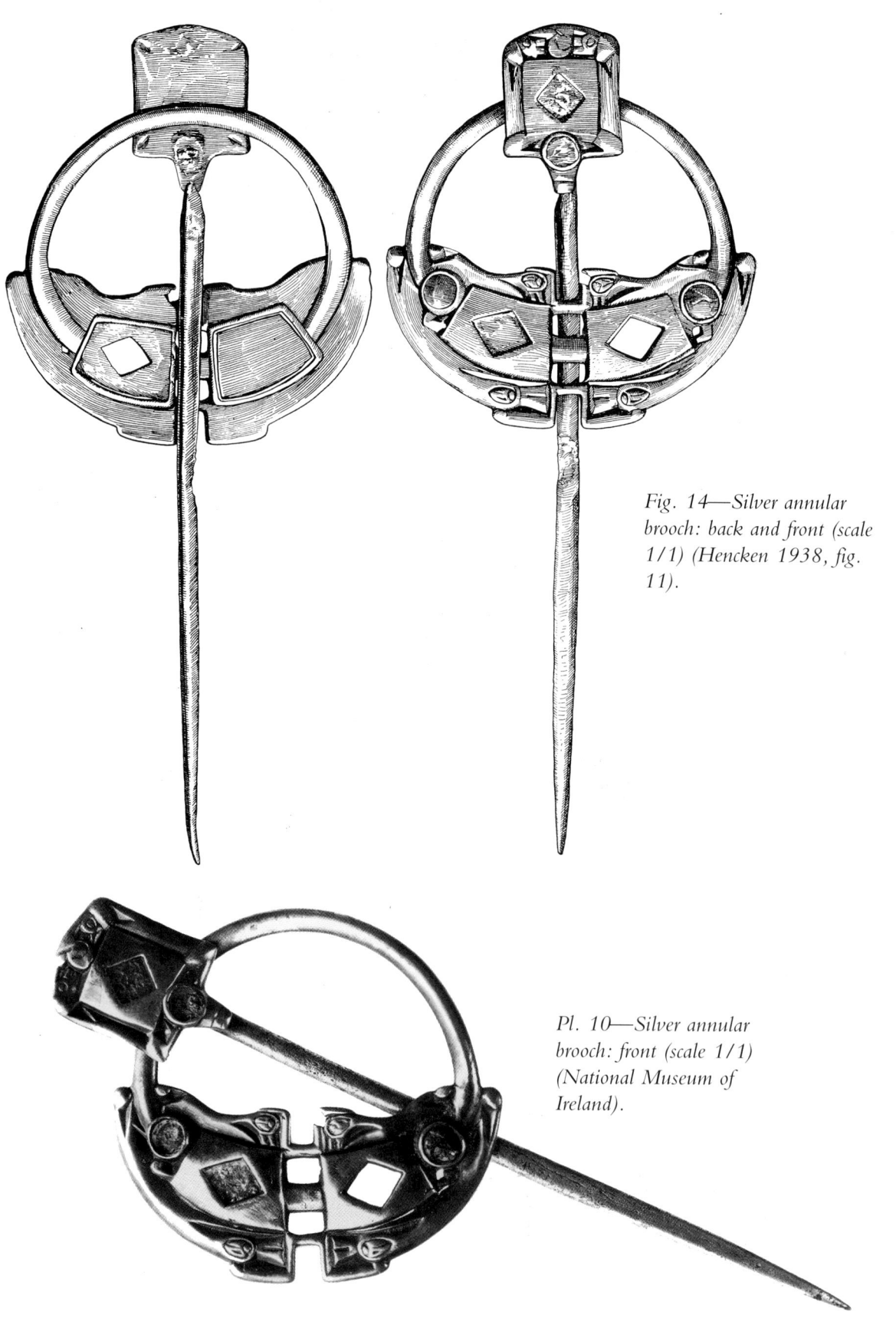

Fig. 14—Silver annular brooch: back and front (scale 1/1) (Hencken 1938, fig. 11).

Pl. 10—Silver annular brooch: front (scale 1/1) (National Museum of Ireland).

fixed pins are decorated with cast interlace or animal ornament (Armstrong 1921–2, pl. XII, figs 2 and 3). The Cahercommaun example is the only brooch-pin with decorated geometric cells of alternating red and yellow enamel. There is, in fact, only one other known enamelled brooch-pin, an old find from Lagore crannog (Hencken 1950, fig. 18, A). Although the Cahercommaun brooch-pin is unique, its decoration of geometric cells enables the pinhead to be linked with a series of similarly decorated personal ornaments, including the head of an annular brooch from County Westmeath (Hencken 1938, fig. 20, A), a group of buckles (Youngs 1997, 198) and the belt-shrine from Moylough, Co. Sligo (Ryan in Youngs 1989, no. 47), which are variously dated to the later seventh or eighth century. A similar date can be suggested for the Cahercommaun brooch-pin.

It is of interest to note that many of the parallels for the enamelled brooch-pin are provenanced to the west midlands, from sites in counties Westmeath, Roscommon and Sligo. To these can be added a trapezoidal mount with geometric cells of yellow and red enamel and blue glass from Liam de Paor's excavations at Inis Cealtra, Co. Clare, and the distribution suggests that the brooch-pin could have been locally produced.

Iron and copper-alloy ringed pins with penannular scrolled heads (E4:646 and 657)

This was the commonest form of iron pin found, and Hencken recorded the discovery of no less than seven examples (Fig. 13, 6; Hencken 1938, 37–8, fig. 22, 126). The site also produced a copper-alloy example (Fig. 13, 7; Hencken 1938, 34 and fig. 19, 190). Unlike the iron penannular brooch from the site, the penannular heads with scrolled terminals on these dress-fasteners are small relative to the length of their respective pins. In addition, the small size of the heads indicates that the latter were merely decorative, and these objects therefore functioned as ringed pins rather than as brooches.

A number of iron pins of this type were found in excavations at Carraig Aille II, Co. Limerick, none apparently stratified (Ó Ríordáin 1949, fig. 10, 123 and 351). Other finds from the site range widely in date, the earliest being a late Roman nail-cleaners and an ibex-headed pin of the fourth or fifth century (*ibid.*, fig. 8, 254, and fig. 9, 520) and the latest a hoard of hack-silver of late ninth- or early tenth-century date (*ibid.*, fig. 7). A copper-alloy pin of this type from Lagore crannog (Hencken 1950, fig. 15, 1200) was also unstratified but must date from after *c.* 650, when occupation at Lagore is believed to have begun (Warner 1986a). Another copper-alloy ringed pin with a similarly scrolled head was discovered in excavations of the Viking Age cemetery at N. Bikjholberget, Kaupang, Norway (Blindheim and Heyerdahl-Larsen 1995, 75 and pl. 66t). Unfortunately, it was a stray find and cannot be closely dated, but if it is an Irish import it must be of Viking Age date. A late date is also suggested by the discovery of two pins of this type—one of iron and the other of copper alloy—in excavations at Dublin on the Christchurch Place site (Fanning 1994, 5 and n. 2) in contexts dating from the tenth century at the earliest. Finally, a copper-alloy disc-headed pin with chip-carved interlace, fitted with a swivelling penannular loop of copper-alloy wire with inward-scrolled terminals (Armstrong 1921–2, pl. XIV, fig. 1, 2), suggests that the form was current in the eighth or ninth century. At present, therefore, all one can say is that the meagre evidence to date suggests that pins with penannular heads with inward-scrolled terminals were current at some stage between the seventh and tenth centuries.

Other iron ringed pins (E4:24)

A number of iron ringed pins were recovered which are difficult to classify because the rings are incomplete. One example (Fig. 13, 8; Hencken 1938, fig. 22, 497) seems to belong to Fanning's plain-ringed, loop-headed class. These 'are known from both pre-Viking and Viking contexts in Ireland and, indeed, the form appears to have been still current in certain areas even after the Anglo-Norman invasion' (Fanning 1994, 16). The earliest iron examples seem to be those from Rathtinaun crannog, Co. Sligo, and from a ringfort at Back of the Hill near Ardagh, Co. Longford, reputedly from levels as early as the fifth/sixth century, while associations at other sites with imported pottery and other ringed pins suggest that the type was in vogue as a popular form of dress-fastener by the eighth century (*ibid.*, 16).

Silver annular brooch (E4:238)

This object was recovered from a layer of ashes on the floor of souterrain B (Fig. 14; Pl. 10; Hencken 1938, 27–30). Although not directly associated, other finds from the same context included a human skull, an iron hook, iron knives, a piece of cut antler and a spindle-whorl made from the head of an ox femur (Hencken 1938, 73). In the original report, Hencken said of its find circumstances that '… it is unlikely to have reached the spot where it was found except during the occupation of the fort' (1938, 24). Having discussed the brooch form, he concluded 'that brooches like that from Cahercommaun belong to IX, and that the Cahercommaun brooch itself was probably made about 800 … *and remains the best evidence for dating the occupation of the fort to IX*' [my italics] (1938, 30). It is clear that this brooch and its date were critical in Hencken's ninth-century dating of the main occupation at Cahercommaun.

The brooch belongs to a fairly homogeneous group of silver brooches to which the term 'Ardagh-type brooches' has been applied after the hoard in County Limerick which produced two examples (Ó Floinn 1990, 190–1). Chronologically, these brooches may be dated broadly to the ninth century, and their distribution is confined to north Munster (*ibid.*, 191).

The condition of the brooch as discovered is of relevance in relation to its date of deposition. The brooch is now reconstructed, but the publication drawing in the report shows that it was found in three pieces—the hoop, pinhead and pin. What is also clear from an examination of the brooch is that the pin is an ancient replacement: while the pinhead and hoop are of silver, the pin itself is of tinned copper alloy. The shank of the original pin would have been fitted into a socket in the base of the pinhead, while the pinhead itself would have been fastened to the hoop by a curved loop projecting from the back of the pinhead. Both loop and socket are now missing, although the scars of both are visible on the original publication drawing (Fig. 14, left). It would appear that the brooch was found in an articulated position, so one can only assume that some form of solder, which decayed after deposition, was used to fit the replacement pin to the pinhead. This would not explain, however, how the pinhead was fitted to the hoop (if indeed it was on deposition). Further evidence of wear is indicated by the fact that the backing plate to the lozenge-shaped recess on one terminal was missing, as was most of the gold inlay from the recesses on both terminals and on the pinhead. In addition, two of the three amber studs on the front of the brooch are missing.

From these losses, the evidence for replacement of the pin and the general worn condition of the brooch, it is clear that it was of some antiquity when it was buried. Although brooches of this type are dated to the ninth century, it is not possible to state how late in the century they continued to be made. Their absence from coin-dated hoards containing hack-silver of the late ninth and tenth centuries suggests that they had gone out of use by the end of the ninth century. The brooches in the Ardagh hoard were deposited towards the end of the ninth century at the earliest, although these may have been preserved as heirlooms. Given the condition of the Cahercommaun brooch, a deposition date late in the ninth or early in the tenth century is likely.

Discussion

From the above, it is clear that the datable metalwork artefacts from Cahercommaun span a period of as much as half a millennium, from the fifth to the ninth centuries. Many of the other artefacts from the site are not as closely datable, so it is not possible to say what other finds might be contemporary with those discussed above.

Little work has been done on fine-tuning the chronology of the small finds of the Early Medieval period from Ireland. Neither has work been done on the possible differences between the periods of manufacture, use and deposition of such artefacts. This is particularly problematic in the case of highly decorated metalwork, such as the silver brooch, which could have remained in circulation long after it was made. Given the number of recently excavated sites with stratified deposits, many supported by radiocarbon or dendrochronology, and the refinement in the dating of imported pottery, a series of discrete artefact assemblages is beginning to emerge which permits some tentative conclusions to be made on the relative dates of certain artefact types. What follows is merely a first attempt to order the material from these stratified sites; it is almost certainly too simple, taking no account of regional variations, and is not meant to be comprehensive.

The material culture of the pre-Viking Age Early Medieval period in Ireland (from, say, the fifth century to the end of the eighth century) may be divided into three phases as follows:

•**EM1**: Fifth/sixth century: stratified deposits containing imported pottery (principally B-ware), artefacts of late Roman type, or radiocarbon-dated, e.g. Clogher, Co. Tyrone, below 'Yellow Layer' (Warner 1979); Millockstown, Co. Louth, phase 1 (Manning 1986); Dooey, Co. Donegal, phases 1 and 2 (Ó Ríordáin and Rynne 1961).

•**EM2**: Later sixth/seventh century: stratified deposits containing imported pottery (E-ware), e.g. Lagore, Co. Meath, period I (Hencken 1950, 6–7); Rathmullan, Co. Down, phase 1 (Lynn 1981–2, 68–77); Gransha, Co. Down, phase 1 (Lynn 1985, 84–6); Moynagh Lough, Co. Meath, phase V (Bradley 1994–5, 166); Garryduff I, Co. Cork, periods I and II (O'Kelly 1963).

•**EM3**: Later seventh–eighth century: deposits stratified immediately above EM2 deposits, e.g. Lagore, period II (Hencken 1950, 7); Rathmullan, phase 2 (Lynn 1981–2, 78–85); Gransha, phase 2 (Lynn 1985, 86–8); Moynagh Lough, phases W, X and Y (Bradley 1991, 18–22).

In addition, there are artefacts from Cahercommaun which can be dated to the early Viking Age:

•**EM4**: Ninth–tenth century: deposits containing artefacts of early Viking Age date, e.g. finds from the Viking cemeteries at Kilmainham and Islandbridge (Bøe 1940, 11–65).

Taking into account what has been said above and looking at all the finds from the site, it is possible to suggest that the finds from Cahercommaun fall into all four broad chronological phases. This is not to say that the finds represent four distinct phases of occupation—the occupation history of the site during the first millennium AD may have been far more complex; alternatively, the presence of some finds may indicate only intermittent or passing human activity on the site. Whatever the exact date range represented by the finds from the site, one thing is certain: there are no artefacts which can be dated later than the tenth century.

The EM1 finds, ranging from the fifth to the sixth century, include the iron penannular brooch. Some of the other iron pins, particularly those with looped wire heads, may also belong to this horizon. Given the very few excavated stratified deposits of fifth- to seventh-century date, it is difficult to suggest what other artefacts from the site might be of this date. The copper-alloy penannular brooch is the sole object that may be assigned to the EM2 period.

The enamelled ring-brooch head belongs to the EM3 period, datable to the later seventh and eighth centuries, and the pins with penannular scrolled heads may belong to this chronological horizon also. A number of other artefact types from Cahercommaun can be included here. The slotted and pronged iron tools, of which seven were found (Hencken 1938, 53 and fig. 12), have been recovered from stratified deposits at Lagore (period II) and Gransha (phase 2). However, examples are known from Viking graves at Islandbridge, Dublin (Bøe 1940, fig. 43), and Håum, Norway (Bergen Museum, B. 7640), indicating that they continued to be used into the ninth century, that is, into EM4.

Of the non-metal artefacts, the eleven bowl-shaped spindle-whorls of bone (Hencken 1938, 44 and fig. 27) may also belong to the EM3 period—stratified examples come from post-E-ware levels at Lagore (period II) and Rathmullan (phase 2). Another spindle-whorl of this type from Donnybrook, Co. Dublin, is interpreted as coming from occupation levels into which a Viking burial of the ninth century was inserted (Hall 1978, fig. 6e; O'Brien 1992). There are no examples of this type of spindle-whorl from ninth-century or later contexts.

There is some stratigraphic evidence at Cahercommaun to suggest that bowl-shaped spindle-whorls are earlier than those made of the cut heads of ox femora (Hencken 1938, 44). Twenty-three of the latter were recovered and Hencken pointed to their presence in Bronze Age levels at Ballinderry 2, while the discovery of another at Knocknalappa Crannog, Co. Clare (Raftery 1942–3, 66 and fig. 3, 4), suggests that the type was found in the Later Bronze Age. Whorls of cut ox femora are notably absent, however, from any stratified excavations of EM1–3 date, suggesting a reintroduction of the type in EM4— whorls found in tenth-century and later levels at Dublin are overwhelmingly of this type.

The silver brooch clearly belongs to EM4, which covers the ninth century, perhaps extending into the early tenth. To the same chronological horizon may be ascribed the iron arrowhead of Viking Age date (Fig. 12), described as a 'tanged tool' in the report. The brooch and its date have been discussed widely, particularly in relation to the date of the occupation of Cahercommaun as well as its implications for the date of souterrains. On the latter, it is now clear that 'the overwhelming weight of Irish archaeological and historical evidence would place the datable souterrains within the bracket of the ninth to the twelfth centuries' (Warner 1986b, 111). There need thus be no great difference in date between the souterrain and the brooch buried in it. As it is now evident that there are artefacts from Cahercommaun that are clearly earlier than the ninth century, and as the silver brooch is, in fact, one of the latest datable pieces of metalwork from the site, one cannot now argue, as Hencken did, that the souterrain and brooch belong to the primary occupation of the fort.

In conclusion, the presence of artefacts ranging in date from as early as the fifth century to the tenth century has been demonstrated. The vast majority of these, however, may be assigned to the later end of this range—EM3 and 4, i.e. between the later seventh and tenth centuries.

THE DATE OF CAHERCOMMAUN: SUMMARY AND CONCLUSIONS
CLAIRE COTTER

A reassessment of the evidence from Hencken's excavations suggests that two principal stages of activity can be identified at Cahercommaun. The first took place in the prehistoric period and is attested to by the flint/chert artefacts, the stone axes and the saddle querns. Each of these assemblages may represent a discrete episode (or a number of episodes) of human activity on the site. Alternatively, they may be the residue of a single phase of activity. If the latter is the case, then Woodman's conclusion that the flint/chert artefacts are very unlikely to post-date the Neolithic period suggests that this activity may have taken place in early prehistory. No cultural layers or structures can be associated with any of the prehistoric artefacts and there is no evidence to indicate what form any associated settlement might have taken. The absence of prehistoric pottery raises the question of whether there was ever a permanent prehistoric settlement on the site, and the possibility that the attested prehistoric activity was of a temporary nature, or took place in a ritual context, cannot be dismissed.

The second recognisable phase of activity at the site dates from the Early Medieval period. In parts 1 and 3 the cultural history of this phase has been approached from a number of different perspectives —architectural, stratigraphic and artefactual—and in part 4 Edel Bhreathnach looks at the Early Medieval settlement from a literary/historical perspective.

The date range of the diagnostic first-millennium AD artefacts from the site spans the period from the fifth/sixth to the late ninth or tenth century (Ó Floinn, *supra*). Difficulties arise, however, when an attempt is made to correlate this with the structural sequence—the surviving buildings do not appear to reflect such a long occupation span. Hencken identified two phases of occupation at the fort (earlier and later) but considered that there was no evidence for the building of new structures or the abandonment of old ones during his later phase (1938, 2). He suggested that the fort was built in the early part of the ninth century AD and was probably occupied for only a few generations at most (*ibid.*). This dating was based mainly on the silver brooch found in souterrain B and considered by Hencken to date from *c*. AD 800. A human skull found in the same souterrain was interpreted as a deliberate 'foundation burial' which had, in all likelihood, been laid down when the fort was built. Both Hencken's earlier and later phases were therefore dated by him to the period after AD 800.

Based on the limited structural and stratigraphic information in the published report, a more extended three-phase sequence has already been suggested for the Early Medieval occupation at Cahercommaun (part 3). Phases B and C in this sequence correspond broadly with Hencken's 'early' and 'late' phases but with two important changes. In the revised sequence, the burial in souterrain B is interpreted as belonging to the final period of the occupation (Phase C), with interment probably taking place after the souterrain had been abandoned. The date of the deposition of the silver brooch is interpreted as providing a *terminus ante quem* for the construction of the souterrain only and not (as suggested by Hencken) for the foundation of the fort. There is a strong likelihood that the souterrain was in use when the brooch was deposited during the later ninth century.

There is also sufficient evidence to argue that there was some occupation on the site prior to the construction of the souterrains and of the stone platform which lay along the interior of the north wall. This pre-souterrain occupation horizon is called Phase A but, apart from recognising its existence, very little light can be thrown on what was happening at the site during this phase.

Ó Floinn's reassessment of the metalwork from Cahercommaun also extends the settlement history further back into the first millennium than was originally suggested by Hencken. Based on his analysis of stratified artefacts from recently excavated sites, Ó Floinn (above) suggests that the material culture of the Early Medieval period in Ireland can be divided into four phases, and concludes that the artefacts from Cahercommaun fall into all four categories. Taking all the above evidence into account, the following broad reconstruction of the site history during the Early Medieval period can be suggested.

Phase A (pre-souterrain phase): fifth/sixth–eighth century
(Ó Floinn's **EM1, EM2** and **EM3**)
No corresponding phase identified by Hencken.

This horizon is evidenced by the penannular iron brooch, the two iron pins with looped heads, and the copper-alloy zoomorphic penannular brooch—all of which are likely to date from the period between the fifth/sixth and the seventh centuries AD—and the head of the enamelled brooch-pin which is of likely seventh/eighth-century date (Ó Floinn, *supra*).

The stratigraphic evidence for Phase A is identifiable only in the northern part of the fort. The two souterrains located there were deliberately hidden from view by a covering layer of rubble. Mixed through this rubble were artefacts, charcoal and animal bones which appear to be residues of earlier occupation. Habitation layers in the adjacent structures 10 and 11 were also sealed beneath stone fill which seems to have been a continuation of the same rubble horizon. Additional evidence for any pre-souterrain activity on the site is difficult to identify. Like the prehistoric assemblage, the four likely fifth–seventh/eighth-century artefacts lack any definite stratigraphical relationship to any of the structures. Three of these objects have no recorded context other than the quadrant in which they were found, and the find-place of the fourth object (the zoomorphic penannular brooch) was recorded only as fill in the north-east quadrant. Three of the four were recovered from the north-east quadrant (this division also included structure 6 and souterrain A), but as this quadrant produced the largest number of finds in more than half the 22 artefact classes (e.g. spindle-whorls, combs, bone pins, iron pins, stone discs etc.) defined by Hencken (1938, 67), no particular significance can be attached to this. The flooring layer for Hencken's 'early' occupation may well have included a buildup of habitation material from this period, but there is insufficient evidence now to determine whether or not this was so. It is also possible that any Phase A structures were either undetectable or undetected during the excavations. Timber houses, for example, would have left little trace, given that the site is located on bedrock, and any stone buildings associated with this phase could have been largely obliterated by later structures. Some of the other artefacts found at the site may also belong to this phase, but as the majority are undiagnostic it is not possible to assess either the duration or intensity of human activity at the site during this period.

The larger question is whether the fort was in existence during this period. If the *in situ* archaeological layers within the lean-to structures 10 and 11, and the artefacts, animal bone etc. in the material buttressing the souterrains are residues of the same occupation horizon, then there was certainly *a fort* on the site prior to the construction of the souterrains in the ninth century. Whether this was an earlier (possibly less impressive) monument or merely a version of the present fort is impossible to say. Currently no Irish ringfort can be undisputedly said to have been constructed prior to the seventh century AD. Evidence from other excavated sites indicates that souterrains were often added to 'early' (seventh/eighth-century) ringforts without, apparently, any other large-scale modifications being carried out. The same may hold true for Cahercommaun, but at present all that can be said is that:

(i) the souterrains are not primary features at the site;
(ii) there is a strong likelihood that there was a fort on the site prior to their construction;
(iii) the ninth-century silver brooch found in souterrain B can no longer be considered as providing the foundation date of the fort itself.

Unfortunately none of the fifth–seventh/eighth-century objects can shed any light on the building history, as (like the prehistoric assemblages) they have no demonstrable relationship to any edifice on the site. A location such as the plateau at Cahercommaun offered extremely favourable conditions for settlement and, as the first part of this paper has shown, the site was the focus of activity on one or more occasions in the prehistoric period. Similarly there may have been a number of different phases of settlement on the site in the Early Medieval period. Given the large number of ringforts in the country (and the high density of forts in the Burren in particular), common sense alone would suggest that some proportion of ringforts were built on already established settlements. The fifth/sixth-century objects could well belong to a pre-fort settlement.

Phase B (main occupation): ninth century
(Ó Floinn's **EM4**)
Hencken's early phase.

To this phase belong the 5/6/7/8 cellular complex of stone buildings and both souterrains. Structures 1, 2 and 3 are also likely to have been in existence at this time, but it is unclear what type of structure or structures stood at the centre of the site. Timber buildings may have occupied much of the southern half of the fort.

In terms of dating, this phase may be bracketed between the construction of the souterrains and their abandonment. The silver annular brooch found in the passage of souterrain B provides a broad *terminus ante quem* for the construction of that feature, and a date in the ninth century seems likely (Ó Floinn, *supra*). The date of the abandonment of the souterrain is unknown, but a date sometime in the later ninth/tenth century seems likely.

The presence of the souterrains and the guard chamber, as well as the fact that the principal dwellings (i.e. those with souterrains) did not impede access to the wall terraces, suggests that this was the main period of occupation within the extant fort. Most of the surviving structures in the interior appear to belong to this phase. As far as can be established from Hencken's sections in the published report, the foundations of the buildings, and of the walls of the fort, rested on the same levelled-off bedrock plane, suggesting that they were built at the same time. As ringforts were first and foremost settlement sites, it could reasonably be expected that periods of intensive occupation would be equally reflected in both the material culture and the visible status of the monument. There is a strong case for arguing, therefore, that the fort *as it survives today* was built sometime during the ninth century AD.

Phase C (later ninth/tenth century– ?)
(Ó Floinn's **EM4**)
Hencken's later phase.

During this phase the southern area was refloored and the rectangular complex (structure 4) may have been constructed at the centre of the site. The door passage was repaved and the flanking walls rebuilt so that the entrance led directly to structure 4. Access to the guard chamber was blocked. Accumulating domestic waste meant that floor levels in the interior rose, so much so that the lower terrace ceased to function as a wall-walk and the ladder recesses or steps were reused as hearths. The insertion of the burial or burials in souterrain B suggests that the souterrain had been abandoned by this stage. During Phase C, therefore, the fort was probably falling into disrepair and its status may also have been declining.

There is no independent dating evidence for this phase (the date of the burial would be a good indication). It is possible that there was very little time difference between phases B and C, with both falling into a ninth/tenth-century bracket. Neither is there any definite indication as to when the fort was finally abandoned. Ó Floinn suggests that none of the artefacts from Cahercommaun can be dated to later than the tenth century. However, it is unclear when 'urban-type' medieval cultural assemblages, with imported pottery and a wider range of manufactured goods, make their appearance on rural settlements in the west of Ireland. During excavations at the stone fort of Dún Eoghanachta on the Aran Islands a thirteenth-century coin provided the only clue that there had been activity on the site in the Later Medieval period, and the remainder of the artefacts belonged to what could be described as a typical 'ringfort assemblage'.

In conclusion, then, on the evidence available at present, the construction date of the fort at Cahercommaun remains a matter of opinion. In the opinion of the writer there is a strong argument to be made in favour of a later date, and Hencken's suggestion that the fort was built *c.* AD 800 may not be far off.

In Part 4, Edel Bhreathnach focuses on Hencken's conclusion that the fort was built by a chief of north Clare and looks at the possible derivations of the place name *Cahercommaun*. The historical explanations for why this location remained favourable for settlement over such an extended period are also examined and, in particular, why such a prestigious fort as Cahercommaun might have been constructed there during the Early Medieval period. The conclusions reached by Bhreathnach will be integrated into a broader discussion, *vis-à-vis* the forts on the Aran Islands, in the final publication of the Western Stone Forts Project.

PART 4. The construction of the stone fort at Cahercommaun: a historical hypothesis

EDEL BHREATHNACH

Introduction: the place-names Cahercommaun and Tullycommon

The date of the construction and occupation of the stone fort at Cahercommaun, Co. Clare, lies sometime between AD 400 and 900. The archaeological evidence, insofar as it can be dated precisely, suggests that most of the activity at the fort took place in the latter part of this period, *c.* 800 (Hencken 1938, 2–3; Cotter, *supra*; Ó Floinn, *supra*). The following study, based primarily on historical evidence, seeks to elucidate reasons why Cahercommaun was occupied at intervals from prehistory to the medieval times and why a substantial fort was built there in the Early Medieval period. The origins of the place-names Cahercommaun and Tullycommon (the townland in which the fort is situated) offer clues to the historical background which resulted in the construction of such a dominant feature as this fort in north Clare.

In his report of the excavations at Cahercommaun, Hencken commented on the fort's name and stated that he had retained the spelling Cahercommaun to avoid confusion, as it appeared in that form on the 6-inch Ordnance Survey map, 'in spite of possible linguistic objections' (Hencken 1938, 3). Cahercommaun lies in the townland of Tullycommon, both place-names seemingly retaining a similar second element, possibly one of two personal names, Commán or Cumann: *Cathair Chommáin* or *Chumainn* and *Tulach Chommáin* or *Chumainn*. The names Cahercommaun (in the form Cahirkamon) and Tullycommon do not occur in texts earlier than the sixteenth century. Westropp (1900–2, 430–1) noted the likely reference to Cahercommaun in *The Irish Fiants of Elizabeth I* in a deed dated to 1585: 'Dermod O'Flanygan of Cahirekamon' (*Irish Fiants*, vol. 2, §4753). The same document refers twice to the townland name Tullycommon: 'Shane ruo M'Shurtan, of Tullagh Coman ... Hubert M'Shurtan of Twllagh Coman' (*ibid.*). Westropp (1900–2, 430) also noted the form *Cahir Comaine* in the late seventeenth-century *Books of Survey and Distribution* (Simington and Mac Giolla Choille 1967, 520). Tullycommon is mentioned in the *Annals of the Four Masters* for 1599 (O'Donovan 1848–51, vol. 6, 2100–1) and in the seventeenth-century *Life of Aodh Ruadh Ó Domhnaill* (Walsh 1948, 202–3, §109), which was used as a source by the annalists. The reference relates to the campaign in which Aodh Ruadh collected many spoils from County Clare, and in both texts the form of the name is *Tulach C(h)umann* (*ibid.*, 202):

> Do rattadh chuicce creacha Cheineoil Fermeic uile durmhor on Disert co Gleann Colaimb Cille ⁊ go Tulaigh Cumann ⁊ ó Chluain Soilchernaigh co Léim an Eich.

> The spoils of all Cenél Fermeic were brought to him from Dysert (barony of Inchiquin) to Glencolumbkille (barony of Burren) and to Tullycommon and from Cloonselherny (barony of Inchiquin) to Leamaneh (barony of Inchiquin).

The place-name *Tulach C(h)umann* is spelt without long vowel *á* and without any indication of genitive singular palatalisation. With regard to the later spelling of these place-names, Westropp in his copious manuscript materials used the forms Cahircommane or Cahercommaun, Tullycommon and very occasionally Tullycommaun (see examples at RIA MS 3.A.40, 299; MS 3.A.44, 11verso; Westropp 1896, 151–7). Local place-name formation, such as the names Cashlaun Gar (*Caisleán Gearr*), a fort close to Cahercommaun, and Glencurraun (*Gleann Chorráin*), the valley in which these forts are located, suggests strongly that the second element of the fort's name at least includes the personal name Commán. The element -*aun* in the Anglicised version originates from the Irish ending -*án* and not from -*an(n)*.

While the evidence is circumstantial in the absence of early references and while it is not entirely certain that the second element of *both* place-names is the same, the possibility that the personal names *Commán* or *Cumann* form part of these place-names provides a reflection, albeit considerably blurred, into the process of name formation associated with some western stone forts. Furthermore, the identification of Commán suggests a historical horizon for the construction and use of some of these forts at a particular period.

The sources for the early history of Munster consist for the most part of entries in the annals, genealogical tracts, legal and pseudo-legal tracts, and saga material which includes an underlying political or genealogical message. Though seemingly meagre when compared to early sources dealing with the northern half of Ireland and though they date primarily from the eighth century onwards, these

Fig. 15—Dynasties of Aran and north Clare c. AD 700.

sources nonetheless enable us to reconstruct the polity of Munster in some detail from *c.* 650. The most important kingship in the province was the kingship of Cashel and, in a manner similar to contention for the kingship of Tara during the same period, old contenders for the kingship of Cashel were being ousted by newly formed confederations. In the north, the confederation which became known as the Uí Néill emerged victorious during the seventh century, while in the south a confederation of dynasties using the umbrella title Éoganachta began to dominate the kingship of Cashel. Other dynasties which were not always categorised as Éoganachta but were sufficiently powerful to be granted equal status in various texts continued to contend for the kingship of Cashel and to exert considerable influence into the eighth century. Most prominent among these dynasties were the Uí Fidgeinti, whose main homelands lay on the southern side of the Shannon Estuary. Along the western coast, a maritime alliance probably existed between population groups such as the Corcu Lóegde, Cíarraige, Alltraige, Corcu Baiscind and Corcu Modruad, whose influence in the inland fertile regions of Munster waned with the emergence of the Éoganachta (Fig. 15).

The Uí Fidgeinti: Éoganacht Ninussa alias Éoganacht Árann?

The importance of the Uí Fidgeinti in Munster, especially prior to the rise of Dál Cais in the ninth century, is evident from a number of genealogical and legal tracts (Byrne 1973, 176–8; Ó Corráin 1975, 21). The annals, and primarily the Munster-orientated *Annals of Inisfallen*, record the names of early kings of the Uí Fidgeinti and their deeds (*vide* 636, 649, 667, 683, 732, 751, 762 *et al.*), many of whom are identifiable in the corpus of secular genealogies (O'Brien 1962, 230–1). The genealogies of three main branches of the Uí Fidgeinti are preserved *in extenso*: the Uí Chairpri and Uí Chonaill Gabra, whose homelands were in west Limerick (Ó Corráin 1969–70, 83–4), and the Uí Chormaic, whose sphere of influence may have been further north in the Burren and the Aran Islands.

The eighth-century text 'The Expulsion of the Déisi' classifies the Uí Fidgeinti as one of the three Éoganachta of Munster: *.i. Eoganacht Raithlind ⁊ Eoganacht Locha Léin ⁊ Eoganacht Hua Fidgeinti co n-Huib Liathain* (Meyer 1901, 116–17, §15). Their high status and their interest in the kingship of Munster are reflected in tracts, dating mainly from the eighth and ninth centuries, on the reciprocal arrangements (*frithfolaid*) between the kings of Cashel and the other kings of Munster. According to the text *Dál Caladbuig* (O'Keefe 1931, 20–1), the king of the Múscraige was entitled to sit beside the king of Cashel unless the kings of Uí Fidgeinti or of Írluachair or Raithlend were present. When this was the case, the king of Múscraige raised his knee as an indication of respect among equals. The same three kings (Uí Fidgeinti, Írluachair and Raithlend) were bound to go on a hosting against *síl Chuind* (Uí Néill) and the Laigin, but only to defend the honour of Munster. If one of them was killed on such a campaign, the king of Munster had to pay compensation to their families (Ó Corráin 1972, 112; Byrne 1973, 197–8). Indeed, such was the importance of the Uí Fidgeinti in Munster and their influence in north Clare and Aran until at least the mid-eighth to ninth century that they were probably known as Éoganacht Árann or Éoganacht Ninussa (see Ó Corráin 1969, 143, for comments on this possibility in another context). Another *frithfolaid* ('reciprocal arrangements') text entitled *Ceart ríg Caisil ó crichaib*, which deals with the tributes due to the king of Cashel from the various parts of Munster, supports this conjecture. This text, which is preserved in the Book of Lecan (230vb39–42) and the Book of Ballymote (190a5), is fragmentary and on the basis of its content possibly dates from the ninth century. According to it, the Corcu Modruad—who are known to have inhabited north Clare during this period—were expected to pay 300 beeves from the Burren, 300 cloaks and 300 milch cows to the king of Cashel. Three hundred boars were expected from the eastern half of the territory, *genmothá a sáerthúatha* 'except from its free *túatha*'. Both manuscripts gloss the word *sáerthúatha* as Éoganacht Árann, suggesting that they continued to enjoy a privileged status into the ninth century and that they were regarded as separate from Corcu Modruad. Those most likely to fit this description were a sub-segment of the Uí Fidgeinti known as Uí Chormaic, who played a significant role in the polity of north Clare and the Aran Islands in the seventh and eighth centuries.

The influence of the Uí Fidgeinti from the Shannon Estuary to Connacht in the seventh and eighth centuries

The Uí Chonaill Gabra: the family of Nechtan Cennfota

As demonstrated by Byrne (1958) in his paper on the Éoganacht Ninussa or Éoganacht Árann and by others (Sproule 1984), the origins and genealogical affiliations of those who regarded themselves as Éoganachta in this early period are complex. The Uí Fidgeinti are a case in point. The main branch of the Uí Fidgeinti, Uí Chonaill Gabra (also known as Éoganacht Gabra), were active in an area stretching northwards from their homelands south of the Shannon Estuary into Connacht. The family of Nechtan Cennfota (O'Brien 1962, 230: 152a6), who were the main dynasty of Uí Chonaill Gabra, exercised considerable power during the seventh century, if the annalistic record is reliable (Ó Corráin 1969–70, 83–4). The *Annals of Inisfallen* (Mac Airt 1951, 88) record in 635 the battle of Cúil Óchtair, a site possibly in the vicinity of Monasternenagh, Co. Limerick (Hogan 1910, 322), fought between the Uí Fidgeinti and the Arada Cliach, their neighbours, who occupied the fertile lands of east Limerick and west Tipperary. An entry in the *Annals of Ulster* (Mac Airt and Mac Niocaill 1983, 118) and in the *Annals of Tigernach* (Stokes 1896, 183) in 635 suggests that the Uí Fidgeinti may have had greater ambitions than encroaching on their neighbours. Lachín mac Nechtain Cinnfota and his nephew Cummascach mac Óengusso meic Nechtain Cinnfota (O'Brien 1962, 388: 327a 21 and 26) were killed at *bellum Segusse* 'the battle of Segais'. The place-name Segais is usually identified with the well at Síd Nechtain—near Carbury Hill, Co. Kildare—from where the River

Boyne issues, and is sometimes used of the Boyne itself. Segais is also the name given to the source of the River Shannon in the Cuilcagh Mountains, Co. Leitrim, and to the district around the River Boyle, which straddles the Curlew Mountains in counties Roscommon and Sligo (Hogan 1910, 594). The well of Segais was known for its supernatural properties, transmitted especially through hazel nuts which fell into it (O'Rahilly 1946, 322; Hull 1962–4). Given Uí Fidgeinti interests in Connacht, apparent from other sources, it is more likely that Nechtan Cennfota's family fell at a battle near the source of the Shannon than the Boyne. A Leinster location for the battle cannot be ruled out completely, however, since the Laigin maintained interests as far south as the Shannon Estuary during this period. The *Annals of Inisfallen* (Mac Airt 1951, 102), for example, comment in 706 *Ár Laigen im Gabair a mMumain* 'A slaughter of the Laigin round Gabair in Mumu', Gabair being the heartland of the Uí Fidgeinti patrimony.

Another member of the Uí Chonaill Gabra dynasty, Óengus mac Nechtain, died in 636 according to the *Annals of Inisfallen* (Mac Airt 1951, 90). Apart from the reference to the death of his son Cummascach at the battle of Segais, Óengus mac Nechtain himself is mentioned in an early genealogical poem ascribed to the seventh-century poet Luccreth moccu Chérai (O'Brien 1962, 204: 149a25):

Óengus crobderg   cathach rí
án ó Gabair   gabtha (ar) ní

Óengus the red-handed, bellicose king,
famous one from Gabar, who was restrained from nothing(?).

His father Nechtan appears as Nechtan Cennocht (Rawlinson B502 reading) or as Nechtan Cendot (Book of Ballymote and Book of Lecan readings) in the same poem. The name of Donennach mac Óengusa, who died in 683, occurs in a list of kings said to have been involved in the promulgation of the Old Irish law *Cáin Fhuithirbe* (Binchy 1958, 53; Breatnach 1986, 42–4). The text reads *co dal Donennaig* 'to a tryst with Donennach', and is glossed in Old Irish *.i. ri Hue Fidgenti ⁊ co ri na Deisi Tuaiscirt* 'i.e. king of Uí Fidgeinti, and to the king of In Déis Tuaiscirt' (Breatnach 1986, 43, §6). Clearly Donennach is king of Uí Fidgeinti. Whether the gloss attempts to claim that he was also king of In Déis Tuaiscirt, who were later Dál Cais, or that another unnamed king is meant remains unclear, although Binchy favoured the latter interpretation (Binchy 1958, 53). Perhaps Donennach wished to be regarded as king of In Déis Tuaiscirt as well as of Uí Fidgeinti. Such was the complexity of dynastic and genealogical affiliations particularly between the population groups Corcu Modruad, Corcu Baiscinn, Déis, Ciarraige and Uí Fidgeinti during this period (Ó Corráin 1968, 46–8), and so intense was the rivalry for dominance of the territory north of the Shannon Estuary as far as the Aran Islands, that kings claimed titles not immediately belonging to their own dynasties. For example, it may not be due solely to their lateness as sources that the *Annals of the Four Masters* (O'Donovan 1848–51, vol. 1, 338) and the *Annals of Clonmacnoise* (Murphy 1896, 117) describe Flann Feórna, the first recorded king of Ciarraige Luachra (d. 741), as *tighearna* 'lord' (*AFM*) or 'prince' (*AClon*) of Corcu Modruad.

Dínertach, another son of Óengus mac Nechtain (O'Sullivan 1983, 1388: 322a2), is the subject of the Old Irish lament reputed to have been sung by Créide, daughter of Gúaire Aidne, king of Connacht (d. 663). Dínertach, according to the prose introduction to the poem, fell *isin tres Aidne* 'in the battle of Aidne' (Murphy 1956, 86), the territory to the east of Corcu Modruad which was later more or less co-extensive with the diocese of Kilmacduagh. It may be noted in passing that this is also an area, similar to north Clare, which has a marked density of place-names containing the element *cathair,* or in its Anglicised form 'caher' (Flanagan 1980–1, 29). In the lament—if it is a lament, since James Carney regarded it as the earliest example of the 'lover-poet' conceit insofar as it was penned by Dínertach's court poet while his lord (Dínertach) was still alive (Carney 1968, 29)—Créide alludes to topographic associations with her dead lover. She recalls time spent in the company of the man *a tóeb thíre Roigne* 'from the land of Roigne'. Dínertach's uncle, Lachín, who died at the battle of Segais in 635, is described in the genealogies as the ancestor of Áes Ragni or Roigne (O'Brien 1962, 388: 327a26). As demonstrated by Ó Corráin, Raigne, Roigne or Mag Raigni corresponded with the parishes of Clonelty (barony of Glenquin, Co. Limerick) and Kilscannell (barony of Connello, Co. Limerick) (Ó Corráin 1969–70, 83). Créide laments towards the end of the poem (Murphy 1956, 86–7, §7):

Canair i n-íath Aidni áin
im thóebu Cille Colmáin,
án bréo des Luimnech lechtach
díanid comainm Dínertach.

> In the land of glorious Aidne, around the sides of Cell Cholmáin, men sing of a glorious flame, from the south of Limerick of the graves, whose name is Dínertach.

Although enveloped by the legend which surrounds Gúaire Aidne's reign, the death of an Uí Fidgeinti noble fighting in Aidne (*pace* Carney's interpretation of the poem) is plausible given the other known activities of Dínertach's family during the seventh century and the first half of the eighth century.

The Uí Chormaic: the family of Commán mac Maínaich

In his extensive study of what he termed 'the chieftaincy of Tulach Commáin'—a territory reconstituted on the basis of the modern townland of Tullycommon—David Blair Gibson was tempted 'by several disparate facts to entertain the hypothesis that there might have been some short-lived Éoganacht chiefdom centred at Cahercommaun' (Gibson 1990, 370). Among the 'disparate facts' noticed by Gibson was the entry in the *Annals of Ulster* (Mac Airt and Mac Niocaill 1983, 162), the *Annals of Tigernach* (Stokes 1896, 149) and the *Annals of the Four Masters* (O'Donovan 1848–51, vol. 1, 306) for the year 705 recording *bellum Corc Modruadh* 'the battle of Corcu Modruad'. The annals record only the death of one Célechair mac Commáin in that battle. This was one of a series of eighth-century battles fought for domination of north Clare. In 721 there was a battle between the Connachta and Corcu Baiscinn, who were being pushed further into west Clare by the rise of In Déis Tuaiscirt (Mac Airt and Mac Niocaill 1983, 174). The *Annals of Ulster* record in 744 the destruction of Corcu Modruad by the Déis and in 763 a battle between the Uí Fidgeinti, Corcu Modruad and Corcu Baiscinn. Furthermore, an entry in the *Annals of Inisfallen* in 751 (Mac Airt 1951, 110) notes the death in Aran of Colmán mac Commáin, who, despite the 46 years between their deaths, could have been the brother of Célechair mac Commáin who died at the battle of Corcu Modruad in 705. Following Byrne (1973, 178), Gibson cited the presence in the region of the Éoganacht Árann or Éoganacht Ninussa as evidence to support his hypothesis of a short-lived Éoganacht 'chiefdom' at Cahercommaun. He also noted that the corpus of medieval Irish genealogies fortuitously preserved Célechair mac Commáin's genealogy, which indicated that he belonged to the Uí Chormaic, a third branch of the powerful Uí Fidgeinti. The Uí Chormaic were descended from Cormac mac Fintait (or Fintain) (O'Brien 1962, 231:152a17–20). Gibson was reluctant, however, to develop his hypothesis on the grounds that 'the few dates from Cahercommaun throw doubt upon this theory, as they show the site to have been inhabited in the late eighth century A.D. One would have to presume that the Uí Cormaic lineage persisted at the site following their defeat [at the battle of Corcu Modruad in 705], and became transformed into Clann hIffernáin [a branch of the Corcu Modruad] or that they were displaced by Clann hIffernáin, who continued the occupation of Cahercommaun' (Gibson 1990, 371).

A study of the ecclesiastical and secular polity of the Aran Islands from *c.* 650 to 1200 being conducted as part of the Discovery Programme's Western Stone Forts Project, which is aimed at providing some historical context for the extraordinary riches of those islands, however, has underscored the significance of Célechair and Colmán mac Commáin and their likely dynastic affiliation.

Colmán mac Commáin, who died in Aran in 751, was a prominent cleric. He is not mentioned in the genealogies of the Uí Chormaic since they only preserve the pedigree of one line of descent, that of Célechair mac Commáin. The name of Colmán's father, Commán, and Colmán's own death in Aran strongly suggest—despite a possible chronological difficulty—that he was Célechair mac Commáin's brother and therefore belonged to the same family. His importance as a cleric is borne out by the sources. He is commemorated in the ninth-century martyrology *Félire Óengusso* on 21 November as *macc Commain a hÁrainn* (Stokes 1905, 236). His eminence as a bishop of Munster is expressed in the quatrain included in the additional notes to *Félire Óengusso* preserved in *Leabhar Breac* (Stokes 1880, clxx):

> Colmán mac Commáin,
> mairg duine nacha cíä,
> epscop samlaid din Muma
> sech ní raba, ní bíä.

> Colmán mac Commáin, woe to the person who does not weep for him, A bishop like him from Munster never was [and] never will be.

The sentiment expressed here, in the mode of the Modern Irish idiom *ní bheidh a leithéidí ann arís* 'his like shall not be seen again', is corroborated elsewhere. Colmán mac Commáin was regarded as one of the four sages of Ireland and was probably a proponent of the *Céli Dé*, a movement of ascetic revival in the early Irish church. The penitential text

Pl. 11—Grave-slab, Teampall Bhreacáin, possibly commemorating Cethernach, a mid- to late eighth-century Uí Fidgeinti king (photograph reproduced with the kind permission of the trustees of the National Museums and Galleries of Northern Ireland).

known as *De arreis* or 'The Old Irish table of Commutations' describes how a particular type of vigil was recommended by Patrick and Colum Cille and others, a tradition which was deposited later with Enda of Aran (Binchy 1962, 62–4; 1975, 281, line 31). According to the same text, this practice was observed by adherents of the *Céli Dé* movement, one of its chief advocates being Colmán mac Commáin, otherwise known as Mocholmóc (Binchy 1962, 64–5; Ó Muraíle 1983, 55):

> Timarnasat ceth(t)ri primsuid hErenn gres fria tu cach mac bethad adcobra(i) nem .i. hua minadain 7 cuimine fota 7 muirdiubur 7 mocolmoc mac commain a haraind.

> The four chief sages of Ireland, viz. Ua Minadan and Cumaine Fota [d. 662] and Murdebar and Mocholmóc mac Commáin [or mac Cumain][d. 751] from Aran have recommended its constant practice to every son of life (?*Céli Dé*) who desires to obtain heaven.

Binchy used the reference to Colmán to suggest that the text *De arreis* was composed *c.* 800 since the latter's death in 751 'provides a *terminus a quo* for the composition of this tract' (Binchy 1962, 70). Whatever about its exact date of composition, this passage confirms the eminent position of Colmán in the eighth-century Irish church and the likelihood that his importance in the church reflected his affiliation to a prominent kindred, the Uí Chormaic. That his fame as a sage or as a custodian of literary or oral tales was well known is understood from the end of the voyage tale *Immram Ua Corra* 'The Voyage of the Uí Chorra'. The tale of this voyage, undertaken by three brothers in repentance for their evil deeds, was related by them to a certain bishop of their people (*epscop dia muinter*), Sóerbrethach, who then told it to Mocholmóc mac Colmáin (*leg.* Commáin) in Aran: *Ro innisside iat do MoCholmóc mac Colmáin i nÁrain* (Van Hamel 1941, 111:526–8). As reflected in these sources, Colmán's eminence also highlights Aran's position as a sufficiently important ecclesiastical centre to attract such a person to it, at least at the time of his death. His distinction as a bishop of Munster and his residence in Aran probably had as much to do with his family's influence in the region as with his own piety or ecclesiastical attributes. One could even postulate, without seeming too far-fetched, that the fragmentary grave-slab from Teampall Bhreacáin on Aran (Pl. 11), which commemorates Cetherna(ch), was erected in memory of Cethernach, Célechair mac Commáin's son and Colmán's nephew (O'Brien 1962, 231: 152a17), who would have died in the mid- to late eighth century. Furthermore, the prominence of his family in the sources, which for this period in this region tend to record only the activities of the most powerful and influential, suggests that Commán, Célechair and Colmán's father and Cethernach's grandfather, left his memorial in the place-name Cathair Chommáin.

The influence of the Ciarraige: Cumann, a possible alternative to Commán?

A branch of the Ciarraige known as the Uí Chummainn were descended from Cumann mac Dega (O'Brien 1962, 309: 160b31–5). It is possible that the personal name Cumann might offer an alternative origin for the second element in Cahercommaun or even more in Tullycommon. That the Book of Leinster classifies other Ciarraige families related to the Uí Chummainn as *De Chorcomrúad* '[Ciarraige] of Corcu Modruad' (O'Sullivan 1983, 1424: 327d48) lends some credence to this idea.

Combining archaeological and historical evidence

The death of Célechair mac Commáin at the battle of Corcu Modruad in 705 draws attention to the other people seeking to establish their authority in this region. The Corcu Modruad probably ruled a territory much more extensive than their known historic lands (covered by the modern baronies of Corcomroe and Burren), but were pushed westwards in the seventh and eighth centuries by the Uí Fidgeinti and In Déis Tuaiscirt (later to become Dál Cais) (Ó Corráin 1975, 21). As noted previously, the annals amply reflect the struggle for dominance which formed the political and military environment of the time during which the fort at Cahercommaun was initially constructed or rebuilt. If the fragmentary text *Ceart ríg Caisil ó críchaib*, which claims that 300 beeves, 300 cloaks, 300 milch cows and 300 boars were sent from the Burren to the king of Cashel, is not purely schematic and is a genuine reflection of the potential economic benefits accruing to the population group who would gain the upper hand in this struggle, it is little wonder that the competition for north Clare was so intense.

Can the activities of identifiable peoples during a specific period in a relatively well-defined region which are reflected in the sources be translated in any way to understanding the archaeological evidence of that same region? The answer is in the affirmative, mindful of a number of constraints. It is altogether too exact to link archaeological patterns with events as seen in the sources. Nothing in human activity is so simple. The landscape—especially in Ireland, which is a small extent of land—predetermines many decisions, be they settlements in fertile locations or proximity to navigable rivers, strategic sites for settled communities or for military purposes. From the prehistoric period onwards, the site at Cahercommaun was occupied sporadically because it afforded some advantage, be it defensive, economic or strategic, which other locations in the area could not offer. Function and dominant activities also predetermine choice of location and the types of structure used. Some western stone forts are likely to reflect the maritime connections, which served economic and military purposes, between peoples of the west coast, who in the historic period can be identified as the Corcu Lóegde, Ciarraige, Alltraige and Corcu Baiscinn (Ó Corráin 1972, 70; Byrne 1973, 170–1). The model suggested by Gibson (1990, 343–53) for 'the chieftaincy' of Tulach Commáin of three nodal points—the capital, Cahercommaun (with its surrounding, but now less visible, settlements), the ceremonial centre, Tulach Commáin, and the principal church, possibly Cell ingen Báeth, Killinaboy—is a starting-point. The difficulty lies in linking this model with a given dynasty or period. Were these fixed points on the landscape upon which various people left their own mark, and how long were the forts in use? Unlike the populations of Britain or the Continent, Irish population groups of the Early Medieval period are not known to have been culturally different from one another, and therefore the archaeological record *appears* homogeneous. Differences may be reflected through a people's exposure to varying external influences (for example, the people of Brega were exposed to Romano-British and Anglo-Saxon cultures); through the manner in which they gained authority in a territory and how stable and extensive their settlements were (for example, defensive versus undefended sites; settled sites; the monumental works of a particularly strong king, which in Ireland seem best reflected in ecclesiastical architecture—grave-slabs, high crosses, Romanesque doorways—rather than in the secular milieu); and through skills acquired in a particular landscape, which of course led to regional variations (for example, stone fort-builders and crannog-builders).

Archaeologists might be mindful that scholars of early Irish language and literature face a similar quandary when seeking to establish the provenance of an early Irish text. The common language is a standard form of Old and Middle Irish in which dialects are hardly detectable (Ahlqvist 1994, 34 (4.7)). Scholars use a range of tests, not always successful, when attempting to establish a provenance, including teasing out the manuscript tradition (Carey 1995), identifying a bias towards a particular dynasty, king, saint or monastery (Ó Corráin 1987), or noting a concentration on the topography of a particular area (Doherty 1986, 368–71). Despite the volume of Irish (and Latin) texts dating from the Early Medieval period, very few can be provenanced and the methodology is still evolving.

If Cahercommaun were approached as a text, what could be deduced about its context and the origin of those who settled there? The earliest reference to the name, *Cahirekamon*, is found in a sixteenth-century text. While acknowledging fully the danger of linking the personal names Commán or Cumann with the place-names Cahercommaun and Tullycommon without the requisite unbroken chronology between the seventh and the sixteenth centuries, sufficient evidence exists from contemporary (seventh-century) and later (eighth- and ninth-century) texts to explain why a site like Cahercommaun might have gained its name from an Uí Fidgeinti sub-king, Commán, or to a lesser degree from a Ciarraige sub-king, Cumann.

The evidence of the earliest sources relating to the polity of Munster (Ó Corráin 1997, 8) shows north Clare from at least the seventh century to have been a territory which was of great interest to competing population groups, the main contenders being the Corcu Modruad, Uí Fidgeinti, In Déis Tuaiscirt, Ciarraige, Corcu Baiscinn, the Connachta and older population groups including the Creccraige and Ercraige. If the archaeological assessment of the fort is that it was built and inhabited between AD 400 and 900—the material evidence favouring the middle and later phases of this period—did it acquire its name from Commán (Uí Chormaic) or Cumann (Ciarraige) as the person who caused its construction, or as a memorial to the person who secured the territory from the Corcu Modruad or others (perhaps Connachta) for the Uí Chormaic or Ciarraige? If this was the case, does the survival of relatively early personal names imply that either the Uí Chormaic or the Ciarraige held onto the fort despite opposition from the Corcu Modruad or In Déis Tuaiscirt? One could speculate that the Uí Chormaic acted as agents for either the kings of Cashel or the Dál Cais (prior to their elevation to the kingship of Cashel) by collecting tribute from north Clare and Aran, and in acting as such retained the status reflected by a substantial fort like Cahercommaun. This hierarchy would fit well with the situation described by the text *Ceart ríg Caisil ó críchaib*, referred to earlier. It may be that tribute was redistributed from the Burren to whoever was king of Cashel through Cahercommaun.

Conclusion

In summary, the place-names Cahercommaun and Tullycommon may retain in their second element the personal names Commán or Cumann, though lack of direct evidence leaves us unable to confirm either possibility. It is plausible to suggest, however, given what is known of the polity of this region from the seventh century onwards, that the fort was constructed either by a branch of the Ciarraige, to whom Cumann mac Dega belonged, or more probably by the Uí Chormaic, the segment of the Uí Fidgeinti to whom Commán mac Maínaich was affiliated. The Uí Fidgeinti case is stronger, considering that their authority from the Shannon Estuary to the Aran Islands in the seventh and eighth centuries was solid enough to cause the construction of a fort of the dimensions of Cahercommaun. This same period witnessed a prolonged struggle for domination of north Clare, presumably for economic and strategic benefits (including possibly the raising of cattle, fishing and maritime alliances), between the Corcu Modruad, the Uí Fidgeinti and In Déis Tuaiscirt, the latter being the final victors, emerging in the ninth century as Dál Cais kings of the territory.

Addendum

Stone forts: other examples of possible dynastic and mythological figures reflected in place-names

If Commán mac Maínaich of the Uí Chormaic is commemorated in the place-name Cahercommaun, it is tempting to hypothesise that other forts gained their names in a similar manner. *Cathair mic Nechtain*, which housed the O'Davoren family until the seventeenth century (MacNamara 1912, 86–93), could conceivably have originated from an association between the latter site and the sons of Nechtan Cennfota. The mythological associations of the name Nechtan, which appears as a personal name in the genealogies of the Uí Fidgeinti, the Ciarraige, the Corcu Modruad, Corcu Baiscinn and Corcu Duibne (O'Brien 1962, 711–12 (index)), needs to be considered as part of understanding the cultural affiliations of these population groups. Nechtan is sometimes regarded as the alternative name for the god Núadu (O'Rahilly 1946, 320 and 516). Nechtan's son was Ochon, or Mac Con (O'Brien 1962, 255: 154d54), who in the guise of Lugaid Mac Con is central to the heroic tale *Cath Maige Mucrama* 'The Battle of Mag Mucrama' (O Daly 1975, 9–10). O'Rahilly (1946, 79) argued that Mac Con was an alternative name for the god Lug, and possibly also for the mythical Cú Roí mac Dáire. O Daly, in the introduction to her edition of *Cath Maige Mucrama*, countered that Mac Con had nothing to do with the word *cú* 'dog, hound' but was the Irish equivalent of the Brittonic *Mabon* or the Celtic deity *Maponus*. She noted the occurrence of the name Nechtan among Pictish kings and of the Pictish name *Tolarggan maphan*, the latter element being parallel to Mac Con. In mythological tales Mac Con's *rechtaire* 'steward' was Nechtan. The names Mochon and Mess-chon appear relatively frequently in the genealogies of the Ciarraige (O'Brien 1962, 254: 154d35–6), whose interest in the west coast and into Connacht was not inconsiderable (Ó Buachalla 1952, 78–81; Ó Corráin 1968, 48; Doherty 1991, 79–80). Mac Con was a favourite name among the O'Driscolls and MacNamaras in the late medieval period and, in the form *Maccon*, survived to the present day among certain families in County Clare (Ó Corráin and Maguire 1981, 127). An incident in the seventh-century *Collectanea* compiled by Tírechán implies that Mac Con was king of Hirot or Erot (Bieler 1979, 154.29–31; 230), the district in which Áth Cliath Medraige (Clarinbridge, Co. Galway) was situated (Hogan 1910, 56). The existence of forts called Caher(a)con (barony of Clonderlaw), Cahermacun (barony of Burren) and Cahermacon (barony of Inchiquin) (for documentary evidence see Westropp 1900–2, 423, no. 28; 431, no. 103; and 436, no. 164) might in some way reflect either the use of the name of an eponymous ancestor or of a historical figure, Mac Con.

Acknowledgements

I wish to thank Siobhán O'Rafferty, Librarian, Royal Irish Academy, for her assistance in delving with me into a voluminous amount of Ordnance Survey Extract materials and Westropp papers, and Cormac Bourke, Ulster Museum, for facilitating the reproduction of the Cethernach grave-slab (Pl. 11).

References

Ahlqvist, A. 1994 Litriú na Gaeilge. In K. McCone *et al.*, *Stair na Gaeilge in ómós do Pádraig Ó Fiannachta*, 23–59. Maigh Nuad.

Armstrong, E.C.R. 1921–2 Irish bronze pins of the Christian period. *Archaeologia* **72**, 71–86.

Barry, T.B. 1981 Archaeological excavations at Dunbeg promontory fort, Co. Kerry, 1977. *Proceedings of the Royal Irish Academy* **81C**, 295–329.

Bieler, L. 1979 *The Patrician texts in the Book of Armagh*. Scriptores Latini Hiberniae 10. Dublin.

Binchy, D.A. 1958 The date and provenance of Uraicecht Becc. *Ériu* **18**, 44–54.

Binchy, D.A. 1962 The Old Irish Table of Penitential Commutations. *Ériu* **19**, 47–72.

Binchy, D.A. 1975 The Old-Irish Table of Commutations. Appendix in L. Bieler (ed.), *The Irish Penitentials*, 277–83. Scriptores Latini Hiberniae V. Dublin.

Blindheim, C. and Heyerdahl-Larsen, B. 1995 *Kaupang-funnene II. Gravplassene i Bikjholbergene/Lamøya undersøkelsene 1950–1957*. Norske Oldfunn 16. Oslo.

Bøe, J. 1940 *Norse antiquities in Ireland* (= H. Shetelig (ed.), *Viking antiquities in Great Britain and Ireland* 3). Oslo.

Bradley, J. 1991 Excavations at Moynagh Lough, Co. Meath, 1980–89. *Journal of the Royal Society of Antiquaries of Ireland* **121**, 5–26.

Bradley, J. 1994–5 Excavations at Moynagh Lough, Co. Meath. *Ríocht na Mídhe* **9** (1), 158–69.

Brannon, N. 1981–2 The excavation of a cashel in Carn Townland, County Fermanagh. *Ulster Journal of Archaeology* **44–5**, 60–4.

Breatnach, L. 1986 The ecclesiastical element in the Old-Irish legal tract *Cáin Fhuithirbe*. *Peritia* **5**, 36–52.

Brindley, A.L. and Lanting, J.N. 1991–2 Radiocarbon dates from the cemetery at Poulnawack, Co. Clare. *Journal of Irish Archaeology* **6**, 13–17.

Byrne, F.J. 1958 The Eóganacht Ninussa. *Éigse* **9**, 18–29.

Byrne, F.J. 1973 *Irish kings and high-kings*. London.

Carey, J. 1995 On the interrelationships of some *Cín Dromma Snechtai* texts. *Ériu* **46**, 71–92.

Carney, J. 1968 Two poems from Acallam na Senórach. In J. Carney and D. Greene (eds), *Celtic Studies: essays in memory of Angus Matheson 1912–1962*, 22–32. London.

Caulfield, S. 1977 The beehive quern in Ireland. *Journal of the Royal Society of Antiquaries of Ireland* **107**, 104–38.

Caulfield, S. 1981 Some Celtic problems in the Irish Iron Age. In D. Ó Corráin (ed.), *Irish antiquity*, 205–15. Cork.

Coffey, G. 1909 *Guide to the Celtic antiquities of the Christian period preserved in the National Museum, Dublin*. Dublin.

Collins, A.E.P. 1955 Excavations in Lough Faughan Crannog, Co. Down, 1951–52. *Ulster Journal of Archaeology* **18**, 45–82.

Connolly, A. 1993 Saddle querns in Ireland. Unpublished M.A. thesis, University College Galway.

Connolly, A. 1994 Saddle quern stones. *Ulster Journal of Archaeology* **57**, 26–36.

Cooney, G. and Grogan, E. 1994 *Irish prehistory: a social perspective*. Dublin.

Cooney, G. and Mandal, S. 1995 Getting to the core of the problem: petrological results from the Irish Stone Axe Project. *Antiquity* **69**, 969–80.

Cooney, G. and Mandal, S. 1998 *The Irish Stone Axe Project Monograph I*. Bray.

Cotter, C. 1989 Gragans West. In I. Bennett (ed.), *Excavations 1988*, 9–10. Dublin.

Cotter, C. 1993 Western Stone Forts Project. *Discovery Programme Reports* **1**, 1–19.

Cotter, C. 1995 Western Stone Forts Project. *Discovery Programme Reports* **2**, 1–11.

Cotter, C. 1996 Western Stone Forts Project. Interim report. *Discovery Programme Reports* **4**, 1–14.

Cuppage, J. *et al.* 1986 *Archaeological Survey of the Dingle Peninsula*. Ballyferriter.

Dickinson, T. 1982 Fowler's type G penannular brooches reconsidered. *Medieval Archaeology* **26**, 41–68.

Doherty, C. 1986 Saint Máedóc and Saint Molaisse. *Breifne. Journal of Cumann Seanchais Bhreifne* **6** (24), 363–74.

Doherty, C. 1991 The cult of St Patrick and the politics of Armagh in the seventh century. In J.-M. Picard (ed.), *Ireland and northern France AD 600–850*, 53–94. Dublin.

Donaghy, C. 1991 Barrel padlocks and their keys in Ireland. Unpublished M.A. thesis, University College Dublin.

Dunlevy, M. 1988 A classification of early Irish combs. *Proceedings of the Royal Irish Academy* **88C**, 341–74.

Dunraven, E. 1875 *Notes on Irish architecture*. London.

Edwards, N. 1990 *The archaeology of early medieval Ireland*. London.

Eogan, J. 1998 Coolnatullagh. In I. Bennett (ed.), *Excavations 1997*, 5–6. Dublin.

Fanning, T. 1981 Excavations of an Early Christian cemetery and settlement at Reask, County Kerry. *Proceedings of the Royal Irish Academy* **81C**, 67–172.

Fanning, T. 1987 Rinnaraw. In I. Bennett (ed.), *Excavations 1986*, 12. Dublin.

Fanning, T. 1988 Rinnaraw. In I. Bennett (ed.), *Excavations 1987*, 13. Dublin.

Fanning, T. 1990 Rinnaraw. In I. Bennett (ed.), *Excavations 1989*, 21–2. Bray.

Fanning, T. 1994 *Viking Age ringed pins from Dublin*. Medieval Dublin Excavations 1962–81, Ser. B, Vol. 4. Dublin.

Flanagan, D. 1980–1 Common elements in Irish place-names: *dún, ráth, lios*. *Bulletin of the Ulster Place-Name Society* **3** (second series), 16–29.

Foster, S.M. 1990 Pins, combs and the chronology of Later Atlantic Iron Age settlement. In I. Armit (ed.), *Beyond the brochs: changing perspectives on the Later Iron Age in Atlantic Scotland*, 143–74. Edinburgh.

Fowler, E. 1960 The origin and development of the penannular brooch in Europe. *Proceedings of the Prehistoric Society* **26**, 149–77.

Fowler, E. 1963 Celtic metalwork of the fifth and sixth centuries A.D. A reappraisal. *Archaeological Journal* **120**, 98–160.

Gibson, D.B. 1990 Tulach Commáin: A view of an Irish chiefdom. Unpublished Ph.D. dissertation, University of California, Los Angeles.

Gleeson, D.F. 1934 Discovery of gold gorget at Burren, Co. Clare. *Journal of the Royal Society of Antiquaries of Ireland* **64** (consecutive series), 138–9.

Grant, C. 1995 Mapping a Bronze Age Burren landscape. *Archaeology Ireland* **9** (1), 31–3.

Grogan, E. and Eogan, G. 1987 Lough Gur excavations by Seán P. Ó Ríordáin: further Neolithic and Beaker habitations on Knockadoon. *Proceedings of the Royal Irish Academy* **87C**, 299–506.

Hall, R.A. 1978 A Viking-Age grave at Donnybrook, Co. Dublin. *Medieval Archaeology* **22**, 64–83.

Hencken, H. O'N. 1935 A cairn at Poulawack, Co. Clare. *Journal of the Royal Society of Antiquaries of Ireland* **95**, 191–212.

Hencken, H. O'N. 1938 Cahercommaun, a stone fort in County Clare. *Journal of the Royal Society of Antiquaries of Ireland* **38** (extra volume), 1–82.

Hencken, H. O'N. 1942 Ballinderry Crannog no. 2. *Proceedings of the Royal Irish Academy* **47C**, 1–76.

Hencken, H. O'N. 1950 Lagore crannog: an Irish royal residence of the seventh to the tenth century A.D. *Proceedings of the Royal Irish Academy* **53C**, 1–248.

Hodkinson, B. 1987 A reappraisal of the archaeological evidence for weaving in Ireland in the Early Christian period. *Ulster Journal of Archaeology* **50**, 47–53.

Hogan, E. 1910 *Onomasticon Goedelicum locorum et tribuum Hiberniae et Scotiae. An index, with identifications, to the Gaelic names of places and tribes*. Dublin and London.

Hull, V. 1962–4 Varia Hibernica no. 5: Early Irish Segais. *Zeitschrift für celtische Philologie* **29**, 321–4.

Irish fiants = *The Irish fiants of the Tudor sovereigns during the reigns of Henry VIII, Edward VI, Philip & Mary, and Elizabeth I with a new introduction by Kenneth Nicholls and preface by Tomás G. Ó Canann* (4 vols) (Dublin 1994 (reprint)).

Jones, C. 1995 Parknabinnia. In I. Bennett (ed.), *Excavations 1994*, 5. Bray.

Jones, C. and Walsh, P. 1996 Recent discoveries on Roughaun Hill, County Clare. *Journal of the Royal Society of Antiquaries of Ireland* **126,** 86–107.

Kelly, E.P. 1974 Aughinish Island. In T. Delaney (ed.), *Excavations 1974*, 20–1. Belfast.

Kelly, E.P. 1987–8 Betaghstown Iron Age cemetery. In 'Excavations bulletin 1977–79: Summary account of archaeological excavations in Ireland'. *Journal of Irish Archaeology* **4**, 65–79.

Kelly, F. 1998 *Early Irish farming*. Dublin.

Kilbride-Jones, H. 1980 *Zoomorphic penannular brooches*. Society of Antiquaries Research Report 39. London.

Lacy, B. *et al.* 1983 *The Archaeological Survey of County Donegal*. Lifford.

Laing, L. 1975 *The archaeology of Late Celtic Britain and Ireland c. 400–1200 AD*. London.

Laing, L. 1993 *A catalogue of Celtic ornamental metalwork in the British Isles c. AD 400–1200*. British Archaeological Reports, British Series 229. Oxford.

Lynch, A. 1988 Poulnabrone, a stone in time. *Archaeology Ireland* **2** (3), 105–7.

Lynch, A. and Ó Donnabháin, B. 1994 Poulnabrone portal tomb. *The Other Clare* **18**, 5–7.

Lynn, C.J. 1978 Early Christian period domestic structures: a change from round to rectangular forms? *Irish Archaeological Research Forum* **5**, 29–45.

Lynn, C.J. 1981–2 The excavation of Rathmullan, a raised rath and motte in County Down. *Ulster Journal of Archaeology* **44–5**, 65–171.

Lynn, C.J. 1983 Some 'early' ring-forts and crannogs. *Journal of Irish Archaeology* **1**, 47–58.

Lynn, C.J. 1985 Excavation of a mound at Gransha, County Down, 1972 and 1982: an interim report. *Ulster Journal of Archaeology* **48**, 81–90.

Lynn, C.J. 1994 Houses in rural Ireland, A.D. 500–1000. *Ulster Journal of Archaeology* **57**, 81–94.

Mac Airt, S. 1951 *The Annals of Inisfallen*. Dublin.

(Reprinted 1977.)

Mac Airt, S. and Mac Niocaill, G. 1983 *The Annals of Ulster (to A.D. 1131)*. Dublin.

MacNamara, G.U. 1912 The O'Davorens of Cahermacnaughten, Burren, Co. Clare. *Journal of the North Munster Archaeological Society* **2** (2), 63–93.

Mandal, S. and Cooney, G. 1996 The Irish Stone Axe Project: a second petrological report. *Journal of Irish Archaeology* **7**, 41–64.

Manning, C. 1986 Archaeological excavation of a succession of enclosures at Millockstown, Co. Louth. *Proceedings of the Royal Irish Academy* **86C**, 135–81.

Meyer, K. 1901 The expulsion of the Dessi. *Y Cymmrodor* **14**, 101–35.

Meyer, K. 1919 *Bruchstüke der älteren Lyrik Irlands*. Berlin.

Moloney, A. *et al.* 1993 Excavations at Clonfinlough, Co. Offaly. *Irish Archaeological Wetland Unit Transactions* **2**. University College Dublin.

Monk, M. 1995 A tale of two ringforts: Lisleagh I and II. *Journal of the Cork Historical and Archaeological Society* **100**, 105–16.

Murphy, D. 1896 *The Annals of Clonmacnoise being the Annals of Ireland from the earliest period to A.D. 1408*. Dublin. (Reprinted 1993.)

Murphy, G. 1956 *Early Irish lyrics eighth to twelfth century*. Oxford.

O'Brien, E. 1992 A re-assessment of the 'great sepulchral mound' containing a Viking burial at Donnybrook, Dublin. *Medieval Archaeology* **36**, 170–3.

O'Brien, E. 1993 Contacts between Ireland and Anglo-Saxon England in the seventh century. *Anglo-Saxon Studies in Archaeology and History* **6**, 93–102.

O'Brien, M.A. 1962 *Corpus genealogiarum Hiberniae*, vol. 1. Dublin. (Reprinted 1976 with introduction by J.V. Kelleher.)

O'Brien, W. 1993 Aspects of wedge tomb chronology. In E. Shee Twohig and M. Ronayne (eds), *Past perceptions: the prehistoric archaeology of south-west Ireland*, 63–74. Cork.

Ó Buachalla, L. 1952 Contributions towards the political history of Munster, 450–800 A.D. *Journal of the Cork Historical and Archaeological Society* **57**, 67–86.

O'Carroll, F. (forthcoming) *Later prehistoric artefacts of the north Munster region*. Discovery Programme Monograph.

Ó Corráin, D. 1968 Studies in West Munster history: I. The regnal succession in Ciarraighe Luachra, 741–1165. *Journal of the Kerry Archaeological and Historical Society* **1**, 46–55.

Ó Corráin, D. 1969 Later Eóganacht pedigrees. *Journal of the Cork Historical and Archaeological Society* **74**, 141–6.

Ó Corráin, D. 1969–70 Raigne, Roigne, Mag Raigni. *Éigse* **13**, 81–4.

Ó Corráin, D. 1972 *Ireland before the Normans*. Dublin.

Ó Corráin, D. 1975 The families of Corcumroe. *North Munster Antiquarian Journal* **17**, 21–30.

Ó Corráin, D. 1987 Legend as critic. In T. Dunne (ed.), *The writer as witness: literature as historical evidence*, 23–38. Historical Studies 16. Cork.

Ó Corráin, D. 1997 Creating the past: the early Irish genealogical tradition. *Chronicon* **1**, 1–32.

Ó Corráin, D. and Maguire, F. 1981 *Gaelic personal names*. Dublin.

O Daly, M. 1975 *Cath Maige Mucrama*. Irish Texts Society 50. Dublin.

O'Donovan, J. 1848–51 *Annala Ríoghachta Éireann. Annals of the kingdom of Ireland by the Four Masters from the earliest period to the year 1616* (7 vols). Dublin. (Reprinted 1990.)

O'Drisceoil, D.A 1988 Burnt mounds: cooking or bathing? *Antiquity* **62**, 671–80.

O'Flaherty, B. 1985 Loher. In C. Cotter (ed.), *Excavations 1984*, 26–7. Dublin.

Ó Floinn, R. 1989 Secular metalwork in the eighth and ninth centuries. In S. Youngs (ed.), *'The Work of Angels': Masterpieces of Celtic metalwork, sixth to ninth centuries A.D.*, 72–91. London.

Ó Floinn, R. 1990 The Tipperary Brooch: a reprovenance. *Tipperary Historical Journal*, 187–92.

O'Keefe, J.G. 1931 *Dál Caladbuig* and the reciprocal services between the kings of Cashel and various Munster states. *Irish Texts* i, 19–21. Brussels.

O'Kelly, M.J. 1958 Church Island near Valencia, Co. Kerry. *Proceedings of the Royal Irish Academy* **54C**, 57–136.

O'Kelly, M.J. 1963 The excavations of two earthen ringforts at Garryduff, Co. Cork. *Proceedings of the Royal Irish Academy* **63C**, 17–125.

O'Meadhra, U. 1987 *Early Christian, Viking and Romanesque art: Motif-pieces from Ireland 2, a discussion*. Theses and Papers in North-European Archaeology 17. Stockholm.

Ó Muraíle, N. 1983 Notes on the history of Doire na bhFlann. In M. Ryan (ed.), *The Derrynaflan hoard I. A preliminary account*, 54–61. Dublin.

O'Rahilly, T.F. 1946 *Early Irish history and mythology*. Dublin. (Reprinted 1976: page references refer to reprint.)

Ó Ríordáin, B. and Rynne, E. 1961 A settlement in the sandhills at Dooey, Co. Donegal. *Journal of the*

Royal Society of Antiquaries of Ireland **91**, 58–64.

Ó Ríordáin, S.P. 1942 The excavation of a large earthen ringfort at Garranes, Co. Cork. *Proceedings of the Royal Irish Academy* **47C**, 77–150.

Ó Ríordáin, S.P. 1949 Lough Gur excavations: Carraig Aille and the 'Spectacles'. *Proceedings of the Royal Irish Academy* **52C**, 39–111.

Ó Ríordáin, S.P. 1954 Lough Gur excavations: Neolithic and Bronze Age houses on Knockadoon. *Proceedings of the Royal Irish Academy* **56C**, 297–459.

O'Riordain, S.P. and Foy, J.B. 1941 The excavations of Leacanabuaile fort, County Kerry. *Journal of the Cork Historical and Archaeological Society* **46**, 85–99.

O'Sullivan, A. 1983 *The Book of Leinster, formerly Lebar na Núachongbála*, vol vi. Dublin.

O'Sullivan, A. and Sheehan, J. 1996 *The Iveragh peninsula: an archaeological survey of south Kerry*. Cork.

Power, D. et al. 1992 *Archaeological Inventory of County Cork: volume 3. Mid Cork*. Dublin.

Raftery, B. 1972 Irish hillforts. In C. Thomas (ed.), *The Iron Age in the Irish Sea Province*, 37–58. London.

Raftery, B. 1984 *La Tène in Ireland: problems of origin and chronology*. Marburg.

Raftery, J. 1942 Knocknalappa crannog, Co. Clare. *North Munster Antiquarian Journal* **3**, 53–72.

Ryan, M. 1981 Poulawack, Co. Clare: the affinities of the central burial structure. In D. Ó Corráin (ed.), *Irish antiquity*, 134–46. Cork.

Simington, R.C. and Mac Giolla Choille, B. 1967 *Books of Survey and Distribution being abstracts of various surveys and instruments of title 1636–1703, vol iv. County of Clare*. Dublin.

Sproule, D. 1984 Origins of the Éoganachta. *Ériu* **35**, 31–7.

Stevenson, R.B.K. 1955 Pins and the chronology of brochs. *Proceedings of the Prehistoric Society* **21**, 282–94.

Stevenson, R.B.K. 1987 Brooches and pins: some seventh- to ninth-century problems. In M. Ryan (ed.), *Ireland and Insular Art A.D. 500–1200*, 90–5. Dublin.

Stokes, W. 1880 *On the calendar of Oengus*. Irish manuscript series, vol. i. Dublin. (*Transactions of the Royal Irish Academy*.)

Stokes, W. 1895–7 The Annals of Tigernach. *Revue Celtique* **16** (1895), 374–419; **17** (1896), 6–33, 119–263, 337–420; **18** (1897), 9–59, 150–97, 267–303, 374–91. (Reprinted 1993, Felinfach reprint, 2 vols, Llanerch Publishers.)

Stokes, W. 1905 *Félire Óengusso Céli Dé. The martyrology of Oengus the Culdee*. London. (Reprinted Dublin 1984.)

Van Hamel, A.G. 1941 *Immrama*. Mediaeval and Modern Irish Series, vol. X. Dublin.

Waddell, J. 1991 The first people, the prehistoric Burren. In J.W. O'Connell and A. Korff (eds), *The book of the Burren*, 59–77. Galway.

Walsh, P. (ed.) 1948 *The life of Aodh Ruadh Ó Domhnaill* (2 vols). Dublin.

Warner, R.B. 1979 The Clogher Yellow Layer. *Medieval Ceramics* **3**, 37–40.

Warner, R.B. 1986a The date of the start of Lagore. *Journal of Irish Archaeology* **3**, 75–7.

Warner, R.B. 1986b Comments on Ulster and Oriel souterrains. *Ulster Journal of Archaeology* **49**, 111–12.

Warner, R. 1988 The archaeology of Early Historic Irish kingship. In S.T. Driscoll and M.R. Nieke (eds), *Power and politics in early medieval Britain and Ireland*, 47–68. Edinburgh.

Westropp, T.J. 1896–7 Prehistoric stone forts of northern Clare. *Journal of the Royal Society of Antiquaries of Ireland* **26**, 142–57.

Westropp, T.J. 1900–2 The cahers of County Clare: their names, features and bibliography. *Proceedings of the Royal Irish Academy* **22**, 415–99.

Westropp, T.J. 1901 Prehistoric remains of north-western Clare. *Journal of the Royal Society of Antiquaries of Ireland* **31**, 273–92.

Westropp, T.J. 1902 The ancient forts of Ireland. *Transactions of the Royal Irish Academy* **31**, 579–730.

Westropp, T.J. 1912 The promontory forts and early remains of the coast of County Mayo. *Journal of the Royal Society of Antiquaries of Ireland* **42**, 185–216.

Westropp, T.J. 1913 Prehistoric remains (forts and dolmens) in the Corofin district, Co. Clare. *Journal of the Royal Society of Antiquaries of Ireland* **43**, 232–60.

White, R.H. 1988 *Roman and Celtic objects from Anglo-Saxon graves. A catalogue and an interpretation of their use*. British Archaeological Reports, British Series 191. Oxford.

Williams, B. 1985 Excavation of a rath at Coolcran, Co. Fermanagh. *Ulster Journal of Archaeology* **48**, 69–80.

Woodman, P.C. 1977 Recent excavations at Newferry, Co. Antrim. *Proceedings of the Prehistoric Society* **43**, 155–200.

Youngs, S. (ed.) 1989 *'The Work of Angels': Masterpieces of Celtic metalwork, sixth to ninth centuries A.D.* London.

Youngs, S. 1997 Recent finds of Insular enameled buckles. In C.E. Karkov, R.T. Farrell and M. Ryan (eds), *The insular tradition*, 189–209. Albany.

4. THE BALLYHOURA HILLS PROJECT
Martin Doody

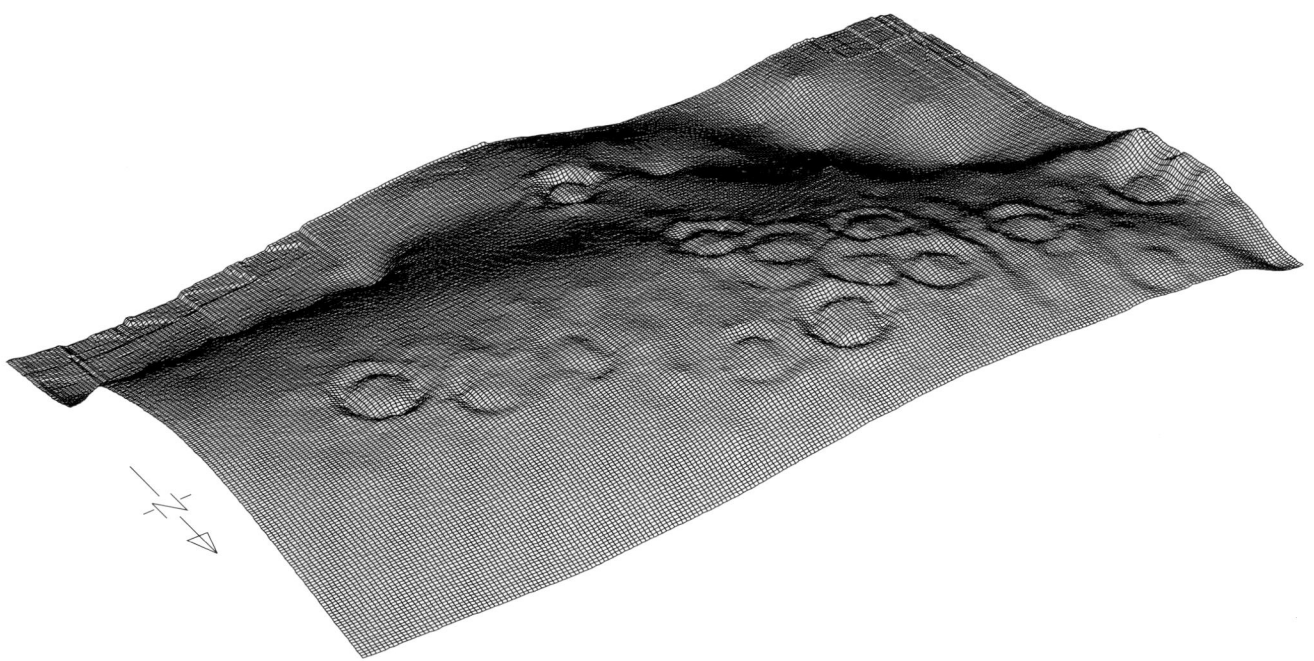

Fig. 1—*Digital Terrain Model—Elton barrow cemetery.*

Introduction

The Ballyhoura Hills Project was established in 1992 to investigate the value of recent archaeological surveys—namely the Cork, Limerick and Tipperary archaeological surveys and the Bruff aerial photographic survey—for identifying hitherto unrecognised sites of potential Bronze Age/Iron Age date.

The project has adopted an interdisciplinary approach, involving geophysical and topographical survey combined with aerial photography and excavation of selected sites. The study has concentrated on a wide variety of site types, including linear earthworks, large-scale crop-mark sites, hillforts and hitherto unrecorded rectangular or subrectangular enclosures, many of which were associated with barrows, mostly in the area to the north of the Ballyhoura Hills. Based on the results of the various investigations, excavations have taken place at the crop-mark enclosures at Conva near Ballyhooly in County Cork (Doody 1995), which were Early Historic in date; at the linear earthwork, the Claidh Dubh, at Ballydague, Co. Cork, which produced a date in the first century AD (*ibid.*); and at the complex of sites at Chancellorsland near Emly, Co. Tipperary (Doody 1993; 1995; 1996).

The most recent work has concentrated on the Chancellorsland complex itself, a number of Chancellorsland-type sites, the Elton barrow cemetery, and the hillforts at Caherdrinny and Carn Tigherna.

Survey

Chancellorsland

The topographic survey was broadened at the Chancellorsland complex to include three further sites (F, G and H). These were initially identified through examination of the medium-altitude aerial photographs and the geophysical survey. The new sites extend the complex of monuments at Chancellorsland to the north and east, and bring the number of enclosures in the immediate area to six and the number of barrows to eight.

Site H was recorded *c.* 120m to the north of Site D as a rectangular enclosure measuring 30.5m east–west by *c.* 25m north–south. Site F was located *c.* 130m east of Site D and appears as a circular enclosure on the 1986 1:10,000 aerial photographs. It did not, however, register on the topographic survey, and the geophysical survey shows the site as a rectangular arrangement of pits measuring 30m north–south by 30m east–west. Site G was recorded

c. 140m to the north of F; it registers on the geophysical survey as a subrectangular enclosure measuring approximately 55m east–west by 50m north–south, and was of comparable dimensions to Site A. As was the case with Site F, there were no surface indications of the enclosure.

Chancellorsland-type sites

A number of sites broadly similar to Chancellorsland Site A, i.e. ditched subcircular or subrectangular enclosures, some of which were associated with barrows and which do not readily fall into recognised archaeological site types, were recognised during the Bruff aerial photographic survey. Fifteen sites were visited and detailed topographic surveys were undertaken at five—Loughanstown, Garrynacahera and Ballingarde in County Limerick, and Moanmore and Lattin in County Tipperary. Geophysical survey was undertaken at Lattin. Although no dating evidence is available for any of the sites, they were sufficiently similar in both size and form to Chancellorsland Site A to suggest a possible Bronze Age date.

Elton barrow cemetery

This small barrow cemetery is located close to the village of Elton in County Limerick. Although impressive from the air, the site is not very obvious on the ground. However, a geophysical survey indicated the presence of at least 22 ring-barrows. Twelve of these were contained within a subrectangular enclosure which appears either to cut through or to be cut by a further two examples. A notable feature of the cemetery is the obvious grouping and successive construction of barrows in confined areas of the site.

The topographic survey highlighted sixteen of the barrows and was especially useful in recognising the construction sequence of the overlapping barrows (Fig. 1).

Hillforts

Three hillforts are included in the Ballyhoura Hills study area. These are at Castle Gale on the summit of Carrig Henry, Co. Limerick (Doody *et al.* 1995), Carn Tigherna on the Nagles Mountains and Caherdrinny on the Kilworth Hills, both in County Cork. All three have been surveyed in detail, and the results of the Carn Tigherna survey are presented below.

The prominent position of the three hillforts affords them extensive views over a wide hinterland. The sites are intervisible and overlook the river valleys of the Blackwater, Funshion and Awbeg, and a large area of the Limerick/Tipperary plains to the north. They are obviously strategically positioned and are likely to have had a distinct territorial significance. The possibility of identifying relationships between the hillforts and other sites in the general area is currently being explored through the Discovery Programme's GIS system. Their location relative to the Claidh Dubh linear earthwork may be significant. The Claidh Dubh effectively cuts off the valley floor between the Nagles Mountains and the Ballyhoura Hills in a north–south direction, while the three hillforts command extensive views over this area from the adjoining uplands. Excavation of a portion of the linear earthwork in the Nagles Mountains suggested a construction date some time prior to AD 100; however, without excavation of the hillforts, any possible chronological association between any or all of these must remain speculative.

A concentration of both prehistoric and later sites was noted in and around the western foothills of the Kilworth Hills, i.e. around Caherdrinny hillfort. For example, there is a concentration of *fulachta fiadh*, although this may be more likely to reflect geographical considerations such as land use and land type in the area rather than actual settlement preference. Similarly, a concentration of Bronze Age burials occurs in an area overlooked by Caherdrinny to the north-east and by Carn Tigherna to the south-east, factors which may point to significant Bronze Age populations in these areas.

Excavation

Chancellorsland Site A

Excavations at the Bronze Age enclosure, Site A, came to a close with a fifth season in 1996. The work in the final seasons concentrated on the structural remains from the interior and the complex stratigraphy of the enclosing ditches.

With approximately one third of the interior excavated, the remains of eighteen structures, or parts of structures, and two palisades have been identified. These consisted of houses and fence-lines and represent successive phases of construction within the enclosure. All of the structures were timber-built and a variety of sizes and ground-plans were found.

Structure 12 was the largest and by far the best preserved of the excavated structures (Pl. 1). It was roughly D-shaped in plan, measuring 6.6m north–south and 5.4m east–west. The northern end was rounded while the southern façade was slightly convex. The entrance was centrally positioned on the

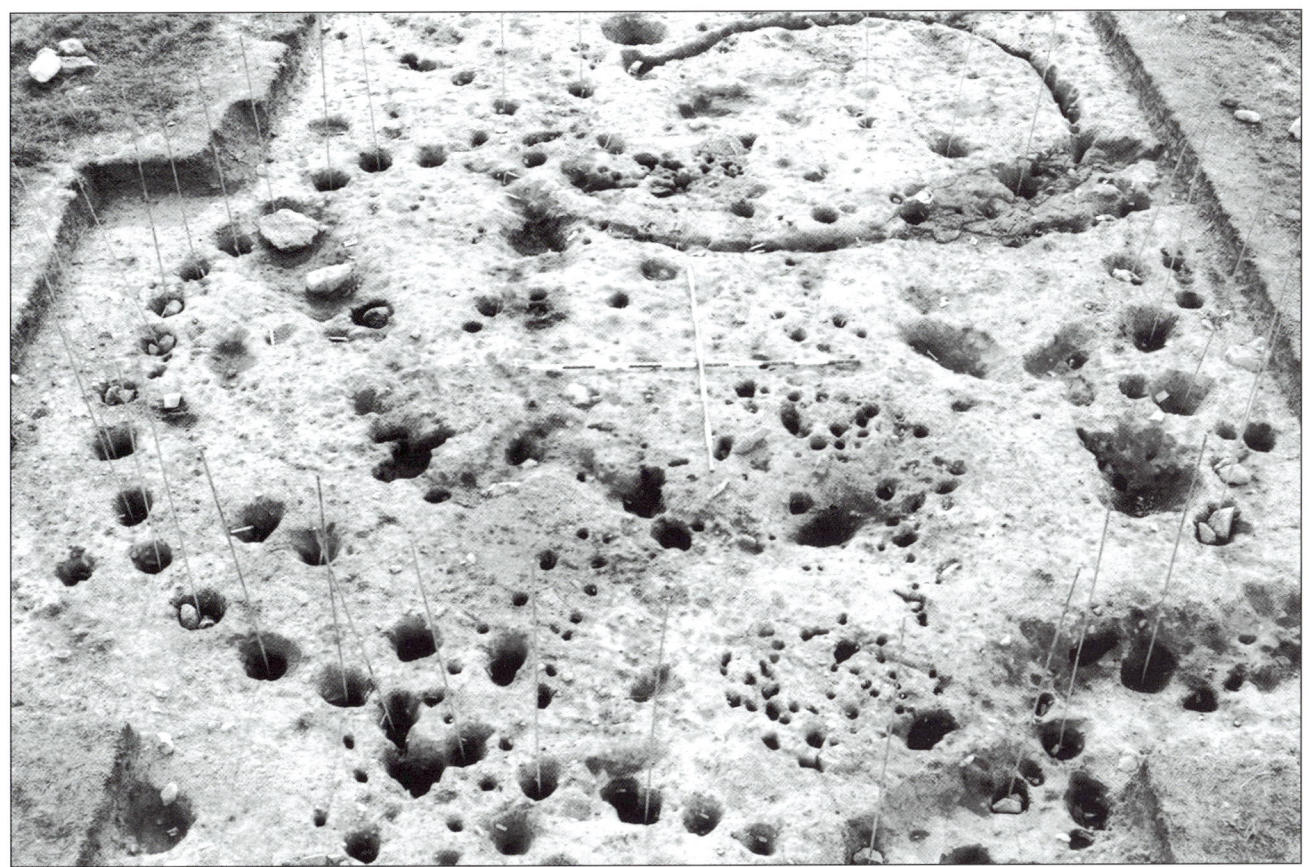

Pl. 1—Chancellorsland Site A—Structure 12 after excavation.

Pl. 2—Chancellorsland Site C—Trench 1, Barrow 4 in background.

southern side. The building was constructed of 44 sturdy timber uprights, set as closely as 0.3m apart. An accelerator date of 3160 ± 40 BP, 1519–1328 BC (GRA-5293), was returned from charcoal from one of the perimeter stakes.

The final season of excavation also focused on the relative chronology of the surrounding ditches. It is now clear that while the site is enclosed by a double ditch, there was never more than one of these open at any given time. Three successive phases of ditch-digging were identified, supporting evidence from the interior of a considerable period of use of the enclosure.

Finds included coarseware pottery, worked flint and chert, bone, stone and amber. Very little metal was found. The waterlogged conditions which prevailed, especially in the inner ditch, favoured the preservation of organic material, and specialist studies are well advanced on many of these, including animal and plant remains, wood, insects and coprolites.

Site C

Excavations were carried out at Site C in 1992 and 1994, and concluded with a nine-week season in 1996. As was the case with Site A, the enclosure here was located on a natural rise where the bedrock is close to the surface. The site, 35m in diameter, is enclosed by a ditch 2.9m wide and 0.55m deep. Several outlying earthworks were recorded on the northern side, including a ring-barrow and a penannular ditch. The stratigraphy of the site is complex and several phases of activity have been identified. The 1994 excavations, for example, confirmed that the ring-barrow post-dated the infilling of the Site C ditch (Doody 1996).

Within the enclosure at least five structures were uncovered, representing successive phases of building. All of these post-dated an earlier phase of activity, when a small ring-barrow was constructed (Pl. 2).

The small number of artefacts and the equally small amount of domestic refuse from Site C suggest short-term, periodic occupation of the enclosure. The radiocarbon dates from the enclosure and outlying earthworks indicate use of the site in the Middle Bronze Age, through the late Iron Age, the Early Christian period and beyond. The earliest stratum, comprising burnt spreads and stake-holes, is broadly contemporary with the use of Site A and has produced a date of 3340 ± 40 BP, 1686–1542 BC (GRA-5294), while an Iron Age date of 1730 ± 80 BP, AD 220–406 (GRA-4230), has been obtained from a ditch associated with the enclosure.

References

Doody, M. 1993 The Ballyhoura Hills Project. *Discovery Programme Reports* **1**, 20–30.

Doody, M. 1995 The Ballyhoura Hills Project. *Discovery Programme Reports* **2**, 12–44.

Doody, M. 1996 The Ballyhoura Hills Project. *Discovery Programme Reports* **4**, 15–25.

Doody, M., Synnott, P., Tobin, R. and Masterson, B. 1995 Topographic survey of the inland promontory fort at Castle Gale, Carrig Henry, Co. Limerick. *Discovery Programme Reports* **2**, 39–44.

A SURVEY OF CARN TIGHERNA HILLFORT, CO. CORK

Barry Masterson

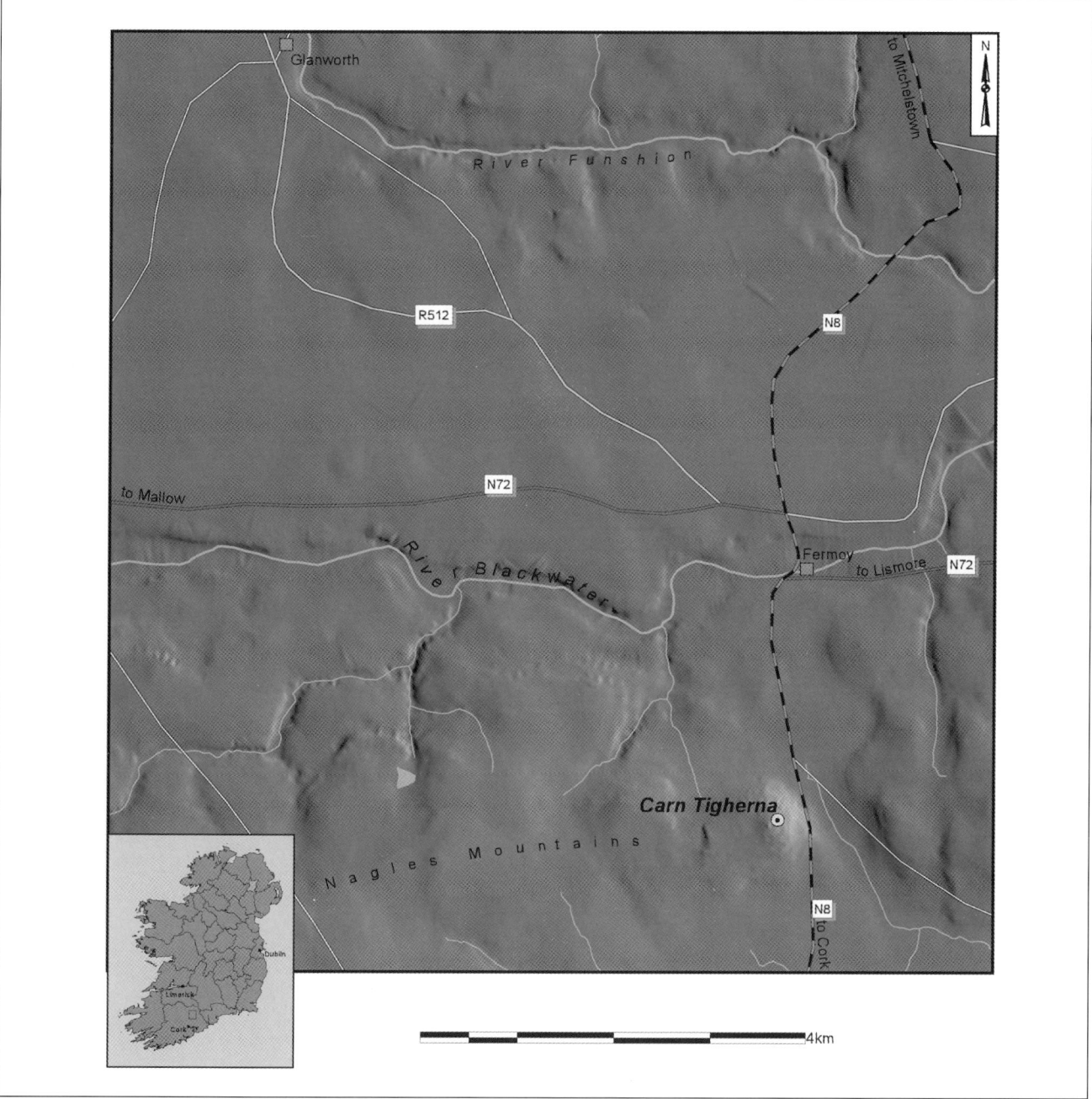

Fig. 1—Location map.

The hillfort of Carn Tigherna (CO35-49-01, NGR 180611, 95895) encloses the summit of Corrin Hill towards the eastern end of the Nagles Mountains, Co. Cork. The hillfort lies between the townlands of Coolcarron to the north and Corrin to the south in the baronies of Condon and Clangibbons, and Barrymore respectively. The summit of the hill rises 180m above the Blackwater River valley, which lies to the north. Westwards, the Nagles continue for 25km to the Boggeragh range, while the eastern slope falls steeply into a 500m-wide pass, connecting the Blackwater and Bride valleys—one of the few passes through the Nagles range (Fig. 1). The local geology is of old red sandstone with quartzite banding. The summit of Corrin Hill commands extensive views in all directions, providing an excellent strategic location for monitoring movement in and out of the Blackwater valley from all sides. The distinctive shape of the hill forms a landmark that is easily recognisable for miles around, also greatly enhancing the visual

Pl. 1—Aerial view of Carn Tigherna (Cork Archaeological Survey).

Pl. 2—Look-out post built into the top of the cairn during World War II (Barry Masterson).

impact the hillfort would have had on the surrounding area.

The forestry plantations surrounding it make the hillfort difficult to see from the surrounding countryside. However, three monuments are still visible on the summit (Pl. 1). The most conspicuous is the 10m-high cross erected in 1933 to commemorate the nineteenth centenary of the death of Jesus Christ. The cross itself is constructed of the local sandstone and was most probably built from material taken from the adjacent stone cairn (CO35-49-02). At present the cairn measures 40m east–west by 26m north–south, standing close to 4m high. Its mass has been much reduced owing to repeated disturbances: stones were removed for the construction of the barony boundaries and the cross, while antiquarian interest in the 1830s resulted in an amateur excavation. In the following century the cairn was further disturbed by the construction of a look-out post, or bunker, which was built into the cairn itself during World War II. This third monument survives as a rectangular structure with stone and mortar walling visible in the body of the cairn (Pl. 2).

The opening of the cairn in the 1830s led to the discovery of a double-compartmented cist burial containing pottery vessels. Gogan (1929) refers to two detailed accounts of the opening of the cairn which differ slightly in detail. An account in Windele's *Topography of Desmond* describes how a double-compartmented cist burial (CO35-49-03) with a capping stone was found after the removal of several hundred tons of stone. One chamber contained fragments of a food vessel bowl, while the other held a well-preserved food vessel vase, containing a quantity of ashes. Another account, given by Lewis in his *Topographical dictionary*, states that when the capping stone was removed two vessels were found, one of which was smashed by the workers to ascertain whether it contained money. Both accounts agree that two vessels were found, one of which survived intact. Gogan discusses the pottery vessels in detail, but their current location is unknown.

The survey

The primary objective of the survey was to record the extent and nature of the hillfort. To date, the only other plan of the fort was an outline plan taken from aerial photography (Raftery 1994, 40, fig. 23). Most of the antiquarian literature relating to Carn Tigherna refers to the burial cairn and the amateur excavations in the last century, without discussing the hillfort itself.

The limit of the survey was the area of clear-fell around the summit, which included the entire area of the hillfort and a clearance of approximately 10–15m beyond the ramparts. The hillfort was under tree cover until 1986, when the monument was acquired by the State and the trees were felled. Since this time, vegetation growth within the area of clear-fell has been in the form of gorse, heather and close-set brambles, making survey work slow and sightings difficult. Small, isolated areas within the survey limits remained unsurveyed owing to the density of the vegetation, which prevented access. Limited clearance was carried out in areas of particular archaeological interest, most notably in the north-west quadrant. At the time of the survey, the forestry plantation encroached on all sides, with the monument just clear, making it impractical to extend the survey further downslope to record a broader topographical context.

The topographic survey was carried out over an eight-week period beginning in early March 1995. Eleven survey control stations were established at strategic locations, providing maximum site coverage. A total station, equipped with a data-logger, was employed to electronically measure and record points on the landscape. Using a selective sampling technique, sample points were chosen at significant changes in terrain form to accurately define the morphology of the site. The sampling density was increased in areas of obvious archaeological interest to ensure that the finer details were accurately represented. In addition to these spot-heights, linework was also recorded on appropriate features, such as walls and ramparts, to define their extent in plan. On average, the distance between sample points varied between 2m and 5m. This interval was also applied to areas where there were no evident archaeological remains to ensure that any previously unnoticed features would be picked up and highlighted through data-processing. Over 6200 points were recorded, which were subsequently downloaded onto a personal computer for processing. The techniques used allowed for the production of results in a variety of formats, including linework plans, contour plans and three-dimensional visualisation through Digital Terrain Models (DTMs) and hill-shaded models (Masterson, this volume).

Survey results

Summary

The results of the survey provide a detailed

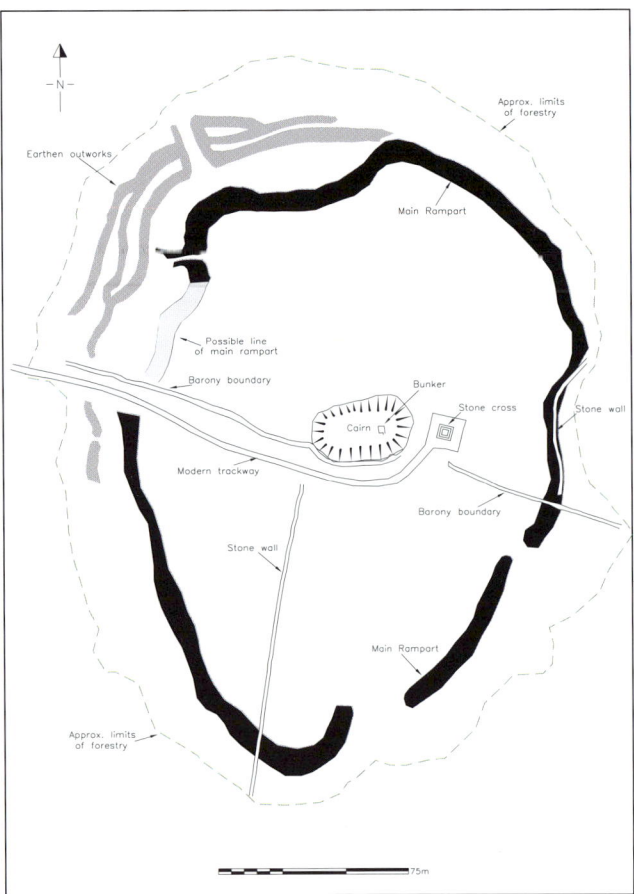

Fig. 2—Outline plan with main features indicated.

Pl. 3—The dumped stone construction of the rampart as exposed on the south-west side of the hillfort (Red Tobin).

representation of the morphology and extent of the hillfort (Fig. 2). In general, the enclosing element consists of a single rampart of dumped stone construction, placing it in Raftery's class I (Raftery 1994, 41). The hillfort measures 250m north–south by 180m east–west, with the primary rampart enclosing an area of 2.92ha (7.2 acres). The total area is 3.39ha (8.4 acres) if the additional area enclosed by the external earthworks on the north-west is included in the calculation. In plan the fort is an irregular oval, narrowing slightly at the south. The north-west quadrant shows evidence of an additional two, and in places three, earthen banks separated by fosses, possibly indicating a greater need for defences/fortification on this, the most accessible side.

Main rampart/primary rampart

The primary rampart of Carn Tigherna is of dumped stone construction (Pl. 3). While it generally follows the contours of the hill, its positioning seems to have been determined by the line of a natural scarp, with the steepest sections at the north, east and south (Figs 3 and 4). This design increases the effective height of the outer face of the rampart, augmenting its defensive nature (Fig. 5). In places the external face rises 4.5m above the surrounding terrain. The interior height averages between 0.4m and 1m. The average base width of the main rampart is approximately 9m. In places the external face has a stepped profile, which is most obvious in the south-east and in the western

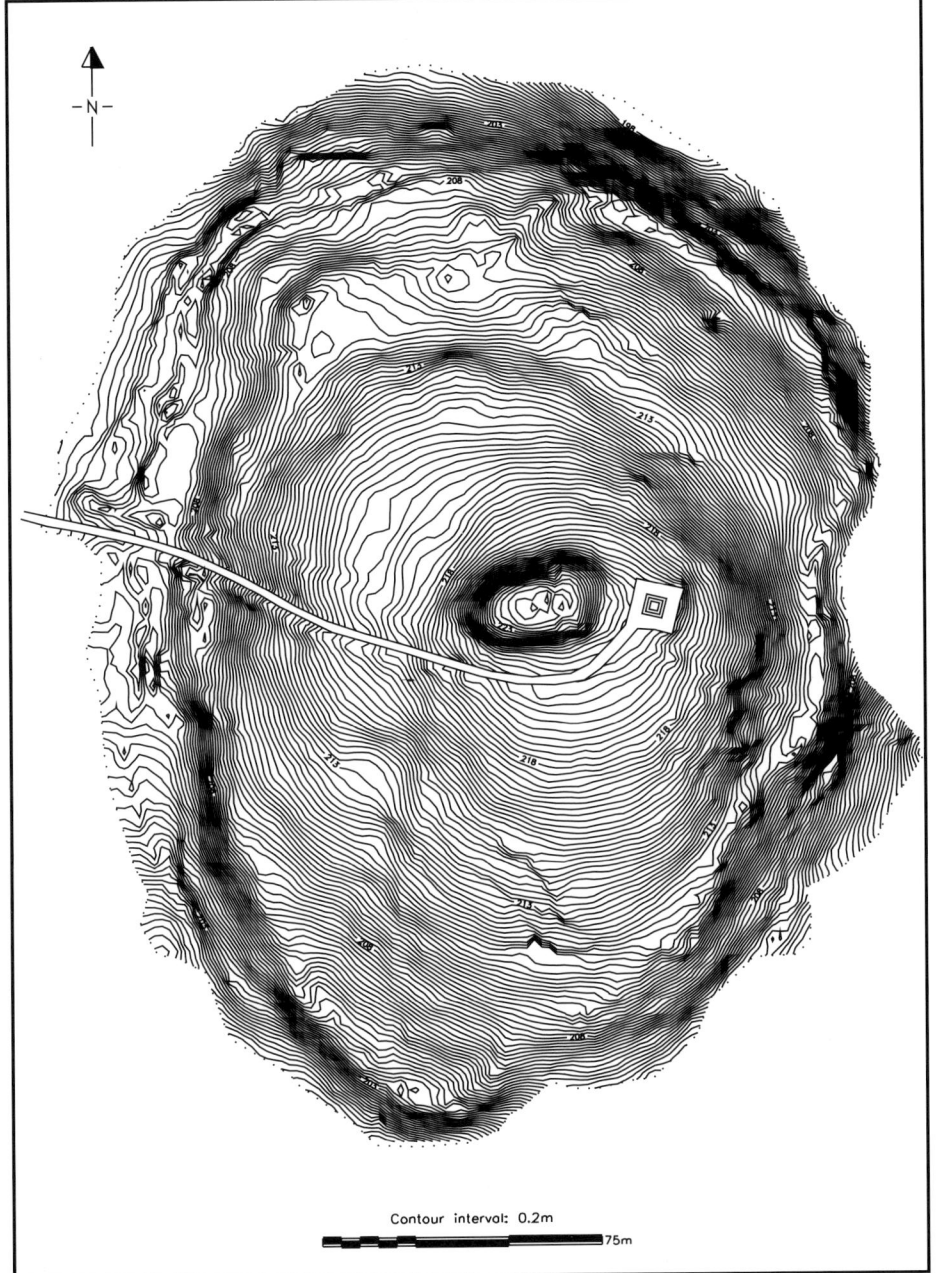

Fig. 3—Contour plan demonstrating height variations.

section. In addition, those areas where the stones of the rampart are exposed (most of the southern half of the site) show evidence of some structural lines within the stonework, suggestive of facing or internal structural features (Pl. 4).

Entranceways

An entranceway passing through the main rampart was located at the north-west of the site (Pl. 5). This sunken passage is 2m wide and extends westwards, outside the main rampart, for *c.* 5m. It is flanked on both sides by low banks. Without excavation, it is unclear whether it is contemporary with the construction of the main rampart or is a later modification.

Other breaks in the rampart

Apart from the north-west entrance there are three other breaks in the line of the main rampart. The largest of these lies north of the modern forestry track and is approximately 40m in length. It is most likely due to modern disturbance. A line of loosely spaced large boulders suggests that the rampart may have continued along the scarp that exists in this location. This is also supported by the hill-shaded model, in which a faint bank can be seen connecting the terminals of the rampart (Fig. 4).

A second break, 18m wide, was recorded at the southern end of the site, at a point overlooking a steep slope on the hillside. There is no visible evidence of rampart remains within this gap, suggesting that it

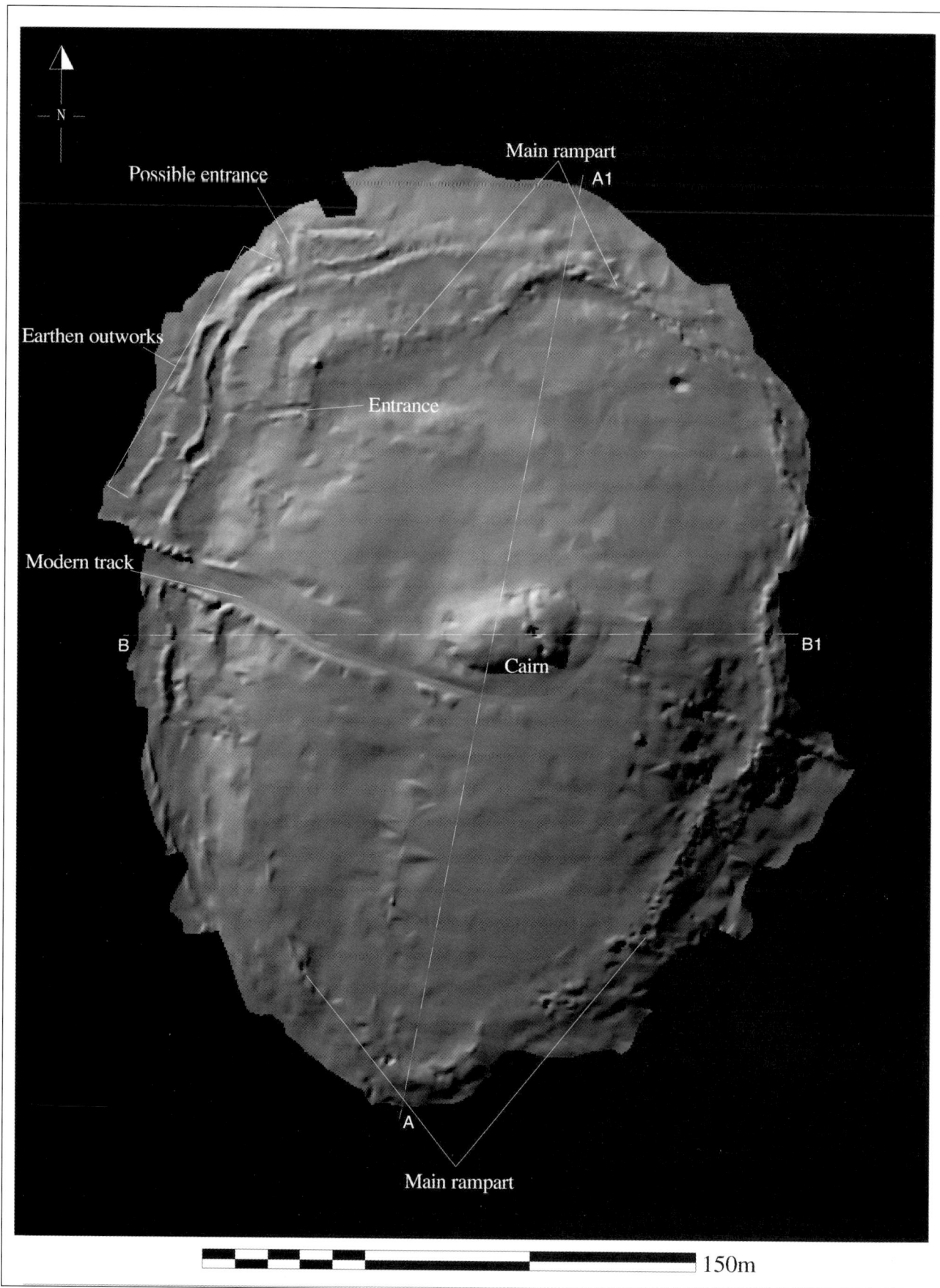

Fig. 4—Hill-shaded plan highlighting structural features.

The Ballyhoura Hills Project

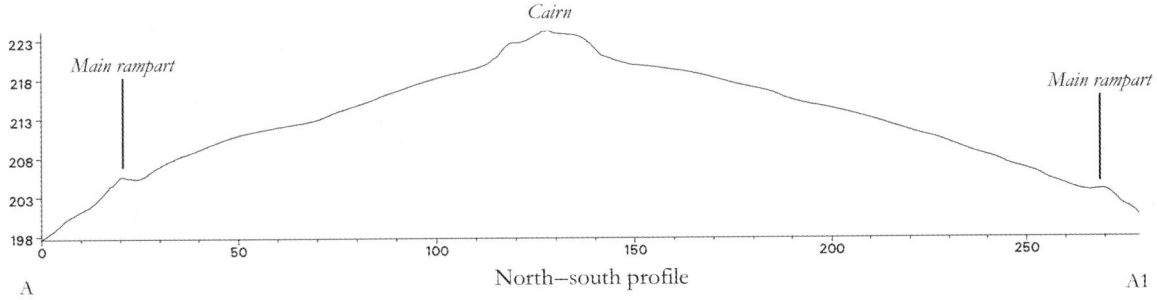

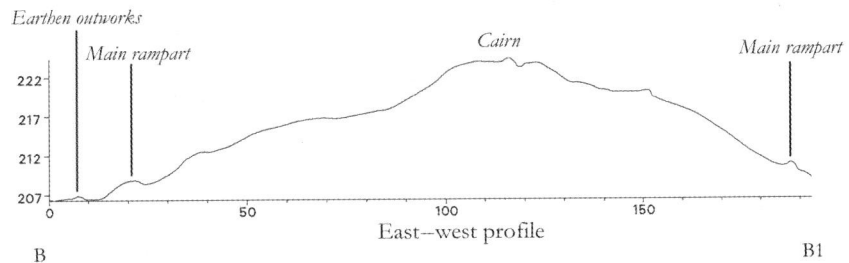

Fig. 5—Profiles through the hill.

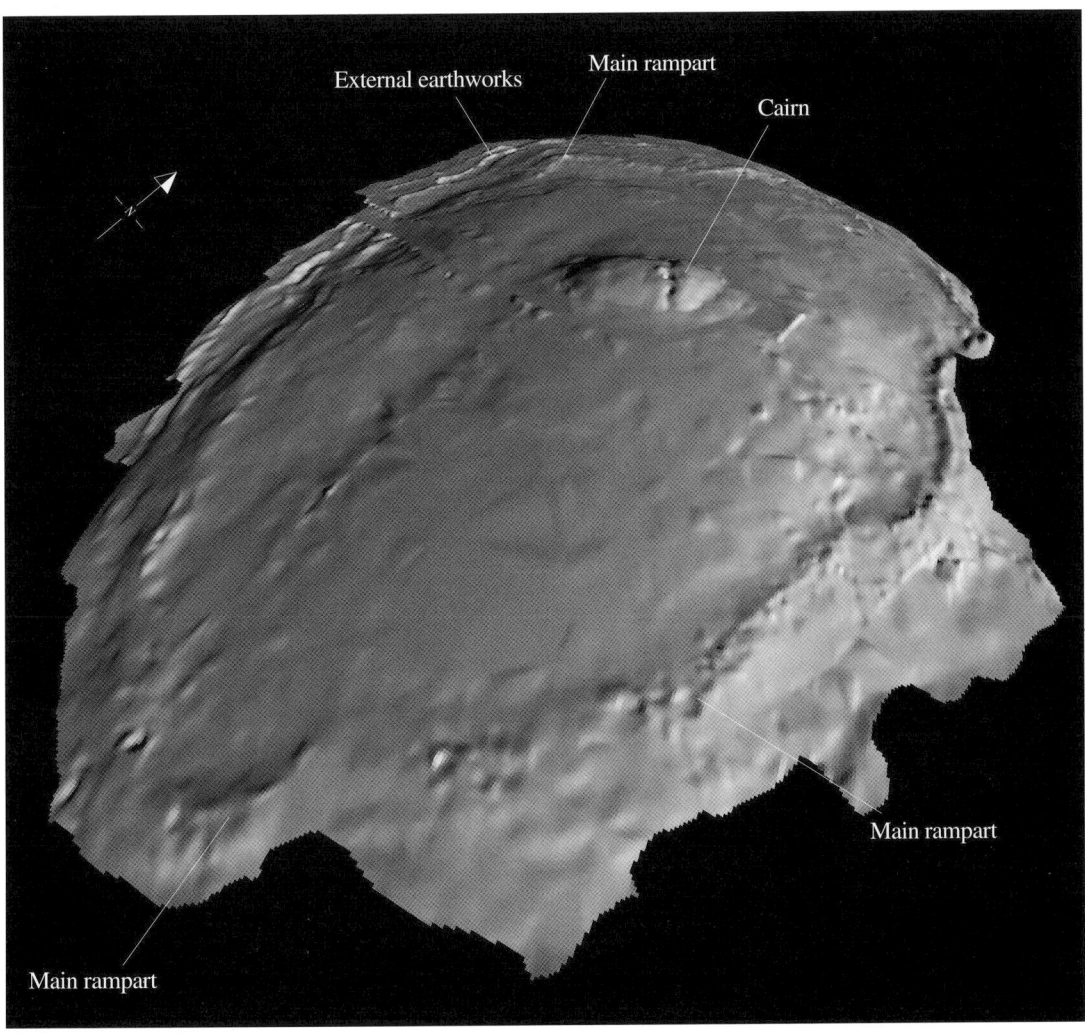

Fig. 6—3-D view of hill-shaded model viewed from the south-east.

Pl. 4—Structural lines visible within the fabric of the dumped stone construction of the main rampart (Barry Masterson).

may be original. The section of rampart to the immediate west of this gap shows a marked inward curving (Fig. 6). This spur is made up of loosely spaced large boulders which appear to be set and which differ from the dumped stone construction of the rest of the rampart. The function of the inward curving and the wide break is unclear. The very width of the break appears to preclude its use as an effective entrance, as would its position overlooking a steep point on the hillside.

A third break in the dumped stone construction of the rampart, 8m wide, lies 17m south of the barony boundary on the eastern slope. The two opposing sections of rampart are slightly offset, with the northern terminal slightly downslope from the southern terminal. The northern terminal is flanked by a standing stone (0.8m x 0.5m x 0.2m) which seems to suggest an entranceway. At present, the gap is closed by a band of closely set boulders, 2.5m wide, which form a wall of sorts and may well represent a blocking of an original entranceway.

Outworks in the north-west quadrant

The north-west quadrant presents a more complex picture of the fortifications. The earthen outworks consist of between two and three banks separated by fosses (Fig. 7). The innermost element, *c.* 3m wide, has a maximum internal height of *c.* 0.25m and an

Pl. 5—The entranceway through the main rampart viewed from the exterior, looking east (Barry Masterson).

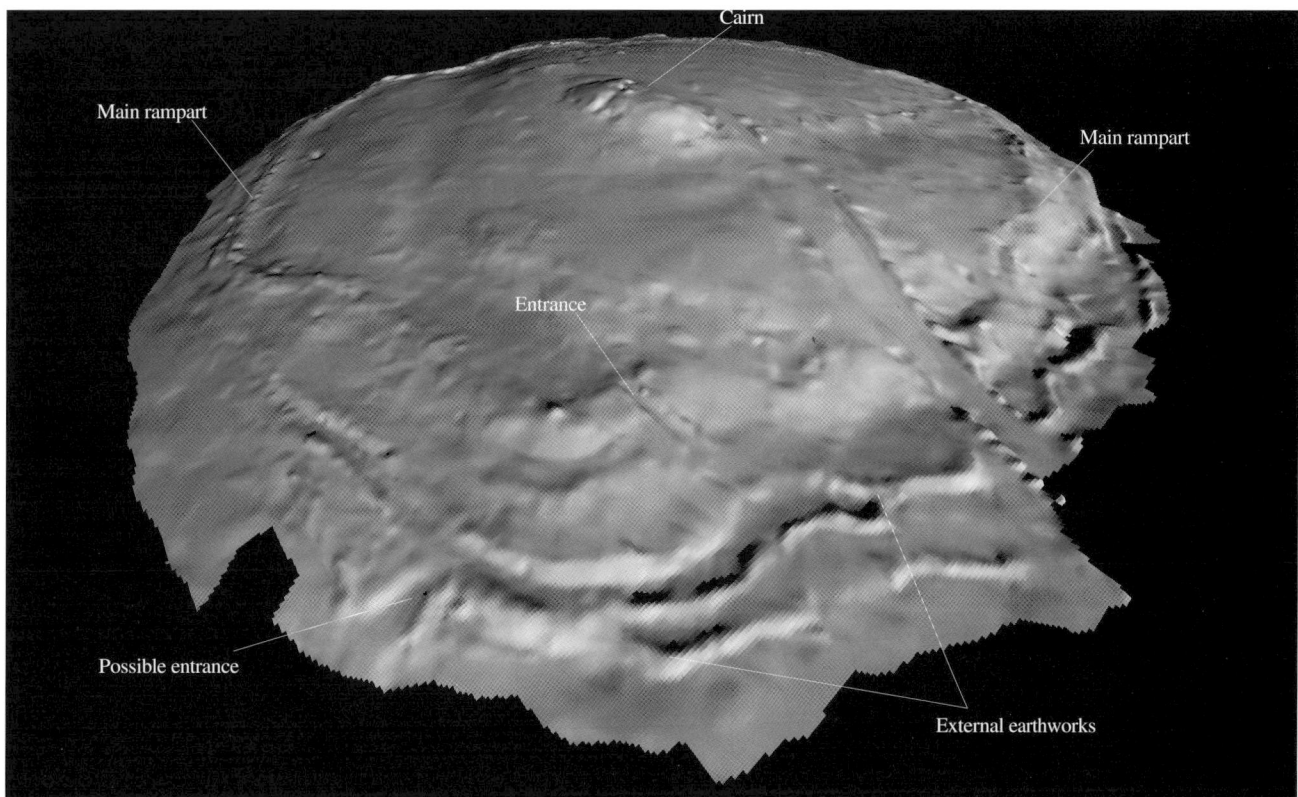

Fig. 7—3-D view of the north-west quadrant.

external height ranging between 0.75m and 2m. It appears that material was scarped out from the slope to form a fosse, with some being used to form the external bank, and some raising the profile of the inner scarp. In places there are two external banks, c. 3–5m wide, with an internal height of 0.3–1.2m and an external height of up to 2m. Sections C–E (Fig. 8) show how the outworks relate to the main rampart, and how the general morphology changes along its course.

An entrance feature through the outworks was recorded in the northern section of this quadrant, consisting of two banks, c. 0.2m high, cutting perpendicularly across the outworks and flanking a passage 5m wide. These parallel banks extend c. 10m outside the enclosing elements but do not appear to continue inside the banks. This entrance is offset approximately 35m north of the entrance through the main rampart. In the absence of excavation evidence it remains unclear whether these outworks represent an original elaborate entranceway or modification of the defences over several periods, although the character of the outworks may indicate that they are a later construct. In either case, the addition of these outworks on this, the most accessible side of the site may indicate a desire to increase the actual or apparent defensibility of the site.

Internal features

The survey of the interior was carried out using gridding techniques in order to highlight any features that were not readily apparent. Evidence from the aerial photograph taken soon after the clearance of the hilltop suggested the possible locations of two enclosures inside the bounds of the hillfort (Pl. 1), a large example to the north-west and a smaller one on the west, just north of the trackway. The topographic survey did not reveal any features that could be identified as either enclosure. It is likely that the photographic evidence is an illusion based on patterns in the vegetation caused by the clearance of the hilltop and the lines of the actual ramparts.

Conclusions

The detailed survey of Carn Tigherna has revealed previously unrecorded features, most notably the external outworks in the north-west quadrant. It has emphasised the complex nature of the defences and the fact that the entrance through the outworks is on a different line to that of the entrance through the main rampart, thereby creating a complex entranceway. This illustrates the possible militaristic nature of the hillfort. The differing characters of the

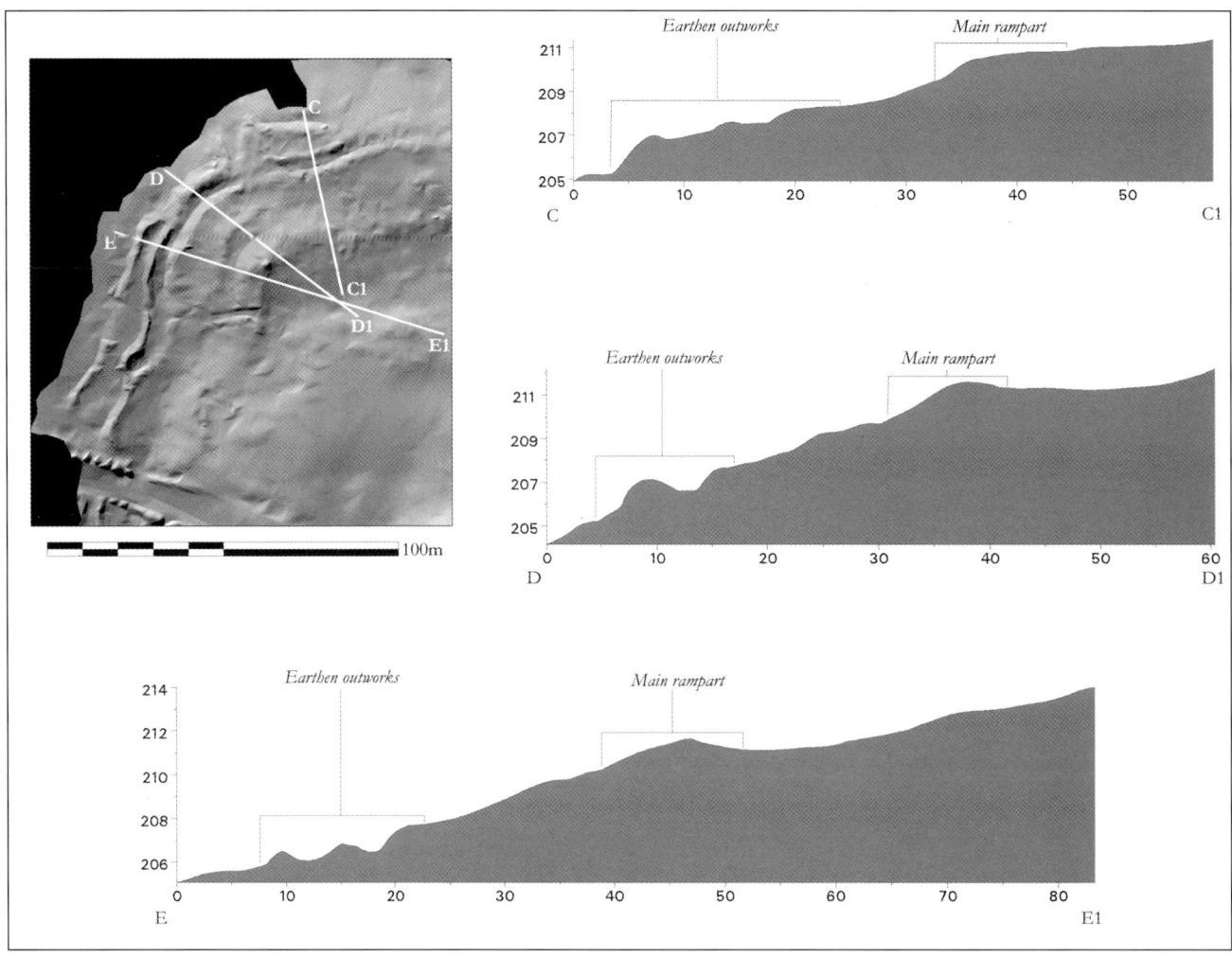

Fig. 8—Profiles through outworks and north-west quadrant.

inner and outer ramparts may indicate an extended use of the site, with refurbishment and elaboration of the enclosing elements over time.

Acknowledgements

The author would like to thank Paul Synnott for his assistance during the execution of the survey and especially Red Tobin for his work on this and other hillfort surveys for the Ballyhoura Hills Project. The Discovery Programme gratefully acknowledges the cooperation of Mr John Greehy of Coillte.

References

Gogan, L.S. 1929 Carn Tighearnaigh Mhic Dheaghaidh. *Journal of the Cork Historical and Archaeological Society* **34,** Part 2, 56–70.

Raftery, B. 1994 *Pagan Celtic Ireland*. London.

5. KNOCKNALAPPA, CO. CLARE: A REAPPRAISAL

Eoin Grogan, Aidan O'Sullivan, Finola O'Carroll and Ines Hagen

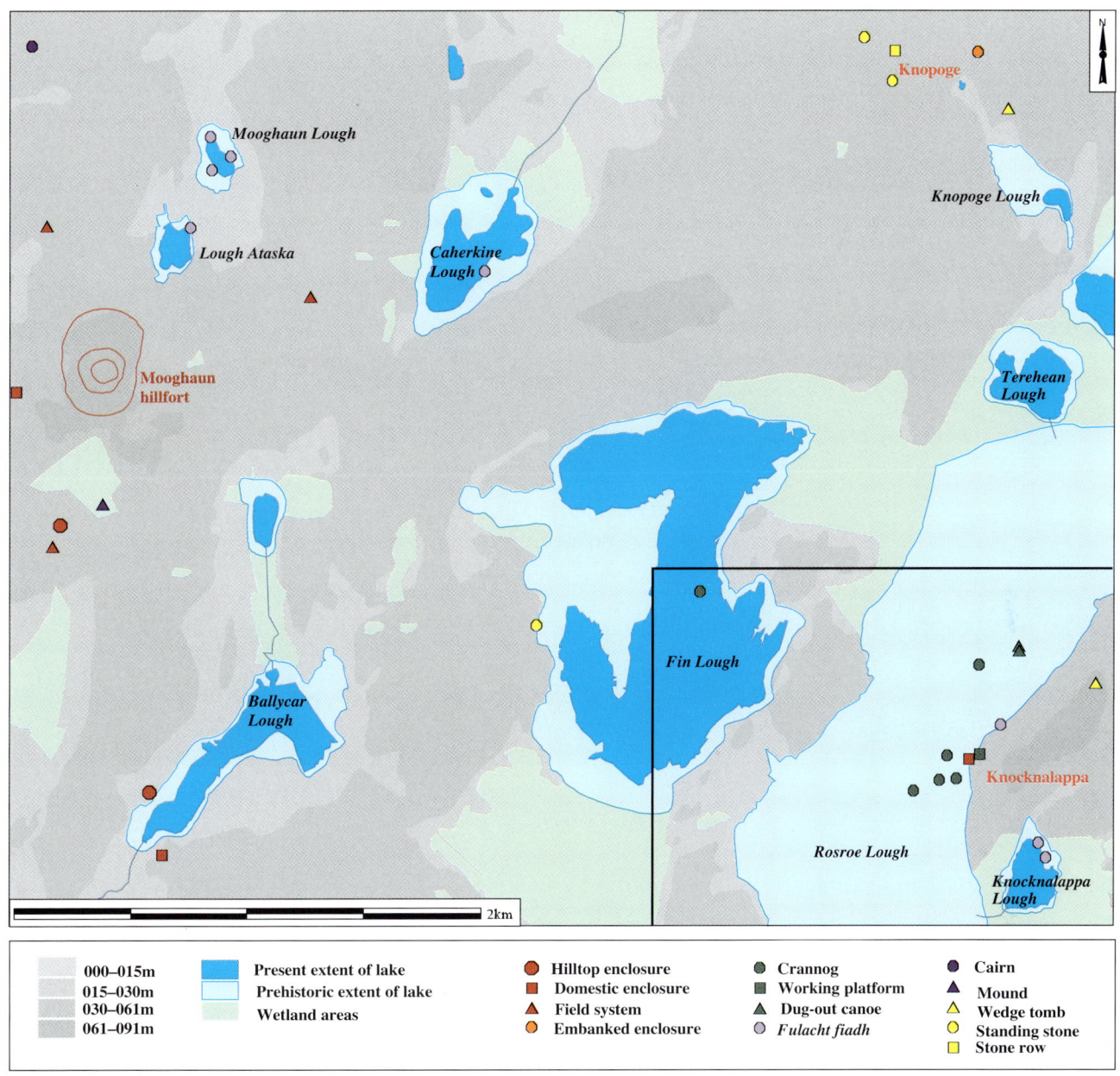

Fig. 1—Location map: the Mooghaun/Knocknalappa area of south-east Clare. Inset: Fig. 2.

Abstract

The late prehistoric lakeshore platform at Knocknalappa, Co. Clare, was excavated in 1937 by Dr J. Raftery of the National Museum of Ireland. Although the site produced a significant assemblage of Late Bronze Age material, the absence of evidence for definite structures led the excavator to conclude that it had never been occupied. A re-examination of the site, together with other sites and artefacts from the area, indicates that the platform was of two phases and that during the second, in the ninth century BC, there was clear evidence for domestic activity.

Introduction

Knocknalappa lies in an area of small lakes and hilly terrain forming part of a broad sweep of lakeland that extends north-eastward from the Fergus Estuary to the Cratloe Hills and constitutes the western boundary of the Shannon Basin (Fig. 1; Pl. 1). The site is on the eastern side of Rosroe Lough, where the lakeshore forms a gentle shelf at the edge of a steep slope. An older shoreline, at the foot of this slope, is clearly marked, and the distribution of later prehistoric sites (see below) suggests that at the time of the construction of the site this was the extent of

Pl. 1—View of the site (centre) from north-east (Aidan O'Sullivan).

the lake (Fig. 2). Rosroe Lough drains from north to south and the main channel flows along the eastern shore. At a lower level, along the bottom of the lake, the channel is divided by a number of small shoals, and the Knocknalappa platform was constructed on the easternmost of these, originally about 100m from the contemporary shoreline. Two further artificial platforms, now beneath the lake level, occur on other shoals further out into the channel (Fig. 2; see below).

Finds from the foreshore

During the summer of 1936 the surface of Rosroe Lough was considerably reduced through local drainage. The area was visited by Seán P. Ó Ríordáin (NMI files) in May, when he identified the crannog, with piles on the northern and southern shores, which had previously formed a small island about 80m from the previous lakeshore. He also noted that two dug-out boats were discovered further north along the same shore. The following week a local antiquarian, J. N. A. Wallace, examined the exposed foreshore, looking for exposed crannogs in the company of Sergeant James Long of the Civic Guards. Wallace noted that the lake level had been lowered by '4–5 feet' and that the island was now attached to the lakeshore and its western side was 'studded with posts' (NMI files). In the course of this reconnaissance the pair discovered a bronze flange-hilted sword, a bronze socketed gouge and a polished stone axe (Wallace 1936–9). The precise location of these finds is difficult to ascertain. They were picked up on the exposed surface of the marl, as were some bones and fragments of wooden vessels (which decayed immediately), perhaps on the western or southern side of the platform. These may have been eroded out of the site. About the same time a third dug-out boat was found on the south-eastern side of Fin Lough, about 800m to the west.

As a result of these discoveries an excavation was carried out on the lakeside settlement site over a five-week period in August and September 1937 by the late Dr Joseph Raftery, National Museum of Ireland.

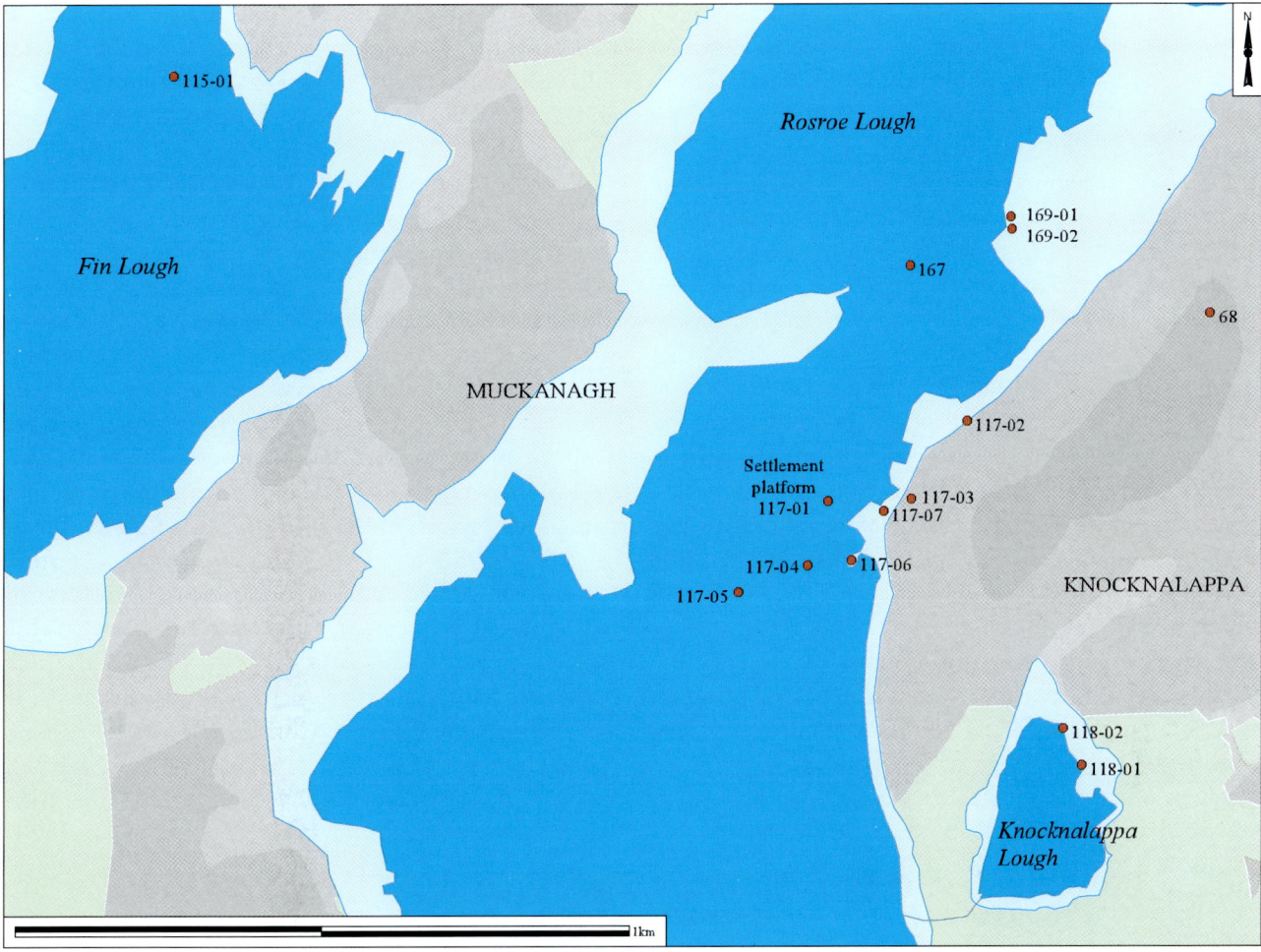

Fig. 2—The Knocknalappa area around Rosroe and Fin Lough. The numbers are the SMR reference for County Clare OS 6" map No. 42.

Recent research

As part of a research programme in the area of south-east Clare centred on the hillfort at Mooghaun South, intensive fieldwork was carried out by the North Munster Project in the area around Knocknalappa. In addition to re-identifying the location of the habitation site excavated by Raftery (1942) and extracting dating samples (O'Sullivan 1997), several new sites were identified. The work included rapid underwater survey. Further research, in the National Museum of Ireland and the Sites and Monuments Record, Office of Public Works (Dúchas), revealed further details regarding these sites, as well as several later prehistoric finds (Grogan et al. 1996, 39–43). Subsequently, an outline assessment of the local landscape context of the site formed part of a general treatment of Late Bronze Age lakeland settlement (O'Sullivan 1998, 85–9).

Description of excavation

Before excavation the site appeared as a low, oval platform measuring 40m east–west by 15–20m north–south, covering an area of c. 1000m^2. The excavation revealed that a natural shoal or rise of lake marl formed the foundation for the mound. Thereafter a thick layer of peat, averaging 1.5m in height, was laid down, within which were found a layer of brushwood and a narrow wooden platform measuring 1.8m by 0.85m. The platform was formed of nine half-split trunks, laid closely side by side. At each corner was a small roundwood stake. Lying on this platform was a thin spread of charcoal and stones as well as the tip of another stake.

The next layer within the peat was a discontinuous deposit of brown peaty soil, in which were found a lignite object (16),* a flint chip (17), a possible hammerstone (18), a bone knife (19), an

---

* The excavation prefix for the Knocknalappa site is E30; this is not shown here. The numbers referred to are the excavation numbers, *not* the numbers used by Raftery (1942).

antler tine (21) and a large portion of a pottery vessel (20). The pot has been poorly reconstructed, although the general profile as published is correct (Raftery 1942, fig. 3:1). The peat was then partly covered by a mixed layer of stones, animal bone and charcoal. This stony layer contained a bronze ring (4), a bronze sunflower pin (5), a lignite bracelet (6), two sandstone saddle querns (7, 11), four 'hammerstones' (8, 9, 12, 13) and 155 sherds of pottery, all but one of them (14) found together and from a single vessel (10). In addition to these, the labels in the NMI indicate that part of a large amber bead (24) and a small flat bronze or possibly lead bead (25) also came from this context.

Surrounding the mound was an arc of vertical stakes to the north, east and west, supplemented by a stone 'breakwater' to the east. Raftery adjudged this to be the revetment for the platform material. On the west side of the platform was an arrangement of posts which could have been used as a boat harbour or jetty. In this area was the stoutest portion of the palisade, which appeared to consist of two distinct lines of posts extending outwards into the lake beyond the western edge of the platform (Fig. 3). At the apex of this curve was an arrangement consisting of two parallel rows of posts, *c*. 1.5m apart, that extended westwards through the lines of the palisade and out into the lake for a distance of *c*. 2m. At the inner end these joined to form a curved end. Lying on and around the outer end of this post setting were several planks and timbers that may have formed the walkway of a small quay.

Finds from around the wooden piles, the 'breakwater' and the area of the 'foreshore' (see below) included about 167 sherds of pottery (10, 38b, 39b, 26, 32, 33, 37), two amber beads (22, 23), a bone spindle-whorl (27), a wooden disc (38a), a thin bronze band (31), a bone handle (28), and five perforated cattle phalanges (29). In addition, there was a quantity of animal bone, amongst which were several showing cut-marks, either from butchery or as part of the process in the manufacture of bone objects.

Above this was a layer of marl overlying the stony layer. A single amber bead (3) was found on or in this marl but it contained no other material. While Raftery (1942, 68–9) considered this to be 'the only possible occupation level on the site', it appears to be a sterile natural layer laid down at some later stage when the level of the lake was higher (see Discussion below). A thin layer of humus covered the marl, within which was found an amber bead (1) and what

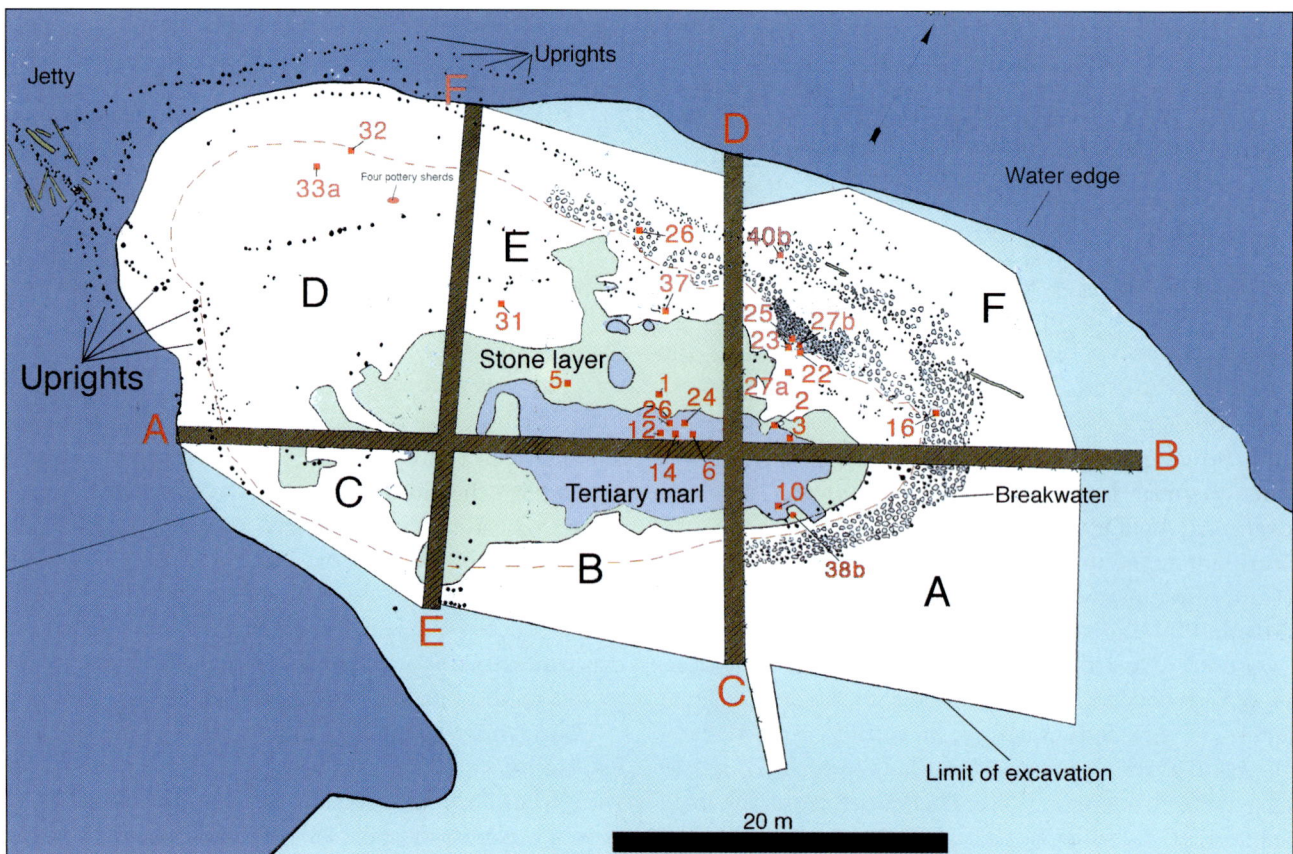

Fig. 3—Plan of the Late Bronze Age platform at Knocknalappa (after Raftery 1942, fig. 1).

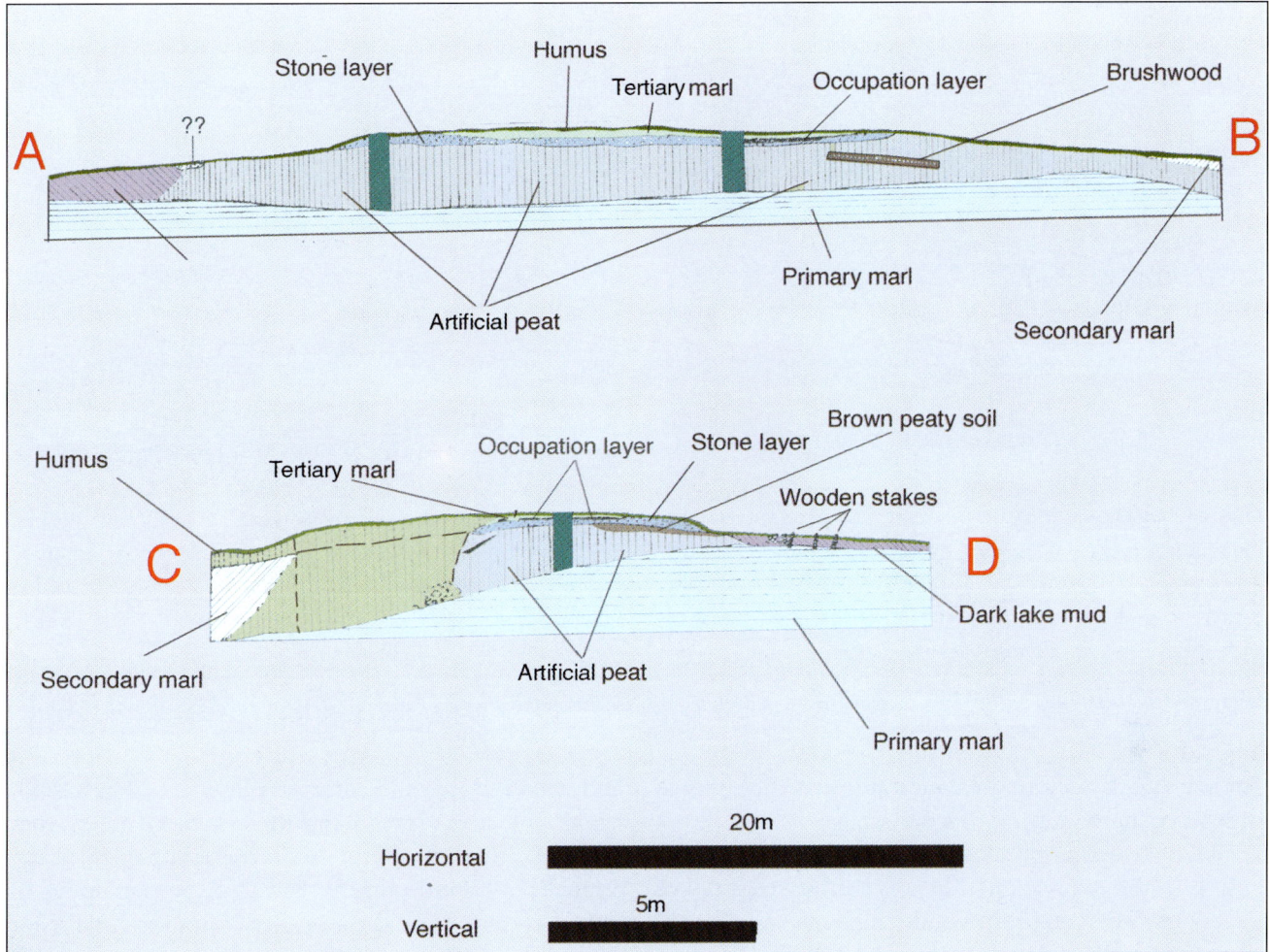

Fig. 4—Sections across Knocknalappa (after Raftery 1942, fig. 2).

was believed to be a rotary quern. This, on examination, proved to be a natural piece.

Animal bone, amounting to 'fourteen bags of bones' (Stelfox in Raftery 1942, 67–9), throughout the site included mainly cattle, sheep, pig, hare and a dog. Birds included raven, cormorant, tufted duck and lapwing. Forty-three charcoal specimens from 'the charcoal layer beneath the sterile marl' were examined by Dr O'Connor (Raftery 1942, 67) and were identified as hawthorn (*Crataegus*, 18), hazel (*Corylus*, 15), ash (*Fraxinus*, 1), holly (*Ilex*, 1), alder (*Alnus*, 2), oak (*Quercus*, 4) and two *Salix–Populus*. Samples from the plank 'platform' included oak (*Quercus*, 5), ash (*Fraxinus*, 2), hazel (*Corylus*, 1), alder (*Alnus*, 1), and four *Salix–Populus*.

All of the material outlined above was believed to have come from the structural layers of the site and no habitation layers were identified (Raftery 1942, 58–9). However, the finds, including the fourteen bags of animal bone and the pottery, a large assemblage of more than 400 sherds, clearly indicate domestic activity incorporated into the building of this site.

The fact that no house structures or hearths were found led Raftery to the assumption that the site had no habitation importance. He interpreted the site either as a temporary platform used for fishing or fowling or as a refuge to be used in time of danger. In his opinion the site was a single-period construction, dated to the Late Bronze Age by the finds represented.

Discussion of excavation

As already noted, in the absence of definite evidence for domestic structures, Raftery (1942, 66) determined that the site had never been occupied and that the finds were contained in the structural layers of the site and derived from 'a pre-existing midden' (location unknown). However, a reassessment of the excavation report itself, together with the site notebook, as well as comparison with other Late

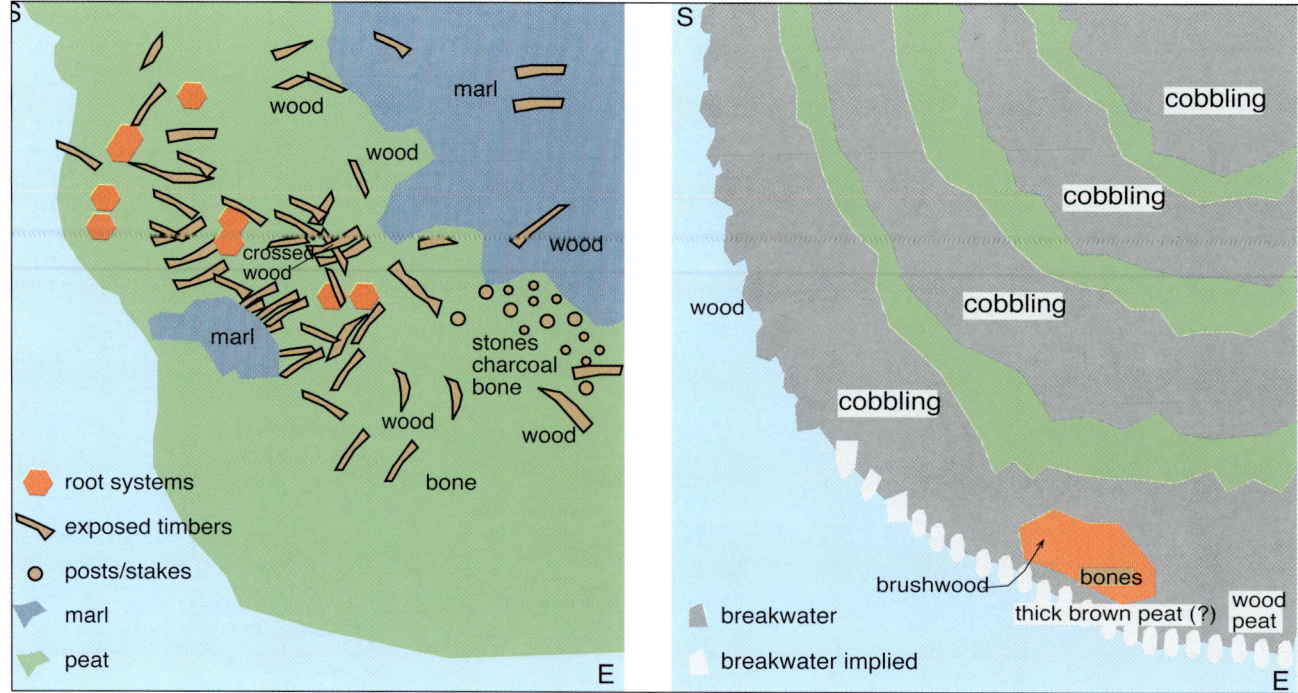

Fig. 5—Sketch-plans of the 1937 excavations, redrawn from Dr Joseph Raftery's notebook (National Museum of Ireland).

Bronze Age lakeshore sites, indicates that the site was indeed occupied during this period.

Two horizons of activity were identified in the course of the excavation. The lowermost consisted of a layer of unwoven brushwood which occurred across the eastern side of the site (Raftery 1942; Fig. 3). This lay on top of a layer of mixed peat and timber, the latter including horizontal logs or unshaped boughs, tree-roots (apparently both alder and ash), and brushwood. Sitting on top of the main brushwood layer was a floor of planks measuring 1.8m by 0.85m and staked to the underlying material by three corner-posts. The tip of another stake, some charcoal and small stones rested on the floor.

The second activity horizon was separated from the plank floor by about 0.15m of peat. This phase was represented by a thick spread of stony material which extended across much of the eastern end of the platform (Figs 3 and 4). Although Raftery's (1942, fig. 1) original ground-plan showing the limits of the spread suggests that it covered an area measuring 21m east–west by 6.5m north–south, the sections clearly show it extending across the full width of the platform, at this point about 20m wide. Thus the spread appears to have covered much if not all of this part of the platform, c. 400m² in area. Partly abutting and partly underlying this was a layer of brown peaty soil. Although again not discussed in the excavation report, the site notebook shows details of extensive loose timbers across the surface of the stone spread and covered by the later sterile marl. These two layers, the stone spread and the associated peaty soil, produced the bulk of the finds, including most of the animal bones and pottery. Most of the remainder of the finds came from the so-called 'foreshore', which is the northern and western surface of the peat platform on which the stone spread was deposited (Fig. 3).

The platform was surrounded by lines of stakes, 5–15cm in diameter, forming an irregular palisade which in some places was two or three stakes deep (Fig. 3). In some places, particularly on the north and west sides, more than one line of stakes was evident. The stakes appear to have been inserted as required along the edge of the platform, and the arrangement gives the appearance of being primarily intended to stabilise the platform rather than to form a defensive barrier. Curving around the eastern end of the platform was a stone breakwater, consisting of a bank of stones 0.5m high and averaging 2.4m in width. On the north-eastern side two distinct banks occurred and had a combined width of c. 5m.

Apart from the stakes of the palisade, other uprights, both stakes and posts, occurred on the platform and occasionally formed short irregular lines or clusters. Surprisingly, there were no stakes or posts shown on the stone platform or in the area subsequently covered by the layer of sterile marl (Fig. 3). This raises an important question regarding the extent of the excavation carried out by Raftery in 1937. It is evident, from his ground-plan and sections

(Raftery 1942, figs 1 and 2), that the surface of the platform was exposed throughout the site and the perimeter, or at least the visible stakes of the palisade, was identified. However, the site notebook, and indeed the published account of the excavation, indicate that only the south-eastern portion of the site ('Section A') was thoroughly excavated, while some detailed work also took place in 'Section E' (Fig. 3). As noted earlier, the site notebook shows a considerable amount of timber on the surface of the stone spread in 'A' (Fig. 5a). This may have included some stakes or posts within the eastern edge of the stone spread. In addition, another working sketch shows the stone spread (labelled 'cobbling') made up of at least three separate layers interspersed with peat. The stone layers appear to have covered successively smaller areas, leaving the impression of a stepped, or 'terraced', arrangement (Fig. 5b). At a lower level, concentrations of bone, wood, charcoal and brushwood were also identified.

The evidence from the site notebook shows that the only portion of the site, including the peat platform, that was fully excavated was along the face of the baulk on the west side of Section A. This was achieved by means of a narrow trench. How the other sections (Fig. 4, A–B, E–F) were produced is uncertain. This may have been by trench along the section faces, or possibly by using test-trenches to provide the general scheme of the sections. Indeed, it is apparent that Raftery, after the initial work in Section A, was very conscious of the short time available for the work and the impossibility of a complete excavation. He described his proposed strategy as essentially cleaning off the surface of the site in the remaining areas (probably Sections B, E and F).

Overall, it appears possible that there were two separate phases of activity at Knocknalappa. The first is represented by the construction of the main peat (and timber?) platform, on which some occupation, indicated by the brushwood layers and the plank platform, occurred. The only other material from this phase is some animal bone, both burnt and unburnt, and at least some of the stakes in the palisade surrounding the platform. One of these (see Fig. 3) was extracted for dating in 1994 and produced a radiocarbon date of 1887–1701 cal. BC (3470 ± 30 BP, GrN-21263), which suggests that this phase of activity could belong to the early stages of the Middle Bronze Age. Owing to the restricted excavation elsewhere on the platform the extent of the activity associated with this phase is, however, very limited.

The evidence indicates that the second phase is represented by extensive deposits of material suggesting occupation over some period of time during which successive layers of stone and timber were deposited on the peat surface of the main artificial platform. Ongoing occupation resulted in the deposition of normal domestic debris—animal bone, charcoal, pottery and occasionally other artefacts. While no definite structures were evident, timbers—possibly including posts and stakes—occurred on the stone spreads. This phase clearly dates from the Late Bronze Age, as shown by the artefacts (see below). In addition, a radiocarbon date of 1033–848 cal. BC (2795 ± 35 BP, GrN-19692) came from a sample of the accretion on the inner face of a potsherd from the site (J. Lanting, pers. comm.). This date is comfortably within the range of a series of dates for settlement with closely related pottery from Mooghaun South, 4km to the north-west (Grogan, forthcoming b).

The artefactual assemblage

The assemblage—pottery, bronzes, amber, lithics, bone and lignite—dates from the Late Bronze Age. The sword has been classified as Class 4 by Eogan (1965, no. 114). It is 40.8cm long and weighs 225g, making it one of the smallest swords recorded. In common with some of the pottery, the gouge and the stone axe, it bears a white, hard accretion, especially on one face. The surface is mottled. The blade is still sharp but nicked, and some damage occurs near the tip. A crack runs across the hilt. The socketed gouge is undecorated and is similar in form to that from Enagh East, Co. Clare (O'Carroll and Ryan 1992), and to examples in the hoard from Dowris, Co. Offaly (Eogan 1983, no. 119, fig. 71). The blade is bevelled on both faces, most noticeably on the back. Some wood remaining in the socket has been identified as ash (*Fraxinus excelsior* L.).

The bronze ring is again paralleled at Enagh East and at Boolybrien, Co. Clare (Eogan 1983, no. 55), although rings like this usually occur in pairs or sets. The pin is categorised as a sunflower pin (Eogan 1974, 112, no. 28), but is atypical in the absence of a central boss. This may be due to severe abrasion of the face, which removed both the boss and any decoration which may have occurred. Two of the five amber beads are large: one, which is broken, is over 3cm in diameter, and the maximum diameter of the other is 4.5cm. Those of the three smaller beads, one broken, are between 0.9cm and 1.1cm. All could have been part of one necklace, such as those from Tooradoo, Co. Limerick (Eogan 1983, no. 103, fig. 58).

Lignite or shale bracelets are relatively common

Site	Location	Palisade	Houses	Jetty	Plain pottery	Date	Earlier activity	Function
Ballinderry 2	Lakeshore		Yes	–	Yes	LBA		Domestic
Chancellorsland	Marshland	Yes + ditch	Yes	–	Yes	LBA	MBA	Domestic
Clonfinlough	Lakeshore	Yes	Yes	–	Yes	LBA		Domestic
Cullyhanna	Lakeshore	Yes	Yes	–		MBA		Domestic
Island MacHugh	Lakeshore	Yes	–	–		LBA		Domestic?
Islandmacgrath	Estuary	Yes	?	Yes	unex.	LBA		?
Killymoon	Marsh edge	Windbreak?				LBA		Industrial
Knocknalappa	Lakeshore	Yes		Yes	Yes	LBA	MBA?	Domestic
Lough Eskragh A	Lakeshore	Revetment				LBA		Domestic
Lough Eskragh B	Lakeshore					M–LBA		Industrial
Moynagh Lough	Lakeshore	Windbreak?	–	–	Yes	LBA	MBA	Domestic
Rathtinaun	Lakeshore	–	Yes		Yes	LBA		Domestic
Aughinish	Dry land	Wall	?	–	?	LBA		Domestic
Ballyveelish	Dry land	Ditch	Yes	–	Yes	M–LBA	EBA	Domestic
Carrigillihy	Dry land	Wall	Yes	–	Yes	MBA		Domestic
Curraghatoor	Dry land	Palisade	Yes	–		LBA		Domestic
Lough Gur J	Dry land	Wall	?	–	Yes	LBA	MBA	Domestic
Lough Gur K	Dry land	Wall	Yes	–	Yes	LBA	MBA	Domestic
Lough Gur L	Dry land	Wall	?	–	Yes	LBA	MBA	Domestic
Lough Gur 10	Dry land	Wall	?	–	Yes	LBA	E–MBA	Domestic
Lough Gur 12	Dry land	Wall	?	–	Yes	LBA		Domestic
Lough Gur cave	Dry land	Wall	Yes	–	Yes	LBA	MBA	Domestic
Lough Gur F	Dry land	–	Building	–	Yes	LBA	–	Industrial

Table 1—Principal features of Late Bronze Age settlement/industrial sites.

on Late Bronze Age sites and occur, for example, at Circle K, Lough Gur (Grogan and Eogan 1987, 364–6, fig. 22), and Emain Macha, Co. Armagh (Waterman 1997, 89, fig. 41). These are generally round or oval in cross-section, although rounded D-shaped sections also occur. The fragment of a larger ring (No. 16; Raftery 1942, fig. 4:4) is closely paralleled by one from Emain Macha (Waterman 1997, 89, fig. 41: 16). The bone knife or spatula (No. 19) is similar to examples from Site C, Lough Gur (Ó Ríordáin 1954, fig. 26), and one from Circle L (Grogan and Eogan 1987, fig. 60:1990). While bone spindle-whorls come from sites of a variety of periods, the toggles (Raftery 1942, fig. 3:5) are so far only paralleled at Ballinderry 2 (Hencken 1942, fig. 5:667).

The material is undoubtedly a domestic assemblage deposited by loss and discard in the course of the occupation of the artificial platform. However, the context of the objects discovered originally on the 'foreshore' is uncertain. It is probable, as Lynn (1983, 52) noted, that these were washed out from the layers within the site. Another possibility is that these three items, the sword, gouge and stone axe discovered in 1936, were a deliberate deposition on or close to the occupation site. Such hoards are not unusual and have been discovered at Rathtinaun, Co. Sligo (B. Raftery, 1994, 32–5), Killymoon, Co. Tyrone (Hurl 1995), and more recently at Dún Aonghasa, Inis Mór, Co. Galway (C. Cotter, pers. comm.). Hoards containing weapons and tools form an element of Late Bronze Age deposition and include those from Blackhills, Co. Laois, Knockmaon, Co. Waterford, and Kish, Co. Wicklow (Eogan 1983, nos 495, 144, 155, fig. 3).

Comparative settlement sites

Several settlement sites provide good parallels. Among these are several lakeshore platforms such as at Clonfinlough, Co. Offaly (Moloney et al. 1993), Cullyhanna, Co. Armagh (Hodges 1958; Hillam 1976), Ballinderry 2, Co. Offaly (Hencken 1942), Island MacHugh, Co. Tyrone (Davies 1950; Ivens et al. 1986), Rathtinaun, Co. Sligo (B. Raftery 1994, 32–5), Moynagh Lough, Co. Meath (Bradley 1996; 1997), and Killymoon, Co. Tyrone (Hurl 1995). These sites have been discussed in detail by O'Sullivan

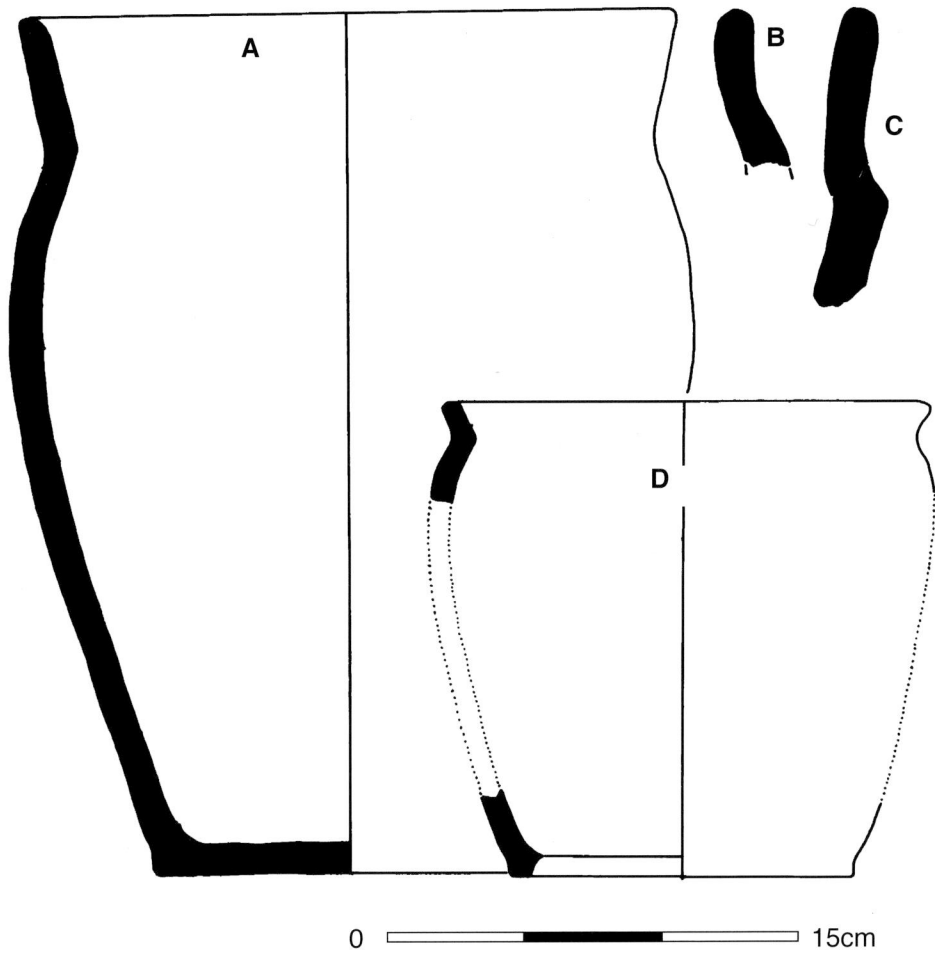

Fig. 6—Comparative profiles of Late Bronze Age necked jars from (A) Knocknalappa, (B) Mooghaun, (C) Emain Macha and (D) Ballinderry.

(1998, 71-96), and were assessed in a wider context by Cooney and Grogan (1994, 149–58). Most of them appear to be domestic settlements, but a largely industrial function is probable for Lough Eskragh B (Williams 1978) and Killymoon. At Islandmacgrath, Co. Clare, a Late Bronze Age palisade enclosure associated with a trackway and a jetty occurs on the edge of the main channel of the River Fergus (O'Sullivan 1996, 67–9). Middle Bronze Age houses and associated activity have also been identified on the Shannon Estuary at Carrigdirty (*ibid.*, 63–7).

An artificial platform at Chancellorsland, Co. Tipperary, defined by a ditch and palisade, was constructed in wet or marshy terrain in the Middle Bronze Age (Doody 1995, 12–18; 1996, 15–22). This was expanded in the Late Bronze Age, with a second ditch enclosing a larger area. The enclosed site at Ballyveelish, Co. Tipperary, also appears to have had a Middle and Late Bronze Age phase (Doody 1987). Other dryland sites, although all overlooking bodies of open water, included the walled enclosures at Carrigillihy, Co. Cork (O'Kelly 1951), Aughinish, Co. Limerick (Kelly 1974), and several sites at Lough Gur which recent research has indicated are of later rather than earlier prehistoric date (Cleary 1995; Grogan, forthcoming a).

The artefacts: comparative assemblages

The material from Knocknalappa is well paralleled at several of the sites mentioned above, particularly the amber beads, the D-sectioned lignite bracelets, small bronze tools and weapons, saddle querns, and bone points, knives and handles.

The increasing numbers of Middle and Late Bronze Age pottery assemblages are demonstrating the transition in ceramic styles, in particular the almost complete disappearance of decoration in the later period (Grogan, forthcoming b). The Knocknalappa pottery is comparatively fine, averaging *c.* 10mm in thickness, and having a relatively smooth surface produced by wetting the surface of the vessel before firing and smoothing it over with the resultant slurry. Of particular significance is the fact that the Knocknalappa vessels are all necked jars (Fig. 6), a form that is unusual in Late Bronze Age contexts. This type is, however, found at Mooghaun, as well as at Ballinderry 2 (Hencken 1942, fig. 2: 7). It forms a very slight element in the assemblages from Emain Macha, Co. Armagh (McCorry 1997, fig. 32:5), and Lough Gur (Circle K; Grogan and Eogan 1987, fig. 16: 1955).

Knocknalappa area survey

Further field survey of the Knocknalappa area, carried out by the North Munster Project between 1993 and 1995, shows that there are several other sites in the immediate vicinity, indicating that the excavated platform was part of an extensive complex. A number of *fulachta fiadh* and small working platforms are located close to the lakeshore, while the identification of a possible large bivallate enclosure on the foreshore may indicate a more significant settlement site close by. The post palisade of the excavated site (42:11701) was re-identified in 1994 and sampled for radiocarbon dating. This produced a surprising Middle Bronze Age date of 1887–1701 cal. BC (3470 ± 30 BP, GrN-21263). This new evidence further suggested that there was settlement activity on this lakeshore throughout the Bronze Age.

As a result it was decided to conduct a rapid underwater archaeological survey on the lakebed to the west and south of the Knocknalappa lake settlement. Aidan O'Sullivan, Donal Boland (the dive leader) and Claire O'Callaghan carried out the survey in June 1996. A number of significant archaeological discoveries were made, including two crannogs (42:11704, 11705) and a partly artificial platform (42:11706).

The sites are listed below, with a brief description.

Discussion

Two phases of activity on the excavated Knocknalappa settlement are apparent, one possibly dating from the Middle Bronze Age, and the more intensive one from the Late Bronze Age. Despite Raftery's reservations, the Knocknalappa platform appears, in the Late Bronze Age, to have been a domestic occupation site on which structures either did not survive or were not identified. Only the south-eastern portion of the site was fully investigated and it produced a range of evidence, including timbers, posts, stakes and artefacts, derived from intensive habitation. Certainly the eastern edge of the platform, an area of at least 400m^2, appears to have been the centre of activity in the Late Bronze Age.

In terms of size, location and method of enclosure, Knocknalappa is similar to other Late Bronze Age lakeshore settlements. The range of material comprising the domestic assemblage is also closely comparable to that from several other occupation sites. Although the artefacts are not particularly numerous, the range and quality compare favourably with other sites of potentially high status, such as Ballinderry 2, Moynagh Lough and Rathtinaun. The suggestion that Knocknalappa forms part of the hierarchy of settlement in the sub-region focused on the contemporary hillfort at Mooghaun (Grogan *et al.* 1996) seems to be borne out by this closer assessment.

In the immediate area of Rosroe Lough it is evident that there was intensive activity, beginning in the Late Neolithic period with the construction of the wedge tomb. The next phase of identified sites is represented by the *fulachta fiadh*, of which at least three have been identified (Fig. 2). These all occur on the now-exposed margins of Rosroe and Knocknalappa loughs, possibly in areas that were subjected to periodic flooding in later prehistory. There are also two other artificial mounds, possibly *fulachta fiadh* or working platforms, and two larger enclosures (42:11706, 11707) that may have been domestic sites. One definite (42:11705) and one possible crannog (42:167), both as yet of unknown date, have also been discovered, while another crannog (42:11501) occurs in the centre of Fin Lough, 1.1km to the north-west.

The *fulachta fiadh* at least are most probably broadly contemporary with the excavated settlement platform. The reported finding of a 'fibula' (similar to the gold bracelets from the Mooghaun hoard) in the wedge tomb indicates the reuse of the tomb in the Late Bronze Age (Westropp 1907, 457) possibly by the occupants of the settlement. It appears that Knocknalappa 1 was the focus of a local Middle to Late Bronze Age complex, which in turn, at least in the latter period, formed a component of the wider landscape dominated by the Mooghaun hillfort.

Archaeological sites in the area around Rosroe Lough (Fig. 2)

The list details the townland, the Sites and Monuments Record Number for County Clare, the site classification and the height OD, followed by a brief description. The date following each entry is the last occasion on which detailed inspection occurred.

Knocknalappa 42:11701
Lakeside settlement platform   OD 30m
The excavated settlement platform (Raftery 1942) survives as a level grassy platform connected to the lakeshore by a low flat neck of seasonally flooded

ground about 100m long. A number of low banks, the remains of baulks left after the excavations, are visible transecting the site. The piles of the surrounding palisade are visible immediately beneath the water on the north and west sides.
14.9.1993

Knocknalappa 43:68
Wedge tomb 'Dermot and Grania's Bed'   OD 61m
The tomb is situated on the north end of a ridge immediately east of Rosroe Lough. It commands an extensive view to the north.

Westropp (1907, 457) noted damage to the tomb before he planned it, and it seems to have suffered further damage since. The northern sidestone, the more westerly of the two southern sidestones, and the stone crossing the west end of the chamber remain *in situ*. The eastern stone of the southern side has collapsed. The transverse slab at the west end of the chamber leans inwards. It would reach somewhat higher than the sidestones even if these were erect. The roofstone, which, from Westropp's plan and sketch, seems to have rested on the three sidestones, is now displaced and rests only on the northern sidestone and the collapsed stone of the southern side.

The chamber decreases in height and width from west to east. It measures 2.8m long to the end of the collapsed southern sidestone, 1.6m wide at the west and 1.2m wide at the end of the sidestones remaining *in situ*.
14.9.93

Knocknalappa 42:11707
Possible enclosure   OD 30m
A large, bivallate, subcircular crop-mark enclosure, visible on aerial photographs, is located on the roughly level terrain on the lake foreshore 200m north-east of the excavated site (42:11801). The site appears to be about 80m in diameter and defined by two ditches. When visited this site was not detectable on the ground.
14.9.1993

Knocknalappa 42:11702
Fulacht fiadh   OD 30m
A roughly U-shaped mound, composed of burnt earth and heat-fractured stone, located on the margins of Rosroe Lough *c.* 200m north of the excavated settlement site (42:11701). The mound stands 1.1m high on the south-east, and is *c.* 6m wide with a maximum length of 9m. Its open side, *c.* 2.3m across, faces north-west.
14.9.93

Knocknalappa 42:11801
Fulacht fiadh   OD 30m
An irregularly shaped mound on the flood-plain close to the north-eastern shore of Knocknalappa Lough, a small lake on the south-east of Rosroe. The mound, composed of burnt earth and heat-fractured limestone, stands *c.* 1.3m high, up to 9m wide and *c.* 16m long, with a subcircular hollow (4m by 3m), presumably the trough area, visible to the south-west on the lake side of the mound.
14.9.93

Knocknalappa 42:11802
Fulacht fiadh   OD 30m
Located in the flood-plain of Knocknalappa Lough, *c.* 50m north of 42:11801. It survives as a low grassy area, slightly curved in plan, composed of three small mounds *c.* 0.3m high, 2m wide and 6.4m long. It may be the remains of a *fulacht fiadh*. No burnt stone was exposed on the site.
14.9.93

Knocknalappa 42:11703
Artificial platform   OD 30m
A crescent-shaped mound, 75m north of the excavated site (42:11701), close to the margin of the lake. Measuring 8m on its longest axis and *c.* 1m high, it has the appearance of a *fulacht fiadh,* but there is no evidence of any burnt stone in its composition. Some struck chert flakes were found on the mound surface.
14.09.1993

Knocknalappa 42:11704
Artificial platform   OD 30m
This is a small circular platform of stone slabs, 5–6m in diameter and 0.5m high (O'Sullivan 1997; 1996). A number of vertical oak and ash posts, 0.06–0.1m in diameter, were recorded on the west side. It is situated out in the lake shallows *c.* 40–50m south-west of the excavated settlement site (42:11701) and separated from it by a dense reed-bed.
9.06.1996

Muckanagh 42:11705
Crannog   OD 30m
This is a large stone and wooden structure in the middle of the lake, situated on a narrow area of shallows (O'Sullivan 1996; 1997). It comprises a central stone feature, a wooden palisade and an outer scatter of posts. It appears to be a crannog or lake platform, 30m in diameter. The core of the site is a series of stone slabs, boulders and small stones, creating a platform *c.* 5–6m in diameter. A wooden

palisade of vertical roundwood and cleft oak and ash posts occurs *c*. 10m to the south. The palisade posts survive to a height of 0.6–0.8m and are 0.1–0.15m in diameter. The level clays to the south have an extensive spread of ash roundwood posts scattered over an area measuring 10m by 20m. These would need to be planned to reveal structural patterns, but there appear to be quite a large number of them, approaching 5–6 posts per square metre. There is also a possible timber jetty to the east, opposing that found at the south-west corner of the excavated site (42:11701).
9.06.1996

Knocknalappa 42:11706
Possible settlement platform   OD 30m
This is a circular, flat-topped platform, *c*. 20m in diameter and 1.5m in height, situated on the lake edge to the south-east of the excavated site (42:11701). A possible ruined stone jetty structure runs out into the lake shallows for a distance of 4–5m. A large proportion of this platform appears to be natural bedrock outcrop, but it is possible that the mound was enhanced for use as a habitation.
9.06.1996

Knocknalappa 42:167
Shoal, possible crannog   OD 30m
A shoal is visible at the narrowest point of Rosroe Lough, 600m north of the excavated site (42:11701). It is visible on aerial photographs and can be clearly seen from the hill at Knocknalappa. It appears to be a roughly circular platform covered by several feet of water. At the time of the visit the lake level was low.
14.09.1993

Acknowledgements

This reassessment of Knocknalappa could not have been carried out without the assistance of the Antiquities Division of the National Museum of Ireland and in particular the Keeper, Eamon P. Kelly. Our especial gratitude to Tom Condit, whose field research contributed much to our understanding of the area. Donal Boland (the dive leader) and Claire O'Callaghan provided invaluable support in the underwater survey. Jan Lanting, Biologisch-Archaeologisch Instituut, Groningen, kindly allowed us to quote the radiocarbon date for the pottery from Knocknalappa. Our thanks to Eoghan Moore, who produced Figs 3–6. Figures 1 and 2 are by Ines Hagen, and we are grateful to Barry Masterson for help in their completion.

References

Bradley, J. 1996 Living at the water's edge. *Archaeology Ireland* **35**, 24–6.

Bradley, J. 1997 Archaeological excavations at Moynagh Lough, Co. Meath, 1995–96. *Ríocht na Mídhe* **9** (3), 50–61.

Cleary, R. 1995 Later Bronze Age settlement and prehistoric burials, Lough Gur, Co. Limerick. *Proceedings of the Royal Irish Academy* **95C**, 1–92.

Cooney, G. and Grogan, E. 1994 *Irish prehistory: a social perspective*. Dublin.

Davies, O. 1950 *Excavations at Island MacHugh*. Supplement to the *Proceedings of the Belfast Natural History and Philosophical Society*. Belfast.

Doody, M. 1987 Ballyveelish. In R.M. Cleary, M.F. Hurley and E.A. Twohig (eds), *Archaeological excavations on the Cork–Dublin gas pipeline*, 9–35. Cork Archaeological Studies 1. University College, Cork.

Doody, M. 1995 Ballyhoura Hills Project. Interim report. *Discovery Programme Reports* **2**, 12–44.

Doody, M. 1996 Ballyhoura Hills Project. Interim report. *Discovery Programme Reports* **3**, 15–25.

Eogan, G. 1965 *Catalogue of Irish bronze swords*. Dublin.

Eogan, G. 1974 Pins of the Irish Late Bronze Age. *Journal of the Royal Society of Antiquaries of Ireland* **104**, 73–119.

Eogan, G. 1983 *Hoards of the Irish Later Bronze Age*. Dublin.

Grogan, E. (forthcoming a) *The prehistoric landscape of Lough Gur*. Discovery Programme Monographs.

Grogan, E. (forthcoming b) The Late Bronze Age pottery assemblage from Mooghaun South. In E. Grogan, *The prehistoric landscape of south-east Clare*. Discovery Programme Monographs.

Grogan, E. and Eogan, G. 1987 Lough Gur excavations by Seán P. Ó Ríordáin: further Neolithic and Beaker habitations on Knockadoon. *Proceedings of the Royal Irish Academy* **87C**, 299–506.

Grogan, E., Condit, T., O'Carroll, F., O'Sullivan, A. and Daly, A. 1996 Tracing the late prehistoric landscape in North Munster. *Discovery Programme Reports* **4**, 26–46.

Hencken, H. O'Neill 1942 Ballinderry Crannog No. 2. *Proceedings of the Royal Irish Academy* **47C**, 1–76.

Hillam, J. 1976 The dating of Cullyhanna hunting lodge. *Irish Archaeological Research Forum* **3** (1), 17–20.

Hodges, H.W.M. 1958 A hunting camp at Cullyhanna Lough, near Newtown Hamilton,

County Armagh. *Ulster Journal of Archaeology* **21**, 7–13.

Hurl, D. 1995 Killymoon — new light on the Late Bronze Age. *Archaeology Ireland* **34**, 24–7.

Ivens, R.J., Simpson, D.D.A. and Brown, D. 1986 Excavations at Island MacHugh 1985—interim report. *Ulster Journal of Archaeology* **49**, 99–103.

Kelly, E.P. 1974 Aughinish Island. *Excavations 1974*, 20–1.

Lynn, C. J. 1983 Some 'early' ring-forts and crannogs. *Journal of Irish Archaeology* **1**, 47–58.

McCorry, M. 1997 Coarse pottery from Phase 3. In D.M. Waterman, *Excavations at Navan Fort 1961–71*, 72–9. Northern Ireland Archaeological Monographs 3. Belfast.

Moloney, A., Jennings, D., Keane, M. and McDermott, C. 1993 *Excavations at Clonfinlough, County Offaly*. Irish Archaeological Wetland Unit Transactions 2. Dublin.

O'Carroll, F. and Ryan, M. 1992 A Late Bronze Age hoard from Enagh East, Co. Clare. *North Munster Antiquarian Journal* **34**, 3–12.

O'Kelly, M.J. 1951 An Early Bronze Age ring-fort at Carrigillihy, Co. Cork. *Journal of the Cork Historical and Archaeological Society* **56**, 69–86.

Ó Ríordáin, S.P. 1954 Lough Gur excavations: Neolithic and Bronze Age houses on Knockadoon. *Proceedings of the Royal Irish Academy* **56C**, 297–459.

O'Sullivan, A. 1996 Later Bronze Age discoveries on north Munster estuaries. *Discovery Programme Reports* **4**, 63–72.

O'Sullivan, A. 1997 Knocknalappa: Bronze Age lake settlements. In I. Bennett (ed.), *Excavations 1996*, 8. Bray.

O'Sullivan, A. 1998 *The archaeology of lake settlement in Ireland*. Discovery Programme Monographs 4. Dublin.

Raftery, B. 1994 *Pagan Celtic Ireland*. London.

Raftery, J. 1942 Knocknalappa Crannog, Co. Clare. *North Munster Antiquarian Journal* **3**, 53–71.

Wallace, J.N.A. 1936–9 Crannog and Bronze Age find at Rosroe (Knocknalappa), Co. Clare. *North Munster Antiquarian Journal* **1**, 38.

Waterman, D.M. 1997 *Excavations at Navan Fort 1967–71*. Northern Ireland Archaeological Monographs 3. Belfast.

Westropp, T. J. 1907 The cists, dolmens and pillars of the western half of the County Clare. *Proceedings of the Royal Irish Academy* **26C**, 447–74.

Williams, B.B. 1978 Excavations at Lough Eskragh, Co. Tyrone. *Ulster Journal of Archaeology* **41**, 37–48.

6. EXCAVATIONS AT MOOGHAUN SOUTH 1995. INTERIM REPORT

EOIN GROGAN

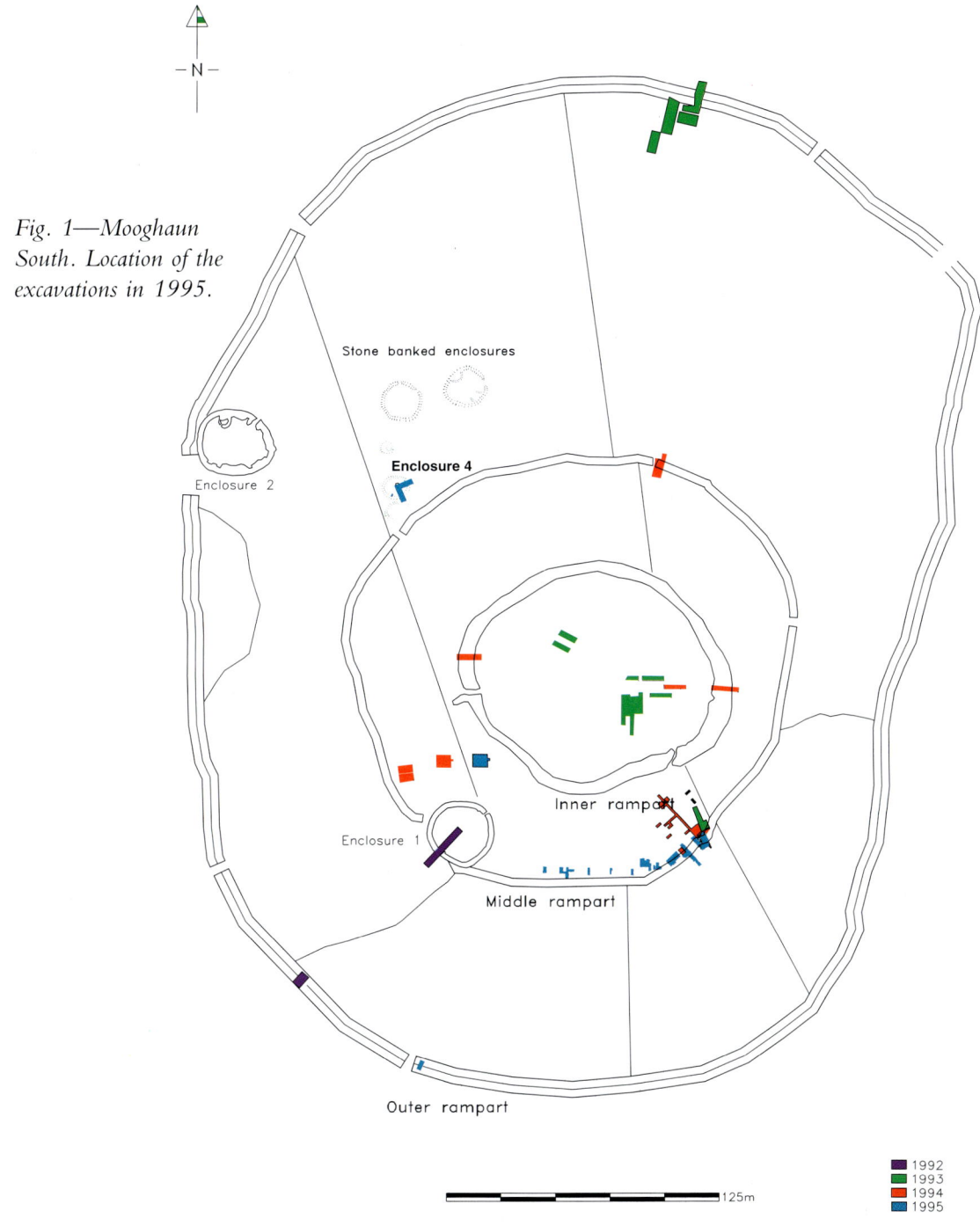

Fig. 1—Mooghaun South. Location of the excavations in 1995.

Introduction

Excavations at Mooghaun took place over an eighteen-week period between May and September 1995. They formed part of a comprehensive programme of investigation which included detailed field survey. Extensive clearance of vegetation took place at various locations within the hillfort, revealing important and previously unrecorded archaeological features. Excavation concentrated on three aspects of the site: the pre-hillfort habitation, the middle rampart, and other occupation evidence within the hillfort. A total area of 230m² was excavated in 1995.

Site C: the middle enclosure (Figs 1 and 2)

Following test and initial open-area excavations in 1994 (Grogan 1996), a series of adjoining cuttings were opened to fully investigate the rampart and the previously identified occupation horizon. An

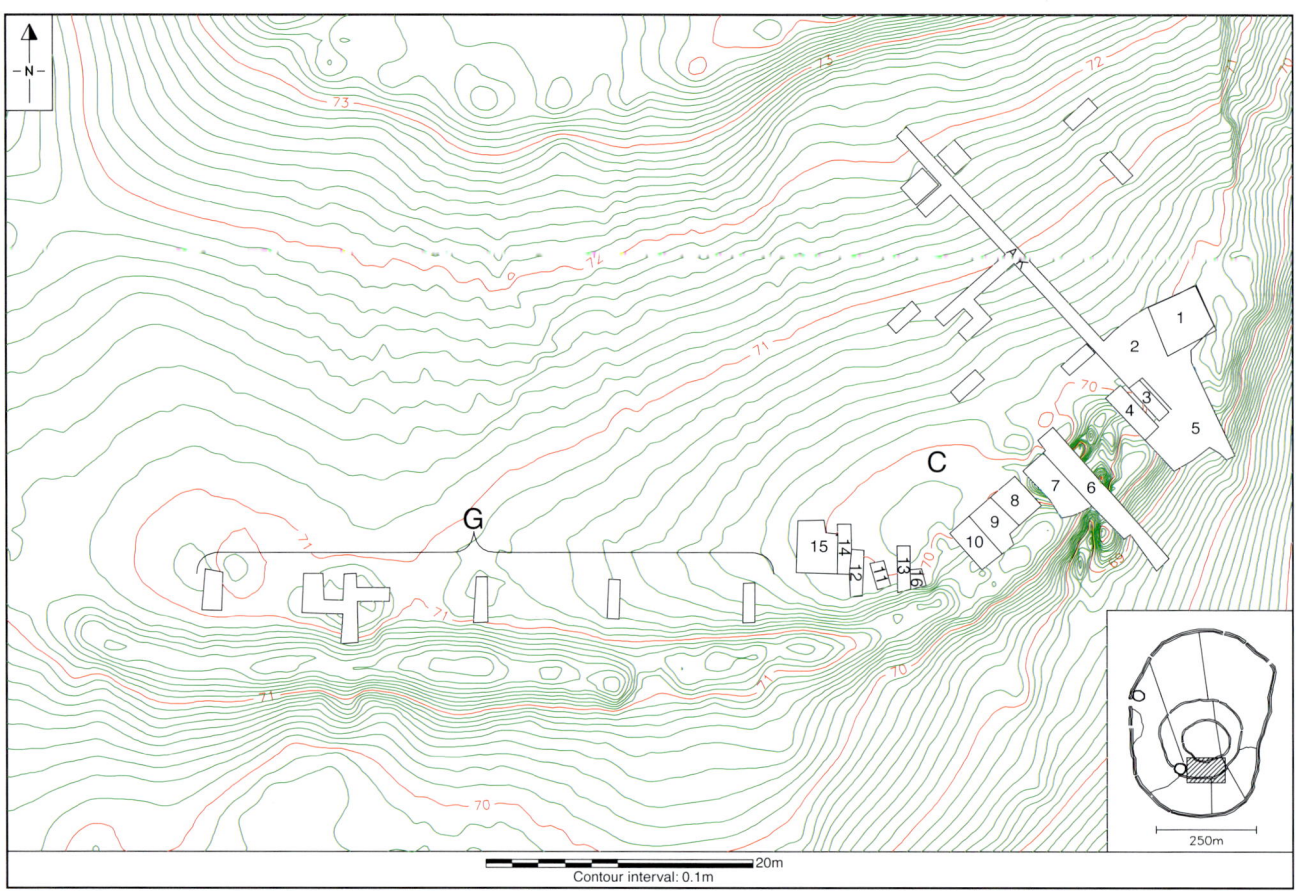

Fig. 2—Mooghaun South. Excavations at Site C.

additional 65m² were opened in the vicinity of the previous work, bringing the total excavated area to *c.* 130m².

Occupation evidence

In this area a natural, south-east-facing terrace extends across the face of the hillslope. The rampart of the hillfort was built along the outer edge of this terrace. Excavation showed that occupation material extends for *c.* 38m along the terrace, covering a total area of *c.* 200m² (Fig. 2). Three principal horizons of activity were identified within an apparently continuous habitation phase. The first is represented by a continuous layer of occupation debris extending over an area of 25m by 2–3m from beyond the north-eastern edge of cutting 1 and the south-western side of cutting 7 (Fig. 3). This appears to pre-date the construction of the rampart. The occupation layers of the second phase abut the primary inner facing of the rampart (F275A), while the third phase post-dates the construction of the secondary facing (F262/275B; see below). The finds include a considerable quantity of animal bone, struck chert and coarse pottery.

During the occupation phase activity occurred along the terrace and extended some way down the steeper southern slope. Along the lip of the terrace the occupation layers contain a series of small areas of paving, which appear to represent ongoing efforts to maintain a level floor (Figs 2 and 3). While these give an overall impression of continuous paving, covering an area of *c.* 10m by 1.5m, the individual coherent elements are often small, consisting of a few slabs laid down on earlier patches. Interspersed between these were thin layers of occupation soil.

Two structures occurred on the inner (northern) portion of the level terrace (Fig. 2). The northernmost, structure 1, was represented by a circle of stake-holes, in some places apparently forming a double wall, *c.* 3.8m in diameter. A second building phase seems to be indicated by a low slab wall overlying the stake-holes on the south-eastern side. A sandstone saddle quern was incorporated into the fabric of this wall. The wall itself was subsequently incorporated into the fabric of the rampart.

Structure 2 was in the central part of the area excavated this year and consists of an irregular circle of stake- and post-holes, *c.* 4m in diameter, apparently representing two or more phases of construction. A substantial hearth (F250-56) occurred towards the centre of this structure. The houses belong to the first or second occupation phase.

A straight 7m stretch of wall (F204/265) constructed of 3–5 courses of limestone slabs occurs towards the south-western side of the 1995 excavation (Figs 2 and 3) and was associated with the final occupation phase. It extends at a tangent to the later rampart and appears to have been faced on the northern side. It may have delimited the southern edge of a structure, or possibly a small enclosure. Further to the west is a shallow, partly rock-cut trench (F202), which curves north and west away from the line of the later rampart. A section of the trench, *c.* 14m in length, was excavated. Its function is uncertain, but it may be associated with the wall. The wall itself was partly dismantled during the construction of the bank of redeposited material forming the inner portion of the middle rampart. The remnants of the wall, surviving to a maximum of three courses, were incorporated within this later feature.

The rampart (Figs 2 and 3)

The rampart had been formed of linear compartments defined by large slabs and blocks infilled with limestone rubble. It was constructed along the outer (southern) edge of the terrace and averages 10m in width. The inner face of the stone portion of the rampart consisted of two closely set vertical walls (F275A, 262/275B) formed by 3–5 irregular courses of large slabs and blocks, surviving to a maximum height of 1.2m (Pl. 1). A low bank comprising a wedge of redeposited occupation material had been piled against the inner side of this facing feature, giving the rampart a maximum width of 13m. The apparent gap in the rampart identified in 1994 (Grogan 1996) was revealed as a later feature, perhaps associated with the cultivation system in the area between the inner and middle ramparts in Site C.

Comment

The evidence from the 1995 season for the sequence of activity around the time of the construction of the hillfort differs somewhat from that identified in previous years (Grogan 1995, 59–61; 1996). Within Site C the earth and stone bank is the final element in the rampart construction, whereas in Sites A, E, H and F it represents the primary stage. This indicates an additional degree of complexity regarding the relationship between the occupation of the hilltop and the hillfort construction. The occupation phase along the middle rampart, at least, appears to have begun before the initial rampart construction but continued into a phase when the occupation was enclosed by the rampart.

Site G: the middle enclosure

Six cuttings were opened along the southern side of the middle rampart between Site C and Enclosure 1 (Fig. 1). The purpose of these was threefold: to determine the extent of occupation evidence along the south-facing terrace, to examine the relationship between any occupation material and the rampart, and to examine the inner face of the rampart itself.

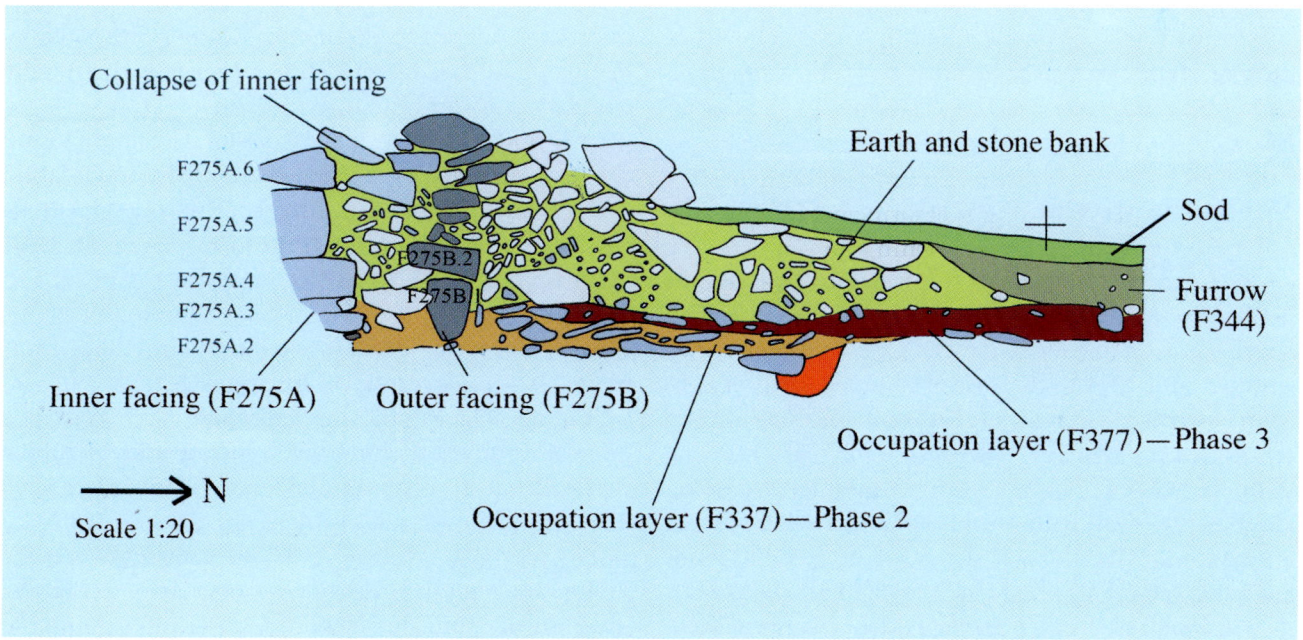

Fig. 3—Mooghaun South. Site C: section through the middle rampart.

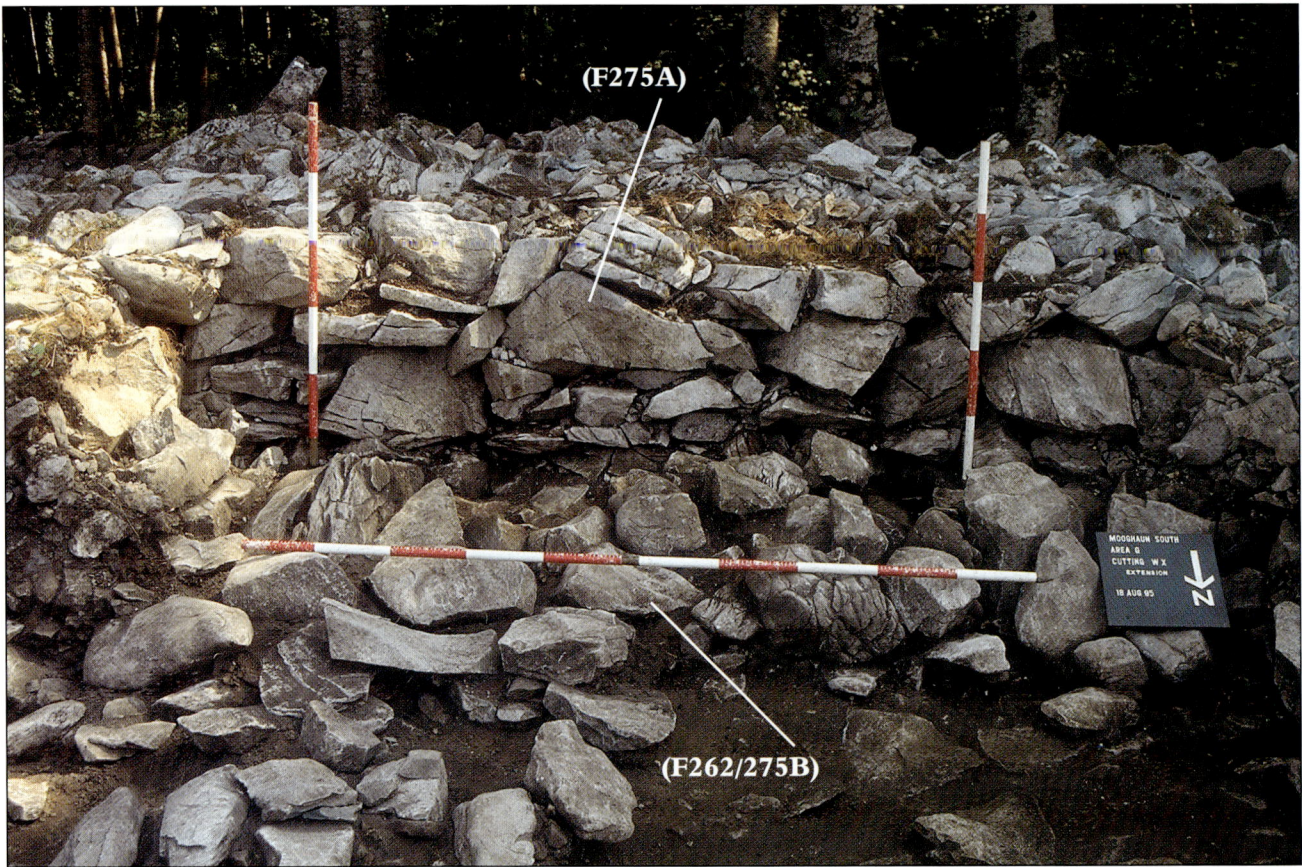

Pl. 1—Mooghaun South. Site C: the primary (F275A) and secondary (F262/275B) inner facings of the middle rampart from the north.

Only the westernmost cutting (No. 1) produced evidence for occupation, in the form of animal bone, some coarse pottery and occupation soils. This area had been extensively disturbed during construction of the rampart, when stone was quarried here. The other cuttings demonstrated the similarity of the rampart to the more intensively excavated cuttings to the east in Site C.

Site D: house site

A third house, similar to those investigated in 1994, was excavated (Fig. 1; Pl. 2). House 2 is 15m south-west of the inner rampart, on level but rocky ground, and 12m to the east of House 1. It is oval in plan, with internal measurements of 3.8m north–south by 3m east–west and an external diameter of 6m. It is constructed of an enclosing double-kerb wall with a rubble fill. The wall is 1.5m in maximum thickness and *c.* 0.4m in height. Finds included fragments of animal bone and worked chert.

Although no further dating evidence was revealed, samples for all three houses have been sent for radiocarbon dating.

Site I: Enclosure 4

Extensive clearance was carried out in the area outside the north-western side of the middle rampart in order to identify a number of features illustrated by Westropp (1908, pl. 9). This revealed three roughly circular enclosures ranging in diameter from *c.* 12 to 25m (Fig. 1; Pl. 3). Two of these, a small enclosure (No. 4) immediately outside the rampart and a larger one *c.* 40m to the north-east (No. 6), appear to correspond in size and location to those identified by Westropp. The third, Enclosure 5, occurs *c.* 25m to the north of No. 4 and represents a new discovery. Excavation in the form of two cuttings totalling 18m² in area was undertaken on Enclosure 4.

Before excavation, the enclosure appeared as a circular structure defined by a low spread of rubble representing a collapsed and partly dismantled wall. The site encloses a fairly level area with a cairn of stones placed off-centre. It is set in a slight natural hollow on a gentle north-west-facing slope so that the interior is slightly lower (*c.* 0.15m) than the surrounding area, except towards the north-west. The enclosing wall is generally very low, but is best

Pl. 2—Mooghaun South. Site D: House 2 from the south.

Pl. 3—Mooghaun South. Site I: Enclosure 4 from the south-west.

preserved on the southern and south-western sides, where it is up to 0.4m in height. The enclosure measures 11.5m (north–south) by 14.5m (east–west) externally, and the interior 7.3m (north–south) by 8.7m (east–west). A small cairn in the centre of the enclosure measured 1.4m north–south by 1.6m east–west, with a maximum height of 0.3m.

A very thin cover of stony organic soil, averaging less than 0.2m in depth, occurred within the interior of the site. While details of the structure were revealed, including the nature of the wall construction, there were no artefacts or internal features other than the cairn. The latter was composed of irregularly placed stones and small limestone blocks, but excavation produced no further information other than some animal bone which may be modern in origin.

Comment

The excavation did not reveal the date or function of the stone enclosure. Its occurrence in the same area as the larger and better-preserved enclosures (Nos 5 and 6) to the north and north-east may suggest that it had some function related to these sites. The proximity of late eighteenth- or early nineteenth-century field walls, *c.* 10m to the west, may in part explain its dilapidated condition.

References

Grogan, E. 1995 Excavations at Mooghaun South, 1993. Interim report. *Discovery Programme Reports* **2**, 57–61.

Grogan, E. 1996 Excavations at Mooghaun South, 1994. Interim report. *Discovery Programme Reports* **4**, 47–57.

Westropp, T. J. 1908 Types of the ring-forts and similar structures remaining in eastern Clare (the Newmarket group). *Proceedings of the Royal Irish Academy* **27C**, 217–34.

7. ARCHAEOLOGICAL APPLICATIONS OF MODERN SURVEY TECHNIQUES

Barry Masterson

Pl. 1—Surveying Carn Tigherna hillfort, Co. Cork, overlooking the Blackwater Valley with the Galtee Mountains in the distance (Barry Masterson).

Introduction

Surveying has traditionally been defined as the science and art of determining the relative positions of points on, above or beneath the surface of the earth, or the establishment of such points. In a more general sense, surveying can be regarded as a discipline that encompasses all methods of gathering and processing information regarding the physical earth and environment. It is the purpose of this paper to explain some of the processes behind such surveys, which are not normally presented in the archaeological literature.

Overview

Archaeologists have always been concerned with representing archaeological monuments in some sort of graphical form, to convey their interpretations of a site, or simply to allow the lay-person to appreciate the subtleties of a monument's structure. The introduction of digital surveying instruments and automated data-logging into the measurement of archaeological monuments and complexes has been a step towards a more flexible record of site morphology and topographical context, rather than the 'static' paper plans which were the previous standard. There are obvious advantages to using these modern survey techniques as an effective recording procedure and as a tool for analysis. They define, through basic geometry, the size, shape and extent of the features under consideration with various degrees of accuracy and detail, depending on the methodology. In an archaeological context, this means that the size, morphology, local setting and structural features of a site can be represented in a variety of formats, simplifying the visualisation process and conveying more information. In addition to this standard end-product, the digital model of the monument or landscape can be augmented by volume analysis, profile generation, intervisibility studies, reconstruction and de-construction, providing valuable additions to our information database. In essence, the data are dynamic, with the advantage that the integrity of the original data set is always maintained, thereby providing a permanent record of the site as it existed at the time of the survey.

The archaeologist should have some understanding of the techniques involved in electronic surveys, their potential and limitations when selecting sites for detailed survey as the detail survey can be a high-cost operation. The archaeologist must assess whether the results justify the expenditure of resources, when a simpler representation of the site may be adequate. Similarly, the surveyor carrying out the work should be able to advise on the details, and should have experience with and a competent understanding of the nature of archaeological monuments and the reasoning behind carrying out such surveys.

Below is an outline of the stages involved in carrying out an electronic topographic survey. Most of the discussion is based on the assumption that a total station (see box below) is the survey instrument; however, the basic principles regarding field recording remain the same, whichever technology is used.

Field procedures

Control survey

Before commencing a detail survey, the survey control requirement must be assessed. The survey control is a network of points from which all subsequent measurements are recorded, similar in concept to the national trigonometric control but on a site-specific scale. The main factor to be considered is whether the control must be permanent or temporary. On a large-scale site, or on sites which are to be excavated, permanent control should be considered mandatory, to allow phases of detail survey to occur over a long period of time. This is especially useful on sites under excavation, where it is important to record excavated detail and site grids within the same coordinate system over different seasons. On smaller sites, which are being surveyed as part of a survey sampling strategy, or for simple representation purposes it is not always necessary to undertake the establishment of permanent control, as quite often the entire survey may be carried out in one observation session.

When establishing a control network, locations are selected which provide maximum visibility of the area to be surveyed and a survey station is established on the ground. A number of such points may be required; in these cases, the *combination* of views from *each* of these stations should cover as much of the site as possible. In addition, when establishing control using an instrument such as a total station, each control station must be intervisible with at least two others for the purposes of determining their exact position in relation to each other. These positions are resolved through a measurement process whereby the angles and distances between the stations are determined and subjected to rigorous processing, resulting in a listing of three-dimensional coordinates and a statistical analysis of each of the station positions. This stage of the survey requires the most precision, as the precision of the control will have a direct bearing on the accuracy of the final survey. With the advent of relatively cheap and easy-to-use Global Positioning Satellite (GPS) technology (see box below), much of the control work on large-scale surveys can be carried out in a shorter time to a comparable accuracy. Survey-grade GPS units will provide national grid coordinates to millimetre accuracy, allowing for an immediate locational reference.

Topographic survey

The topographic survey is the stage where the elements of the site and immediate surroundings are recorded. The basic procedure for carrying out a topographic survey remains constant, regardless of site type or size. In basic terms, sufficient points and lines must be recorded to allow a complete computer simulation of the ground surface. It is the quality of the points location and its bearing on the definition of the surface morphology that is most important, however, not the number of points. It is quite conceivable to have a similar quantity of data points defining monuments of vastly different scales. For example, a 40m-diameter enclosure may be fully represented by 800 data points, while a small burnt mound measuring 10m by 10m may take as many as 400, owing to the level of detail and scale required for the final results. The surveyor must choose what level of detail is required, assess the amount of variation in the surface of the site and choose data points, possibly adopting a selective sampling procedure, that will accurately represent the ground surface. For a three-dimensional survey, these points must define *changes* in the surface morphology. Recording changes in the horizontal and vertical direction of features is the absolute minimum requirement, which should be further supplemented by the addition of points that describe the *shape* of the features to give a more realistic representation. Thought should also be given to the surrounding terrain, to provide a context for the monument. This surrounding area can often be generalised by spreading out the sampling distance of surveyed points. Linework-only plans present a simpler scenario, in which the changes in direction of

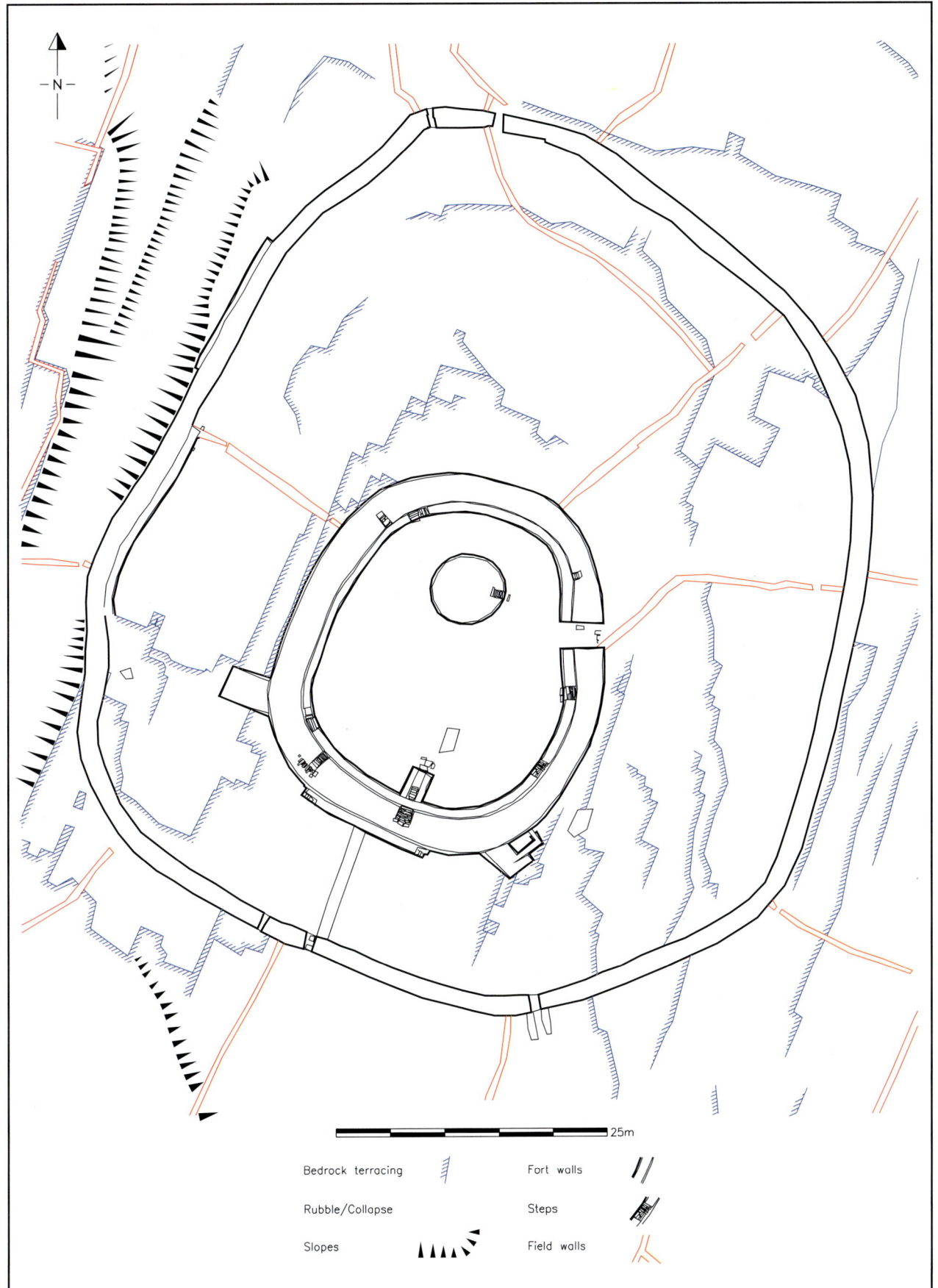

Fig. 1—*Digital linework plan of Dun Eochla, Inis Mór, Co. Galway, based on a survey carried out in 1994 for the Western Stone Forts Project.*

Pl. 2—*Aerial view of Dun Eochla, Inis Mór, Co. Galway (Claire Cotter).*

outlines and hard detail need only be considered in the horizontal plane. This will reduce the amount of time required for a site survey but, considering the benefits and variety of output forms provided by three-dimensional data, the full 3-D survey offers a greater return for a relatively small increase in expenditure.

The instrumentation used for carrying out the detail survey will normally be a total station. The exact model or type used will depend on the resources of the archaeological project and the accuracy requirements of the survey. In general, even relatively low-cost electronic instruments are more than adequate for most detail survey tasks. In either case, the decisions regarding sampling strategies remain the same, as do the recording processes. Most modern instrumentation will come equipped with a data-logger—a field computer attached to the instrument that will automatically record and store the measurement data in addition to providing software tools for limited processing and analysis. These data-loggers require the surveyor to assign a sequence of coding defining additional information about the individual points. In general, these codes will define a point as being either a control station, a discrete point (spot-heights for example) or part of a line (defining the outline of a feature). The coding may be as complex as desired, with new codes being created to describe any number of features. Some forethought is advisable, however, as parameters for every code must be defined to allow the processing software to compile a structured database of the recorded points. A standardised coding system is often more effective, as it simplifies future work and reduces the time spent redefining codes on completion of the survey.

Processing

A wide range of software packages is available for the reduction of survey measurements. The choice is usually determined by the resources available and the features required. In general, most packages tend to be geared more towards the engineering fields of surveying, providing facilities for calculating volumes, setting-out information and highway design. For the archaeo-surveyor, the basic modules of such packages will usually suffice, as these will produce raw results in the form of a basic outline plan and a database of the three-dimensional coordinates of every point surveyed. These results may be followed up in numerous ways using more specialised modules or

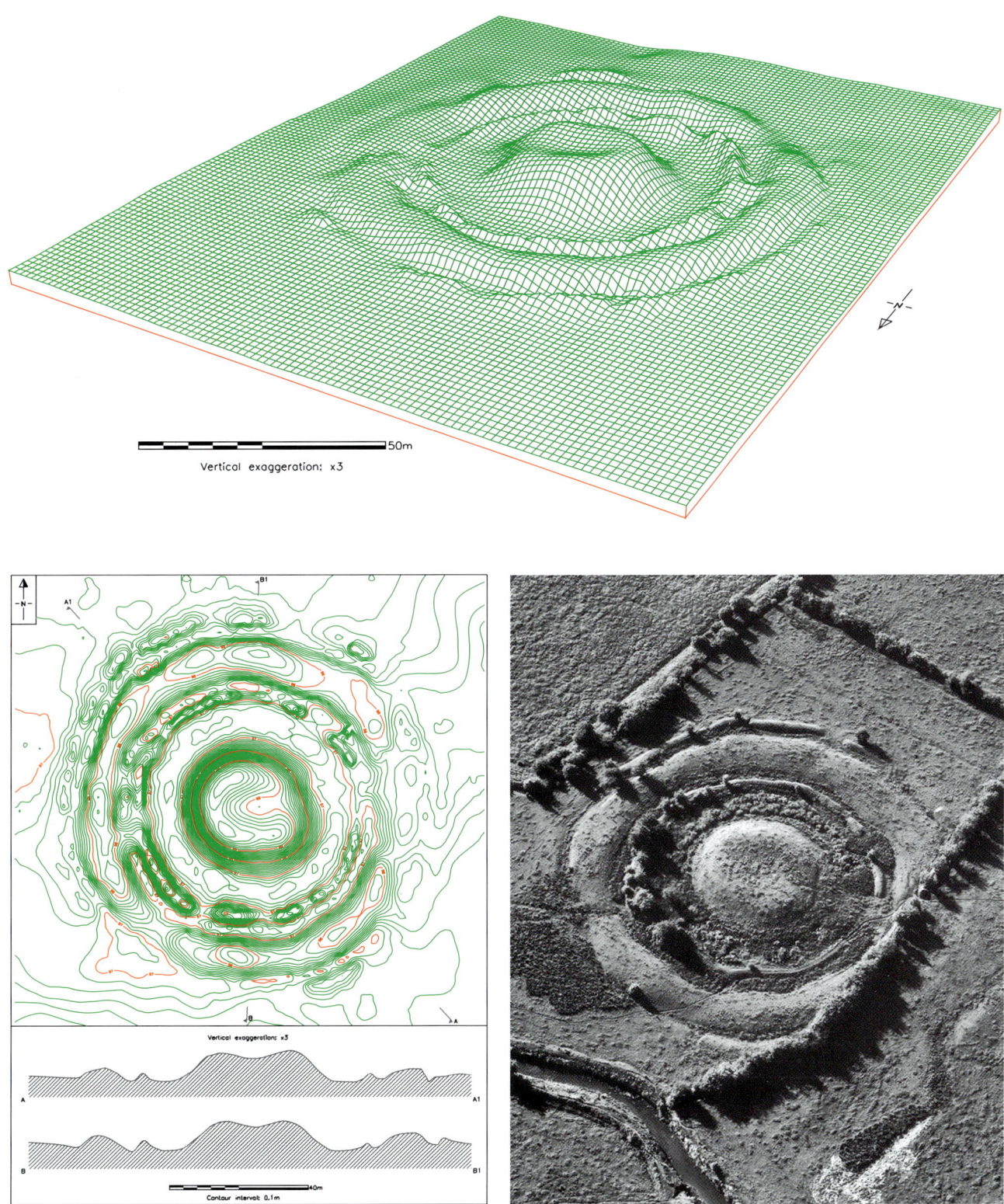

Fig. 2—*Digital Terrain Model (DTM) and resulting contour plan and profiles of the complex earthen enclosure and mound at Rathanny, Co. Limerick, based on a survey carried out in 1995 for the North Munster Project. The photograph shows an aerial view of Rathanny, CUCAP AVT 27 (reproduced with the permission of the Cambridge Committee for Aerial Photography).*

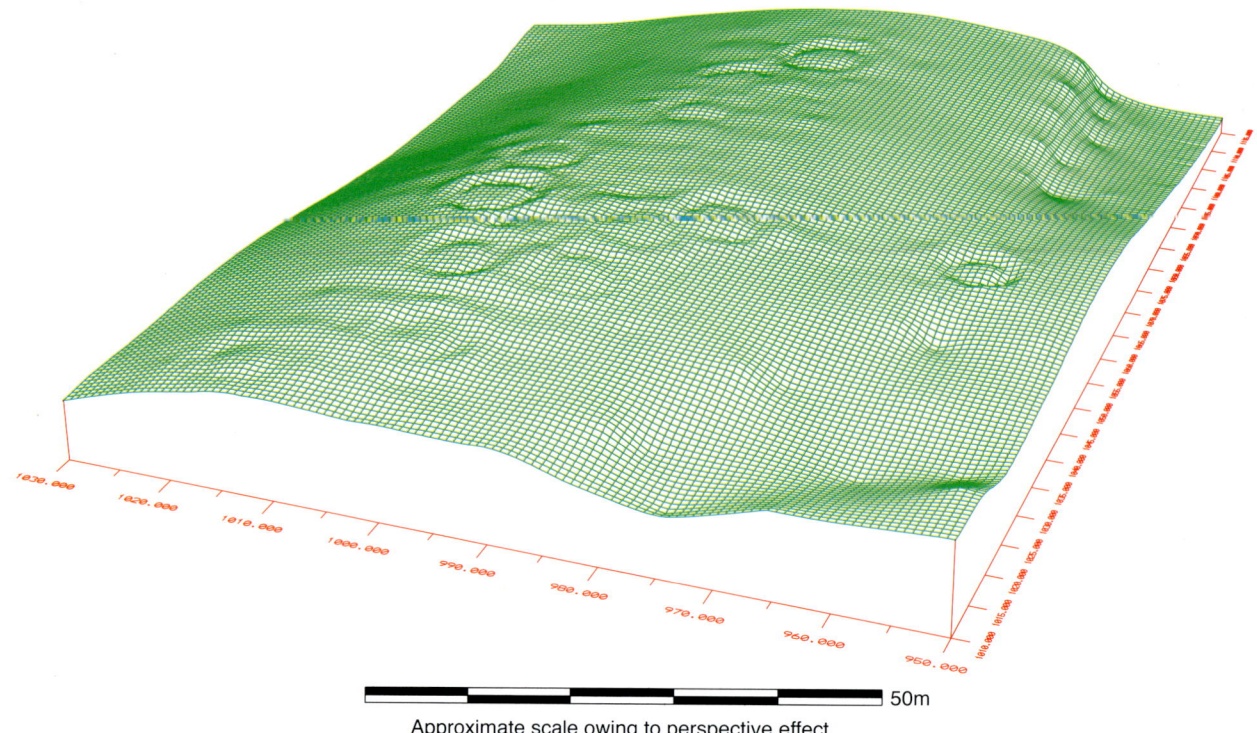

Fig. 3—DTM of a barrow cemetery at Elton, Co. Limerick, based on a survey carried out in 1996 for the Ballyhoura Hills Research Project. Fourteen ring-barrows can be seen, most of which straddle a dry ridge that runs through a waterlogged area.

software packages dedicated to terrain modelling and visualisation.

Linework plans can be finalised using a Computer Aided Design (CAD) package to provide a basic outline of the site's features, most acceptable for hard, well-defined detail such as walls and boundaries. Utilising standard drawing conventions, these digital drawings are visually comparable to hand-drawn plans, with the advantage that they can be quickly reproduced with varying degrees of detail at different scales (Fig. 1; Pl. 2). For the archaeologist, the main strength of the digital survey lies in the ability to create a Digital Terrain Model (DTM) of the site. This is effectively a computer rendering of the site, based on the survey measurements, which can yield additional data in a variety of formats, both graphical and numerical. A number of methods are available for generating a DTM, each with varying advantages (triangulation and various gridding methods, for example). In basic terms, a surface model is calculated from the sample point distribution, with the heights on the surface interpolated from the surrounding spot-heights. A common analogy is that of draping a rubber sheet over the distribution of points. This virtual sheet will take the shape of the terrain, represented by the data points. The exact method used for calculating the surface is determined on the basis of producing a model which will honour the surveyed points as closely as possible while being visually concise and unambiguous in its portrayal of archaeological features.

Virtual perspective views of this three-dimensional model can be generated by varying the viewpoint of the observer to produce an illustrative graphic of the site, thus providing a simple method for visualising site context and morphology. In addition, this technique has the advantage that the parameters of the model can be varied to aid in the visualisation process. For example, the vertical axis of the DTM can be exaggerated to highlight low-relief features that might otherwise go unnoticed. There are two basic methods for displaying this type of model. The first is to present it as a wire-mesh grid, with lines running parallel to the axes of the grid at regular intervals. This provides the observer with a sense of perspective, as the lines converge in the distance (Figs 2 and 3). Additional information may be added to the basic DTM to aid in the interpretation of the site, such as the locations of features or finds in plan, and stratigraphical information in the vertical axis (Fig. 4). The second form of DTM visualisation is the hill-shaded model, where the DTM is treated as a solid

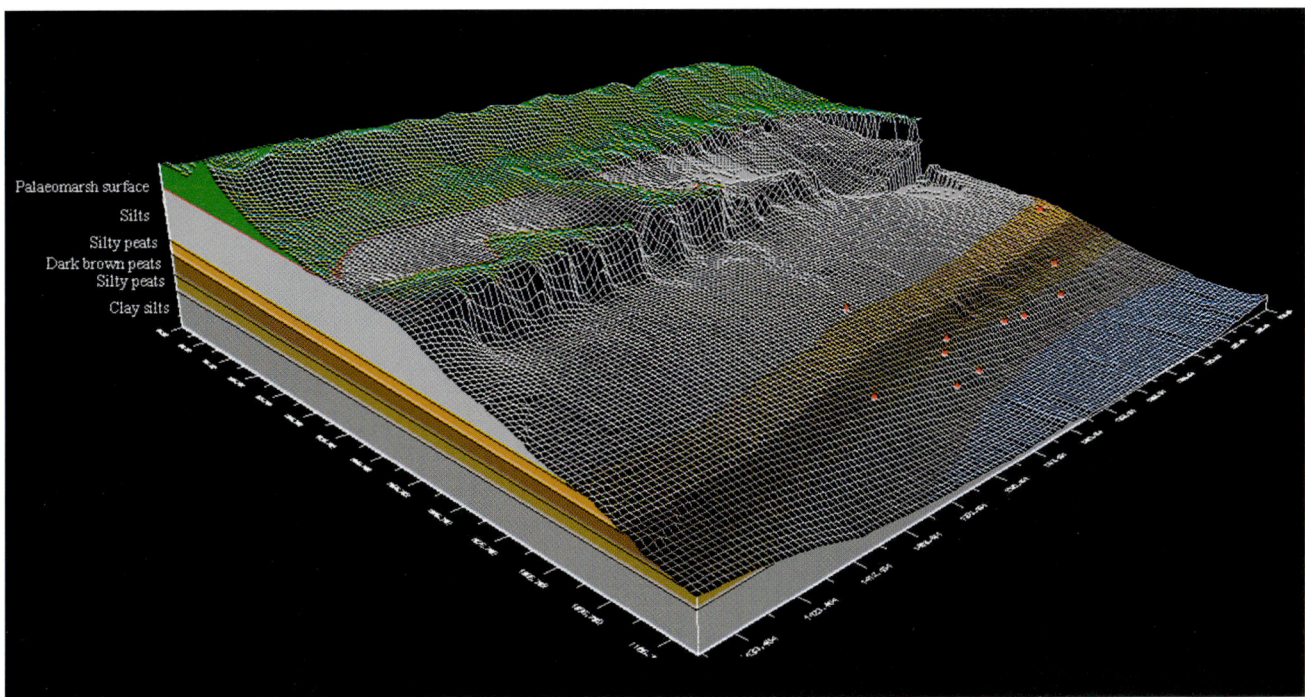

Fig. 4—Digital Terrain Model (DTM) of a section of the foreshore at Carrigdirty Rock, Co. Limerick. Based on topographical survey and palaeoenvironmental stratigraphical coring results, this model indicates the exposure of layers of peats and clays on the lower foreshore, and the location of early prehistoric artefacts and bone.

surface rather than a wire mesh. It is then possible to render the surface and simulate the rays of light from a virtual sun within the computer environment. This has the effect of creating an image that falls within our conceptions of reality more readily than the more abstract visualisations provided by the wire-mesh DTM. The hill-shaded model can be presented in either plan form, for a 'scaleable' representation (Fig. 5), or as a perspective view for general visualisation. Setting the virtual light source to a low altitude, thereby casting longer 'shadows', can highlight subtle ground features. Analogous to taking aerial photographs with a low-altitude sun, this technique has the advantage that the image produced is of a virtual model, whereby the sun can be positioned at an altitude and bearing that would not occur in nature. This can enhance aspects of the site that an aerial photograph could not, in addition to being a representation devoid of any vegetation that might obscure details of the site (Doody et al. 1995).

As well as being useful for visualisation purposes, the DTM is the underlying structure for creating contour plans, which can be generated to any desired contour interval. When generating very small contour intervals, it is necessary to bear in mind the level of detail that the site was originally surveyed to, since the survey point distribution may not realistically support the resolution desired. A small contour interval is often desirable, as it will display the finer details of monument morphology, similar to exaggerating the vertical axis of a DTM. While the contour plan may not always provide the same ease of visualisation as a perspective view of a DTM, it presents a geometrically correct graphical model from which dimensions and relative height differences can be scaled (Fig. 6).

All of the above methods of representation have the advantage that they are not limited by scale. In theory, as the digital model is a computer simulation of reality, views can be produced from any viewpoint, at any scale. In addition, the topographical survey provides a framework for clarifying the spatial relationships of information from other data sources. Superimposing other forms of data can allow for a greater understanding of how these data relate to the physical presence of the site, perhaps best exemplified by geophysical data (Newman 1993; 1995; 1997) (Figs 7 and 8).

Volume determination

The possibilities for further numerical analysis offered by the digital model are practically limitless, as any query regarding the physical properties of a

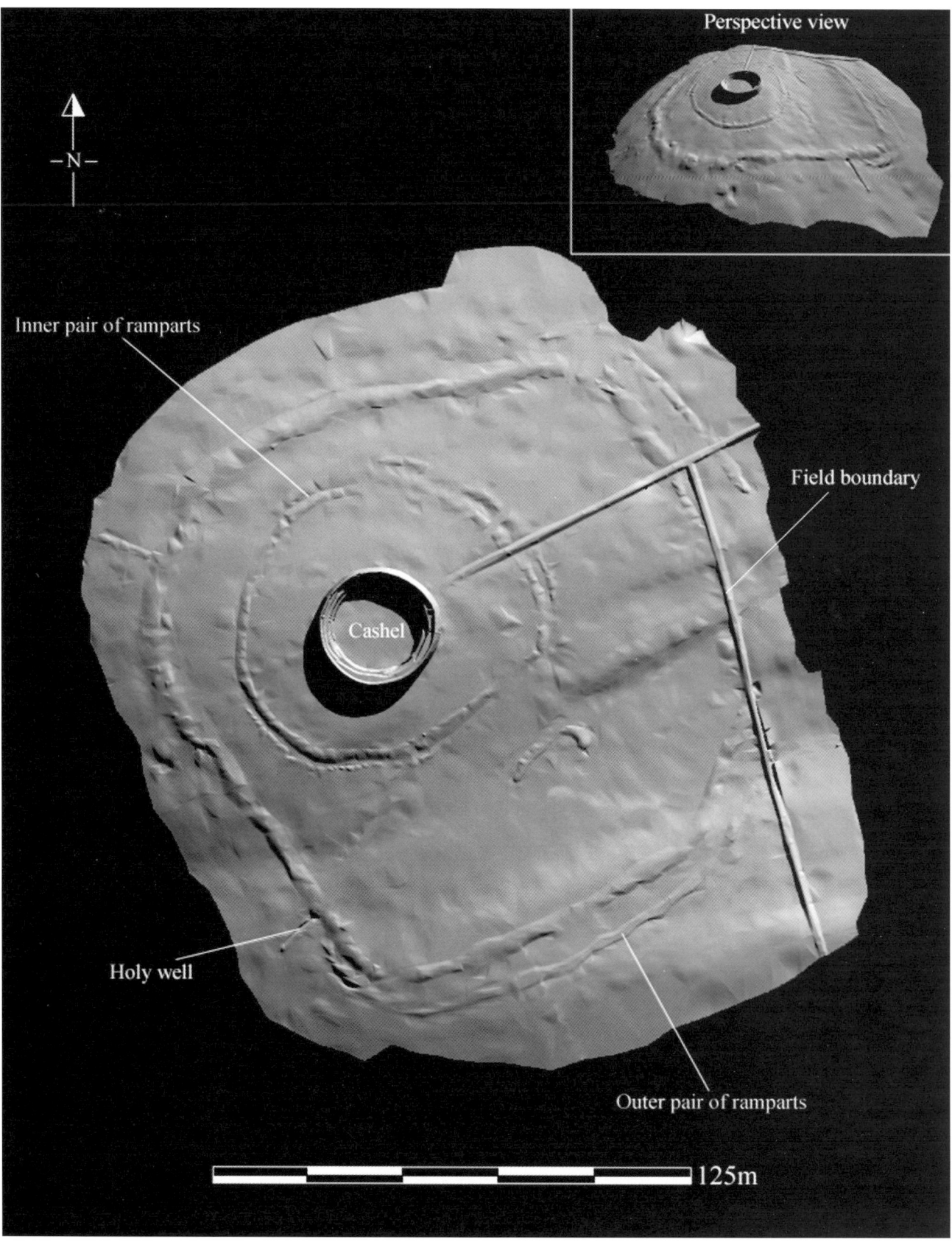

Fig. 5—Hill-shaded model of Grianan Aileach, Co. Donegal, based on a survey carried out in 1996 for the Western Stone Forts Project.

The total station (Pl. 3)

The total station is an instrument combining an electronic theodolite, an electromagnetic distance-measuring (EDM) unit and a microprocessor. The instrument measures angular values in the horizontal and vertical planes through electronic means. Distances are determined by transmitting either a microwave or an electro-optical beam to a reflective target. Most EDM units are capable of measuring distances up to 2km with one target prism. This can be increased to approximately 9km with a larger bank of prisms.

Using these angles and distances, the built-in microprocessor can calculate horizontal distances, height differences, coordinates and relative position differences in real time. The real power of this system, however, lies in the addition of the electronic data-logger, a portable field computer that automatically records all measurement data and notes, vastly increasing the speed at which the detail survey is carried out. The data-logger also possesses limited processing power for in-field checks and processing. In addition, many of these loggers can be programmed to provide customised support for the archaeologist or surveyor.

Global Positioning System

The Global Positioning System makes use of satellite technology for the determination of positions on the earth's surface. In basic terms, a satellite receiver tracks several satellites which are in orbit around the earth. The receiver computes its coordinates in relation to the GPS co-ordinate system and then converts to the coordinate system chosen by the surveyor. This system is ideal for the establishment of control networks, as the instrument can be set up and left for a given length of time as it tracks the satellites, without the need for establishing lines of sight. In addition, a portable receiver can be used in conjunction with a base station to carry out detailed survey, in much the same way as a total station is used. It should be noted, however, that certain control requirements must be met in order for this particular detail survey method to attain the accuracy provided by total station methods. Problems may also occur where buildings or trees compromise the view to the satellites.

Pl. 3—Total station equipped with a data-logger (Barry Masterson).

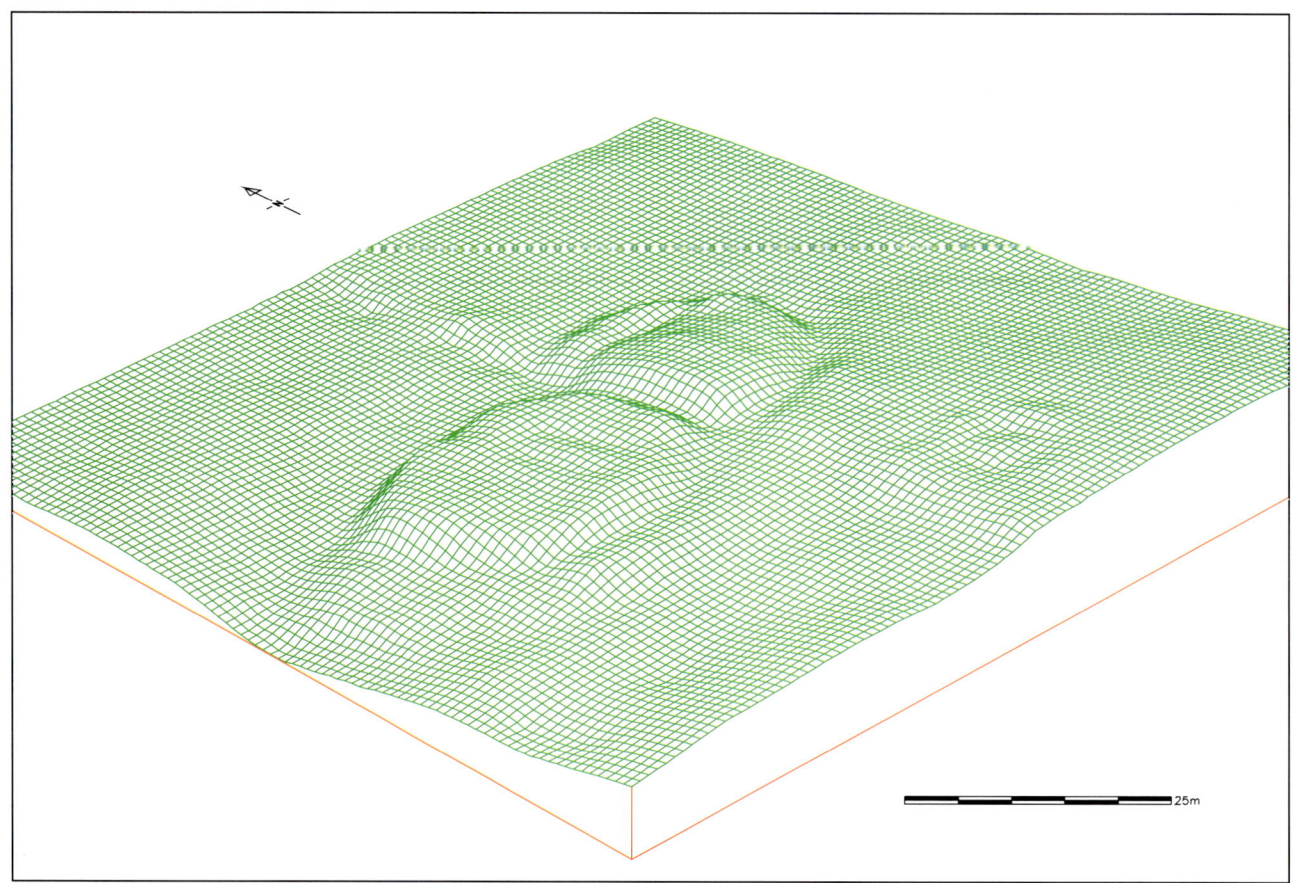

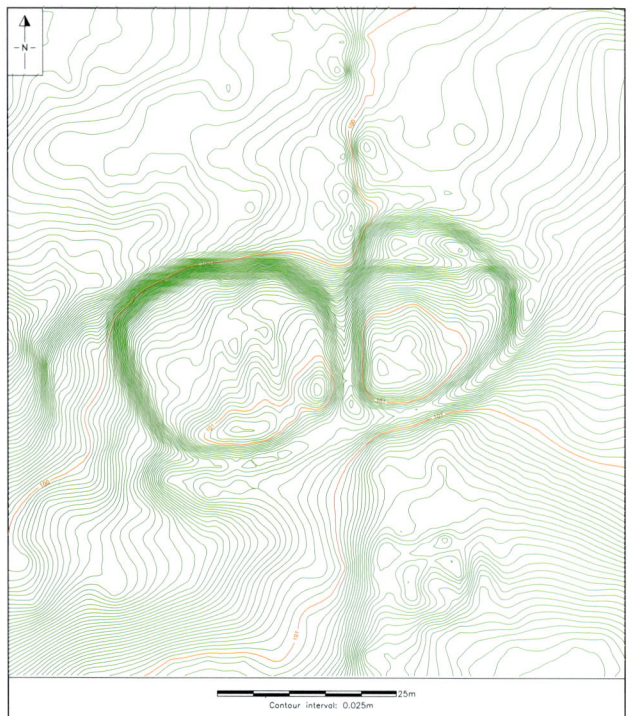

Fig. 6—DTM and contour plan of an enclosure and barrow at Moanmore, Co. Tipperary, surveyed in 1996 for the Ballyhoura Hills Project.

monument can be applied. Detailed below is one of the most useful queries, that of determining the volume of material used to construct a monument. Since any detailed survey defines a mathematical model of a surface, it is possible to apply functions/formulae to the data in order to extract further information. Here is an example of how the digital data can be used to accurately calculate the volume of material contained within a structure. It should be noted that it is possible to calculate the volume of material contained within the structure from most sources of survey data; the method used to calculate the volume will depend on how the survey was carried out or what format the data/results are in.

There are two basic methods available for calculating the volume of material within a monument's structure. The first is based on contours, often used when the survey has been carried out using non-digital instrumentation or when data from older surveys are the only source of information. From a contour plan, the area enclosed by each contour line on the monument is measured either electronically, with a digitiser, or mechanically, using a planimeter. The volume of the structure can then be calculated by applying the trapezoidal rule:

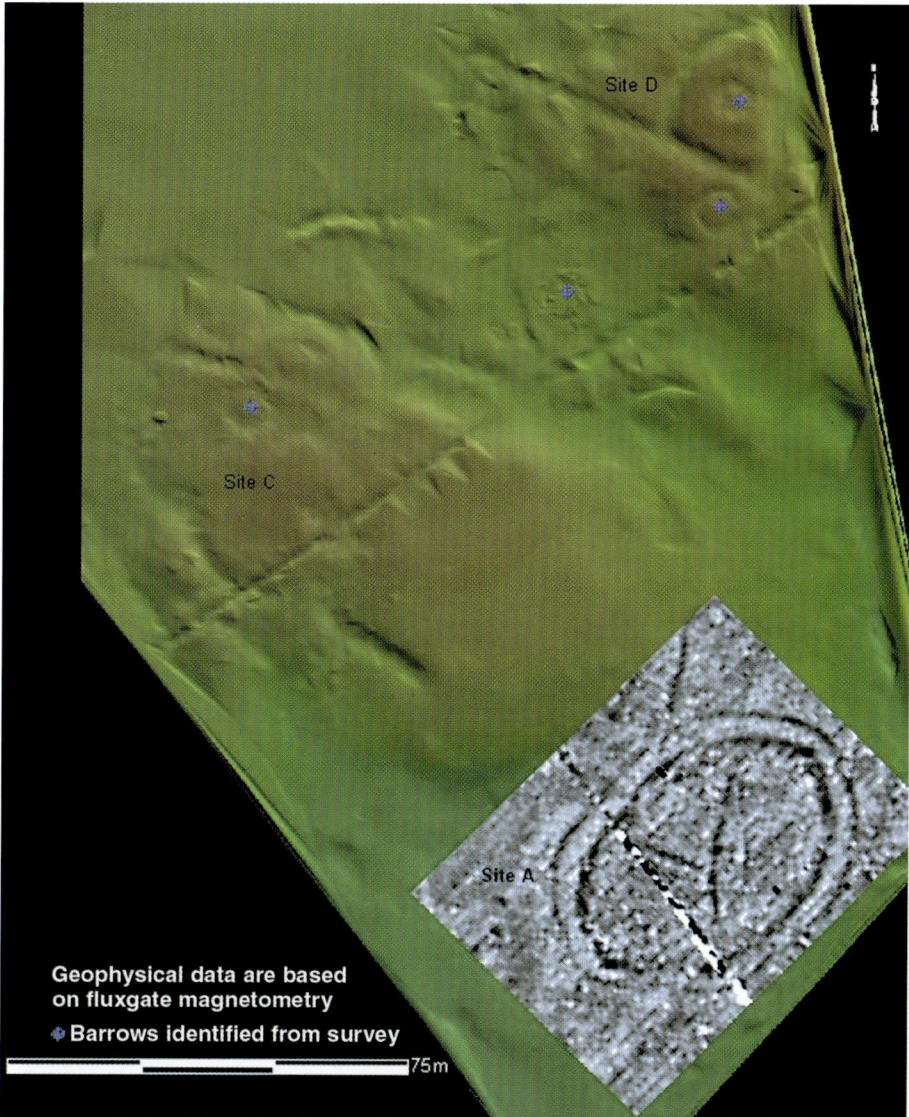

Fig. 7—Shaded relief map of the Chancellorsland complex, Co. Tipperary, with the magnetometry survey of site A superimposed over the model.

Fig. 8—Perspective view of a shaded relief map of the Chancellorsland complex, Co. Tipperary, viewed from the south-west with the magnetometry survey of site A superimposed over the model. Site C is visible in the left foreground while the barrows of site D can be seen in the background.

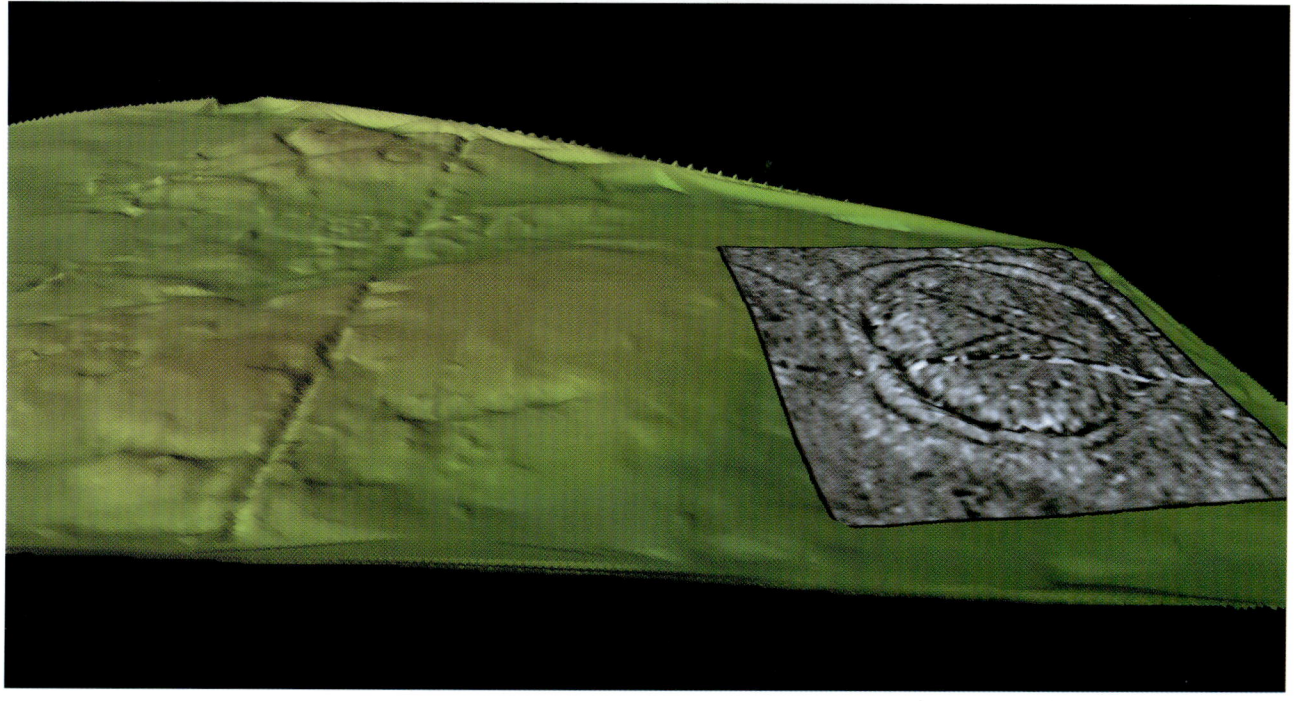

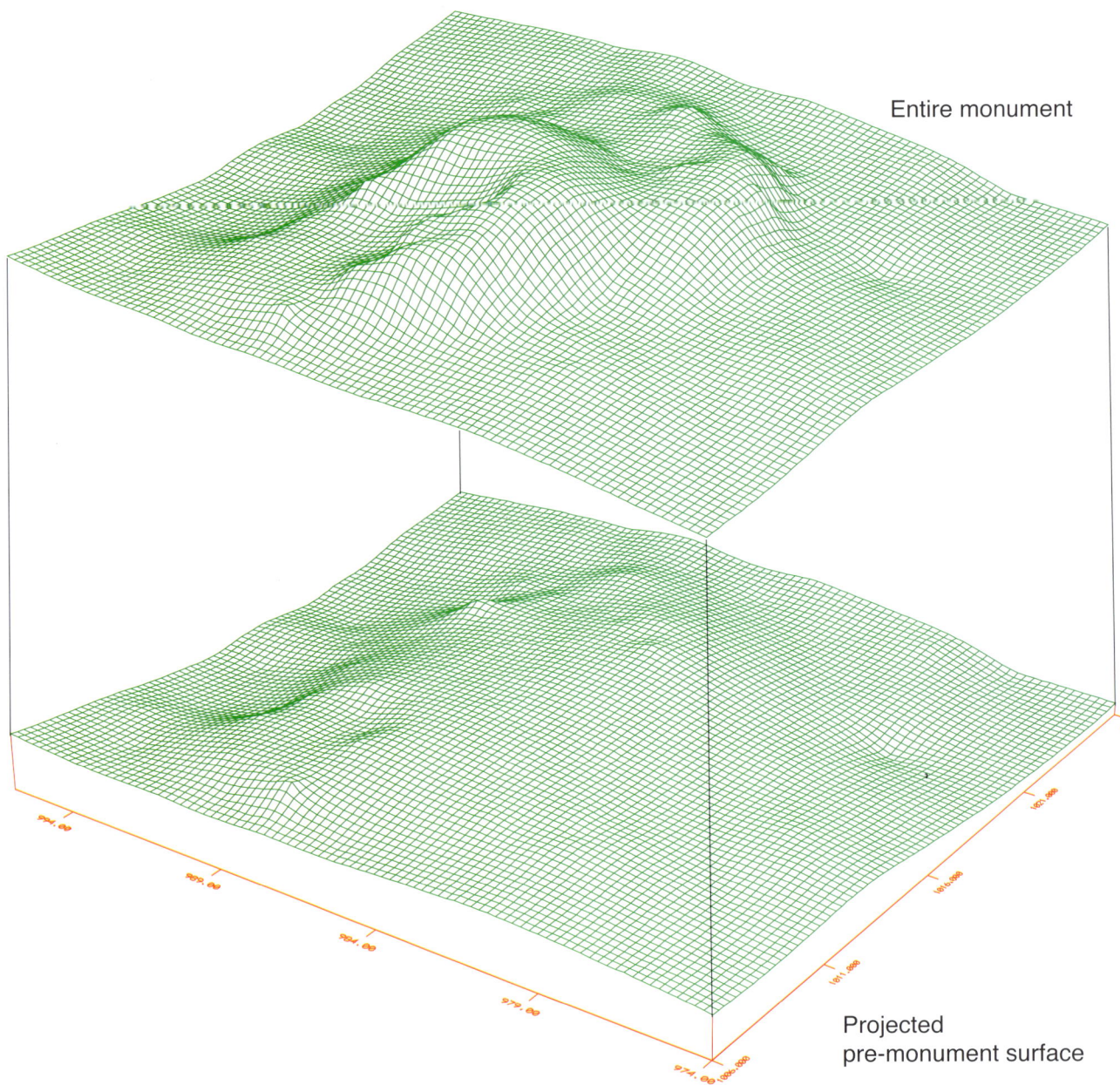

Fig. 9—A DTM of a fulacht fiadh near Magh Adhair, Co. Clare, overlying a projected pre-monument ground surface. Used for volume calculations, these models are based on a survey carried out in 1994 for the North Munster Project.

$$V = I/2(A_1 + 2(A_2 + ...A_{n-1}) + A_n),$$

where

V is the volume to be calculated,
I is the contour interval,
A_1 to A_n are the enclosed areas of the contour levels 1 to n.

When a site has been digitally surveyed, a more rigorous method can be applied which makes direct use of the raw survey data. Since the DTM accurately models the ground surface, it provides an excellent base for directly calculating volumes without passing through the intermediate stage of generating contours. Several formulae are available for this process, the simplest being a variation of the trapezoidal rule as outlined above. The volume of the model can be determined by the trapezoidal rule, using the area enclosed by vertical sections rather than the horizontal sections defined by the contours.

This formula can be adapted to give the volume above a projected or pre-monument construction ground surface by comparing two DTMs of the area under consideration, one with the monument as surveyed, the other with the monument effectively removed from the landscape by omitting data points that define the surface of the monument from the

DTM generation process (Fig. 9). The result is a projected ground surface, on which the monument is assumed to be resting. The difference between the volumes of the two models is effectively the volume of the mound. The main advantage of this calculation over the contour method is that the latter restricts the determination of the volume to the lowest contour interval on the monument. This is acceptable if the site is positioned on level terrain, but problems occur on sloping ground where no single contour will fully enclose the lower portion of the site. Using a projected ground surface negates this effect, as the resultant data are of the difference between the projected surface and the actual surveyed surface, ensuring that the volume calculated is of the monument alone.

It should be noted that, although these calculations are mathematically sound, the results are an approximation, as the survey data available may not truly represent the actual extent of the monument, and contours are a result of interpolation. Many factors will have affected the apparent volume of an archaeological structure. The actual location of the site will provide some indication of how much soil buildup, erosion or slippage will have occurred, thus altering the apparent volume of the structure. This said, the results will be an accurate assessment of the volume of the visible remains of the monument as it stands at the time of the survey. These volume data can provide additional information which may aid in site interpretation, such as calculating the man-hours required for the construction of the monument.

See the case study below for an example of how these calculations may be applied in the particular case of burnt mounds/*fulachta fiadh*, where the volume of the mound can provide direct information on the usage of this type of site.

Application of techniques to excavation

As stated above, when carrying out an excavation, a detailed survey of the ground surface of the site should be considered a prerequisite, as it provides a permanent and precise record of the site at the time before the disturbance caused by excavation. However, survey technology has a role to play throughout the entire course of the excavation, thereby maintaining the standard of data-recording. It goes without saying that the coordinate system used for surveying the site as a whole should also be used as the control grid for any geophysical work that may be carried out, in addition to providing the framework for standard excavation planning techniques such as the planning frame or baseline and offset methods. To bring this one step further towards a complete digital representation of a site, we could envisage the complete survey, electronically, of excavated surfaces. These surface models could then be compiled to recreate a digital representation of the site stratigraphy. When integrated with database technology in a Geographical Information System (GIS) this will allow for the study of the entire monument or complex at both a surface and subsurface level, allowing for a greater understanding and more complex interpretation.

The only limitations to using a total station for the recording of excavated detail would appear to be logistical problems. On a large-scale excavation it may not be practical, or cost-effective, to have a single surveyor continuously recording as the excavation progresses, as such detailed survey work is quite time-consuming. In addition, the excavation method may not allow the meaningful survey of layers in a manner that would be conducive to this particular form of visualisation. In either case, it would be advisable to back up such surveys with the traditional planning methods as, by default, it forces the detailed examination of every square metre of the excavated surface, which should allow a greater understanding of the subtleties of contextual relationships than would the relatively non-interactive electronic surveying techniques.

Another possible method for capturing the information required to model excavated areas could be to utilise photogrammetrical techniques. Photogrammetry is a non-contact survey method using overlapping pairs of photographs that can be viewed, and measured, in three dimensions. With the appropriate instrumentation, it would be possible to model the excavated surface in much the same way as a standard detail survey. This method has the advantages of being capable of high accuracy while being relatively fast in capturing the raw data. To date, however, little use has been made of such methods on excavations in Ireland, mainly owing to expense and the preparation required to facilitate the correct operation of the method. Some use has been made of photo-mosaics, most notably the work carried out by Burenhult (1980) at Carrowmore, Co. Sligo. This is particularly suitable for verification of field drawings and general site portrayal; depending on the control points within the photographs, it can also be used as a source for two-dimensional plans. Such techniques are frequently used for the surveying of building façades, where direct measurement is difficult, but can be adapted to the horizontal for

Case study: burnt mounds

Fig. 10—Contour plan of the fulacht fiadh *near Magh Adhair, Co. Clare, based on a survey carried out in 1994 for the North Munster Project. The survey also highlights that the* fulacht *is a two-phase site, with the earlier mound to the south-east subsumed by a later kidney-shaped mound to the north-west.*

The above volume calculations are an ideal method for gaining further information regarding usage calculations for fulachta fiadh/burnt mounds. The calculation of the amount of usage of the site is dependent on the volume of the mound of burnt stone, the size of the trough in which the water was heated, the percentage of the volume of the trough that has to be filled with stone before the water has reached a usable temperature, and finally the type of stone used in the heating process. By necessity, if the site remains unexcavated, some or all of the parameters of the calculation will have to be approximations or estimates interpolated according to data derived from experiments or other excavated sites. The mound itself may be surveyed in detail, but soil buildup will most likely reduce the apparent volume of the mound. Under ideal conditions, all measurements would be available during an excavation, with the full shape and extent of the surface of the mound exposed and surveyed in fine detail to provide an accurate surface model in addition to detailed measurement of the trough area. After the removal of the mound material the pre-monument ground surface would also be surveyed in detail, thereby providing an ideal combination of surfaces to carry out an exact volume calculation.

In either case, the actual method of calculation is relatively simple.
(1) The volume of the material within the burnt mound must be calculated.
(2) The volume of stone required for one use must be determined.
(3) The volume of the mound is divided by the volume of stone required for one usage to determine the approximate minimum number of uses.
(4) A multiplication factor, determined by the stone type used, is applied to the minimum number of uses to determine a more realistic approximation of the actual number of uses of the site.

The volume of the mound itself may be determined by the methods detailed above. The first difficulty is determining the volume of stone required for one use. In the absence of excavation data for the site under examination, the average-sized trough is assumed to measure 1.9m x 0.9m x 0.9m, giving a volume of 1.539m^3. Experiments have shown that approximately two thirds (66%) of the trough has to be filled with stone before the water is hot enough for use (O'Kelly 1954), giving an average volume of approximately 1m^3 of stone required to heat the water in one usage. This value is simply divided into the volume of the mound to arrive at a minimum number of uses, as if each stone was used for one heating only.

To arrive at a more realistic value, this minimum number of uses is modified according to the type of stone used. Experiments have shown that different stone types have varying resistances to successive heatings and coolings, thus varying the number of times they can be used before fracturing to unusable sizes and being discarded onto the mound (Buckley 1990). In the following examples, the predominant basal rock type is limestone, which can survive six successive heatings and coolings before becoming unusable. Again, without excavation the ratios of different stone types used remains unknown, and therefore a precise calculation is not possible.

Results

The table below is a breakdown of the data from field surveys carried out as part of a site-sampling strategy within the Mooghaun landblock under investigation by the North Munster Project of the Discovery Programme. In all cases the sites were unexcavated and so the specific information on the make-up of the mound was unavailable. The dominant stone type is assumed to be limestone, as this is the basal rock type of the area.

The results of such calculations can only lead to more questions as, on their own, they are simply interesting facts about the monument under consideration. Each site will have its own peculiarities that will change how the data are treated. For example, depending on the local conditions, these usage approximations may indicate a long period of use, most notably where the use of such a site is obviously seasonal (where the burnt mound is covered by seasonal expansion of a lake or turlough, for example). Taken in a broader context, the volume data themselves provide a useful element for a comparative analysis of the levels of activity within a landscape, possibly using fulachta fiadh volumes as an indicator of activity within a specific period. This would require a systematic survey of a representative sample of the fulachta fiadh/burnt mounds within a given study area.

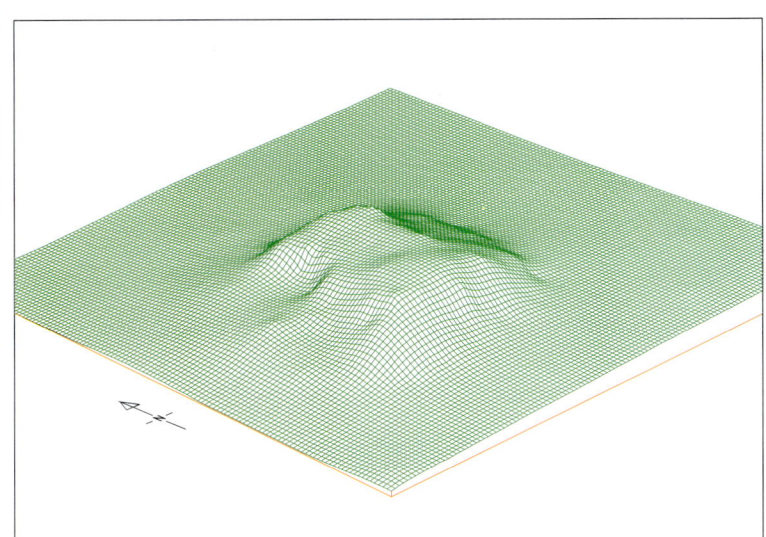

Fig. 11 (top)—DTM of a fulacht fiadh *at Castlefergus, Co. Clare, based on a survey carried out in 1994 for the North Munster Project.*

Fig. 12 (bottom)—Contour plan of a fulacht fiadh *at Ballyhickey, Co. Clare, based on a survey carried out in 1994 for the North Munster Project.*

Site name	Calculated volume of mound	Inferred min. no. of uses	x6 = approx. no. of uses
Magh Adhair (Fig.10) (two-phase site)	30.14m³	30	180
Castlefergus (Fig. 11)	77.56m³	78	468
Ballyhickey	55.35m³	55	330
Mooghaun	15.60m³	16	96

planning purposes. Moving away from the 'classic' photogrammetrical systems, software is currently available that allows the archaeologist to use photogrammetric techniques within a limited budget. Using standard non-metric cameras and few surveyed control points, this software enables the production of accurate 3-D models of artefacts or structures. As the technology advances, it is likely that photogrammetry will provide an important tool for the recording of excavated material. At present, the main applications of such techniques are likely to be limited to small-scale excavations or the recording of delicate artefacts *in situ* before removal from the ground.

Conclusion

There has been a dramatic increase in the uses of electronic surveying techniques within Irish archaeology. From detail surveys to position-fixing, from site representation to analysis, the uses of this technology are practically boundless, limited only by the imagination of the user. The small sample of possible applications described above highlights how these techniques can be used to further enhance the way we interpret archaeological remains, opening new avenues of research.

Since the technology has become more affordable, and computer software has simplified many tasks, digital surveying techniques have become one of the most cost-effective methods for the visualisation of archaeological monuments. As a non-destructive method that gathers much information about the morphology and physical attributes of a site, digital survey provides an excellent means for a greater understanding of a site as a whole. When a digital survey is available prior to excavation it can focus the questions of the excavator to enable the targeting of specific areas that will potentially yield the most answers. Users of this technology often overlook the other, non-graphical, uses of the data (volume calculations, as mentioned above, being only one example) which can open up so many more new approaches to site investigation. Future research will ultimately benefit from current archaeological projects adopting such technology as a standard, the digital data providing an excellent basis for an archive that can be stored efficiently and accessed for further processing and analysis by future generations.

References

Buckley, V. M. 1990 Experimentation. In V. Buckley (ed.), *Burnt offerings,* 170–2. Dublin.

Burenhult, G. 1980 *The archaeological excavation at Carrowmore, Co. Sligo, Ireland. Excavation seasons 1977–79,* 15–18. Stockholm.

Doody, M., Synnott, P., Tobin, R and Masterson, B. 1995 A topographic survey of the inland promontory fort at Castle Gale, Carrig Henry, Co. Limerick. *Discovery Programme Reports* **2**, 39–44.

Newman, C. 1993 The Tara Survey. Interim report. *Discovery Programme Reports* **1**, 70–93.

Newman, C. 1995 The Tara Survey. Interim report. *Discovery Programme Reports* **2**, 62–7.

Newman, C. 1997 *Tara: An archaeological survey.* Discovery Programme Monographs 2. Dublin.

O'Kelly, M. J. 1954 Excavations and experiments in Irish cooking places. *Journal of the Royal Society of Antiquaries of Ireland* **84**, 105–46.